Death, Afterlife, and the Soul

Religion, History, and Culture
Selections from The Encyclopedia of Religion

Mircea Eliade
EDITOR IN CHIEF

EDITORS
Charles J. Adams
Joseph M. Kitagawa
Martin E. Marty
Richard P. McBrien
Jacob Needleman
Annemarie Schimmel
Robert M. Seltzer
Victor Turner

ASSOCIATE EDITOR
Lawrence E. Sullivan

ASSISTANT EDITOR
William K. Mahony

Death, Afterlife, and the Soul

EDITED BY
Lawrence E. Sullivan

Religion, History, and Culture
Selections from The Encyclopedia of Religion

Mircea Eliade
EDITOR IN CHIEF

MACMILLAN PUBLISHING COMPANY
New York
COLLIER MACMILLAN PUBLISHERS
London

Macmillan Publishing Company
866 Third Avenue, New York, N.Y. 10022

Collier Macmillan Canada, Inc.

Library of Congress Catalog Card Number: 89–34209

Printed in the United States of America

printing number
1 2 3 4 5 6 7 8 9 10

Library of Congress Cataloging-in-Publication Data

Death, afterlife, and the soul / edited by Lawrence E. Sullivan.
p. cm. — (Religion, history, and culture)
"Selections from the Encyclopedia of religion."
Bibliography: p.
ISBN 0-02-897403-4
1. Death—Religious aspects—Comparative studies. 2. Funeral rites and ceremonies. 3. Future life—Comparative studies. 4. Soul—Comparative studies I. Sullivan, Lawrence Eugene, 1949– II. Encyclopedia of religion. III. Series.
BL325.D35D43 1989 89-34209
291.2'3—dc20 CIP

CONTENTS

PUBLISHER'S NOTE

Since publication of *The Encyclopedia of Religion* in 1987, we have been gratified by the overwhelming reception accorded it by the community of scholars. This reception has more than justified the hopes of the members of the work's editorial board, who, with their editor in chief, cherished the aim that it would contribute to the study of the varieties of religious expression worldwide. To all those who participated in the project we express again our deepest thanks.

Now, in response to the many requests of our contributors and other teachers, we take pride in making available this selection of articles from the encyclopedia for use in the classroom. It is our hope that by publishing these articles in an inexpensive, compact format, they will be read and reflected upon by an even broader audience. In our effort to select those articles most appropriate to undergraduate instruction, it has been necessary to omit many entries of interest primarily to the more advanced student and/or to those who wish to pursue a particular topic in greater depth. To facilitate their research, and to encourage the reader to consult the encyclopedia itself, we have thus retained the system of cross-references that, in the original work, served to guide the reader to related articles in this and other fields. A comprehensive index may be found in volume sixteen of the encyclopedia.

Charles E. Smith
Publisher and President
Macmillan Reference Division

INTRODUCTION

The Centrality of Death in Life

Few fascinations grip the living more forcefully than the fate of the dead. Does the soul exist, and does it continue to exist after death? Wht is the soul like? What awaits us after our bodies are gone?

In 1926, Sir James George Frazer, like the British anthropologist Edward Tylor before him, concluded that fearful questions about the "otherworld" of death was one reason why religion exists at all (the other reason being human involvement in "this" world, as reflected in what Frazer called the "worship of nature"). We have no way of knowing whether Frazer was correct about the origins of religion, but we can be certain that fearful respect for the dead and hope for life after death stir human thoughts and passions. We have only to think of Stonehenge, the Egyptian pyramids, Dante's *Divine Comedy,* Mozart's *Requiem,* or the funeral origins of New Orleans jazz to see that the experience of death has inspired art, poetry, music, and architecture in every culture and period. At the same time, speculation about the afterlife and the desire to commune with or give tribute to the dead enrich the cultures of the living.

We mortals may not be aware how completely our lives are structured around death. New Englanders may forget, for example, that nearly every one of their towns is centered on the cemetery. Names of the dead are commemorated in stone and fixed on memorials or plaques in town squares or in memorial parks, churches, or synagogues located at the heart of every community. On a grander scale, Washington, D.C., like so many capitals of vital nations, is framed by death. Its landmarks include memorials to George Washington, Abraham Lincoln, John F. Kennedy, the Unknown Soldier, and deceased veterans of our major wars.

The centrality of death in social life need not be grisly, nor need it constitute a morbid fascination. Art, architecture, poetry, and stories recall the dead; memorial holidays mark the calendar with festive celebrations in honor of them. These forms that fill our space and time direct the family, individual, or society toward a singular point. Our extraordinary monuments as well as our everyday landscapes ground the creativity of community and nation on this inescapable truth of human reality: all humans die.

Death is always imagined within one culture or another, but despite its universality, death has a different story in each religious tradition. Each religion pictures the origins of death in a different way: the disobedience of the first ancestors in a blissful garden; the opening of a bundle or box that should have stayed closed; the race between two animal messengers (e.g., a tortoise and a hare), one bringing the message of life, the other of death; or stealing a look at the first old people before they had the time to don the new skins of youth once again. Furthermore, each religious tradition offers a different account of the history of significant deaths. The details of important deaths become enduring themes in cultural history, and the meaning of those deaths become the stuff of cultural reflection. Central inspirations in Western art, for example, include the crucifixion of Christ, the image of the slain savior in his mother's arms, and the death of saints and martyrs. These motifs have fascinated artists and spectators for two thousand years. Death-centered art is not unique to Western countries. Near Xian, China, for example, a whole army, consisting of thousands of exquisite life-size statues, has been standing underground in battle formation for millenia. Uncovered only recently, the figures are spread across an entire plain. The portrait on each statue has unique features. The likenesses of dead soldiers protect the likeness of the emperor in death even as their living models fought to defend him in life.

One could multiply examples of the importance of the dead and the images of death in each religious tradition. Muslim holy places may possess the remains of a saint or even a hair of the prophet Muḥammad. Buddhist stupas contain some relic of the Buddha. Every Roman Catholic altar, even in small neighborhood communities, contains the bone fragment of a canonized saint. Veneration of the dead is a key feature of religious life in many communities in Africa, Melanesia, and elsewhere.

Just as there is no escape from the reality of death at life's end, so there is no end to death imagery while we remain alive. We need not travel to faraway places to see this. Every day, films and novels serve up concrete images of death in myriad poses. An evening's television dramas provide a variety of scenarios of deaths both gentle and violent. The deaths of family, friends, and workmates bring death closer. As long as we are alive we have some involvement with death, a concern that pervades every level of being human—from the economic and the artistic to the intellectual and psychological; from inheritance patterns, estate taxes, and life-insurance payments to uncontrollable sorrow and bad dreams.

Peering into death—that deep silence into which every voice passes—stirs up waves of word and image. Even without our conscious effort, images of dying, afterlife, and the dead ripple into our nightmares and sweet dreams. Those tempted to think that science has put an end to mystical fascinations with life after death should look again. Medical technology is opening a new frontier for thoughts about life after life. This is happening in several ways. Biologists Peter and Jean Medawar argue that death and visions of an afterlife account for human beings' unique sense of direction in the cosmos. "Only human beings guide their behaviour by a knowledge of what happened before they were born and a preconception of what may happen after they are dead," they write, "thus only human beings find their way by a light that illumines more than the patch of ground they stand on" (Medawar, 1977).

Even more sensational "revelations" about death have occurred as a result of modern medicine. Advances in the medical technology of resuscitation, for instance, have resulted in an increasing number of people who have survived "death." Are these individuals scouts for a new human awareness? Kenneth Ring thinks so (Ring, 1984). He suggests that these individuals, brought back from "death" by extraordinary new technologies, are prophets and seers for a new planetary vision. Are they? The question, together with the answers offered by researchers such as Ring and Raymond Moody (Moody, 1975), have captivated large public audiences. In far-reaching statistical surveys, the uniquitous Gallup poll has tracked the increasing number of those living who have experienced "death" (Gallup, 1982). Death is not dead in the world of modern science.

What "dead" patients see and experience after they "die" has become a subject of systematic, scientific study. The International Association for Near-Death Studies was founded in 1978 and its membership has soared since then. Cardiologist Michael B. Sabom and psychiatric social worker Sarah Kreutziger, for example, conducted five years of joint research in the intensive care and kidney dialysis units at two Florida hospitals. They based their findings on debriefings with a carefully screened sample of seventy-eight patients who had "died" (Sabom and Kreutziger, 1977a, 1977b; Sabom, 1982). Many of these studies concur on key elements of "after-death" experiences. A significant number of those who have "died" report the same highlights: unspeakable joy, immersion in brilliant light, sensation of weightlessness, vision of one's own soul, meeting a guide, undertaking a journey (across a bridge, a river, through a tunnel), undergoing a judgment, gaining an umparalleled vision of the whole of reality, taking up residence in another kind of space (Zaleski, 1987: 97–135; Sullivan, 1988: 524–548). What shall we make of all the new information (and perhaps new kinds of experience of "death") that modern science provides?

We moderns do not stand apart from all the other humans in our curiosity about death. In one form or another, these questions are posed in every culture. Why does life end? What is the significance of the final moment of death? Is this intimate nestling of death in life absurd or significant? Does death arrive from afar, merely a visiting stranger to life, or are death and life close friends who have known each other all along? Is there a form of life—a soul, perhaps—they share in common? Are life and death, in fact, related in fruitful ways? Does death, too, include forms of life? How can we know?

Given the centrality of questions about death throughout human history it is strange that we often refuse to treat the topic seriously. Worried, perhaps, about the uncertainty of any knowledge about death and the afterlife, we fail to probe that uncertainty with the knowledge of human history that we already have. The paradigm of uncertainty may be, in fact, the fate of the soul after death. But notice the irony of our stance. By backing away from careful consideration of the fate of the soul after death, because it may be indeterminate by our standards, we have left ourselves with few tools to understand the descriptions of death, afterlife, and the soul left to us by countless generations. Yet these ideas have been central motivations for cultures everywhere. In other words, in trying to hold on to certainty in such matters, we place beyond our reach much of what we know about human beings, about ourselves. We leave ourselves poorly equipped to understand human culture and less able to probe the working and meaning of the imagination, that labor that is distinctively human.

Far from being an end, death marks the beginning of a breakthrough for the human imagination. Postmortem existence is a thoroughly imaginal existence (McDannell and Lang, 1988; Himmelfarb, 1983). Only through the distinctively human labor of imagination do the living envision life after death and the mythic geographies of death. Poking through the breakpoint of death into the otherworld is an act that orients the human being in this world, brings into full power the imagination of the living, and enables human labor to take new account of material existence. But because endings are intrinsically probative, this breakthrough is also the greatest test of the value of the imagination and all its symbolic capacities (Sullivan, 1988; 468–649). That is why death so often arises for the first time in the context of a trial, resulting from failure to pass a test or to endure an ordeal. But it is the imaginative basis of human creativity that is itself put on trial when death renders a judgment on the value of symbolic expression. Is death the final undoing or the ultimate triumph of those imaginative capacities?

This book presents a broad range of views on death, afterlife, and the soul. These views belong to human cultures around the globe and across time. The point is less to provide definitive answers than to open new avenues of inquiry and to stimulate new creative possibilities. Answerable or not, the questions about death must be pursued, for the inquiry seems constitutive of human nature and culture as we know them. Humanity appears to be that species that reflects on its own significance. As a mortal being, what is the meaning of mortality? By exploring the outer limits of existence and of certainty, humans try to look further than they can see. They explore and extend the margins of human possibilities and in this very act of confronting their own end come to grips with their own purpose and understand their own significance.

REFERENCES AND SUGGESTED READINGS

Gallup, George, Jr., and William Proctor. *Adventures in Immortality: A Look beyond the Threshold of Death.* New York, 1982.

Himmelfarb, Martha. *Tours of Hell: An Apocalyptic Form in Jewish and Christian Literature.* Philadelphia, 1983.

McDannell, Colleen, and Bernhard Lang, *Heaven: A History.* New Haven, 1988.

Medawar, Peter, and Jean Medawar. *The Life of Science.* London, 1977.

Moody, Raymond A., Jr. *Life After Life.* Atlanta, 1975.

Ring, Kenneth. *Heading Toward Omega: In Search of the Meaning of the Near-Death Experience.* New York, 1984.

Sabom, Michael B. *Recollections of Death: A Medical Investigation.* New York, 1982.

Sabom, Michael B., and Sarah Kreutziger, "Near-Death Experiences," *New England Journal of Medicine* 297, 19 (1977a): 1071.

Sabom, Michael B., and Sarah Kreutziger, "The Experience of Near Death," *Death Education* 1 (1977b): 195–203.

Sullivan, Lawrence E. *Icanchu's Drum: An Orientation to Meaning in South American Religions.* New York, 1988.

Zaleski, Carol. *Otherworld Journeys: Accounts of Near-Death Experience in Medieval and Modern Times.* New York, 1987.

ONE

DEATH, FUNERALS, AND THE DEAD

1 DEATH

Th. P. van Baaren

The statement that there is no life without death and no death without life is as banal as it is true. Its truth is self-evident; its banality arises from the fact that life and death can be—and, as a rule, are—defined as mutually exclusive states of being, which turns the statement into a truism. The widespread belief in the continuity of life after death does not diminish the validity of this definition, because life after death is conceived of as a mode of being essentially distinct from life on earth, the life between birth and death. [*See* Afterlife.] This is true also when life after death is thought of as a replica of life on earth, for the replica can never be exact.

Given the inevitability and definitiveness of death, it is not surprising that in all cultures, so far as our knowledge goes, the idea of dying has captured the thoughts and imagination of human beings. Indeed, during certain periods, such as the European Middle Ages, as demonstrated not only by the church but also by art and literature, this is true to a high degree. In a relatively small number of religions—among which are three of the most important in world history: Buddhism, Christianity, and Islam—preoccupation with death has led to the conviction that life after death (that is, eternal life, which no longer is subject to the restrictions of time and even is the real life as compared with human existence on earth) must be considered as far greater in importance than life on earth. This tradition still colors to a high degree the mental outlook and moral judgment of countless millions in modern times. Yet from the point of view of history and anthropology the regarding of death as more important than life is far from common. The majority of religions firmly accent life here and now.

It is true that in a few cultures, the Indian ones among them, both life and death can be relativized. Even then, however, life and death are considered different modes of being. We must keep in mind also that immortality, eternal life in the strict sense of Christianity and Islam, is not a common concept. A great many cultures believe that life after death, too, may come to an end.

In a great number of cultures there seems to exist a connection, if not direct then, in any case, indirect, between the first coming of death into this world and the origin of both the countless imperfections that are part of the world of man and, more especially, evil. In her thorough study entitled *The Origins of Evil in Hindu My-*

thology, Wendy Doniger O'Flaherty writes, "The Hindu mythologies of evil and of death are closely related." On the same page she remarks further, "The myths of death and evil share the same recurrent motifs and often offer the same solutions to the different problems posed" (O'Flaherty, 1976, p. 212).

Put differently, the original perfect order of the entire cosmos, as perceived by a great number of cultures, excludes disorder and death, and death is thought to result once the order has been broken down or invalidated. As has been noted by many scholars, the coming of evil and of death is often closely connected with the appearance of sexual desire and hunger. In any case, death seems to be something whose existence requires explanation. According to the general belief, and practically all cultures conceive it in this manner, the appearance of death is the worst and most basic break in the original normality of human life as it was meant to be in principle.

Although many individuals die in peace, willing resignation in the face of death is rare as a motif in mythology. A myth from the Ivory Coast tells of the time when death was unknown and of its first coming. When Death approached, everyone fled into the bush except one old man who could no longer walk, and he asked his young grandson to make him a mat to lie upon. When Death came the child was still busy working on the mat, and so they both died.

THE ORIGIN OF DEATH

In 1886 Andrew Lang presented a classification of myths about the origin of death, and in 1917 Franz Boas published an article on these myths among the North American Indians. Hermann Baumann in 1936 and Hans Abrahamsson in 1951 presented classifications of the African myths about the origin of death, including maps that show the geographic division of the several motifs found on this continent. Because such classifications according to specific motifs result in a long list, even when just a single continent is treated, I have opted for a more systematic classification. Although death can be personified as the god of death, as is the case in a great number of religions, for purposes of classification this makes little or no difference. As can be expected, a number of myths combine the characteristics of more than one motif, and where examples of this occur I have classified them according to what I consider to be the main motif.

An analysis of the reasons given for the coming of death into this world, according to the classification system that I have adopted, shows a number of types:

1. Death is considered the natural destination of man, or, at least, it is considered to be in accordance with the primordial will of the gods and as such is to be accepted, if not without demur then without the necessity of further explanation. Death forms, as it were, an indispensable part of the divine administration (or the divine economy) and is simply acknowledged as such.
2. The death of a god or some other mythic being has given rise to the existence of death in the human world as well, and so it is not in any respect due to the behavior of man.
3. Human death is the result of conflict among divine beings.
4. Death is the result of man being cheated by a god or some other mythic being, or of the carelessness or stupidity of such a being.

5. Death is the result of some human shortcoming, sometimes a rather futile one in our eyes. It remains somewhat doubtful, however, whether in strict terms this impression of futility is justified and to what degree it is due to imperfect understanding, insufficient knowledge of the culture in question, or incomplete reporting by our sources.
6. Death is the result of a wrong judgment or a wrong choice made by man.
7. Death results from some kind of guilt, usually, but not exclusively, human guilt. Yet the question of guilt can be difficult to decide. In certain cases there is only a sin of omission, which can also be seen as a simple case of human shortcoming, of being at fault, at most a venial sin. There may be—to show the difficulty—more than one argument given for the origin of death, such as, for example, curiosity and disobedience. Curiosity in itself is a minor shortcoming, if it is one at all, but when it leads to disobedience it becomes decisively important; according to the various myths, disobedience is the actual sin that deserves death. In my discussion of this reason for the coming of death, I shall mainly treat sins of commission. Apart, then, from a number of cases in which the question of whether we can actually speak of human guilt must be left as a matter of opinion, the three main reasons given in which this point is clear are disobedience, sexual offense, and killing.
8. Man dies because he himself has desired death.

A few myths pose such specialized and detailed problems that they cannot be treated satisfactorily within the scope of a general introductory article. This holds, for example, for some myths current in South Asian religious traditions.

Death as a Natural or God-Willed Designation. While modern scientific understanding teaches us that individual organic life is finite not only by necessity but even in essence, all the possibilities envisaged by religious thinking involve the belief that death is an interruption of natural life, that it is, in fact, unnatural. The unwillingness of many nonliterate peoples to accept the possibility of a "natural" death shows this clearly. Originally, so the myth frequently runs, man was destined for a paradisiacal existence until some untoward occurrence changed that destiny.

Similar is the conviction that death is the ordained and god-willed destiny of man, as is the case in a number of religions. Death as a rule remains the enemy of man. The Lugbara of East Africa, although they believe that practically all matters of importance are in the hands of the ancestors, consider death an act of God. In various parts of Indonesia we find the belief that human beings are somehow identical with the cattle of the gods. Whenever the gods in heaven slaughter an animal, a man on earth dies.

The Luba of the southeastern Kongo region tell a mythical story of an old woman who had lost all her loved ones and remained alone on earth. She could not understand why this had to happen to her and so left her home in order to find God and ask him the reason for her sad fate. She had a long and weary journey, but in the end she found God and was able to pose her question. She had to be content, however, with the same answer Job received when he complained to God that he did not understand why he, the example of faith and piety, should be so sorely plagued: God then answered that he is mighty and cannot be called to account by man. So, too, the old Luba woman had to console herself with the knowledge that her fate had been willed by God.

In Greece also we find this resignation in the face of death. In a famous passage of the *Iliad* (5.146–149), Homer compares the generations of humans to the leaves on a tree: when the season of winter storms begins, leaves fall from the tree, and, in the same way, one human generation must make way for the next.

The classic, often-quoted example of this theme occurs in the Babylonian *Epic of Gilgamesh,* where, after the sudden death of his friend Enkidu, Gilgamesh roamed the world in search of the secret of eternal life but, in the end, without success. Gilgamesh did discover the herb of life, whose name means "as an old man, man becomes young again." Yet even though after countless difficulties and dangers he succeeded in acquiring the small plant, which grew on the far side of the waters of death and made man young again, he lost it to a snake while returning to the world of the living. The snake stole the herb while Gilgamesh slept, and since then snakes have no longer died but have simply changed their skin. This motif of the snake is found in a number of variations in many cultures all over the world.

Gilgamesh was obliged to accept the conviction of man's mortality and to abide by the will of the gods, who had decided on that mortality. The Gilgamesh epic phrases it thus:

> Gilgamesh, where are you roaming?
> You shall not find the life you search after!
> When the gods created mankind,
> they destined death for man,
> but life they kept firmly in their own hands.

Although ancient Egypt knew no myth to explain the origin of death, the texts make it clear that death was seen as a negative element, an abnormality that unfortunately is inherent in creation. One of the Pyramid Texts states clearly that no death existed in primeval time, before the gods, the world, and mankind were made. The Egyptians were consequent: the created gods—who were distinguished from the primeval ones, the creator-gods themselves—were also mortal, at least ultimately.

A myth from Tahiti tells of the gods Hina and Tefatou and their disagreement over the fate of man. Hina proposed that man should rise again after his death, but Tefatou answered that because the earth and all plants must die, man should share the same destiny. Hina had to be content with the moon, which "dies" and yet rises again.

The concept of death as resulting from the will and power of a god may lead to religious problems. The tribes of Patagonia (South America), now practically extinct, believed that death was the work of the supreme god Waitaunewa, but they did not accept this belief meekly and passively. On the contrary, when one of their loved ones died they not only wailed but also protested: they accused the god of murder and avenged themselves by killing the animals that belonged to him. In this context it must be mentioned that the problems of death and of all suffering in the world are closely connected with theodicy, as is the problem of the origin of evil.

Death as The Result of a Divine Death. There is a concept that man dies because a god or some other mythical being died first, and in this no question of fault or guilt is ascribed to human beings. The German anthropologist Adolf E. Jensen (1963) has given the name *dema* to a class of mythical beings who, by their deeds in a primeval time, originated human life and culture as we know it now; their deeds, however, ended with their own death. Some myths relate that the *dema* were murdered, but others say that they suffered a voluntary death. The life and death of the *dema* provide the divine paradigm for human experience, for man follows the pattern set by these mythical originators. There is a parallel between divine and human fate: because a god once died, human beings, too, are now subject to death. There are also examples of this theme that are not connected with the concept of *dema* gods. In a myth of the Shuswap Indians of North America, for example, we are told that the son of a heavenly chief died for reasons unknown. His was the first death, but since then all human beings have had to die.

Death as The Result of a Divine Conflict. Human death may also be seen as resulting from a conflict between gods. A myth from the island of Ceram in eastern Indonesia relates an argument between a stone and a banana regarding the way in which man should be created. The stone killed the banana, but on the next day the children of the banana were ready to continue the fight. In the end the stone fell into an abyss and admitted defeat, but with one condition: man would be as the bananas wanted him to be, but he must die just as a banana does.

The Shilluk of the upper Nile have a tradition that explains the origin of death in terms of a quarrel between the god Nyikang and his brother Duwat. In an election for a new king Duwat was chosen and Nyikang passed over. To avenge himself Nyikang stole part of the regalia and departed with his supporters. Duwat went in pursuit of his brother but failed to overtake him. Seeing this, he threw his digging stick after Nyikang and said, "Take this stick to bury your people!" And in this way death came into the world.

A myth from the Musarongo of the lower Kongo region also tells about divine conflict that ended in death for mankind. The Dogon of Mali tell of a quarrel between the gods in which the penis of the god Ogo was crushed. This led first to the death of the god himself and then to the death of man as well. The Blackfeet Indians of North America tell about a time when an Old Man and an Old Woman disagreed on every occasion. The man wanted the best for human beings and intended to give them life, but the woman had other plans and, as always, had the last word. A well-known variation of this pattern is found in the myths in which the quarreling beings are twins.

Another variant of the quarrel between gods is the conflict between the Sun (or some other divinity) and the Moon concerning human life. In these stories Sun and Moon are, of course, mythical beings. A number of these myths can be found in Africa, each one connecting the destiny of man with that of the Moon. This type of myth can also be found all over the world, however, because speculation about the connection of the moon's phases with human life and death is nearly universal. [*See* Moon.] A myth from the Fiji Islands in the South Pacific acquaints us with the story of two gods, Moon and Rat, who quarrel about the fate of man. Moon wants man to grow old, disappear, and then be young again, after his own example, but Rat insists that men should die as rats do, and his voice prevails.

A myth from the Caroline Islands in the western Pacific states that in the beginning the life and death of man ran parallel to the phases of the moon, but then an evil spirit succeeded somehow in contriving that man should die and never wake up again. The Numfor of Sarera Bay (formerly Geelvink Bay) in Indonesia relate a myth that very much resembles the one from the Carolines. This myth recounts how a werewolf succeeded in cheating man and thus seducing him into disobedience, and in this manner men lost their power of rejuvenation.

Death as The Result of a God's Cheating or Carelessness. Death sometimes is attributed to divine cheating. Here, of course, the well-known mythical figure of the trickster looms up. According to the myths of the Indian tribes of central California, Sedit, the trickster, personified by the coyote, brings death into the world through his intrigues. Hence the Maidu tell how he destroyed the hill on top of which was a lake with the water of life, which could have prevented mankind from dying. Numerous North American Indian myths describe Coyote or another trickster as the bringer of death. The trickster combines creative and destructive characteristics. As the divine figure who introduces disorder and chaos into an ordered world, he, like the creator himself, is an indispensable part of the cosmos, which is conceived of as a totality in which mutually opposed elements are united. [*See* Tricksters.]

In West Indian Voodoo religion Gèdè is the god of death as well as the trickster. Maya Deren, in her fascinating book on Voodoo, *Divine Horsemen: The Living Gods of Haiti* (London, 1953), calls Gèdè "corpse and phallus; king and clown." He is the lord of darkness and the lord of crossroads. He reminds every man that death will give way to no one, not even to the richest, most powerful, and most illustrious men. The combination of the trickster and the god of death is apt, for the cruelest joke of the gods is that they have ordered creation in such a way that not only the possibility but even the inevitability of death is built into it, so that every human being must eventually die.

In another myth of the Dogon we are told that the first human beings, the Andumbulu, did not die but instead were transformed into snakes. One day the god Amma offered to sell a cow to a young woman. The woman asked the price, and the god told her that the price was death. The woman bought the cow and shortly afterward her husband died. She remonstrated with the god, but he reminded her of the price that he had asked and she had agreed to pay. Amma refused to cancel the agreement and take the cow back, and so death came into this world.

In other cases we find reports that death resulted from the carelessness or stupidity of some mythical being. This type of myth is called "the message that failed" (Baumann, 1936). The messenger is often a snake or a lizard, both animals that change their skin. The basic idea here is the belief that the supreme deity intended to give man eternal life but some subordinate god inadvertently spoiled his intentions. The Wute of East Africa explain the origin of death in the following manner: God sent a chameleon to man with the message that mankind would live eternally. The chameleon, however, was in no hurry. First it stopped and bought itself a splendid headdress, and then it ambled on at its leisure. After two weeks it finally arrived at its destination. In the meantime the snake had learned of the gift that was meant for man and had gone to man and pretended that it had been sent to convey the message that mankind would be subject to death without resurrection. As punishment both the snake and the chameleon were cursed by God: now men will readily kill them. The message itself, however, could not be reversed, and man was fated to die.

A myth of the Ashanti of Ghana tells of the paradise in which man first lived. This happy state came to an end when a few women objected to God's presence while they ground corn for food. God then retired from the world and went to heaven. He remained benevolently inclined toward man, however, and sent a goat to tell him that he need not fear death, because it meant only that he would live on in heaven. The goat was in no hurry and took time off to have a good meal. God saw this, and so he sent a sheep with the same message, but the sheep instead told man that death would mean the definitive end of existence. Shortly thereafter the first death occurred, and God instructed mankind on how to bury the dead. In a myth of the San of southern Africa the messenger is a hare, which many cultures consider a lunar animal.

A myth from the island of New Britain in the western Pacific belongs to a type more frequently found in Melanesia. It ascribes the coming of death to the stupidity of a messenger, rightly called To Purgo ("stupid one"), who is the wise and benevolent god's twin. Without any malice To Purgo confuses his message and pronounces death for man and everlasting life for the snake. In a myth of the Annamese of Southeast Asia the messenger's mistake is not involuntary: he changes the message because the snakes threaten him.

A myth from central Africa provides a typical example of how man's "deathlessness" was lost because of levity and lack of care. God gave a toad an earthen jar and instructed the creature to be very careful of it because it contained death. The toad met a frog hopping cheerfully along and the frog wanted to take over the job of carrying the jar. The toad hesitated but in the end gave in. The frog hopped off happily juggling the jar and then dropped it. The jar broke, and death got out.

Death as the Result of Human Shortcoming. In another category, death may be seen as having its origins in human nature. That is, it is believed to result from a human shortcoming. This shortcoming, however, can hardly qualify as human guilt. A myth from the Solomon Islands (with parallels from other islands of Melanesia) tells that originally both man and snakes changed their skin as they grew old and, thus reborn, became young again and again. But once a woman left her baby in the care of her mother while she went out to work. The old woman played with the child until it fell asleep and then she went out to the river to bathe and change her skin. The baby woke up after the grandmother had returned and so did not recognize her, for she appeared in the shape of a comely young woman. The child then howled and yelled and remained inconsolable. Finally, furious and desperate, the grandmother returned to the river and put on her old skin. But, so she told the child, from then on all human beings would grow old, and only snakes would preserve the capacity of renewing themselves by sloughing off their skin.

In Africa we find a type of myth that explains the coming of death into the world by saying that during the night God proclaimed to all men the news of life without death, but because they slept on without troubling themselves about this divine revelation they missed the proclamation of their own eternal life. This myth presupposes a certain connection between sleep and death. This connection is, of course, widely recognized and remarked on, but only here and there is it related to the problem of the origin of death. The Greeks held the notion that Sleep (Morpheus) and Death (Thanatos) were brothers, and this motif is known elsewhere as well. A myth from the Ekoi of the Cross River region of West Africa tells that once upon a time God asked the people whether they knew what it meant to die, and they all answered in the negative. God told them to gather in the palaver house of the village, and every few hours he put the same question to them, until they were quite overcome by sleep. Then he told them that they had learned what death is, for death and sleep are similar.

Another motif in this category is that which Hans Abrahamsson calls "discord in the first family." The Lotuko of Uganda tell about a family quarrel that led to death as the irrevocable end of human life. Once upon a time a child died, and the mother implored the supreme god to bring her baby to life again. The god granted her request, but the child's father, for reasons that are not clear, was dissatisfied and killed the child; and this second death proved decisive. Then, according to the myth, the supreme god said, "For the future, whenever a Lotuko dies, he must remain dead."

A myth from the Lake Sentani region of Indonesia reports that the first human beings were unable to understand the language that their father used to tell them the secret of eternal life. This man had died but came to life again the next day. He tried to communicate with the snakes and other animals that now are able to shed their skin. These understood him well enough, but once he told the secret he himself forgot it; and so he had to die once more and this time remain dead forever.

One of the most interesting motifs associated with the appearance of death on earth is the notion that death punishes man for having made death into an occasion for pageantry and merriment. The illogic of this idea is avoided in a number of myths by assuming that it was the death of an animal that occasioned such sport. The Bena Kanioka of the middle Kongo region consider the first death the result of a human transgression. It could have remained an isolated occurrence, however, if man had not made the burial an occasion for feasting and merrymaking. To punish man, death was made permanent. A related motif occurs in a myth from upper Burma: in the beginning of time, when death was still unknown, an old man played a practical joke on the sun god by pretending to be dead. The sun god became angry when he discovered this joke and turned the pretended death into a real one, thus inaugurating death. Here again we see that levity in the face of any death is punished by the appearance or persistence of death in the world of man.

Death as The Outcome of a Wrong Choice. Death can be viewed as the outcome of a wrong choice made by human beings themselves. The Holoholo, a subtribe of the Luba, say that God gave man the chance to choose between two nuts, one in each of his hands; one symbolized life and the other, death. Man, or, in this case, woman, chose the wrong hand, and so death became the destiny of all mankind, while the snake, which was also present at this scene, received the gift of unrestricted renewal of life.

A myth of the Toraja of Sulawesi (formerly Celebes) tells another story of a wrong choice. One day God dropped a stone down from heaven onto the earth as a gift for mankind, but man did not know what to do with this unlikely present and, clearly and openly showing a lack of appreciation, rejected it. Shortly afterward God presented man with the banana, and this he welcomed. Man, however, had not understood the implication of this choice, that is, that he had turned down the offer of life without death, the stone's mode of being, and had accepted instead the manner of existence in which death and birth alternate. The banana tree is widely known as a symbol of death and renewal, because its cuttings grow into new trees, and the pruned tree forms new shoots.

The motif that James G. Frazer, in *The Golden Bough* (1890), his classic study in the history of religion, called "the fatal bundle or the fatal box" belongs in this subdivision to some degree; partly, too, it belongs with the stories of death resulting from disobedience. The Ngala of the upper Kongo region explain the coming of death in a myth that tells how God offered a man working in the forest two bundles, a large one that contained a number of useful and pretty things such as knives and beads, and a small one that contained everlasting life. The man dared not decide on the spot which bundle to take, and so he went to the village to ask advice. In the meantime a few women came along, and God offered them the same choice. They unpacked the large bundle and found mirrors with which they could admire themselves and cloth from which they could make dresses, and so they chose the large bundle. In this way man failed to qualify for eternal life and was subject to death.

Death as the Result of Human Guilt. As can be expected, a great number of myths cite human guilt as the cause of death. The anthropologist Paul Radin must have been mistaken when he wrote that nowhere except in the Bible has man been held responsible for the origin of death. This guilt, it is true, can be conceived of in a variety of ways. In Africa, among the Yoruba of Nigeria and the Lobi of Burkina Faso, for example, we find myths in which human death follows on general moral decadence.

The Tamanaco, a now-extinct tribe of the Orinoco River region of South America, told a myth of how in the beginning the earth was created by two divine brothers. One of them, Amalivaca, once lived for a time among men. Before he left them to return to the world of the gods, he announced that he would take off his skin, and he instructed them to do the same whenever they wanted to become young again. One woman, however, seemed to doubt the value of this advice. So the god became angry and told her that she would die; and because of her lack of belief in the words of the god, death came into this world. Three variations on the theme of death caused by guilt can be identified.

Disobedience. A common motif is the belief that death was caused by man's disobeying God. There may be subsidiary motivations present, as, for example, curiosity or carelessness, but disobedience remains the primary point.

The best-known example of the coming of death as a punishment for disobedience is, of course, the biblical myth of Adam and Eve in Paradise as told in the *Book of Genesis*. Some deduce from this story that God had originally intended to give Adam and Eve everlasting life, although this is not expressly mentioned.

Genesis 2:16–18 states without any ambiguity: "You may eat from every tree in the garden, but not from the tree of knowledge of good and evil; for on the day that you eat from it, you will certainly die." Eve was tempted by the serpent and ate the forbidden fruit. She found it good and gave some to Adam, who accepted it willingly. God, as could not be otherwise expected, detected their disobedience and cursed all three: the serpent, Eve, and Adam. Strangely enough, however, and here an ambiguous element appears, death is not expressly named in the formulas of cursing that God uses, but is indicated only in symbolic metaphor: "You shall gain your bread by the sweat of your brow until you return to the ground; for from it you were taken. Dust you are, to dust you shall return" (*Gn.* 3:19).

Only after God had made tunics of skin for Adam and Eve to wear did he reflect on the necessity of chasing the first human beings from the Garden of Eden lest they eat from the tree of life as well: "The man has become like one of us, knowing good and evil; what if he now reaches out his hand and takes fruit from the tree of life also, eats it and lives forever?" (*Gn.* 3:28). The inconsistencies, which are rarely absent from myth, make the *Genesis* story rather enigmatic after all. In God's first proclamation the tree of life is not forbidden, although its existence is mentioned. So we must judge that it was a matter of chance that man did not eat from the tree of life, which was not forbidden, before his disobedience regarding the other special tree led to the judgment pronounced in *Genesis* 3:14–19. However, God's pronouncement that man must certainly die on the day that he eats the forbidden fruit of the knowledge of good and evil is shown up as a rather hollow threat. God, in spite of his threatening words, has to take special measures to prevent man from living on in eternity. This short analysis of the creation myth in *Genesis* shows that the connection between human disobedience and the origin of death is at best rather loose and must lead us to doubt whether the best-known example of death's origin as the result of disobedience is really the best one.

Medieval theologians speculated extensively as to exactly which sin led to the Fall, for disobedience as such is not one of the seven mortal sins. Some medieval theologians ascribed the fall of man to pride *(superbia)* or lust *(luxuria)*. In Buddhism, also, lust and death are closely connected. O'Flaherty writes, "Lust and death are combined in the devil" (O'Flaherty, 1976, p. 213).

Among the Carib of Guyana a myth can be found that tells how the creator-god Purá wanted to give eternal life to man, but because man disobeyed the god's instructions on how to attain this goal, all men became subject to death. Among the Lamba of Zambia is a myth that tells how man received a number of small bundles from God. The messengers to whom the bundles were given were forbidden to inspect them: they had to be handed unopened to the "chief on earth." The messengers, overcome by curiosity, failed to obey and opened the bundles, one of which contained death. The Ekoi tell that God commanded man never to kill and eat a white sheep. Man disobeyed God and was punished by the coming of death for all men.

We also find the notion that death is the punishment for premature burial. The Kongo of the lower Kongo region know a myth about how the creator-god Nzambi ordered man not to bury a child who had died because the child would return to life in three days. But the parents did not believe him, and they disobeyed, and so death became irrevocable. This theme recurs in a myth from the Fiji Islands. And the Dogon have a myth that tells how death originated from the learning of a forbidden language.

The motif of the forbidden fruit is not restricted to the Bible. The Efe, a Pygmy tribe of central Africa, tell that the creator designated the fruit of one tree as forbidden. It happened, however, that a pregnant woman once experienced an irresistible desire to eat the forbidden fruit, and she prevailed upon her husband to pick it for her. The result was that God sent death into the world as punishment for their disobedience. Although this myth slightly resembles the biblical one, it is probably not derived from missionary sources, either Christian or Muslim. Important details of the biblical story are absent: the tree of knowledge, for example, is not mentioned. Various other details differ as well, such as that of the woman's pregnancy. Moreover, numerous versions of this myth can be found in Africa.

Another variant of the theme of disobedience is the Pandora motif, usually called the "box" of Pandora, although the Greek poet Hesiod, who tells this story in his epic *Works and Days* (80–105), speaks of a jar. Pandora received the jar from Zeus, who strictly forbade her to open it. She disobeyed him, and all kinds of misfortune and evils escaped into the world when she removed the lid. The only positive thing in the jar was hope. Although death is not expressly mentioned in this case, the myth of Pandora clearly belongs to the type called "death in a bundle or box."

Sexual Offense. The guilt that brings about death may be a sexual offense committed by man, but this transgression may also be projected back into the world of the gods. Thus, according to a myth of the Dogon, death came into existence as a result of primordial incest committed by the god Ogo.

In Africa we find a myth that tells about God forbidding the first human beings to copulate. When they disobeyed this injunction, death came into existence. A myth from the Nupe of Nigeria relates that God first created the tortoise, then man, and then stone. To the tortoise and man he gave the gift of life, but not so to stone. At this time death did not yet exist, and so the tortoise and man became very old and then young again. They were not content with this state of affairs, however, and went to God to ask him for a child. God told them that they could have children but that then they would have to die. He asked them whether they still wanted children, since they knew that having them would bring about their death. Nevertheless, both creatures insisted that they wanted children. Thus it happened: they begot children, and when the children were born, the fathers died.

A myth from the Baiga of central India connects the beginning of death with the first human copulation. A Baiga man and woman had congress in the forest, a thing unknown before. The earth started to tremble, and they died immediately. Since then, death has formed part of human life. And the Tucano Indians of Colombia ascribe the first death to lasciviousness.

Killing. The first death is also ascribed to a killing, often considered a murder. In many cases a mythical being is killed in the primeval time related in myth. A myth from the Mentawai Islands, near Sumatra, relates that the first human beings came forth from a bamboo plant and immediately fled into the bush. There they lived a miserable existence until the god Siakau took pity on them and taught and helped them. Later the god changed himself into an iguana, a sacred animal on these islands, and in this shape he was accidentally killed by two of the four original human beings. They had not recognized Siakau in his new shape and had wrongly accused him of destroying their gardens. Their punishment was instant death. The other two persons fled, but death had entered the world forever.

Among the Arawak of Guyana we encounter a myth about the creator-god. Once when he visited earth to see how his creatures were faring, man, who was wicked, attempted to murder him. Consequently the god deprived mankind of the gift of eternal life and instead bestowed it on snakes and similar creatures, which since then have been able to change their skin. The Algonquin Indians of North America tell about a conflict that occurred at the beginning of time, during which the aquatic animals drowned a wolf, the little brother of the culture hero Mänäbush. In this manner death was brought into the world.

In a number of cultures we find the belief that there was once a time when human life knew neither death nor birth: life went on forever, and procreation and birth were unknown. Then some disturbance happened, some transgression, usually a killing, was committed, and this occurrence changed the situation and introduced a new mode of life in which birth and death alternated. A good example is the story of Hainuwele ("maiden") in a myth from Ceram, as told by Jensen (1939). In short, this myth relates how the people envied Hainuwele because she was luckier and richer than all others. During a communal gathering the dancers formed a spiral and forced Hainuwele to the center, where they had dug a deep hole. The girl was pushed into the hole while loud singing drowned her cries for help. The grave was filled in with earth and stamped down by the dancers. This primeval murder marked the beginning of the alternation of death and birth.

Death as a Desire of Man. The last category of myth we must consider recounts how man desired death because he did not want to prolong a life that had become burdensome. Abrahamsson (1951) has drawn attention to African myths of this type, according to which man, plagued by disease or suffering from the indignities of old age and, thus, weary of life, wants to die and so calls out for death to come to him. A myth of the Mum of Cameroon relates that God could not understand why so many men became cold and stiff, but Death (here personified) showed him how the old and miserable people cried out for release from this existence. The Ngala tell that man asked for death because there was so much evil and unhappiness in the world. The Nuba of the upper Nile connect the death wish with the fact of overpopulation.

One myth, probably African but the clearest version of which is known from Morocco and put in Muslim terms, tells the story of a virgin who had lived for five hundred years. Moses happened to find her anklets, taken off before her death, and prayed to God to be allowed to see the dead girl. God granted his request and caused the girl to rise from her grave. In a conversation with Moses she said that she had lived far too long and had grown tired of living. Then Moses beseeched God to let man die sooner. Although this myth does not treat the introduction of death on earth, it clearly shows how weariness of life may become a reason for wishing to die; and in mythical terms this nearly always means a reason for the first appearance of death.

CONCLUSION

As can be expected, still other motifs related to the origin of death are mentioned in mythology. Myths from India connect the coming of death with the overpopulation of the earth and the resulting starvation. In contrast with the Nuba myth mentioned above, this Indian myth has the gods deciding to send death. A myth from the inhabitants of the Sarera Bay region relates how the god Tefafu, after several false starts, finally succeeded in creating perfect human beings. The god, however, became envious of his own creatures and decided to destroy them by a great flood. He spared only two, a brother and sister. He wanted them to marry, and when they demurred at committing incest, he told them falsely that it was all right. The new generation of mankind, born from this incestuous marriage, was no longer perfect;

it was evil and subject to both disease and death. So Tefafu was satisfied and went to sleep.

As to the question of the age of the myths on the origin of death, a general answer, in my opinion, cannot be given, and even a restricted one remains full of uncertainties. Baumann (1936) has tried to date these myths in accordance with the *Kulturkreiselehre,* but as this theory no longer commands much authority, the results gathered in this manner must remain doubtful.

We can assume with a modicum of certainty that, given the primary importance of death for all human beings, the search for its origin originated in a very early phase of human culture; but it is impossible to put even a tentative and approximate date on that time when man first considered death as an unnatural break in life, an inexplicable abnormality, for which an explanation was needed.

[*For cross-cultural discussions of mythical views of death and the afterlife, see* Underworld *and* Otherworld.]

BIBLIOGRAPHY

Abrahamsson, Hans. *The Origin of Death: Studies in African Mythology.* Uppsala, 1951. Authoritative treatment of the African myths on the origin of death.

Baumann, Hermann. *Schöpfung und Urzeit des Menschen im Mythus der afrikanischen Völker.* Berlin, 1936. One chapter treats the origin of death.

Bendann, Effie. *Death Customs* (1930). Reprint, London, 1969. A general introduction.

Boas, Franz. "The Origin of Death." *Journal of American Folk-Lore* 30 (1917): 486–491. First special treatment of the Amerindian myths on the origin of death.

Dangel, R. "Mythen vom Ursprung des Todes bei den Indianern Nordamerikas." *Mitteilungen der anthropologischen Gesellschaft in Wien* 58 (1928): 341–374. Treats the Amerindian myths on the origin of death.

Jensen, Adolf E. *Hainuwele: Volkserzählungen von der Molukken-Insel Ceram.* Frankfurt, 1939. The myth of Hainuwele.

Jensen, Adolf E. *Myth and Cult among Primitive Peoples.* Chicago, 1963. Among other things, contains a thorough treatment of the dema.

Lang, Andrew. *La mythologie.* Paris, 1886. First classification of myths on the origin of death.

Muensterberger, Warner, *Ethnologische Studien an indonesischen Schöpfungsmythen.* The Hague, 1939. Contains material on the origin of death.

O'Flaherty, Wendy Doniger. *The Origins of Evil in Hindu Mythology.* Berkeley, 1976. Also treats the origin of death.

Preuss, Konrad Theodor. *Tod und Unsterblichkeit im Glauben der Naturvölker.* Tübingen, 1930. Still a useful introduction, although dated in regard to theory.

2 HUMAN SACRIFICE

KAY A. READ

Human sacrifice, defined as the killing of humans or the use of the flesh, blood, or bones of the human body for ritual purposes, has been a widespread and complex phenomenon throughout history. Most contemporary scholars try to explain human sacrifice in terms of earlier theories of sacrifice in general. Though the explanations given for the purposes of sacrifice have been almost as varied as the phenomena themselves, they may be reduced to nine common themes drawn from four of the classic works on sacrifice. These themes may be illustrated with descriptions of human sacrificial practices in differing cultural contexts.

E. B. Tylor (1832–1917) theorized that the origin of religion lay in the primitive tendency to "animate" the entire world with "soul-ghosts." Human sacrifice released these soul-ghosts so that they might join their ancestors and function as a gift to gain particular ends, as homage to a deity, or as a form of renunciation.

THEORETICAL PERSPECTIVES

According to W. Robertson Smith (1846–1894), sacrifice originated in totemism. Sacrifice was a communal meal shared between the people and their god, who was simultaneously their totemic animal and their kinsman. Smith postulated two types of sacrifice. The first, the honorific, was a gift either on a friendly basis of exchange or as a part of homage to a powerful deity. The communion meal became a cannibal feast when a tribe, such as the wolf tribe, offered to the god the appropriate food—the members of the sheep tribe, for example. The second, the piacular or expiatory sacrifice, took on a mystical, sacramental flavor when a tribe's own totemic animal was offered as a redemption for a misdeed. The animal, who as a kinsman was also a representative of the people themselves, was killed and then shared in a communion in which people achieved atonement by physically assimilating into their own bodies the totemic form of themselves. The sacrificed animal was reborn by being assimilated into the living bodies of the people who ate it, and since those people were identified with the totemic animal, they too were reborn through this ritual.

James G. Frazer (1854–1941) developed a theory of regeneration of fertility according to which the sacrificial offering possessed tremendous potency. Sacred kings and human vegetative gods were killed to pass on their power to a younger successor, to incorporate their potency into the living who consumed their bodies, and to prevent their decay in old age since decay would endanger the fertility of earthly existence. Frazer also suggested that animals and plants were eventually substituted for the original human sacrificial offering because of the fear inherent in killing humans.

In their essay on Vedic and Hebrew sacrifice (1898), Henri Hubert and Marcel Mauss considered sacrifice to be a religious act which, through the consecration of an offering, modified or transformed the condition of the person who accomplished that act by joining the divine and mortal via the sacrifice. Moreover, the self-sacrifice of a god in human form was the ideal abnegation, for it was an offering of one's own life.

Nine basic purposes of human sacrifice have been commonly cited from these early theorists: (1) humans are sacrificed in order to release souls for the service of the dead ancestors; (2) human sacrifice is a gift that binds deities to people in an exchange or that serves to propitiate the gods either as homage or as renunciation; (3) human sacrifice is a communion meal in which the power of life is assimilated and thus regenerated; (4) the offering of human sacrifice serves as an expiation of past transgressions and has a redemptive character; (5) it brings about atonement, (6) the regeneration of earthly fertility, or (7) immortality; (8) it transforms human conditions; and (9) it unifies the divine and mortal. Although some new approaches have been added taking into consideration factors such as the role that cosmology plays or the ordering capacities of human sacrifice, contemporary interpreters of human sacrifice still find these themes fruitful in a variety of cultural settings.

HISTORICAL CORROBORATION

The burials at Chan Chan (fourteenth–fifteenth centuries) in Peru are illustrative of the theme of soul-release and kinship with the dead. In this capital of the Chimu empire, many adolescent females were sacrificed and buried with their king. It is known that later, during Inca domination (fifteenth–sixteenth centuries), the king was considered alive after death and was treated as a participant in the affairs of his surviving kin. A kinship was established between the dead and the living in the Shang period (c. 1500–1000 BCE) in China as well. According to David N. Keightley (1978), in the Shang political system the dead and the living formed a bureaucracy together. The dead received "salaries" in the form of human sacrifices for their jobs as intercessors between the king and the high god Ti. Without this, earthly prosperity could not continue. At An-yang (c. 1500–1400 BCE), the entombment of an entire company of soldiers, four charioteers, their companions, the horses, and the chariots has been unearthed. [*See* Afterlife, *article on* Chinese Concepts.]

The themes of expiation, redemption, and communion were central in the sacrificial tradition of the early Christian church. The early martyrs believed that their sufferings were evidence that the millennium was close at hand. By recapitulating Christ's death, they shared in his resurrection and were instantly transported into his presence. Ignatius of Antioch (Antakya, Turkey) echoed the themes of redemptive communion when he joyously declared that he looked forward to being crushed by the teeth of beasts so that he might become wheat for God's bread.

Themes of redemption and abnegation can also be found in the self-sacrifices of the samurai in Japan. Drawing on a warrior tradition dating back to the eleventh century that stressed kinship and extreme loyalty in the face of failure, the Bushidō cult arose in the peaceful Tokagawa period (1600–1867). Since there were few wars for the samurai to fight, Confucian ideals were joined with the earlier warrior ethic to create a martial cult in which the warrior was to give complete loyalty to his lord by rendering service in office rather than in war. If *seppuku* (ritual suicide) was demanded, the samurai were to comply without question. The reasons for *seppuku* might include atonement for transgressions, the avoidance of capture in war, the death of one's lord, or a final protest to a lord who failed to follow the samurai's good advice—an act of selflessness intended to bring the foolish lord back to his senses. *Seppuku* became a refined art in which the samurai, with tremendous self-control, slashed his own belly. Often an assistant then decapitated him in such a way that the head was left hanging by a bit of flesh. In one incident forty-seven samurai chose this ritual to avenge the disgraceful death of their lord. The kamikaze pilots of World War II also followed this ancient warrior tradition. [*See also* Bushidō.]

In the Hawaiian Islands, sacrifice stands for transformation, communion, and the capacity to reorder what has been disordered. In Hawaiian theology, gods, humans, and nature are one human species. Gods are no more than differentiated manifestations of the undifferentiated cosmic Pō (of which people and nature are extensions) so that the entire world is related by kinship. The sacrificial ritual begins with some perceived lack, which is understood as a kind of disorder. The offering is consecrated to the god, who eats a part of the sacrifice, thus assimilating into himself its *mana* (effective potency). The sacrifice then passes back to the participants, who assimilate it. In this communal sharing, life is reordered and thus regenerated via the mutual assimilation of the sacrifice—an assimilation made possible by the shared kinship of gods and humans. A transformative reordering is made.

The evidence for human sacrifice in Vedic India (c. 1500–600 BCE) is still largely contested. However, by drawing on both textual and archaeological sources, Asko Parpola has suggested that rituals that were precursors of the Agnicayana (Vedic fire sacrifice) included the killing of humans. These earlier rites were part of a yearly cycle of two seasons devoted to war and agriculture, the two divisions marked by sacrifices in which the Aśvamedha (horse sacrifice) was equated with the *puruṣamedha* (human sacrifice). Death and regeneration were central concepts in these two sacrifices as they were in the Agnicayana. Even today, the Agnicayana symbolically involves human sacrifice: the mythic sacrificial dismemberment of Puruṣa (Cosmic Man) is recalled as the fire altar is constructed brick by brick, an act that reorders both Puruṣa and the cosmos. Five heads originally were buried under the altar—those of a man, a horse, an ox, a sheep, and a goat. Today a live tortoise is buried because of its cosmic and regenerative symbolism. The first layer of bricks represents Puruṣa's thousand eyes, and the finished altar is shaped like the firebird who will carry the sacrifice to heaven. J. C. Heesterman has suggested that human sacrifice was eliminated in the Brāhmanas (c. 900–700 BCE), which substituted animals and rice cakes, in an attempt to control the fear of disorder inherent in the ritual killing of humans. [*See* Vedism and Brahmanism *and* Puruṣa.]

The themes of order and disorder also play a role in Aztec sacrifice as does the theme of sacrificial exchange. A central myth of the Aztec tells of the birth and destruction of four ages prior to the Fifth Sun, the age of the Aztec. Each previous age is named for the way in which the sun was totally destroyed. The Fifth Sun, called the "age of movement," was also doomed to destruction by earthquakes and famine. The sun of this age was born by the willing self-sacrifice of the gods, and so shall people sacrifice themselves for the gods in return. In a cosmic exchange, gods are the maize of people's existence while people are tortillas for the gods to eat. But just as all people are born, eat food, grow old, and die, so too will the Fifth Sun meet its demise, no matter how much it is fed. The Aztec universe was thus unstable—wobbling between periods of order and disorder. Only human sacrifice could stay the end, and that only temporarily. In this eschatological setting, massive sacrificial rites were performed that may have offered people a chance to take some control of their inevitable destruction, a chance to control the uncontrollable.

Human sacrifice may seem remote to civilized sensibilities. Nevertheless, as a human act it must be at least partly intelligible to other humans. On 18 November 1978, in Jonestown, Guyana, 914 members of the People's Temple took their own lives by means of a cyanide-laced fruit drink. Most of them did so willingly. The complex reasons for this massive sacrifice of human lives are both disturbing and challenging to one's capacity to understand. Yet some familiar themes may be recognized. The people of Jonestown, like the Christian martyrs, believed in a utopian world on "the other side." Like the samurai, they chose death as a "revolutionary act" to protest against the racism that they had failed to overcome, and like the Aztecs, they preferred to choose the time and place of their own deaths. As Jim Jones said during that "white night": "I haven't seen anybody yet didn't die. And I like to choose my own kind of death for a change."

[*See also* Suicide.]

BIBLIOGRAPHY

E. B. Tylor's theories of animism and sacrifice as a release of souls is discussed in his *Religion in Primitive Culture* (1871; Gloucester, Mass., 1970), vol. 2, pp. 1–87. The section on sacrifice (pp. 461–496) describes this phenomenon in terms of Tylor's views on its traits, mechanisms, permutations, and survivals. The short article "Sacrifice" in the *Encyclopaedia Britannica,* 9th ed. (Boston, 1886), is W. Robertson Smith's initial and concise explication of his theories of sacrifice in general, including those of human sacrifice. For James G. Frazer's theories of sacrifice, see his twelve-volume work *The Golden Bough: A Study in Magic and Religion,* 3d ed., rev. & enl. (London, 1911–1915). Henri Hubert's and Marcel Mauss's *Sacrifice: Its Nature and Function* (Chicago, 1964) is a short study of the structure and function of Vedic and Hebrew sacrificial rituals and is a classic work that has had widespread influence.

A short article by David N. Keightley, "The Religious Commitment: Shang Theology and the Genesis of Chinese Political Culture," *History of Religions* 17 (February–May 1978): 211–225, gives a concise discussion of the religious perspective that may have provided a basis for, among other things, human sacrifice in the Shang period of early China. Jacquetta Hawkes's *Atlas of Ancient Archeology* (New York, 1974) gives a short description of the Anyang site and includes a bibliography. A comprehensive discussion of martyrdom and its sacrificial theology in the early Christian church can be found in W. H. C. Frend's *Martyrdom and Persecution in the Early Church* (Oxford, 1965). H. Paul Varley's book *The Samurai* (London, 1970), written with Ivan I. Morris and Nobuko Morris, is a popular treatment of the cult of the warrior and its conceptual changes throughout Japanese history from the fourth to the twentieth century. Valerio Valeri's *Kingship and Sacrifice: Ritual and Society in Ancient Hawaii* (Chicago, 1985) is an extensive study of the structure and function of Hawaiian sacrificial rituals, with particular attention to the role of the king. Valeri includes a fine discussion of Hawaiian theology as well.

A lengthy treatment of a contemporary performance of the ancient Vedic fire ritual can be found in Frits Staal's two-volume *Agni: The Vedic Ritual of the Fire Altar* (Berkeley, 1983). This book also includes source material for the historical background of the possibility of human sacrifice in early India. It also includes an article by Asko Parpola, "The Pre-Vedic Indian Background of the Srauta Rituals" (vol. 2, pp. 41–75), which discusses the relationship between the horse sacrifice and human sacrifice.

An extraordinarily rich source of information on the Aztecs was compiled by a sixteenth-century Franciscan father, Bernardino de Sahaguń, in his *Historia general de las cosas de la Nueva España,* translated by Arthur J. O. Anderson and Charles E. Dibble as *Florentine Codex: A General History of the Things of New Spain,* 13 vols. (Santa Fe, N.Mex., 1950–1982). Volumes 2, 3, and 7 are particularly good for ritualistic and mythic sources on human sacrifice.

3 SUICIDE

Marilyn J. Harran

The topic of religiously motivated suicide is a complex one. Several of the major religious traditions reject suicide as a religiously justifiable act but commend martyrdom; among them are Judaism, Christianity, and Islam. These religions distinguish between actively willing to end one's life in suicide and passively accepting one's death as the divine will by means of martyrdom at the hands of another. Nonetheless, the actions of some of the early Christian martyrs and the deaths of the Jews at Masada in 74 CE blur this distinction. [*See also* Martyrdom.]

In contrast to religiously motivated suicide one may speak of heroic and altruistic suicide, the act of a person who decides that he or she has an ethical responsibility to die for the sake of community or honor. One must also differentiate between religiously motivated suicide and suicide that may be virtually forced upon an individual by the norms of society and may constitute either a duty or a punishment. One thinks of *satī*, widow burning in India, and of *seppuku*, self-disembowelment, when it occurred as a punishment in Japan. In these cases too, however, no simple distinction holds true. *Satī* became an accepted practice within medieval Hinduism, upheld by the brahmans, and accounts indicate that even into modern times it was often a voluntary practice. By her self-sacrifice the widow both achieved an honored status for herself and atoned for the sins and misdeeds of herself and her husband. *Seppuku* was often the voluntary last act of a defeated warrior who chose to demonstrate both his fealty to his lord and his mastery over himself.

Like the major Western traditions, both Buddhism and Confucianism condemn suicide, but there are examples of self-immolation by Buddhist monks and of the seeking of honorable death by Confucian gentlemen. In contrast to these traditions, Jainism regards favorably the practice of *sallekhanā*, by which a Jain monk or layperson at the end of his lifetime or at the onset of serious illness attains death by gradual starvation.

These few examples demonstrate the complexity of the topic of religiously motivated suicide and the difficulty in distinguishing it from martyrdom or sacrifice, on the one hand, and from heroic or altruistic suicide, on the other. In addition, the occurrence in 1978 of the mass suicides at Jonestown, Guyana, raises the question of the relation between religious motivations for suicide and general fear of persecution, combined with mass paranoia. This question applies equally well to the mass suicide of Jews faced with persecution in York, England, in 1190 and to the mass suicides of Old Believers in Russia in the late seventeenth century.

On the whole, what we may term religiously motivated suicides constitute but a small proportion of the total number of suicides. In his classic work *Le suicide,* Émile Durkheim discussed the social causes for egoistic, altruistic, and anomic suicides. His work and that of many other scholars demonstrate that suicide has most often occurred for reasons other than religious ones. These include the desire to avoid shame, to effect revenge, to demonstrate one's disappointment in love, and to escape senility and the infirmities of old age. Suicide as a means of avoiding shame and upholding one's honor was considered a creditable act in societies as different as those on the Melanesian island of Tikopia, among the Plains and Kwakiutl Indians of North America, and in ancient Rome.

Scholars have argued that the incidence of and attitude toward suicide are largely dependent on the individual's and society's view of the afterlife. Where death is perceived as a happy existence, scholars such as Jacques Choron believe, there is an inducement to suicide. In the first known document that apparently reflects on suicide, the Egyptian text entitled *The Dialogue of a Misanthrope with His Own Soul*, death is seen as attractive because it will lead to another and better existence. The tendency toward suicide is strengthened when suicide is regarded either as a neutral act or as one worthy of reward. Suicide rates also increase when this life is regarded as no longer acceptable or worthwhile. For example, Jim Jones, the founder of the Peoples' Temple, urged his followers in Guyana to commit suicide in order to enter directly into a new and better world, where they would be free of persecution and would enjoy the rewards of the elect. In the Jonestown community, suicide on a mass scale was appreciated as a religiously justifiable act that would be rewarded in the afterlife.

ANCIENT GREEK AND ROMAN CIVILIZATION

While the ancient Greek writers and philosophers did not consider suicide an action that would lead to a better existence, they did see it as an appropriate response to certain circumstances. The fact that Jocasta, the mother of Oedipus, chose to commit suicide upon learning of her incestuous relationship with her son was understood and appreciated by the ancients as an appropriate response to a disastrous situation. Heroic suicide in the face of a superior enemy and the choice of death to avoid dishonor or the agony of a lengthy terminal illness were accepted as justifiable actions. Through the voice of Socrates, Plato in his *Phaedo* did much to form the classical attitude toward suicide. Socrates himself chose to drink the hemlock, but he also affirmed the Orphic notions that man is placed in a prison from which he may not release himself and that he is a possession of the gods. The decision to commit suicide is thus an act against the gods, depriving them of their prerogative to end or to sustain human life. The key word for both Plato and Socrates is *necessity.* A person may appropriately end his life only when the gods send the necessity to do so upon him, as in fact they did to Socrates. Plato's disciple, Aristotle, argued even more strongly against suicide. He regarded it as an offense against the state, since by such an act a person fails to perform his obligations as a citizen. Thus it became a social outrage—a view that has continued to dominate thought in the West until the most recent times.

Whereas the Pythagoreans and Epicureans opposed suicide, the Stoics regarded it favorably under certain circumstances. The Stoic was obliged to make a decision that properly addressed the demands of the situation; at times the decision might be to commit suicide. Both Zeno and his successor, Cleanthes, are reported to have done so.

Heroic suicide and suicide to avoid dishonor or suffering became frequent within the society of the Roman empire. Seneca, in particular, moved beyond the insistence on a divine call or necessity for suicide to the assertion that suicide at the appropriate time is a basic individual right. For Seneca, the central issue was freedom, and he affirmed that the divine had offered humankind a number of exits from life; he himself chose to exercise the right to suicide. His successor, Epictetus, placed more limits on suicide, stressing again the belief that one must wait for the divine command before acting: the suffering that is a normal part of daily life for much of humanity does not of itself constitute a sufficient reason for suicide—although exceptional pain and suffering offer justifiable cause. For Epictetus, Socrates was the best model and guide in deciding when one might legitimately choose to end one's life.

JUDAISM

Whereas suicide was at the very least tolerated, and often applauded, among the ancient Greeks and Romans, the Hebrew people disapproved of it. Judaism draws a clear distinction between suicide, which it defines as self-murder, and martyrdom, which it defines as death on behalf of one's faith and religious convictions. Nonetheless, the Hebrew scriptures, which contain few references to dying by one's own hand, do describe several instances of heroic suicide. The king Abimelech, gravely wounded by a woman, called upon his armor-bearer to kill him (*Jgs.* 9:52–54). Although he did not literally kill himself, his command to his aide may be regarded as effecting what he could not perform himself, so that he might not die in dishonor. The death of Samson (*Jgs.* 16:28–31) may certainly be judged a heroic suicide, since by his act he brought about the demise of a large number of the enemy Philistines. The gravely injured Saul fell upon his own sword in order to avoid a disgraceful death at the hands of his enemies (*1 Sm.* 31:4), and his armor-bearer, who had failed his master's request to kill him, then fell upon his own sword. The death of Ahithophel, the counselor to David and then to David's son Absalom, would appear to be a suicide motivated by disgrace. When Absalom refused to follow the advice Ahithophel gave him regarding his battle with David, Ahithophel returned home, set his affairs in order, and hanged himself (*2 Sm.* 17:23). The last suicide recorded in the Hebrew scriptures, the death of the king Zimri, occurred because of the loss of a decisive battle (*1 Kgs.* 16:18).

Although Hebrew scriptures do not explicitly forbid suicide, the Judaic tradition came to prohibit it, partly in the belief that God alone gives life and takes it away, and partly on the basis of the sixth commandment, which forbids unjustified homicide. However, rabbinic law regards persons committing suicide as most frequently being of unsound mind and thus not responsible for their actions. Under these circumstances, they may still receive normal Jewish burial rites. Furthermore, suicides committed under duress, as for example to avoid murder, idolatry, or adultery, were considered blameless and indeed even praiseworthy. The mass suicide at Masada in 74 CE and other mass suicides in Europe during the Middle Ages were considered in this light.

Concerning Masada, the historian Josephus Flavius recounts, on the basis of the report of a few survivors, that on the eve of the Roman assault on that hill the leader of the vastly outnumbered Jewish resistance, El'azar ben Ya'ir, called the community together and reminded them of their vow not to become the slaves of the Romans. That night many of the soldiers killed their families and committed suicide. Others drew lots to decide who would kill his fellows and then die by his own hand. It is impossible to say how many of the over nine hundred defenders allowed themselves to be killed and how many ended their lives by suicide. In spite of the Jewish prohibition against suicide, Masada came to be regarded as a heroic sacrifice, and it remains a living symbol of a people's response to oppression.

Although accounts of individual suicide within Judaism are rare, there are examples of mass suicides during times of persecution. During the First Crusade, in 1096, Jews who had obtained sanctuary in the bishop's castle at Worms chose mass suicide over baptism; similar instances of suicide to avoid baptism occurred in various Rhineland towns, such as Mayence, and in York, England, where in 1190 some 150 Jews set fire to the building in which they had sought safety and then consigned themselves to the flames. Yet other instances of mass suicide occurred during the Black Death, when popular superstition blamed the outbreak of the plague on the Jews. Although abuse and persecution were certainly major motivating factors during the periods of the Crusades and the Black Death, these mass or multiple suicides appear to have arisen from a deep religious desire to remain true to the faith. They point again to the difficulty in distinguishing between, on the one hand, suicides motivated by fear of persecution and, on the other, suicides motivated by religious convictions and ideals, deaths that in the latter case the tradition judges to be acts of martyrdom. Certainly the deaths at Masada must be regarded as both faithful obedience to religious affiliation and identity and the culmination of a desire to give the Jews' enemies a hollow victory.

CHRISTIANITY

Christianity repudiates suicide on much the same biblical grounds as does Judaism. The only suicide recorded in the New Testament is that of Jesus' betrayer, Judas Iscariot; it is described in such a way as to indicate that it was a sign of repentance for his deed (*Mt.* 27:3–5). The church father Tertullian referred even to Jesus' death as voluntary—a description approximating that of suicide, since clearly a divine being controls his own life. In his book *Conversion* (1962), Arthur Darby Nock points to the "theatricality" present in some of the actions of the early martyrs, as in "the frequent tendency of Christians in times of persecution to force themselves on the notice of the magistrates by tearing down images or by other demonstrations" (p. 197). Bishop Ignatius of Antioch, writing to his fellow Christians in Rome, pleaded that they do nothing to hinder his martyrdom but allow him to be consumed entirely by the beasts. But whereas Tertullian asserted that only martyrs would reach paradise before the Parousia, Clement of Alexandria sought to stem the tide of those rushing to martyrdom by differentiating between self-motivated suicide and genuine martyrdom for the faith.

In his *City of God,* which appeared in 428 CE, the church father Augustine wrote against suicide in a way that became determinative for the tradition. He discussed various situations in which a Christian might find himself or herself, and concluded that suicide is not a legitimate act even in such desperate circumstances as those of a virgin seeking to protect her virtue. Augustine argued that suicide is a form of homicide, and thus prohibited by the sixth commandment; that a suicide committed in order to avoid sin is in reality the commission of a greater sin to avoid a lesser; and that one who commits suicide forfeits the possibility of repentance. Subsequent church councils, as well as such eminent theologians as Thomas Aquinas in the thirteenth century, sided with Augustine. Suicide, in contrast to martyrdom, came to be regarded as both a sin and a crime. Dante placed suicides in the seventh circle of the inferno in his *Divine Comedy,* and popular opinion throughout Christian Europe regarded suicides in the same light as witches and warlocks. Indeed, their corpses were treated in a similar manner: suicides were frequently buried at crossroads with stakes driven through their hearts to prevent their ghosts from causing harm. The last recorded instance of such a burial in England occurred in 1823, and the law mandating confiscation of the property of a convicted suicide remained on the books until 1870.

In spite of ecclesiastical censure, religious impulse did lead to suicides, sometimes on a mass scale. Some thirteenth-century Cathari or Albigensians may have chosen suicide by starvation. Even more dramatic are the accounts of the Old Believers *(raskol'niki)* in late seventeenth-century Russia who chose death by fire over obedience to liturgical changes introduced by the archbishop Nikon, with the subsequent backing of the tsars. According to tradition, on several occasions one to two thousand people who had been besieged by government troops, as at Paleostrovskii monastery in 1688, locked themselves within chapels or monasteries and burned them to the ground, consigning their own bodies to the flames.

Although martyrdom as a testimony to one's faith continues to be honored within Christianity, suicide as an individual act undertaken for nonreligious motives is regarded as a sin, and until recently it was regarded as a crime unless done in ignorance of its implications or in a state of lunacy. Few Christian theologians and philosophers challenged this view. John Donne, who served as dean of Saint Paul's in London, was a notable exception. In his book *Biathanatos,* written in 1608 but not published until 1644, Donne challenged the Augustinian belief that suicides cannot repent; he argued that a totally negative attitude toward suicide places limitations on the mercy and charity of God. New attitudes toward suicide were subsequently expounded by a variety of philosophers such as David Hume, who argued that suicide is not a crime. However, although the Christian attitude toward suicide may now be characterized as more compassionate than during earlier periods, the act of suicide, in contrast to martyrdom, continues to be regarded as a serious sin.

ISLAM

Islam joined Judaism and Christianity in prohibiting suicide *(intiḥār)* while glorifying those who die the death of a martyr *(shahīd)* or witness to the faith. While scholars debate whether or not the Qur'ān itself specifically forbids suicide, they agree that the *ḥadīth,* the traditions that preserve the words of the Prophet on a wide variety of issues, prohibit suicide. According to these sources, Muḥammad proclaimed that a person who commits suicide will be denied Paradise and will spend his time in Hell repeating the deed by which he had ended his life. By the tradition's own standards, religiously motivated suicide is an impossibility, since the taking of one's own life is both a sin and a crime. Nonetheless, as with Judaism and Christianity, the line between suicide and martyrdom is not clear. Since it is believed that the Muslim martyr who dies in defense of the faith is rewarded with immediate entrance into Paradise, where he will enjoy great pleasures and rewards, it would not be surprising if some Muslims readily participated in battles even when badly outnumbered, in the hope that they might die while fighting.

Within Islam the Shīʿī sect emphasizes the self-sacrifice and suffering of its imams, the successors to Muḥammad. The death of Ḥusayn, the grandson of the Prophet, and the third imam, was regarded by his followers as an act of voluntary self-sacrifice that could be termed a religiously motivated death. Although he died on the battlefield, his death was subsequently interpreted as a goal he both desired and actively sought; the passion play enacted as the climax of ʿĀshūrā' (tenth of Muḥarram) depicts his death as actively willed. In a translation of this play (*Muhammedan Festivals,* edited by G. E. von Grunebaum, New York, 1951) Ḥusayn says: "Dear Grandfather [Muḥammad], I abhor life; I would rather go visit my dear ones in the next world" (p. 92). Within Shiism, and the Ismāʿīlī sect, Ḥasan-i Sabbāḥ in the twelfth century formed the order of the Assassins, which was devoted to establishing its own religious and governmental autonomy, in part by killing both Crusaders and Sunnī Muslims. The death of a member of this order was regarded not as a suicide, even when his mission had been one almost certain to result in his death, but rather as a glorious martyrdom that would earn him both the veneration of society and the delights of Paradise. The tradition cites many accounts of a mother who rejoiced on hearing of the death of her son, only to put on mourning clothes when she learned subsequently that he had not died and thus had not attained the glorious state of martyrdom.

HINDUISM AND JAINISM

In discussing Judaism, Christianity, and Islam, I have pointed to the close relationship between suicide and martyrdom and the difficulty frequently encountered in distinguishing between them. Regarding the religions of the East, the difficult issue is the relation between suicide and sacrifice. In Hinduism, the Brāhmaṇas laid the foundation for religiously motivated suicide by declaring that the fullest and most genuine sacrifice is that of the individual's self. The *Śatapatha Brāhmaṇa* outlines the procedure by which one renounces the world, forsaking one's belongings and departing into the forest. Certainly Hinduism affirms that suicide must be a thoughtful decision—as in the resolve of a person to end the sufferings of old age—or that it must be a religiously motivated act. One Upaniṣad condemns those who attempt suicide without having attained the necessary degree of enlightenment. The Dharmasūtras firmly prohibit any suicide other than one religiously motivated. In ancient and medieval Hinduism a number of methods of committing suicide were regarded favorably, such as drowning oneself in the Ganges, jumping from a cliff, burning oneself, burying oneself in snow, or starving oneself to death. Various places of pilgrimage, such as Prayāga (present-day Allahabad) or Banaras, were seen as particularly auspicious places for ending one's life.

Two types of suicide in Hinduism, very different in form and intention, are worthy of special examination. The first is the death by suicide of the enlightened person, the world renouncer. Such a person, in his quest for release from *saṃsāra,* has devoted himself to increasingly difficult acts of penance and to a thorough study of the Upaniṣads. Once he has attained the goal of freedom from all desires, he may begin the great journey in the direction of the northeast, consuming nothing other than air and water. According to the lawgiver Manu, a brahman might also follow this procedure when he begins to be overcome by a serious illness.

The second form of suicide in Hinduism that deserves special attention is *satī,* widow burning. It appears to have been a form of suicide motivated by both social and religious considerations. Although the custom is not unique to India, it nonetheless was practiced there most frequently and over the longest period of time. The practice may go back as far as the fourth century BCE, but it began to grow in popularity only after about 400 CE. According to Upendra Thakur in his study *The History of Suicide in India,* "*satī* in its latest forms was a mediaeval growth though it had its germs in ancient customs and rituals" (1963, p. 141). The practice of *satī* might take one of two forms. In one, *sahamaraṇa,* the woman ascended the funeral pyre and was burned alongside the corpse of her husband. In the second, *anumaraṇa,* when the wife learned that her husband had died and his body had already been cremated, she would ascend the pyre and die alongside his ashes, or with some belonging of his. Certainly, at least in some cases, *satī* was motivated by genuine feelings of grief and affection on the part of the widow. Although the practice remained voluntary, in some areas social pressure may have made *satī* more the rule than the exception. No doubt the practice also gained popularity because the life of a widow was both lonely and degrading. On the other hand, the blessing or curse of a woman on her way to perform *satī* was believed to be very powerful, and her act of sacrifice was believed to purify both herself and her husband. Thus, although the act of *satī* may not always have been religiously motivated, it did have its religious reward. The British, during their rule of India, made a determined effort to abolish the practice, finally outlawing it as homicide in 1829.

Perhaps the tradition that most explicitly condones religiously motivated suicide is Jainism. Following the teaching of their saint Mahāvīra, who lived in the sixth century BCE, the Jain monk and the Jain layperson lead, in differing degrees, a rigorously ascetic life in order to attain liberation and to free the soul from karma. Members of the laity as well as monks are encouraged to practice *sallekhanā* (austere penance), in order to attain a holy death through meditation. Jains believe it is their duty to prevent disease or the infirmities of old age from undermining the spiritual progress they have attained through asceticism and meditation. Jainism prescribes strict rules for when *sallekhanā* is appropriate. As Padmanabh S. Jaini indicated in his book *The Jaina Path of Purification,* Jainism distinguishes between impure suicide, by which the passions are increased, and pure suicide, the holy death attained with "inner peace or dispassionate mindfulness" (Jaini, 1979, p. 229). *Sallekhanā* involves gradual fasting, often under the supervision of a monastic teacher, until the stage is reached whereat the individual no longer consumes any food or drink and thus gradually attains death by starvation. Jains perceive *salle-*

khanā to be the climax of a lifetime of spiritual struggle, ascetic practice, and meditation. It allows the individual to control his own destiny so that he will attain full liberation or at the very least reduce the number of future reincarnations that he will undergo.

BUDDHISM AND CONFUCIANISM

Turning to Buddhism and Confucianism, we find that suicide is legislated against in both traditions, but that there are notable exceptions involving religiously motivated suicide. Gautama Buddha, in his personal search for salvation, deliberately chose against the practice of fasting unto death. Nonetheless, under certain extraordinary circumstances, Buddhists see religiously motivated suicide as an act of sacrifice and worship. We find indications of this positive attitude toward suicide, or self-sacrifice, in some of the accounts of the Buddha's previous lives contained in the Jātakas (Birth Tales). The stories of the Buddha's previous lives as a hare *(Śaśa Jātaka)* and as a monkey *(Mahākapi Jātaka)* both describe suicide as an act of self-sacrifice to benefit another, and only in the story of the monkey does this act lead to death. Another famous account is that from the *Suvarṇaprabhāṣa,* a Mahāyāna *sūtra,* which describes the suicide or sacrifice of the Buddha, during his life as the prince Mahāsattva, in order to feed a hungry tigress unable to care for herself. Following this model, Buddhism in its various forms affirms that, while suicide as self-sacrifice may be appropriate for the person who is an *arhat,* one who has attained enlightenment, it is still very much the exception to the rule.

Confucianism based its attitude toward suicide on another consideration, that of filial piety and obligation. The person who commits suicide robs his ancestors of the veneration and service due them and demonstrates his ingratitude to his parents for the gift of life. The duty of a gentleman is to guide his life according to *li,* the code or rules of propriety. In rare cases, suicide was required of the gentleman who failed to uphold these rules. In some instances a gentleman might commit suicide to protest improper government, since above all a gentleman was obliged to uphold the virtue of humaneness. Thus, in these unusual instances suicide was the correct way to demonstrate adherence to the precepts of Confucianism.

Although the Japanese tradition of *seppuku,* or *harakiri,* should be regarded in its voluntary form as heroic rather than as religiously motivated suicide, it nonetheless does contain certain religious elements. The standard by which all acts of *seppuku* (disembowelment) were judged was set by the heroic Minamoto Yorimasa during a desperate battle in 1180. While suicide was usually performed as an individual act by a noble warrior or *samurai,* there are examples in Japanese history of mass suicides, such as that of the forty-seven *rōnin* who accepted the penalty of *seppuku* in order to avenge the death of their lord in 1703.

While Christian missionaries in Japan, from the time of the arrival of the first Jesuits, sought to prevent *seppuku,* the Zen Buddhist tradition continued to regard it as a form of honorable death. The selection of the *hara,* or belly, as the point at which the sword was plunged into the body reflected the belief that the abdomen is the place where one exercises control over one's breathing and is, indeed, the central point of self-discipline. More generally, as Ivan I. Morris states in his book *The Nobility of Failure,* the abdomen was considered in the Japanese tradition as "the locus of man's inner being, the place where his will, spirit, generosity, indignation, courage, and other cardinal qualities were concentrated" (Morris, 1975, p. 367). Thus, by committing oneself to the performance of *seppuku,* which became a clearly defined ritual, one demonstrated in this final act the greatest degree of self-control, discipline, and courage.

CONCLUSION

This article has focused directly on religiously motivated suicide. It has omitted references to suicide among elderly Inuit (Eskimo) and among young Tikopia islanders, to cite only two examples from a vast number of possibilities. In these cases, as in many others, although the suicides may be heroic or altruistic, they do not demonstrate a clear religious motivation. Suicides by reason of financial failure, or loss of honor or of a loved one, occur among the Kwakiutl and Iroquois Indians, as well as among Bantu-speaking peoples of Africa. Occurrences of suicide are not limited by geography or time, but of the many suicides that have taken place throughout the ages, only a small proportion can be judged to be religiously motivated.

The examples of religiously motivated suicide discussed here demonstrate the wide variety of forms and purposes that the act may take. Many of the examples, from both East and West, illustrate the difficulty in distinguishing between suicide that is religiously motivated and suicide that is motivated by heroism, altruism, or fear of persecution and suffering. The deaths at Jonestown in 1978 raise anew the problem of how we are to differentiate between religiously motivated suicide and suicide induced by paranoia and terror. There is no simple distinction between suicide and martyrdom, on the one hand, or between suicide and sacrifice, on the other. In formulating these distinctions and in evaluating the morality and religious value of certain acts that result in death, each person brings to bear his or her own religious and ethical values and tradition. Such personal judgment must, however, be conjoined with the awareness that what may be perceived by one observer as needless self-sacrifice or even self-murder may be judged by another as the noblest example of religiously motivated suicide in behalf of beliefs, values, or tradition.

BIBLIOGRAPHY

There is a vast literature on suicide, but relatively little of it focuses on the act as religiously motivated. Any student of the topic must begin with Émile Durkheim's *Le suicide,* translated by John A. Spaulding and George Simpson as *Suicide: A Study in Sociology* (New York, 1951). It is the classic work on the varieties of suicide analyzed from a sociological viewpoint. Jacques Choron's chapters on "Suicide in Retrospect" and "Philosophers on Suicide" in his volume *Suicide* (New York, 1972) are quite helpful in understanding the place of suicide in the West at different times. A volume edited by Frederick H. Holck, *Death and Eastern Thought: Understanding Death in Eastern Religions and Philosophies* (Nashville, 1974), contains several chapters that refer to suicide. Alfred Alvarez also discusses the themes of religious motivation for suicide and religious prohibition of the act in his book *The Savage God: A Study of Suicide* (London, 1971). He includes personal reflections on his own suicide attempt, and describes his friendship with the poet Sylvia Plath, who committed suicide in 1963.

Among the older studies of the topic, still useful are *Suicide: A Social and Historical Study* by Henry Romilly Fedden (London, 1938) and *To Be or Not to Be: A Study of Suicide* by Louis I. Dublin and Bessie Bunzel (New York, 1933).

There are relatively few sources that consider religiously motivated suicide in specific traditions. For the Western religious traditions, the reader should refer to the bibliography of the article *Martyrdom* as well as to the various primary sources mentioned throughout this article. In addition, for Judaism, the reader will find useful Yigael Yadin's *Masada: Herod's Fortress and the Zealots' Last Stand* (New York, 1966) and Cecil Roth's *A History of the Jews in England* (Oxford, 1941), which discusses the events at York. On Christianity, particularly informative is Samuel E. Sprott's *The English Debate on Suicide from Donne to Hume* (La Salle, Ill., 1961). William A. Clebsch has prepared a new edition of John Donne's work, translated as *Suicide* (Chico, Calif., 1983), with a very helpful introduction. Robert O. Crummey presents a fascinating account of suicides among the Raskol'niki in his book *The Old Believers and the World of Antichrist: The Vyg Community and the Russian State, 1694–1855* (Madison, Wis., 1970). See especially his chapter entitled "Death by Fire." On Islam, the most useful secondary source remains Franz Rosenthal's "On Suicide in Islam," *Journal of the American Oriental Society* 66 (1946): 239–259. For the Assassins, one should consult the comprehensive historical account by Marshall G. S. Hodgson in *The Order of Assassins: The Struggle of the Early Nizârî Ismâ'îlîs against the Islamic World* (1955; New York, 1980).

For the Eastern traditions, in addition to the volume edited by Holck and the primary texts mentioned in the article, the following books are useful sources for individual traditions. For Hinduism, see both the older account by Edward Thompson, *Suttee: A Historical and Philosophical Enquiry into the Hindu Rite of Widow-Burning* (London, 1928), and the more comprehensive study by Upendra Thakur, *The History of Suicide in India: An Introduction* (Delhi, 1963). For Jainism, Padmanabh S. Jaini offers a detailed account of *sallekhanā* in his book *The Jaina Path of Purification* (Berkeley, 1979). The Buddhist account entitled "The Bodhisattva and the Hungry Tigress" may be found in the volume edited by Edward Conze, *Buddhist Scriptures* (Harmondsworth, 1959). For the Japanese attitude toward suicide and death, see the fascinating work by Ivan I. Morris, *The Nobility of Failure: Tragic Heroes in the History of Japan* (New York, 1975), and for the study of *seppuku* among the warrior class, see *The Samurai: A Military History* by S. R. Turnbull (New York, 1977).

4 FUNERAL RITES

Louis-Vincent Thomas
Translated from French by Kristine Anderson

Death is not only a biological occurrence leaving the corpse as a residue that must be administered to; it is also, and more importantly, a sociocultural fundamental because of the beliefs and representations it gives rise to and the attitudes and rituals it brings about. It is of course understood that rites are the immediate extension of beliefs, and that funeral rites, in particular, are the conscious cultural forms of one of our most ancient, universal, and unconscious impulses: the need to overcome the distress of death and dying.

We will here take the word *rite* in its anthropological sense; that is, in a larger sense, quite apart from liturgical or theological concerns. A rite, then, is a ceremony in which behaviors, gestures and postures, words or songs uttered, and objects handled, manufactured, destroyed, or consumed are supposed to possess virtues or powers or to produce specific effects. Centered on the mortal remains or its substitute, then on whatever survives of those—material traces or souvenir relics—funeral rites may reveal three finalities. First, it is believed that they preside over the future of the departed, over both the metamorphosis of the corpse and the destiny of the person, whenever death is defined as transition, passage, or deliverance. Second, they attend to the surviving close kin, mourners who must be consoled and reassured. Finally, they participate in the revitalization of the group that has been disturbed by the death of one of its own. Very often in traditional societies, in Africa and more often in Asia (notably in China), the funeral rites are presented as a theater of renewal, with acted parts, mimes, dancers, musicians, and even clowns.

Funeral rites are so important that the presence of the participants becomes a strict obligation, particularly in traditional societies. In traditional Africa, funeral rites are the most resistant to the pressure of acculturation. A function of the rite essential to the social group is easily seen; after all, numerous psychiatrists affirm that many problems derive from the guilt arising when one hurries over obsequies or comes out of mourning too soon.

Chief Moments in Funeral Rites

Funeral rites may comprise numerous ceremonies. The Toraja of Sulawesi (Celebes) see four fundamental stages. During the first, the deceased is said to be ill: washed, dressed, and adorned, he may be nurtured for as long as a year. Then comes the first festivity, lasting from five to seven days, with sacrifices, lamentations, songs, and dances; this marks the difficult passage from life to death and ends with a provisional interment inside the house. During the following intermediary period, these festivities increase. Finally the ultimate ceremony is performed, requiring several months of preparation during which winding-sheets, cenotaphs, and, most notably, an effigy (the famous *tau-tau*) are employed, not without ostentation; it concludes with the burial and the installation of the deceased in the beyond.

The succession of funerary acts sometimes takes on a bureaucratic tone, particularly in Chinese Taoism, where the main part of the rite is devoted to drawing up documents and contracts with the gods. Especially noteworthy are the consultation of cosmic forces in order to determine propitious days and places for the rites; the *kung-te,* or acquisition of merits for the deceased; the *p'u-tu,* or offerings for wandering souls; and the ritual for liberating the soul.

Nevertheless, to determine the chief moments of funerals, anthropologists use the formulation, however incorrect, of the double funeral, which implies rites of separation followed by intervals varying from a few weeks to several years, followed by rites of integration that put an end to the mourning.

SEPARATION RITES

In most traditional societies, the passage from decay to mineralization dictates the two chief moments in the funerary ritual. The first funeral, or separation rite, is for the purpose of "killing the dead," as the Mossi of Burkina Faso say—in other words, killing what remains alive in the dead person by breaking the emotional bonds that unite him to the community. While the corpse decays, simultaneously corrupt and corrupting, it is terribly vulnerable and dangerous. Two attitudes, contradictory yet complementary, orient the conduct of the living toward the dead: solicitude and rejection, shown in a symbolic or realistic manner according to points of view that vary with each ethnic group.

Solicitude begins immediately after death, tinged with commiseration and fear: the dead person is given food, gongs are sounded to scare away evil spirits, the corpse is washed and purified, and its evolutions are watched, especially if the body lies in state for a long time (from three to twelve days among the Miao of Southeast Asia). It is dressed, its natural orifices are stopped, and, most important, the wake is organized. This can be the occasion for big reunions and a largescale ritual. For the Maori of New Zealand it is an intensely dramatic ceremony, the key moment of the funeral rite, accompanied by songs, cries, lamentations, elegies, and more or less generous meals, depending on the fortune of the deceased. To multiple meals the Inca of Peru added games of dice with very complex symbolism. The outcome of the game was supposed to orient the soul of the deceased so as to help him attain heaven. The dead person participated by influencing the manner in which the dice fell, thereby revealing whether he was well or ill disposed toward the player. The deceased's possessions were divided according to the results.

When respectful solicitude has soothed the dead, rejection asserts itself. Once the last homages are rendered, the deceased is invited to rejoin his ancestors or to prepare for his afterlife (metamorphoses, reincarnation, sojourn with God, etc.). To overcome his hesitation, a number of methods are used: one may tie him down securely or mutilate him (poke his eyes out, break his legs); lose him by returning suddenly from the cemetery by a detour; or arrange to deposit him at the foot of a mountain or on the far side of a river he cannot cross. In compensation, sometimes an effigy remains at home as a substitute for him, or he may be promised an annual invitation. Because the decaying of the corpse constitutes a risk that its double will prowl in the village, the relatives submit to the constraints of mourning, which puts them outside the social circuit. The specific purpose of these interdictions is to separate all those contaminated by the corpse's decay. Curiously enough, in India the Toda have a single term, *kedr,* which simultaneously designates the corpse, the state of mourning, and the interval between the first and second funerals. A statement made by a dying Maori chief to his son likewise clarifies the problem: "For three years your person must be sacred and you must remain separated from your tribe . . . for all this time my hands will be gathering the earth and my mouth will be constantly eating worms . . . then when my head falls on my body, awake me from my sleep, show my face the light of day, and you shall be *noa* [free]" (Hertz, 1970, p. 33). Therefore, when mineralization, whether natural or artifically accelerated, sets in, it is a sign that the deceased has fulfilled his posthumous destiny. He has passed the initiatory tests imposed on him; he has rejoined the ancestors or the gods; or perhaps he is ready for metempsychosis or reincarnation.

RITES OF INTEGRATION AND THE CESSATION OF MOURNING

In almost all traditional societies, double funerals are held. After a delay varying from a few weeks to ten years, according to the ethnic group and the resources at the family's disposal, a final ceremony takes place that confirms the deceased in his new destiny and confers on his remains a definitive status. Like the integration of the dead person, this ritual consecrates the reintegration of the mourners into the group: order is reestablished and interdictions are lifted. As a rule, the bones are exhumed and then treated in different ways according to local traditions: washed, dried, sometimes covered with ocher, they are preserved as visible relics, placed in containers, buried again, or even pulverized and mixed with ritual beverages. In sub-Saharan Africa, the latter custom is quite prevalent, especially among Bantu-speaking peoples. Among the Bamileke of Cameroon, the inheritance of skulls according to rigorous rules symbolically secures the collective memory and the continuity of the clam. In Madagascar the Famadihana (which has been wrongly translated as "turning over the corpses") gives way to costly festivities: when a family decides to celebrate the cult of its dead, they proceed from opening the tombs and changing the winding-sheets to rewrapping and reburial with great ceremony, before an audience in a state of great jollity. For two days songs, dances, music, processions, and festivities punctuate the ritual manipulations.

In Borneo, the Olo Nyadju give themselves up to analogous states on the occasion of Tiwah. Along with some degree of fasting, the majority of Indonesian ethnic groups do the same thing. This bone cult, which is generally referred to as an ancestor cult, flourishes among the American Indians, in China, and elsewhere, and still has its equivalent in Europe. There is hardly any difference between the old Chinese who carefully brushes his ancestor's bones and the skeleton washer of Neapolitan cemeteries who, two years after the burial, when the corpse has dried out, washes the bones in front of the families before putting them in a marble urn. In the French provinces, the custom of the anniversary meal and mass is clearly a response to the same fantasies of reestablishing order.

Indeed, the ritual of secondary obsequies ending in definitive burial has a twofold justification in the imagination. First of all, the transfer of the bones to another place completes the purification process. It is as if the earth has been corrupted by the decaying body, necessitating the removal of the purified bones to an unsullied location. Second, although the provisional inhumation is always individual, the final burial is very often collective. Such is the custom of the Goajiro Indians in Venezuala: three years after death, the bones are sorted and dried, then exposed during a funeral wake. They are then transferred into a large urn, where the remains of all the dead from the matriclan or the matrilineage are gathered together. Thus, communal reunion of the sublimated remains follows the isolation of impure decay.

On the other hand, Western ossuaries, by virtue of their anonymous character, have hardly any impact on an individualistic society. At the very most, as "display cases" they provide the "exposition of the bones" as an aid to meditation. "Let us come to the charnelhouse, Christians; let us see the skeletons of our brothers," says a Breton song. In any case, if inhumation in a common ditch is judged shocking and infamous by us, the collective ossuary does not scandalize anyone. In fact, it can be seen as a solution to the problem of cemetery space and an orientation for a new cult of the dead. The possibility has even been raised of reintegrating the sacred into cemeteries in the form of an "ossuary-necrology" that would reassemble the community of the dead and make the living sensitive to the bonds uniting them to the past.

With the second funeral, therefore, the fate of the deceased has been settled. To borrow the vivid language of the Mossi of Burkina Faso, the ritual of integration "makes the dead live again." From then on, grief no longer has reason to exist. The marginal period has permitted the mourning work to be finished. But, in any case, is not ritualization, like elegance, a way of charming anguish? At this stage, interdictions are always relaxed. After undergoing purifying baths and multiple reparation sacrifices, the mourners are reintegrated into the group. Thanks to the symbolic support of the bone, life on every level henceforth reasserts all its rights—both the life of the metamorphosed deceased and the life of the group from which he emerged. Once the decaying flesh and the signs of death have disappeared, the imperishable vestige is left with its charge of symbols. Funeral rites thus have the capacity "to reduce any object at all to significance, let it pass over to the other side of the gulf" (Maertens, 1979, p. 236). This can be clearly seen in the following set of processes: decay → mineralization; excluded mourners → reintegrated mourners; oversignificant corpse → hypersignificant remains.

In Vietnam, ritual constitutes what is called the "transfer of life": while the body is buried in a tomb defined according to the rules of geomancy, the soul, set on a tablet that itself is enclosed in a box covered with a red and gold case, becomes the protective ancestor that one venerates and prays to at the family altar.

A qualifying remark must be inserted: the conditions of death (place, moment, means) orient the meaning of the rite. The evil dead person, for example, can be deprived of a funeral, or may have the right to only a truncated or clandestine funeral; he will never become an ancestor or know happiness. Status, age, and sex also play a determining role in the elaboration of ceremonies.

Some Key Rites

Only a few fundamental rites concerning the good death will be considered, because of their quasi-universality and the depth of the fantasies that they express.

ATTENDANCE AT DEATH, CERTIFICATION OF DEATH, AND INTERROGATION

If to die far away from home or to die a violent death is usually equivalent to a bad death in traditional societies, it is not only because uncertainty is alarming but also, and more importantly, because the dying cannot be helped. Mothering, making secure, and taking charge of the dying person, who is consoled, caressed, and helped to die for the same reason he was helped to be born, is a universal constant. This attitude has a religious aspect. To take only one example, we know the importance to elderly and very sick people of the Christian last sacraments, including the purifying aspersion that evokes baptism and redemption through the Passion and the Resurrection, as well as the profession of faith and, when possible, the Eucharist. As for the anointing of the sick, let us recall that this new ritual, although it abandons the expiatory aspect and gives only a circumstantial role to the effacement of sin, nevertheless insists on help by grace.

It is important to make sure that the deceased is really dead. Besides interpreting tangible signs like the stopping of the breath and the heart, one can call on the diviner, the priest, or the doctor. There are also other ways of making sure: right after the death of a Chinese, one of his close kin climbs the roof of the house to "call back his soul"; if it does not return, there is no doubt about his death. While for the Toraja of Sulawesi the deceased is not dead but only ill (as noted), among the Tibetans and the Miao (Hmong) the deceased must be informed that he is really dead because he doesn't know that he is: "The illness fell on the rocks and the rocks could not bear it. Then it slid into the grass, but the grass could not carry it. And that is why, O Dead One, the illness has come to you. The earth could not bear the illness, so the illness reached your soul. That is why you have found death" (Georges, 1982, p. 183). Then, with great kindness and consideration, they explain to him what he needs for the great journey: bamboos to communicate with the survivors or the gods, the "wooden house" (coffin), the hemp shoes, alcohol, food, and the cock that will show him the way. The announcement of the death also obeys precise rules. Women's lamentations punctuated by cries, drums, and bells, as well as symbolic formulas and the sending of messengers, are the most frequent practices.

In traditional societies, another notable belief is that the corpse is simultaneously alive and dead. It no longer has a voice, but in its fashion it speaks. No one hesitates to question it in order to learn why it died or, sometimes, its desires concerning the transmission of its possessions; only little children and fools escape this rite, because "they don't know what they say." Among the Diola of Senegal, the dead person, tied to a bier, is supported by four men, and people take turns asking it questions. If the corpse moves forward when questioned, the response is positive; if it moves backward, it is negative; if it wavers in the same place, it is indicating hesitation. Among the Somba of Benin, "no" is expressed by a rocking from left to right, and "yes" by a rocking from back to front. For the Senufo of the Ivory Coast, leaning to the left indicates the deceased's agreement, and leaning to the right, his disagreement. It sometimes happens that the dead person bears down on one of those present in order to demand that questions be put to him (the Diola) or requires that the carriers be changed in order to pursue the rite (the Lobi of Burkina Faso). Substitute objects sometimes replace the corpse at the time of the interrogation, on condition that they participate in its vital forces. An assegai with the hair of the deceased is an adequate substitute for the Boni of Guyana, while a tree trunk containing his nails and body hairs suffices for the Bete of the Ivory Coast. If the death was willed by God or the ancestors, a frequent occurrence among the Egba of Benin and the Orokaiva of New Guinea, the group feels reassured. But if it resulted from a crime, witchcraft, or violation of a taboo, the fault must be immediately atoned for and the guilty punished. In its way, by its voiceless word the corpse plays an important role in social regulation.

LAYING OUT THE DEAD: PURIFICATION AND MOTHERING RITUALS

The funeral rite proper begins with the laying out of the corpse, which, in its essential aspect, is equivalent to an authentic purification, a symbolic prelude to rebirth. A holy task among the Jews and especially in Islam, it is a matter of divine obligation, thus of *'ibādāt,* involving a relationship with God and not just a social function. Laying out the corpse is universal and rigorously codified in ancient societies. In the West Indies, especially in the Antilles and in Haiti, this ritual is reminiscent of that of the midwife. Death, like birth, demands a certain ceremonial that is no less than the "transitory reintegration in the indistinct," to borrow Mircea Eliade's expression. By placing, for example, a vat of water underneath the couch where the corpse is lying, one symbolically reestablishes the sources of life (amniotic fluid). One is again assured that the soul, which has just left the body, will not disappear into nothingness, and that the deceased, thus purified, will be reborn in another world.

Among the Agni-Bora of the Ivory Coast, there is a similarity between the grooming of the newborn baby and the grooming of the deceased: holding the naked body on their knees, old women wash it with three successive rinses, perfume it, and dress it. For the baby, the rite is always accompanied by singing; the washing is done from the head to the feet with the right hand. In the case of the deceased, however, the rite is executed in silence with the left hand, and proceeds from the feet to the head. This is because birth is an arrival, and rebirth a departure. In the European countryside the laying out is still the work of the "woman who helps" (the midwife), who is also the "woman who does the dead." The laying out of the dead is again an act of mothering.

Among the Miao, the deceased is rubbed with a warm towel without being undressed; then is dressed in new clothing finished off with a richly decorated kimono. The head is wrapped in a turban, and—an important detail—the feet are shod in felt or leather shoes with curled tips, like those sold by the Chinese. Sometimes the duty of one of the relatives is to make these shoes. The dead must depart with good shoes for the trip about to be undertaken. A harquebusier comes up to the deceased and forewarns deferentially: "Now we are going to fire a few shots that will accompany and protect you for the whole length of your trip. Don't be afraid."

DISPLAY OF THE DECEASED: THE CORPSE DETAINED

Aside from punitive exhibition (desecration of the corpse) in the case of a bad death, when a devalued dead person is deprived of a funeral, the display of the corpse reflects the noblest intentions (valorization of the corpse).

In traditional societies, where death is a public affair involving the whole community, display of the corpse is almost a general rule. It is stretched out on a mat, on a funeral bed, or in a coffin, placed in the mortuary in a special case or in the open air, or suspended at the top of a tree or on a scaffold in the middle of the village square. Sometimes it even presides over its own funeral. The presentation varies according to places and beliefs, but most often it is done in state, with all the symbols that recall the deceased's social function. In Senegal, the dead Diola appears much as if he were alive, but with his most beautiful clothes, his bow and arrows if he was a good hunter, his farming implements and sheaves of rice if he was a good farmer. The horns of cows he sacrificed during his life and heads of cattle are exhibited to emphasize his wealth. The ostentatious display of belongings is frequent. Sometimes the dead person is displayed in the midst of his herd, as among the Karamojong of Uganda and certain Indians of North America. The length of time for displaying the dead and his goods may vary according to his wealth: among the Dayak of Borneo, it ranges from one to six years. Another custom, peculiar to the Sioux, is to suspend the head and tail of the dead person's horse on the same scaffold on which he is exposed. Display of the dead seems to serve a double function: to show the dead that he is being rendered the homage due him by offering him to view in his best light, and to show him as a model of the role he played in the group. The dead person is glorified as having accomplished his mission, and the aura with which he is endowed is reflected on the collectivity, which thus reaffirms the identity and cohesion it so needs upon losing one of its members.

In southern Sulawesi, the Toraja still use the effigy, or *tau-tau,* especially for the deceased of high rank. This figure, made of breadfruit wood according to strict rules, must resemble the deceased as much as possible (same sex, height, face), though often with improvements. Dressed in the dead person's clothing and adorned with jewels, necklaces, and bracelets, it is the object of numerous rites whereby it is in turn animated and made to die, wept over and consecrated. At the end of a very long ceremony, the corpse, swathed in its winding-sheets, is raised on a platform below which is placed the *tau-tau.* Both then preside over the buffalo sacrifices and receive their part of the offerings. Finally, when the corpse goes back to the sepulcher for the last time, its representative is permanently exhibited as near as possible to the tomb. For the Toraja, the effigy becomes more than a ritual object associated with death; it is, if not the deceased, at least its visible double.

In the West today, the embalmed corpse lies in state in funeral homes. It is still a matter of rendering homage to one no longer alive, and of facilitating the mourning work by conserving a better image of the departed: the mortician's work spares the dead person the stigma of death for a time and gives the impression that he is sleeping in peace. The essential thing is that the dead person should be present, recognizable to his family (to a certain extent, a disfigured corpse is tantamount to an absent one). The certainty of his death can be borne more easily than the uncertainty surrounding his absence and silence.

In this respect, wakes have a soothing value, supposedly for the departed and certainly for the survivors. The sacred and the profane are mixed. In Spain, rosaries and responses are recited. People speak of the deceased, because to speak of him is to be with him again. And if sometimes the conversation turns to funny stories, this does not imply a lack of respect for the dead but a pleasant relationship with him. At one extreme, these wakes are almost feast days. Perhaps this is because in some villages, like the Aragonese village of Leciñena, the immediate neighbors cook the celebrated *tortas,* a kind of brioche made only on feast days (the Feast of the Virgin, a marriage) and for a death wake.

When there are mourners, especially female ones, display of the dead facilitates the sincere and organized expression of emotions through praise of the departed, invitations to return among the living (visits, possession, reincarnation), reproaches or invectives concerning his cruelty in leaving his close kin, and advice for his posthumous destiny. This is how the rhapsodist addresses the deceased Miao after the ritual offering of the cock: "Take it and eat. Henceforth you will have the cock's soul with you. Follow it. Hurry and look for the silk suit you wore at birth. You will find it hidden under the earth [an allusion to the placenta of the newborn, which is always carefully buried near the house in which he was born]. Now leave" (Georges, 1982, p. 187). Again dressed in his silk garment and guided by the cock, the soul of the dead person then sets out on the long journey the singer is chanting about. Finally, before the final farewells, the dead person may be transported into the village and the fields, visiting for the last time the places where he lived, and communing with himself before the altars where he made sacrifices.

FOOD GIVEN TO THE DEAD AND IN HOMAGE TO THE DEAD

We will mention only briefly the offering of victuals to the dead, whether during the funeral or at the moment of burial. To help the deceased on his long journey, the Aztec burned food with him—usually a fat little dog with a tawny coat—to help him cross the rivers on his infernal route. This rite, common to almost all cultures, corresponds to a widespread belief: the offerings are the indispensable viaticum that permits the dead to survive the transitory journey into the world of the ancestors. The sacrifices offered simultaneously play the same role, albeit symbolically.

Better yet is the common meal that accompanies funerals almost everywhere. A practical necessity justifies it: those who have come to honor the dead and console the close kin must be fed. The importance of the feast is often such that it takes on the dimensions of a potlatch: in numerous ethnic groups, brief rites are initiated at the time of death, and the funeral services are deferred until sufficient reserves of rice, palm wine, and cattle have been set out. In the view of traditional mythologies, it is a communal event in which the dead person participates: a seat, plate, or part of the food (often the best) is reserved for him, or a descendant represents him, or the table is set in the presence of the corpse—diverse customs showing an intention to intensify the relationship with the deceased and to persuade the group that he is not completely dead. In Western societies, the funeral meal is a means of appeasing grief by reinforcing the bonds that unite the living in the absence of the dead. The meal following the death is like a birth for the talkative and hungry community of the living, which has been wounded, split up, and interrupted by the death.

But all these reasons are valid only on an obvious level. On the symbolic level, the funeral meal is a way of retaining the dead person, and on these grounds, it is a substitute for the cannibalistic meal. In Haiti, the funeral meal is appropriately termed a *mangé-mort,* just as in Quebec, where the expression *manger le mort* is still in use. In fact, the manducation of the corpse is connected to a universal fantasy that psychoanalysts neatly term "the exquisite corpse" (an expression borrowed from surrealist poetry). Obeying the pleasure principle, the fantasy mechanism of the exquisite corpse responds to the trauma of loss through the desire for incorporation of the lost object. Amorous fusion with the other is then achieved in an exaltation that, in the real world, would perhaps be secret. The dead person is fixed and assimilated in his best features; he who devours him makes him his own in spite of all taboos. In this connection, let us recall a strange Mexican custom that does not even disguise the necrophagic intention. On the Day of the Dead, an extraordinary commercial activity mobilizes the whole population: superb confections are sold that represent the skulls and skeletons of the dead, ravishing or burlesque in appearance, with first names engraved in order to help the customers make their choices.

Controlling Decay

Decay is the justification for all funeral rites. Everything is brought into play in order to tame it (display of the corpse), hide it (winding-sheets, the sarcophagus), forbid it absolutely (embalming and mummification, incineration, cannibalistic ingestion), retard it (corporal attentions), or accelerate it (towers of silence; see below). A profound need underlies all these approaches to decay: to stabilize the deceased in an indestructible medium—a stage marking the reconciliation of the community with his death. These remains—mummy, relic, ashes, or bones—all civilizations, without exception, persist in preserving.

TAMED OR ACCELERATED DECAY

Conditions of exposure may eventually accelerate the mineralization of the corpse. Sunlight and even moonlight, as well as a smoky fire, are believed to contribute, but the body is sometimes also offered to birds of prey and other carnivores, or to ants. In the Tibetan tradition, corpses were torn apart by the *ragyapas* ("dismemberers") and thrown to the dogs, so that the bones would be stripped much faster. But the most spectacular example is given us by the towers of silence built in the seventeenth century, particularly in Iran by the Zoroastrians. According to the sacred texts of the *Zand,* the corpse is the essence of impurity. It is therefore out of the question to pollute "the things belonging to the good creation" by carrying out the final burial of a decomposing body. Hence the custom of exposing the body in a remote location known to be frequented by carnivorous animals. Vultures, in particular, are the purifiers that disencumber the dead person of rotting flesh, the medium of demonic infection. From this came the practice, which spread little by little, of building towers of rock especially designed to isolate corpses and avoid their contaminating presence during the purification process. The interior of the "tower of silence," or *dakhma,* consists of a platform inclined toward a central pit. Cells *(pāvis)* hollowed out in three concentric circles receive the corpses—men in the outer zone, women in the middle zone, and children toward the central pit. In this case, in which the custom of second obsequies no longer takes the symbolic form of the commemorative meal, the dried bones are thrown down twice a year into the depths of the pit. There, under the combined effect of the sun and the lime that is spread there, the bones are transformed into dust. The pit branches into four canals for the evacuation of rainwater, which is received and purified in four subterreanean pits where carbon and sand clarify it. Formerly, the remains were removed periodically, to be kept in an ossuary: cleansed of all impurities, they testified that the soul was ready for the final ceremonies. [*See* Dakhma.]

DECOMPOSITION ACCEPTED BUT HIDDEN

Obviously, the cemetery is a place where remains are preserved and concealed. The feminine and maternal valence of the earth responds to a universal fantasy: "Naked I came out of the maternal womb; naked I shall return there" (*Jb.* 1:21). In African cosmogonic thought, burial in Mother Earth, the source of fertility and dwelling place of the ancestors, takes on a quasi-metaphysical significance. The same symbolism serves for other forms of interment, such as the deposit of the corpse in grottos or in funeral jars that evoke the uterine cavity. The earth is indeed the place *par excellence* for transformations. Not only does one plow seeds into it at the time of sowing, but it is also a mediator in all rites of passage: the corpse is entrusted to it at the time of the funeral, as are neophytes' nail clippings, hair, and other fleshly remains from initiation rites and the placenta and umbilical cord at birth. Burial can also, in a sense, transform the land. Thus the Hebrews did not begin to bury their dead until as a people they became sedentary; burial is always connected to the ownership of land, that is, to the appropriation of a "promised land," without doubt, a way of salvation.

One could go on forever describing the infinite variety of types of cemeteries (mass burial sites or scattered individual crypts, as in Madagascar; at the heart of the village or far-flung) and types of tombs (simple ditches to elaborate mausoleums to modern, efficient columbaria for cremated bodies). In many systems of burial the distinction between social classes is still, as it were, heavily felt.

The corpse's position in the tomb is no less variable: seated; stretched out on its back or side; in the fetal position; even on its stomach, as was once the case in our own culture for adulterous women; or standing, in the manner of some military men or heroes of the American West. The orientation of the body can also be important. For some emigrant groups, it is toward the country of birth. For populations that traditionally ascribe birth to sunrise and death to sunset, the deceased must have his head to the east in order to be in position for rebirth. On the other hand, medieval Christians who wanted to be buried facing the direction from which salvation came placed the head toward the west so that the deceased could face Jerusalem. Similarly, Muslims are buried on their right side, turned toward Mecca.

The necropolis does not exist in India or Nepal since ashes are thrown into the sacred rivers, nor is it commonly of importance in sub-Saharan Africa. But where it does exist, the cemetery is still a symbol charged with emotion, sometimes arousing fear and melancholy, sometimes calm and reflection. In this regard one must praise Islamic wisdom, by which the very texture and functions of the cemetery maintain a state of relative osmosis between the living and the dead. The cemetery *(maqbarah)* is often designated by the more euphemistic term *rawḍah* ("garden"). Certainly, its ground has often been consecrated to that use by a pious tradition, but it is not closed. The dead rest there on the bare ground in a simple winding-sheet, thus returning to the elements. In both senses of the term, it is open to nature. But it is open to society, too. The belief prevails that bonds exist with the bodies of the deceased before the Last Judgment and that for the living to visit the tombs is a praiseworthy act and, what is more, a deed that will be considered in their favor then. The cemetery is also a traditional place to go for a walk: women often meet there on Fridays.

PROHIBITED DECAY

Setting aside the still rare phenomenon of cryogenation (in which the deceased wait in liquid nitrogen until the time when people will know how to restore them to life), there are three common forms of prohibited decay.

Cannibalism, Decay, and Mineralization. Robert Hertz (1970) has emphasized the particular function of cannibalism that spares the dead person the horror of a slow and ignoble decomposition and brings the bones almost immediately to their final state. This is obviously true for endocannibalism, when it is practiced on revered dead persons. There is no doubt that the purpose of cannibalism is to prohibit rotting. On the one hand, consumption of the flesh occurs as soon as possible after death, and, since the flesh is usually cooked, putrefaction does not begin in the course of consumption. On the other hand, inquiries among populations with a tradition of cannibalism clearly reveal the finality of the act: "In this way, we knew where he [the dead] was and his flesh would not rot," said the Australian Turrbals (Hertz, 1970, p. 24, n. 1). This is also the view expressed by the Merina, according to a historical Malagasy document of the last century: "Our kinsman is dead; what shall we do with his body, for he was a man we loved?" Some answered, "Since he is dead, let us not bury him but let us eat him, because it would be sad to see him rotting in the ground." (ibid., p. 28).

Cannibalism promotes mineralization, but intentions toward the corpse in this regard differ according to whether endocannibalism or exocannibalism is involved.

Endocannibalism refers us back to the traditional scheme of the double funeral: on the first occasion, the dead person is buried in the earth or, similarly, in the belly, where human digestion prepares its accelerated passage to mineralization; on the second occasion, the remaining bones are handled with respect and receive the final obsequies. The destruction resulting from the manducation is only a mutation of forms that symbolically achieve a kind of conservation: incorporation. In a sense, ingestion could be interpreted as embalming transferred to the oral register. As for exocannibalism, however, the situation is different, at least concerning the treatment of the remains. The cannibal feast undoubtedly implies incorporation and, by its reference to myths of origin, it can take the form of a veritable primitive mass in which the bread and wine are really flesh and blood. But whereas the vital force animating the enemy's corpse is assimilated, his bones and uneaten parts may be abandoned or held up to ridicule. The Ocaina Indians of the Peruvian Amazon suspend the enemy's penis from a necklace worn by the victor's spouse; the mummified hands are used as spoons, the bones as flutes, and the painted and exposed skull serves as a ritual bell. [*See* Cannibalism.]

The Cremated Corpse. According to many mythologies, the purifying fire is above all liberating. In Bali, as long as the fire has not reduced the corpse to ashes, the dead person is impure; he continues to wait, his spirit not yet separated from his body. According to many beliefs, fire is the promise of regeneration and rebirth. [*See* Fire.] Through fire, a superior level of existence can be attained. According to Greek mythology, Herakles stretched himself out on the pyre of Mount Oeta, while

Zeus announced to the other gods that Herakles was about to become their equal: the fire would relieve him of his human part, immortalize him, and make him divine. The same theme is found in the Upaniṣads, the classic texts of Hinduism. It is therefore not the impurity of the corpse that is implicated in the cremation ritual, but the impurity of the body and the human condition. Ashes are the proof of that impurity; if the body were perfect, it would burn without ashes.

The destiny of the remains varies. In Japan, the bones are traditionally divided between two containers, one of which is buried at the place of cremation and the other in the natal village of the deceased. In Thailand, part of the remains are collected in an urn kept at home, while the remainder is buried at the foot of the pyre, kept in a reliquary monument, or even thrown into a river. In India, custom formerly demanded that the ashes be deposited in a tomb. Later a rule was imposed that still persists today: since fire is the son of the waters, funeral rites should summon first one and then the other. Also, the ashes and noncalcinated bones are sprinkled with water, and cow's milk and coconut milk as well, before being thrown into the Ganges, the sacred river that flows from Śiva's hair. The same procedure is followed in Nepal and in Thailand, where other sacred rivers conduct the deceased downstream toward his celestial residence. In Bali, the remains are thrown into the sea after having been meticulously sorted by the relatives, washed in sacred water, arranged on white linen, and inserted into a dried coconut adorned with flowers. Finally, there is the particular case of the Yanoama Indians of Venezuela, who crush the remaining bones after the incineration of their warriors, in order to consume them mixed with game dishes or beverages in the course of a communal meal.

Cremation can be assimilated to all other modes of provisional burial, and people who burn their dead conform in many respects to the classic scheme of the double funeral, but with different means and a shortened duration. The first funeral, corresponding to the ritual of the exclusion of the dead, soothes the corpse and leads it to a purification that can be accomplished only by the process of decay. Those who cremate the dead find the equivalent of the first funeral in the rites that accompany the handling of the body during the generally short period between death and combustion on the pyre. The second obsequies, which concern the charred and purified remains, correspond to the rites of integration of the dead in his status in the beyond, while mourning is lifted for the survivors.

Preservation of Bodies. Egyptian embalming practices are famous. The long, difficult techniques only make sense, however, in the framework of the osirification ritual that makes the dead person a god through assimilation with Osiris. Before, during, and after the technical manipulations, an extremely complicated ceremony took place, which undoubtedly explains the long duration of the treatment and the great number of participants. Invocations, readings, and prayers punctuated each act of the embalmers, whose very gestures were strictly regulated. Afterlife was not possible unless the liturgy was observed in its minutest details. "You will not cease living; you will not cease to be young, for always and forever," cried the priest at the end of the embalming. Then the last ceremony could be performed: the opening of the mouth. In the purification tent or at the entrance to the tomb, the gestures of the officiating priest were accompanied by aspersions, offerings, and sacrifices, fumigations with incense, and magico-religious formulas. With the end of his adz the priest touched the dead person's face in order to reintroduce the vital energy.

In addition, mummies discovered in South America and the testimony of Spanish chroniclers affirm that the Inca, for example, embalmed their dead. The technical success of their mummies seems not to have been as spectacular as that of the Egyptian mummies, especially if one remembers that the Inca empire occurred relatively close to our own time (at the end of our Middle Ages). The body was treated with different ingredients (honey, resin, and herbs) and painted with *roucou* (a vegetable dye); the viscera, preliminarily removed, were prepared and kept separate in a receptacle. The dry climate and the burial methods (a hole in a rocky wall, or a funeral jar) were favorable for preservation. Like the pharaohs, the sovereigns were the objects of particular care. An illustrated story from the sixteenth century, whose author, Huaman Poma, was of Inca origin, recounts the royal funeral ritual: the embalmed Inca, adorned with his emblems, lay in state for a month; at his sides were placed women and servants, likewise embalmed, to serve him in the other world. Although the techniques were rudimentary, there is good reason to assume that a very precise ritual was used to increase efficacity. Thus, the funeral offerings deposited next to the body appeased the maleficent spirits that caused decomposition. Indeed, since the life principle (the *aya*) remained in all parts of the corpse, rotting involved the destruction of the individual. On the other hand, if the body was preserved, the spirit of the dead could be reincarnated in a descendant. This belief in a second birth appears to explain the fetal position of corpses found in tombs and funeral jars.

Whatever the modalities, we can agree with Robert Hertz that it is legitimate "to consider mummification as a particular case derived from provisional interment" (Hertz, 1970, p. 20). If the interval separating death from final burial corresponds to the duration necessary for mineralization or desiccation, then a symmetry exists between the Egyptian rite and that of certain archaic ethnic groups. It is only when the embalming is concluded "that the body, having become imperishable, will be conducted to the tomb, that the soul will leave for the country of Ialou, and that the mourning of the survivors will come to an end." The waiting period, that is, the time necessary to achieve mineralization, can be reduced only by a manipulative intervention; it has not changed meaning at all, even if in this case the corpse is the equivalent of the body in its apparent totality (a mummy) or in part (a trophy head), rather than the residue of bones and ashes.

Conclusion

I have, as it were, painted a composite picture of funeral rites, in which it can be seen that they border on the *stricto sensu* sphere of the sacred. It may in fact be argued that, thanks to rites—those of former times especially, and to a lesser degree those of today—everything is brought into play in order to put death (even if accepted) at a distance, and eventually to make fun of it or tame it by permitting the community, when it feels concerned, to pull itself together. This is why funeral rites can shift the drama of dying from the plane of the real to that of the imaginary (by displacements and metonymy, symbols and metaphors), and it is in this that their efficacity resides. To reorganize the society disturbed by death and to console the survivors even while the deceased is being served and his destiny oriented—these are the two fundamental aims of funeral customs. In all regions, then, such rites are simultaneously defined first as liturgical drama with its places and scenes, its actors and their scripts, and also as individual or collective therapies (one might recall Nasser's moving funeral). In this respect, traditional cultures have inexhaustible resources of rich symbolism that the modern world has forgotten.

Indeed, modern life, especially in an urban milieu, entails multiple mutations that are probably irreversible on the level of ritual, and perhaps disquieting for the psychic equilibrium of our contemporaries. Many practices are simplified or omitted: the wake is impossible at the hospital or in tiny apartments, condolences and corteges are practically eliminated. Consider, for example, today's laying out of the dead: for the impurity of former times, the pretext of hygiene is substituted; for respect for the corpse as subject, obsession with or horror of the corpse as object; for family deference, the anonymity of an indifferent wage. In the same way, the signs of mourning have fallen into disuse—we have passed from "mourning clothes in twenty-four hours" to twenty-four hours of mourning!—and it is unseemly to show one's sorrow. People care less and less about the deceased, who sink into the anonymity of the forgotten; fewer and fewer masses are said for the repose of their souls, while the scattering of ashes eliminates the only possible physical support for a cult of the dead. If, at least on the imaginary plane, rites once primarily concerned the deceased, today they primarily concern the survivors. Thus, to take only one example, the new Roman Catholic ritual of anointing the sick tends to deritualize and desacralize death itself as an essential mutation. It is truly the disappearance of death, considered as a passage, that is witnessed by others.

Without a doubt, man today is condemning himself to a dangerous cultural void concerning rites and their symbols. We may well ask if our funerals, expedited in the "strictest intimacy," do not dangerously deprive us of a ritual that would help us to live.

[*See also* Rites of Passage *and* Ancestors. *For symbols and myths associated with funeral rites, see* Bones; Ashes; Tombs; *and* Death.]

BIBLIOGRAPHY

Ariès, Philippe. *Western Attitudes toward Death: From the Middle Ages to the Present.* Translated by Patricia Ranum. Baltimore, 1974.

Ariès, Philippe. *Essais sur l'histoire de la mort en Occident.* Paris, 1975.

Gennep, Arnold van. *Rites of Passage.* Translated by Monika B. Vizedom and Gabrielle L. Caffee. Chicago, 1960. See chapter 8.

Gennep, Arnold van. "Du berceau à la tombe." In *Manuel de folklore français contemporain,* edited by Arnold van Gennep, vol. 1, pp. 111–373. Paris, 1976.

Georges, Elaine. *Voyages de la mort.* Paris, 1982.

Guiart, Jean, ed. *Les hommes et la mort: Rituels funéraires à travers le monde.* Paris, 1979.

Hertz, Robert. "Contribution à une étude sur la représentation collective de la mort." In *Sociologie religieuse et folklore,* edited by Robert Hertz. Paris, 1970.

Maertens, Jean-Thierry. *Le masque et le miroir.* Paris, 1978.

Maertens, Jean-Thierry. *Le jeu du mort.* Paris, 1979.

Thomas, Louis-Vincent. *Anthropologie de la mort.* Paris, 1975.

Thomas, Louis-Vincent. *Le cadavre.* Brussels, 1980.

Thomas, Louis-Vincent. *La mort africaine.* Paris, 1982.

Thomas, Louis-Vincent. *Rites du mort: Pour la paix des vivants.* Paris, 1985.

Urbain, Jean-Didier. *La société de conservation.* Paris, 1978.

Walter, Jean-Jacques. *Psychanalyse des rites.* Paris, 1977.

5 TOMBS

Tamara M. Green

Ritual disposal of the dead seems to be a phenomenon unique to humans; inhumation (burial in the earth) in various forms has been universally practiced except where supplanted by other rites, such as exposure of the dead to birds of prey. It is clear from evidence dating back as far as the Paleolithic period (for example, artifacts found buried in the grave, the position of the corpse, and so on) that disposal of the dead has always primarily served a ritualistic rather than utilitarian function; indeed, historical and anthropological investigation reveals that such burial rituals reflect any given society's view of the nature not only of death, but also of the totality of human existence within the cosmos.

THE LIVING AND THE DEAD

The great variety of equipment found in the earliest graves suggests that human beings have always been unable to accept death as the end of life. In addition, it may be deduced from the widespread ritual of inhumation that the new dwelling place of the dead was seen typically as beneath the earth. The location of the burial site itself indicates whether the worlds of the living and the dead were regarded as separate and hostile to each other or as part of a continuum. Thus, when there is affection or reverence for the dead or some benefit is thought to accrue from their presence, burial may take place within the house or within the family compound (as in China). When, however, the dead are regarded as objects of fear and death is viewed as a source of pollution for the living, the place of disposal is a location that thereafter is seen as belonging to the dead.

Accordingly, burial in the earth may be understood by some cultures as the recognition of the eternal cycle of life and death in which human beings, as part of nature, participate. Just as the earth lives and dies and is reborn again, so humans may be seen to undergo the same process. The mythic image of humankind as autochthonous, born out of the earth or created out of dirt or clay, is then carried to its logical conclusion by the practice of returning humans to the place that had once brought them forth. And in those cultures where earth is associated with the female principle, humankind can be seen as being received back into the mother who gave birth to it. Thus we find even in those cultures that cremate their dead the common practice of burial of the ashes within a grave.

In other cultures, however, burial of the dead may also reflect the desire of the living to separate themselves from the dead, to establish strict boundaries between the terrestrial and subterranean worlds, and to ensure that through proper disposal the dead will not harm the living. Thus we may note such practices as the constriction of the dead through binding or weighting down with stones as well as the strict injunctions concerning the disposal of the dead, which are found in all cultures and which may be interpreted as a display both of kindness toward the dead in hastening their departure from this world and of fear in preventing them from remaining in this world where they may do harm. The concept of the necropolis or city of the dead may be seen as the natural consequence of such beliefs; the modern cemetery represents the continuity of such belief.

Often geography, topography, and conditions of life may combine with worldview to produce the mode of disposal of the dead. Exposure of the dead, for example, may reflect the fear of polluting the sacred elements of earth or fire with death (as among the Parsis) but also may be the consequence of a soil too hard to be excavated (as among the inhabitants of the far northern hemisphere). Similarly, burial within caves may be a reflection of the belief in caves as openings into the subterranean world of the dead, but such a practice cannot develop without the existence of caves (or their potentiality). Cremation may be more convenient for the nomad, but it is also practiced by settled peoples who believe it a necessary prelude to freeing the spirit from the body.

ABODES OF THE DEAD

Although ritual burial is evident during the Paleolithic period, little can be deduced about the function of the grave other than what is cited above. It may be remarked, however, that there is widespread evidence of cave burial during this period. Nevertheless, there seems to have been no attempt, even in the later Paleolithic period, to establish boundaries between the living and the dead by separating them from areas of settlement; it would seem that the living and dead often shared the same space. It is not until the Neolithic period that the understanding of the nature of death is marked not only by the contents of the grave but by what is visible to those who are still living; it is during this period that we see the development of the tumulus, or mound, grave as the most characteristic form of burial. It is possible that the tumulus grave arose in part out of humanity's need to establish psychic boundaries between itself and the world of the dead by placing them either in a specified area (for example, within a stockade or ditch) or in a mortuary house reserved for the dead, which was then covered over with mounds of earth. The houses or enclosures, made of either stone or timber, found within these mounds suggest that they were considered dwelling places of the dead, while their location within areas of settlement would seem to indicate that the dead, once properly buried, were regarded as protectors of the land in which they were interred; the location of their tombs would serve to reinforce the family's claim to the land. The Chinese practice of *feng-shui,* geomancy, which reveals to the practitioner where to locate graves, temples, and houses in order that the dead, the gods, and the living may find their rightful places of habitation, is predicated on such a belief. Further, the tomb as the residence of the dead is demonstrated by the widespread practices of making offerings at the site of burial (sometimes even pouring the offering into the grave itself through specially constructed apertures) and of invoking the dead at the grave.

The tumulus burial, which expressed itself in a variety of forms during the prehistoric period, found its architectural continuity in such varied structures as the *tholos* or beehive-shaped tomb of the Mycenaean Greeks and the pyramid of the ancient Egyptians. The mound, the *tholos,* and the pyramid may be interpreted both as abodes of the dead and as re-creations of the archetypal cosmic mountain. The primeval mountain may be envisioned as the source from which all life arises (as in Egypt), the center of the world (as in China), or the link between the worlds of the gods, the living, and the dead. The rounded form of certain of the tumuli may also serve to re-create the dome of heaven; it seems certain that this motif survived in the rounded tombs of the Roman and Byzantine emperors. Finally, the mound may serve as a marker that simultaneously signifies the reverent remembrance of the dead and a warning to the living that the site belongs to the dead. The stone circles of the Neolithic period, such as those at Stonehenge and Avebury in England, clearly seem to delineate the boundaries between the two worlds. To enter into the sacred circle was to enter into another world. [*See* Megalithic Religions.]

The tumulus as a place of contact between the sacred and profane worlds may also be seen in the Buddhist stupas, which were originally dome-shaped mounds surrounded by a railing but were later also built in the shape of towers. Stupas were said to have been erected at the request of the Buddha himself as a place for the enshrinement of his and his disciples' relics. In their construction they may be considered models of the cosmos, and they are venerated as sacred places of pilgrimage. The pagoda is a later development of the form. Similar in function is the Tibetan *chorten,* a monument erected over relics of the Buddha or his saints or as a cenotaph (empty grave) to mark a sacred spot. Built in the form of a spire, its top is decorated with a tongue-shaped spike, which is said to represent the sacred light that emanated from the Buddha. [*See* Stupa Worship.]

The link between the world of the dead and the primeval mountain may also be noted in the rock-cut chamber tombs, found among the various Semitic cultures of the ancient Near East, whose facades, re-creating the monumental entrances of temples, have been carved on the faces of cliffs and whose chambers burrow into the rock itself. Into this category may be placed as well the tower-tombs found throughout the Roman world and especially in the East; these are decorated on the outside with various mythological and religious symbols and contain burial chambers within.

The recognition of the tomb as the abode of the dead, in whatever form the dead may survive, is given further credence by the great variety of articles buried in the tomb: there seems to be a universal connection between the status of the individual and the quality of grave goods, while the expected continuation of earthly occupation is often reflected by the tools found in the grave. The interior decoration of tombs, clearly meant to gratify the dead and found among a great number of ancient cultures, depicts ordinary activities, such as banquets and athletic contests. Such representations suggest that the world of the dead is not so different from the land of the living as to be unrecognizable.

The function of the tomb as a dwelling place is further revealed by the widespread custom of placing the remains of the dead, either beneath the earth or above, in containers that imitate in architectural form the dwelling places of the living (for example, Etruscan cremation urns and Phoenician sarcophagi). The concept of residency in the tomb, however, is often contradicted by a concomitant belief in a land where the dead reside. This difficulty is sometimes resolved through the consideration of the tomb as a temporary shelter to be occupied only until the physical remains have decayed or the time of judgment has come, or it may be seen as an abode that is only sometimes inhabited by the dead. Within the burial mounds of the ancient Scandinavians, the dead were sometimes placed in ships that seem to symbolize the voyage to the other world. In some sects of Islam, on the other hand, it is necessary to prepare a tomb of ample size, which resembles a house with its arched roof, in order that the corpse may sit up when responding to the examining angels, but the dead remain within that tomb until the time of final judgment.

THE SHIFT TO THE LIVING

The location of the grave, its contents, its internal decoration, and the disposal of the remains within it present clear evidence of the concerns and beliefs of the living about the dead. The complex history of funerary architecture and art, however, would seem to indicate a gradual shift in emphasis from the internal, timeless world of the grave to the temporal world of the living. Whereas the tumulus served to enclose the dead within their world along with any goods that they might need there, burial practices after the prehistoric period reveal increasingly elaborate construction and decoration of the exterior of the tomb, while the furnishings of the interior grow increasingly modest. The shift is certainly not clear-cut: a pile of stones above the grave may serve to keep the dead within but is also the simplest form of remembrance of the dead contained there. Similarly, highly decorated sarcophagi are found both buried in the earth and uncovered in aboveground structures.

The changing nature of the grave may be seen through a brief survey of Greek burial practices. During the Bronze Age, we find every sort of burial—monumental *tholos* tombs, rock-cut chamber tombs, and simple pit graves (both lined and unlined)—with a great variety of grave furniture and offerings; both inhumation and cremation were practiced. During the protogeometric period (twelfth to ninth centuries BCE), we find our first evidence of grave markers, in the form of amphorae placed on small tumulus graves. By the geometric period, we find clay vases decorated with a variety of scenes from the funeral ritual, but there are still a number of objects buried in the grave. The archaic period (seventh to mid-fifth centuries BCE) produced the clearest indication of a shift in belief and practice: while vast sums of money were then being spent on the outward appearance, objects placed within the grave for the benefit of the dead became increasingly scarce, a trend that continued into the classical age (mid-fifth to late fourth centuries BCE). Although built tombs replaced the burial mound, the principle of burial remained: the dead were buried beneath the structure, not within it.

So elaborate were some of these monuments that sumptuary laws were enacted at the end of the sixth century BCE and periodically renewed; these limited the amount of money and labor that could be expended on the burial and the grave marker. During the Hellenistic period, when the grandeur and even the divinity of kings became an acceptable concept, the further elaboration of the notion of the tomb as the abode of, and monument to, the dead was seen in the development of the mausoleum, an aboveground structure that contained or covered the burial chamber. Imitating various forms of domestic and sacred architecture, the mausoleum takes its name from Mausolus, the fourth-century BCE dynast of Caria, in Asia Minor. Perhaps the most spectacular combination of the themes discussed above, however, is found in the first-century BCE funeral monument of Antiochus I of Commagene, built in the Taurus Mountains at Nimrud Dagh in present-day Turkey. There, upon three terraces surrounding the high tumulus that contains the funerary chamber, sat colossal statues, originally between eight and ten meters high, of the gods and the deified Antiochus. Also adorning the terraces are various mythological creatures of the Greek and Persian traditions as well as a zodiacal lion giving the royal horoscope.

The art found decorating graves during the archaic and classical periods (amphorae, freestanding statuary, and carved, freestanding stones called stelae) reflects the development of a standardized funereal iconography: the most frequent representations, found painted on vases, in relief, and on freestanding statuary, are sirens singing laments for the dead, sphinxes, heavily draped female figures of mourning, *kouroi* and *korai* (idealized male and female forms), and the representation of *dexiōsis* (two adults linked by the clasping of hands or by the clasping of a symbolic object, such as a bird, perhaps indicating the link between the worlds of the living and the dead). In addition, the frequent appearance of inscriptions commemorating the dead emphasizes the memorializing function of the monument. These motifs in turn were absorbed into the Western tradition of religious iconography: the fierce sphinxes and winged lions of the Near Eastern and Greco-Roman funereal traditions became the guardian angels standing watch above the Christian grave.

In all cultures, the themes of funerary iconography generally reflect the concerns of both the living and the dead. Thus we find the symbols of belief in a life beyond death represented through the elaborate portrayal of religious rituals, banquets of the living and the dead, and gods of the underworld as well as the simple depiction of the fruits of immortal nature, such as olive branches, grapes, flowers, vines, and cornucopias. The eternity of the cosmos is reflected in some cultures by the appearance on the monument of astrological symbols, such as the crescent moon or zodiacal signs; while in Christianity, for example, the symbol of the faith, the cross, reflects the belief in everlasting life promised by the crucifixion. Sometimes the monument may merely be an indication of the faith of the one buried; for example, we find in Hellenistic and Roman Palestine the representation of specifically Jewish motifs, such as the *menorah* (seven-branched candelabrum) and the shofar (ceremonial horn), along with the traditional pagan symbols of immortality. One such sarcophagus is carved with two Greek Nikes (figures representing victory) who hold a roundel containing a large *menorah* above a scene of Bacchic wine making.

The temporality of human existence, however, is often a theme of funereal art as well. In the Greco-Roman world, for example, a portrait of the deceased on the gravestone was common, as were scenes from everyday life, sometimes denoting occupation or social status. Medieval effigies of the deceased upon the tomb represent the continuity of this tradition. Humanity's need to continue to participate in both the sacred and the profane worlds, even after death, is amply illustrated by its tombs and funerary monuments.

[*See also* Death; Funeral Rites; Caves; Pyramids; Temple; *and* Towers.]

BIBLIOGRAPHY

Brandon, S. G. F. *The Judgment of the Dead.* London, 1967.

Cumont, Franz. *Recherches sur le symbolisme funéraire des Romains.* Paris, 1942.

Edwards, I. E. S. *The Pyramids of Egypt.* New ed. New York, 1972.

Hartland, E. Sidney, et al. "Death and Disposal of the Dead." In *Encyclopaedia of Religion and Ethics,* edited by James Hastings, vol. 4. Edinburgh, 1911.

Kurtz, Donna C., and John Boardman. *Greek Burial Customs.* Ithaca, N.Y., 1971.

Toynbee, Jocelyn M. C. *Death and Burial in the Roman World.* Ithaca, N.Y., 1971.

6 RELICS

JOHN S. STRONG

Relics may loosely be defined as the venerated remains of venerable persons. This should be taken to include not only the bodies, bones, or ashes of saints, heroes, martyrs, founders of religious traditions, and other holy men and women but also objects that they once owned and, by extension, things that were once in physical contact with them.

According to the principles of contagious magic, any personal possession or part of a person's body can be thought of as equivalent to his whole self, no matter how minute it may be, or how detached in time and space. Thus a bone, a hair, a tooth, a garment, a footprint can carry the power or saintliness of the person with whom they were once associated and make him or her "present" once again.

Scholars eager to discuss the "origins" of relics have often pointed to the magical use of such objects by "primitive" peoples in rituals of war, healing, rainmaking, or hunting. They have gathered examples from all sorts of ethnographies to show that fetishes and talismans, amulets and medicine bundles were sometimes made of human bones, hair, or organs. They have thereby concluded that the impulse in man to preserve and use "relics" must be very ancient indeed. They may well be correct, but it is important to try to view such examples within their individual cultural contexts, and not to generalize too quickly from them about the development of relic worship as a whole.

In fact, the veneration of relics is not equally emphasized in the various religions of the world. Highly featured in some traditions (such as Buddhism and Catholicism), it is virtually absent in others (Protestantism, Hinduism, Judaism), and found only incidentally elsewhere (Islam, ancient Greece). In this article, therefore, we shall deal primarily with the Roman Catholic and Buddhist traditions. But before doing so, it may be helpful to examine briefly some of the reasons for the other traditions' diversity.

PROTESTANTISM, HINDUISM, AND ISRAELITE RELIGION

The Protestant reformers condemned the veneration of relics partly for theological reasons and partly because it was closely associated in their minds with the sale of indulgences and with other ecclesiastical practices of which they disapproved. From the start, their criticism was thus polemical, and, appealing to reason, it lambasted in particular the fantastic proliferation of relics that had developed in medieval Catholicism. For instance, John Calvin (1509–1564), who wrote a treatise on relics, mockingly commented that in his day the quantity of wood contained in relics of the True Cross was so great that even three hundred men could not have carried it.

In Hinduism, opposition to relic worship occurred for quite different reasons. Though Hindus commonly honor the memories of great saints and teachers and visit sites of pilgrimage associated with them, they do not generally venerate their bodily remains. On the one hand, the doctrine of reincarnation and the belief in the ultimately illusory nature of things of this world simply do not promote relic worship. On the other hand, and probably more importantly, death and things associated with it are, in Hinduism, thought to be highly polluting. For this reason, in fact, Hindu funeral customs stress the total destruction of the body, which is most commonly cremated. The ashes from the pyre and any unburned fragments of bone, though they are treated with respect for a while, are all eventually disposed of, often in a nearby river, ideally in the Ganges.

In ancient Israel, there also existed a concern for purity and for separating the dead from the living. Bodies were not cremated, but they were quickly and carefully buried in the hollowed sides of caves or burial chambers. There it was expected that they would decay, dry up, and disintegrate; thus tombs were commonly reused by family members. Pronounced rites of mourning and lamentation did take place, but, generally speaking, the tomb and the corpse were thought to be unclean, and contact with them was defiling (*Lv.* 21:1–4, *Nm.* 19:11–16). Hence, there was little room for any enthusiasm for relics.

It may also be, however, that too great a veneration of the remains of the dead—as in the occasionally mentioned practice of making food offerings in the tombs—was thought of in certain ancient Israelite circles as bordering on idolatry or paganism, and hence to be condemned.

ISLAM

Much the same concern can be found in Islam; certain Qur'anic scholars periodically denounced the veneration of relics, especially of the bodies of saints, as ***shirk*** (polytheism), that is, as treating the grave as an idol rather than worshiping God alone. Nevertheless, the cult of relics did manage to grow within the Muslim fold, and it continues to be popular today.

In addition to the various "traces" *(athar)* left by Muḥammad, such as hairs, teeth, autographs, and especially footprints, Muslims have long venerated the remains of saints. This, it should be pointed out, is a cult of bodies rather than of bones, and focuses on the tombs of holy persons that dot the countrysides of those Muslim lands where their worship plays an important role. Though ritual patterns at these tombs may vary, often believers will circumambulate the saint's enshrined coffin, leave votive offerings there, and pray for cures, for help with family problems, or more generally for "blessing" *(barakah)*. While some Muslim theologians may claim that such petitions are not technically made to the saint but through the saint to God, it is clear that, in the minds of the faithful, the saint himself is thought to be present in the tomb and able to respond effectively.

In some instances, owing to their great popularity, certain famous saints are reputed to be buried in more than one place. Thus, for example, the body of the great

Shīʿī martyr, Ḥusayn ibn ʿAlī (d. 680 CE), while usually thought to be enshrined in Karbala, is also reputed to rest in Medina, Damascus, Aleppo, and a number of other places, and his head is said to be in Cairo, where it remains a popular center of piety.

Nonetheless, because of orthodox objections, the cult of relics in Islam seems never to have mushroomed in quite the way it did in Christianity or Buddhism, and it has retained a somewhat ambiguous status. This ambiguity is perhaps best summed up in the recurring legends of mausoleums that were destroyed by the very saints they entombed—the saints themselves thereby posthumously objecting to their own cult (and at the same time showing their even greater glory).

ANCIENT GREECE

In ancient Greece, the veneration of relics was closely connected to the cult of heroes, whose reputed remains—often bones larger than life-size—were enshrined and honored in towns as a guarantee of their protection and an enhancement of their prestige. Thus Lesbos had the head of Orpheus, Elis the shoulder bone of Pelops (which had been found by a fisherman and identified by an oracle). Tantalos's bones were at Argos, while the remains of Europa were the focus of the great Hellotia festival in Crete. All of these were thought to ward off disease and famine, to encourage fertility and welfare, and sometimes to bring about miraculous cures.

Occasionally the relics of great heroes were the object of searches and, when found, had to be translated to their place of enshrinement. Plutarch, for example, describes in some detail the quest for the bones of Theseus, a hero whose armed ghost many Athenians believed to have helped them achieve their victory at Marathon. Finally, when his remains were discovered on the island of Siphnos, they were transported to Athens with considerable pomp and celebration and enshrined in the center of the city.

In addition to the bones of the heroes, weapons and other objects associated with them were honored. Thus, in a variety of temples, visitors could marvel at Orpheus's lyre, Achilles' spear, Helen's sandal, Agamemnon's scepter, the Argonauts' anchor, the stone swallowed by Kronos, even the tusks of the Erymanthian boar captured by Herakles. Such items were, perhaps, more objects of curiosity than of cults, but they served the important function of drawing pilgrims and of concretizing the myths and glories of a former age.

EARLY CHRISTIANITY

In Christianity, we find an example of the fully developed veneration of relics. Its origins within the Christian tradition are usually traced to the cults that arose around the tombs of the early saints and martyrs. [*See* Persecution, *article on* Christian Experience.] These cults are often compared to the similar hero cults of the Hellenistic world. They stem, however, not only from a desire to venerate the memory of the departed saint, but also from a hope to partake of some of the power and blessing he or she derived from a close and ongoing relationship with God.

It was thought to be beneficial in the early church to be physically close to the saints. Hence, from the start, Christians paid visits to their tombs; there they celebrated the Eucharist on the stone slabs covering their graves. Sometimes, they even decided to settle permanently in the vicinity of these graves. In this way, tombs became altars, and whole cities arose where once had been cemeteries.

Alternatively, the bodies of the saints were sometimes brought to the faithful; they were translated from their graves to existing cities and enshrined in churches there. Thus existing altars also became tombs, and the custom of celebrating mass over the bones of the martyrs was reinforced. In fact, by the fourth century, in the Eastern church, the Eucharist could only be celebrated on an altar covered with an antimension—a cloth into which were sewn fragments of relics. And in the West, the common custom was to enclose relics in a cavity in the altar top itself—a practice that became formalized in 787 when the Second Council of Nicaea declared the presence of such relics to be obligatory for the consecration of a church.

With the toleration of Christianity throughout the Roman empire beginning in the reign of Constantine (272–327), the demand for and veneration of relics grew. Especially in the fourth and fifth centuries, not only were the known remains of martyrs venerated but lost relics of ancient saints started making their appearance. Thus the body of Saint Stephen—the first Christian martyr—was discovered as though it had been waiting for this time and was enshrined in a number of important centers.

At the same time, relics connected with Christ's passion came to be highly esteemed: the crown of thorns, the nails that pierced his hands and feet, and especially the wood of the True Cross on which Christ had died and which, according to legend, had been discovered by Constantine's mother, Helena. The cross was said to have been made of the wood of the Tree of Life, taken belatedly from the Garden of Eden by Adam's son Seth. It was, thus, a powerful symbol of both the death of Christ and the rewards of eternal life. Along with other relics, it was credited with miraculous cures, even resurrections. It was also used as a talisman for magical protection; Gregory of Nyssa's sister Macrina (c. 327–379) always wore around her neck an amulet consisting of a splinter of the True Cross encased in a ring, and she was clearly not the only noblewoman to do so. It comes as no surprise, then, that by the middle of the fourth century, according to one account, wood from the True Cross filled the world (though miraculously the original cross itself still remained whole and undiminished in Jerusalem).

The growth of the cult of relics in the early church, however, was not without controversy and opposition. On the one hand, it was clearly an offense to traditional Roman sensibilities about keeping the dead in their proper place. For example, Julian the Apostate (r. 361–363) denounced the Christians for filling the world with sepulchers and defiling the cities with the bones and skulls of "criminals." On the other hand, even within the Christian community, there were those such as Vigilantius (early fifth century) who were very critical of the worship of relics, claiming that it was grossly superstitious and bordered on idolatry. However, Jerome, in an angry reply to Vigilantius, argued that Christians did not "worship" relics but "honored" them. Doctrinally, then, if not always in practice, a distinction was made that still stands today between the *veneratio* paid to the saints and their relics and the *adoratio* espoused for God and Christ.

Other church leaders, however, were concerned about the veritable traffic in relics that was developing in the fourth and fifth centuries, especially in the East. In 386, therefore, the emperor Theodosius passed legislation restricting the translation of dead bodies and the selling, buying, or dividing of the remains of martyrs. This, however, seems to have had little effect; at the end of the century, Augustine was still complaining of unscrupulous monks who wandered and traded in "members of martyrs if martyrs they be," and over a century later, the emperor Justinian had to issue another decree regulating the exhumation and transfer of saints' bodies.

It is important to realize the many dimensions of these practices and their larger religious and social significance. As Peter Brown has pointed out, the translations of relics that started in the fourth century helped to spread Christianity by making it more mobile and decentralizing it (Brown, 1981, p. 88). Because of this, not only local holy men but centrally important saints could be worshiped in places far away from the ancient foci of the faith. It was not necessary to journey to Palestine or Rome to honor the memory of Jesus or of the early martyrs; they could be found—present in various physical objects—more close to home, indeed in any consecrated church. In this, the translation of relics was a perfect complement to the popular practice of pilgrimage; it brought the saints to the people instead of taking the people to the saints. At a somewhat different level, the translation of relics also served to establish an intricate network of "patronage, alliance, and gift giving that linked the lay and clerical elites of East and West," which was crucial in the development of the church (Brown, 1981, p. 89). In this, the remains of saints acted as a sort of symbolic exchange commodity.

At the same time, as Brown has also pointed out, the exhumation, dismemberment, and translation of relics has played an important role in divorcing them from too direct an association with death. Precisely because relics are fragments of bones and not whole corpses, precisely because they are in altars or reliquaries and not in coffins, the connotations of death are suppressed, and in the relics the saints can be thought to be "alive."

THE MIDDLE AGES

By the time of the Middle Ages, the veneration of relics had become so widespread, popular, and intense that more than one scholar has called it the true religion of the medieval period. Especially in Europe, churches, monasteries, cathedrals, and other places of pilgrimage seemed to develop an almost insatiable thirst for relics that might add to their sanctity, prestige, and attractiveness to pilgrims. This increasing demand led, in fact, to a renewed search for the bodies of ancient saints in places such as the catacombs in Rome. Quickly, a transalpine trade in bones developed, manned by relic merchants and professional relic thieves, who were eager to supply the needs of Carolingian bishops and abbots and later of Anglo-Saxon kings. Then, with the Crusades, still new sources of relics became accessible—Jerusalem and Constantinople being the most important of these.

Throughout the Middle Ages, relics, in fact, were significant sources of revenue. Offerings made to the shrine of Thomas Becket, for example, accounted for almost half of Canterbury's annual income in the late twelfth century, and this proportion increased when special indulgences were granted to pilgrims there. It is not surprising, then, that persons in power were willing to invest considerably in the acquisition of relics. Louis IX of France (r. 1226–1270), for example, reportedly offered the count of Fondi fifteen thousand florins for the bones of Saint Thomas Aquinas, but, alas, in vain.

When relics were obtained, they were often magnificently enshrined. The reliquaries in which they were encased were some of the most richly adorned products of medieval art; sometimes entire buildings were conceived of as reliquaries, such as the splendid Sainte Chapelle in Paris, which was built to house Christ's crown of thorns.

Given such enthusiasm and piety, it is perhaps not surprising that fraudulent and false relics should also appear. Chaucer, in his *Canterbury Tales,* tells of a relic monger who in his trunk had a pillowcase that he asserted was Our Lady's veil. Other sources mention exhibitions of vials that were said to contain a sneeze of the Holy Spirit, or the sounds of the bells of Solomon's temple, or rays from the star that guided the wise men from the East. One church in Italy even claimed to possess the cross that Constantine saw in his vision.

More generally, however, piety and rival claims led to a bewildering multiplication of the remains of saints. During the Middle Ages, it was rare, in fact, for a saint's body or bones to exist in one place only. At least nineteen churches, for example, claimed to enshrine the jaw of John the Baptist. The body of Saint James was found most famously at Santiago de Compostela in Spain, where, like a magnet, it drew pilgrims from all over Europe along well-established routes; it was also venerated, however, in at least six other places, with additional heads and arms elsewhere. Saint Peter, of course, was honored in Rome, but despite (or because of) his fame there, pilgrims could also venerate significant portions of his body at Arles, Cluny, Constantinople, and Saint-Cloud. While his thumb was to be seen in Toulon, three teeth were in Marseilles, his beard was in Poitiers, and his brain was in Geneva (although John Calvin later claimed it was but a piece of pumice stone).

Relics of more minor saints—six hands of Saint Adrian, various breasts of Saint Agatha—abounded as well. The list is almost endless, and Collin de Plancy easily filled three volumes of a dictionary of relics with references to them.

As for relics of Jesus and the Virgin Mary, they, too, were extremely popular during the Middle Ages, though the doctrine of their bodily ascension to heaven presented some difficulties. In their cases, bones were, for the most part, not legitimately acceptable. Great emphasis, however, could be laid on any object that had once been in contact with their persons.

In the case of the Virgin, these relics tended to emphasize her maternal, nurturing, and domestic characteristics. Thus vials of her breast milk (spilled on various occasions) could be found in countless churches throughout Christendom, later causing Calvin to comment that, had she been a cow all her life, she could not have produced such a quantity. Almost as popular was her tunic (especially that worn at the time of the Annunciation). Threads from it were occasionally worn in protective amulets. Roland, in Spain, for example, fought with a sword in whose hilt was a piece of the Virgin's robe (along with a hair of Saint Denis, a tooth of Saint Peter, and some of Saint Basil's blood). Finally, in Loreto, in central Italy, the whole of the house in which the Virgin had raised the young Jesus in Nazareth could be visited. It was believed to have been miraculously transported there through the air from Palestine in 1296.

In the case of Jesus, the relics were of a more varied character. Some, such as his swaddling clothes and the boards of the manger in which he lay in Bethlehem, brought to mind the figure of the Christ child. Others called up more complex associations, perhaps; no fewer than seven churches claimed to possess his circumcised foreskin, and the one at Coulombs in the diocese of Chartres was venerated by pregnant women hoping for an easy childbirth. Still others simply recalled various episodes recorded in the Gospels: bread crumbs left over from the loaves he had used in feeding the five thousand, one of the pots in which he had turned water into wine, the cloth that had covered the table at the Last Supper, the towel he had used on that occasion to wipe the apostles' feet, the body of the ass on which he had entered Jerusalem.

The greatest veneration and enthusiasm, however, were reserved for relics associated with Christ's passion. Some of these, such as the crown of thorns, the spear that had pierced his side, the nails and wood of the True Cross, had long been popular. But now no detail of Christ's agony escaped attention, and in various churches, pilgrims could also venerate the pillar to which he had been tied, the reeds with which he had been whipped, Veronica's veil on which he had left an image of his face on the way to Calvary, the seamless robe that the soldiers divided, the sponge with which he was offered vinegar, the blood and water that flowed from his side, and, finally, the burial shroud in which he lay in the tomb and on which he left the full imprint of his body. This shroud, now in Turin, was perhaps the last major relic of Christ's passion to come to light. It was first exhibited in the fourteenth century and has, in recent years, become the subject of intensive debate and scientific analysis.

It is sometimes difficult to realize the fervor with which medieval man approached many of these relics. Part of their attraction, of course, lay in their reputed miraculous powers, especially in the form of cures, but there was more to it than this. Relics enabled the pious to relive—to recall experientially—events that were central to their faith. They were visible manifestations of the presence of Christ and of his saints that could, in the words of one bishop, "open the eyes of the heart." They thus provided effective focal points for religious devotion and emotion. Suger, the abbot of Saint-Denis in Paris, has described the scene there in the early twelfth century. The old church, he states, was oftenfilled to overflowing by the faithful, who pressed in closely to implore the help of the saints and strove hard to kiss the nail and crown relics of the Lord. Women found themselves trampled underfoot or squeezed to the point of suffocation, while the brethren themselves, pressed hard by the crowd, periodically had to make their escape with the relics through the windows.

BUDDHISM

Christianity is but one of two major traditions in which relics have played a prominent and popular role. The other—Buddhism—became one of the great propagators of relic worship throughout Asia. Unlike Hinduism, which, we have seen, had little room for relics, Buddhism was from the start fascinated by, and preoccupied with, death. This does not mean that Buddhists did not share some of the Indian repugnance for dead bodies. They tried, however, to overcome that repugnance, meditating on the impurity and impermanence of the body, dead or alive. The remains of the Buddha and of other enlightened saints, however, were thought not to be impure but worthy of the highest veneration.

The focus in Buddhism has been by and large on the relics of the Buddha himself, even though Buddhists in ancient India did also honor the relics of his disciples, and though still today, in some places, believers will search the ashes of great monks for their *śarīradhātu* (either bits of bone or tiny pieces of what is thought to be metamorphosed bodily substance).

According to tradition, when the Buddha passed away into final *nirvāṇa,* he told his disciples who were monks not to preoccupy themselves with his physical remains but to follow his teaching. After his cremation, therefore, his relics were left to the laity. Almost immediately they became the object of a dispute among various North Indian monarchs, each of whom wanted all the physical remains of the Buddha for his own kingdom. According to the *Mahāparinibbāna Sutta,* this squabble was resolved not by the monks but by a brahman named Droṇa who divided the Buddha's relics into eight equal shares and distributed them to eight kings, instructing each to build a stupa (a domed funerary mound) over his portion.

The fate of these eight "Droṇa stupas" (as they were called) is uncertain. According to one legend, however, soon after his conversion to Buddhism, the great Indian emperor Aśoka (third century BCE) collected from them the relics, which he then redistributed throughout his empire, this time dividing them into eighty-four thousand shares and building eighty-four thousand stupas to enshrine them. Thus, the Buddha's physical body (his relics), along with his teaching (his Dharma), was spread throughout the Indian subcontinent in a systematic and ordered way. It is clear, however, that Aśoka was also using Buddhism and the relics symbolically in order to impose his own authority over the kingdom.

In addition to this legend of the eighty-four thousand stupas, there are a number of other quite different traditions concerning the fate of the Buddha's relics. These focus not so much on his ashes as on the fortune of certain of his bones and teeth. One tooth, for instance, ended up enshrined in Sri Lanka, where today it is an object of veneration by pilgrims who come to the Temple of the Tooth in Kandy to make offerings of flowers and incense. Once a year, in the summer month of Äsala, it is paraded in pomp around the city in what remains one of the chief Sri Lankan festivals.

Throughout the precolonial history of Sri Lanka, possession of the Buddha's tooth was seen as an indispensable attribute of kingship. Its cult was the privilege and duty of the legitimate ruler and was thought to ensure social harmony, regular rainfall, bountiful crops, and righteous rule. Its possession meant power. Thus, when the British finally took Kandy in 1815 and captured the tooth, they found to their surprise that resistance to them soon stopped.

The official cult of the tooth relic was and is today carried out by an entire hierarchy of priests. Several times a day, in a series of ceremonies that closely resemble the Hindu pattern of worship of the gods, they ritually entertain the tooth, bathe it, clothe it, and feed it. In this, it is quite clear that the Buddha is thought to be somehow present, despite the doctrine that he has completely transcended the realm of rebirth.

As with the saints in Christianity, this presence of the Buddha in his relics is sometimes emphasized by the occurrence of miracles. For instance, according to the *Mahāvaṃsa* (Great Chronicle) of Sri Lanka, when King Duṭṭhagāmaṇi (first century BCE) was about to enshrine some Buddha relics in the great stupa he had built, the casket in which they were kept rose up into the air; it opened of itself, and the relics came out, took on the physical form of the Buddha, and performed all sorts of miracles that had been performed by the Buddha himself during his lifetime. According to some traditions, it might be added, much the same miracle is expected to take place at the end of this present world cycle, when, just prior to the advent of the next Buddha, Maitreya, all of the dispersed relics of the present Buddha will miraculously come together again to form his body one more time, before disappearing forever into the depths of the earth.

Sri Lanka, however, was by no means the only Buddhist nation to enjoy the possession of prestigious Buddha relics. A number of hairs of the Buddha were enshrined in splendor in the great Shwe Dagon pagoda in Rangoon, Burma; and in Lamphun in northern Thailand, several relics of the Buddha became the object of great veneration and elaborate legends. In both of these places, as in many others throughout the Buddhist world, the presence of Buddha relics is closely linked to the first introduction of Buddhism into the country. In other words, the relics were not just objects of veneration for a few but were symbolic of the establishment of the faith in a whole region.

The situation was somewhat different in China, where Buddhism was always in competition with a number of other faiths and ideologies. Nevertheless, in Ch'ang-an (present-day Sian), the ancient capital of the T'ang dynasty, the emperor's periodic reception for the Buddha's finger bone relic (generally kept at a monastery outside the city) was perhaps the greatest religious festival during the ninth century. As Kenneth Ch'en put it in his *Buddhism in China,* "Whenever this relic was put on public display, the people . . . would work themselves into such a state of religious frenzy as to belie the statement that the Chinese are rational and practical in their conduct" (Ch'en,1964, p. 280). Devotees threw themselves on the ground, gave away all their possessions, cut off their hair, burned their scalps, and made fiery offerings of their fingers. It was, in fact, this sort of display that in 819 led the Confucian scholar Han Yü to petition the throne to put an end to such celebrations, pointing out that it was demeaning for the emperor to have anything to do with the bone of a barbarian.

Another famous relic of the Buddha in China was a tooth that was originally brought to Nanking in the fifth century and then taken to Ch'ang-an. Lost for over eight hundred years, it was rediscovered in 1900 and is presently enshrined in a pagoda outside Peking. In the late 1950s and early 1960s, the Chinese government, eager to improve its relations with Buddhist nations of South and Southeast Asia, allowed it to go on a tour to Burma and then Sri Lanka, where it was worshiped by hundreds of thousands of people.

Not all of the Buddha's relics, however, have been bodily remains. In several places in South and Southeast Asia, great stone footprints, reputed to be his, are still venerated today. In northwest India, he is said to have left his shadow or reflected image on the wall of acave that was a popular pilgrimage site from the fourth to the eighth century. There, given the right amount of devotion and meditation, pilgrims were thought actually to be able to see the Buddha himself in his shadow. Nearby was a rock on which one could discern the pattern of the cloth in the Buddha's robe where he had set it out to dry. Also in the same region was the Buddha's begging bowl, which the Chinese pilgrim Fa-hsien saw during his trip to India (399–414). Fa-hsien recounts a legend concerning the bowl's miraculous migration over the centuries throughout the Buddhist world. According to this, at the end of the present age, it is destined to ascend to the Tuṣita Heaven, where it will be a sign for the future Buddha Maitreya that the time for him to come down to earth is at hand.

CONCLUSION

In both the Christian and Buddhist traditions, as well as to a lesser extent in Islam and ancient Greece, the examples of relics we have considered present a great variety of aspects and have been caught up in a whole gamut of symbolisms. In relics, believers have found the ongoing presence and power of Jesus, of the Buddha, of the saints of different traditions. Everywhere relics have performed miracles of various kinds; they have been used to ward off evil, to effectuate cures, and to ensure the prosperity of individuals, cities, and even nations; they have legitimized the rule of kings and emperors; they have helped spread and popularize religion; they have been bought, stolen, traded, and fought over, and have held social, economic, and political importance.

But for all these many functions, it must be noted that relics remain marked with a certain ambiguity. They are often objects that are normally considered to be impure—dead flesh, bones, and body parts—and yet they are venerated as holy. In this very paradox, however, we can see some of the ways in which relics work to heighten the holiness and purity of the saints; if even their impurities are venerated, how much purer and more venerable they must be themselves!

Somewhat the same reasoning can be applied to a second and more basic ambiguity found in relics. They are clearly symbols of death and impermanence; they are what is left after the saints and founders of the tradition are no more. Yet, as we have seen repeatedly, they also make manifest the continuing presence and life of these absent beings. In asserting that the saints are "alive in death," or, in the case of Buddhism, that they are paradoxically present despite their final *nirvāṇa,* relics in both traditions manage to bridge a gap that is one of the great divides of human existence.

[*See also* Bones. *For discussions of religious architecture connected with the veneration of relics, see* Architecture; Tombs; *and* Stupa Worship.]

BIBLIOGRAPHY

Surprisingly little has been written of a general comparative nature on relics. Mention should be made, however, of the two articles by J. A. MacCulloch and Vincent A. Smith: "Relics (Primitive and Western)" and "Relics (Eastern)," in the *Encyclopaedia of Religion and Ethics,* edited by James Hastings, vol. 10 (Edinburgh, 1918). They are still useful, although dated.

For the study of relics in Christianity, a number of more specialized works are helpful. Peter Brown's *The Cult of the Saints: Its Rise and Function in Latin Christianity* (Chicago, 1981) is a good place to begin, while André Grabar's *Martyrium: Recherches sur le culte des reliques et l'art chrétien antique* (Paris, 1946) remains a standard and readable classic. On the True Cross, see Anatole Frolow's *La relique de la Vraie Croix: Recherches sur le développement d'un culte* (Paris, 1961) and, from an art historical perspective, the Pierpont Morgan Library's *The Stavelot Triptych, Mosan Art and the Legend of the True Cross* (Oxford, 1980) by William Voelke. For a still useful introduction to the place of relics in medieval Christianity, see chapters 6–8 of George G. Coulton's *Five Centuries of Religion,* vol. 3 (Cambridge, 1936). For a fascinating listing of various relics through the ages (but one marked by a highly prejudiced commentary), see J. A. S. Collin de Plancy's *Dictionnaire critique des reliques et des images miraculeuses,* 3 vols. (Paris, 1821–1822). This also contains, in an appendix, a reprint of John Calvin's treatise on relics. For a fine study of the medieval traffic in relics in western Europe, see Patrick J. Geary's *Furta Sacra: Thefts of Relics in the Central Middle Ages* (Princeton, 1978). Finally, among the many recent works to appear on the Shroud of Turin, mention might be made of Ian Wilson's *The Shroud of Turin: The Burial Cloth of Jesus Christ?* (Garden City, N.Y., 1978).

For the study of relics in Buddhism, several specialized sources are also available. A useful discussion of various sources concerning the division of the Buddha's relics after his death can be found in chapter 11 of Edward Joseph Thomas's *The Life of Buddha as Legend and History* (London, 1927). For a study of Aśoka's enshrining of the relics in eighty-four thousand stupas, see John S. Strong's *The Legend of King Aśoka* (Princeton, 1983), pp. 107–119. A detailed description of the rituals associated with the Buddha's tooth in Sri Lanka can be found in H. L. Seneviratne's *Rituals of the Kandyan State* (Cambridge, 1978). This work surpasses all earlier ones on this topic. A helpful introduction to the temple of the Buddha's relic in Lamphun, Thailand, is Donald K. Swearer's *Wat Haripuñjaya* (Missoula, Mont., 1976). For Buddhist relics in China, see Kenneth Ch'en's *Buddhism in China: A Historical Survey* (Princeton, 1964).

Finally, two useful works for the study of relics in Islam deserve mention: Ignácz Goldziher's "On the Veneration of the Dead in Paganism and Islam," in volume 1 of *Muslim Studies* (Chicago, 1966), and, on the cult of the saints in Egypt, Jane I. Smith and Yvonne Haddad's *The Islamic Understanding of Death and Resurrection* (Albany, N.Y., 1981), appendix C.

7 ANCESTOR WORSHIP

Helen Hardacre

The term *ancestor worship* designates rites and beliefs concerning deceased kinsmen. Rites of ancestor worship include personal devotions, domestic rites, the ancestral rites of a kinship group such as a lineage, periodic rites on the death day of the deceased, and annual rites for collectivity of ancestors. Generally excluded from the category are rites for the dead having no specific reference to kinsmen, and beliefs about the dead in general that lack any special reference to kinship.

GENERAL CHARACTERISTICS AND RESEARCH PROBLEMS

Ancestor worship has attracted the enduring interest of scholars in many areas of the study of religion. In the late nineteenth century, it was identified as the most basic form of all religion, and subsequent studies of the subject in specific areas have provided a stimulating point of access to related problems of religion, society, and culture.

The worship of ancestors is closely linked to cosmology and worldview, to ideas of the soul and the afterlife, and to a society's regulation of inheritance and succession. In East Asia ancestor worship is found combined with the practice of Buddhism, and ancestral rites compose a major part of the practice of Confucianism. It is generally acknowledged that ancestor worship functions to uphold the authority of elders, to support social control, and to foster conservative and traditionalist attitudes. In addition, ancestor worship is clearly linked to an ethic of filial piety and obedience to elders.

The institution of ancestor worship is properly regarded as a religious practice, not as a religion in itself. It is generally carried out by kinship groups and seldom has a priesthood separable from them. It is limited to the practice of the ethnic group; there is no attempt to proselytize outsiders. Its ethical dimension primarily refers to the proper conduct of family or kinship relations. It does not have formal doctrine as such; where texts exist, these are mainly liturgical manuals. In most cases ancestor worship is not the only religious practice of a society; rather, it exists as part of a more comprehensive religious system.

The meaning of *worship* in *ancestor worship* is problematic. Ancestor worship takes a variety of forms in different areas, and its attitudinal characteristics vary accordingly. The ancestors may be regarded as possessing power equivalent to that of a deity and hence may be accorded cult status and considered able to influence society to the same extent as its deities. Typically, the conception of ancestors is strongly influenced by ideas of other supernaturals in the society's religious system. Ancestors may be prayed to as having the power to grant boons or allay misfortune, but their effectiveness is regarded as naturally limited by the bonds of kinship. Thus, a member of a certain lineage prays only to the ancestors of that lineage; it would be regarded as nonsensical to pray to ancestors of any other lineage. Accordingly, members of other lineages are excluded from the ancestral rites of kinship groups of which they are not members. The religious attitudes involved in the worship of ancestors include filial piety, respect, sympathy, and sometimes, fear.

The rites of death, including funerary and mortuary rituals, are regarded as falling within the purview of ancestor worship only when memorial rites beyond the period of death and disposition of the corpse are carried out as a regular function of a kinship group. Thus, the funerary rites and occasional memorials common in Europe and the United States are not regarded as evidence of ancestor worship. However, when ancestors are collectively and regularly accorded cult status by their descendants, acting as members of a kinship group, such practices are regarded as ancestor worship.

Dead or stillborn children, miscarriages, and abortions are generally conceptually distinguished from ancestors. For the most part these exceptional deaths are accorded very abbreviated funeral rites, if any, and they generally receive little memorial ritual. Like those who die in youth before marriage, their fate is regarded as especially pitiable and as a source of possible harm to the living.

The study of ancestor worship involves several different questions. How are the ancestors viewed in relation to their descendants? Is ancestor worship in some sense a reflection of actual relations between fathers and sons? In what circumstances are the ancestors viewed as capable of harming their descendants, and is the ancestors' benevolence or malevolence linked to descendants' sense of guilt toward them? What can be learned about relations of jural authority from studies of ancestor worship? What is the character of domestic rites? These often seem to reflect a feeling that the dead are still "living" in some sense, that they can be contacted and their advice sought. Studies in this area illumine attitudes toward death and reveal a very general perception that the dead gradually lose their individual characteristics and merge into an impersonal collectivity. A recent topic of research concerns the differing attitudes of women and men toward ancestors.

ANCESTOR WORSHIP IN THE HISTORY OF THE STUDY OF RELIGION

In *Principles of Sociology* (1877) Herbert Spencer wrote that "ancestor worship is the root of every religion." According to his view, the cult of heroes originated in the deification of an ancestor, and in fact all deities originate by an analogous process. Spencer's euhemerist theory rested on the idea, familiar in the scholarship of his day, that religion as a whole has a common origin from which its many forms derive. Knowledge of this original form would provide the key to understanding all subsequent developments.

Somewhat earlier Fustel de Coulanges wrote in *La cité antique* (1864) that the ancient societies of Greece and Rome were founded upon ancestor worship. Furthermore, when the beliefs and practices of ancestor worship were weakened, society as a whole was entirely transformed. In the view of de Coulanges, Greece and Rome were founded upon a common belief in the soul's continued existence after the body's death. The family that continued to worship its ancestors became society's basic unit, expanding gradually to the clan divisions of gens, phratry, and tribe. Eventually cities were founded, governed as quasi-religious associations by patrician families.

In *Totem and Taboo* (1913), Sigmund Freud postulated that the belief that the living can be harmed by the dead serves to reduce guilt experienced toward the dead. That is, in kinship relations characterized by conscious affection there is inevitably a measure of hostility; however, this hostility conflicts with the conscious ideal of affectionate relations and hence must be repressed. Repressed hostility is then projected onto the dead and takes the form of the belief that the dead are malevolent and can harm the living.

Meyer Fortes considerably refined Freud's hypothesis on the basis of African material. In *Oedipus and Job in West African Religion* (1959), Fortes found that among the Tallensi belief in the continued authority of ancestors, rather than fear of them, is the principle means of alleviating guilt arising from repressed hostility.

Among the Tallensi relations between fathers and sons are affectionate, but, because a son cannot attain full jural authority until his father's death, sons bear a latent resentment of their fathers. However, this resentment does not manifest itself as belief in the malevolence of the dead. Instead, the Tallensi believe that the authority of the father is granted to him by his ancestors, who demand from the son continued subordination. Thus the function of ancestor worship is to reinforce the general, positive valuation of the authority of elders, quite apart from the individual personality of any specific ancestor. A related function is to place a positive value upon subordination of the desires of the individual to the collective authority of tribal elders. This value is useful in ensuring the continued solidarity of the group.

In *Death, Property, and the Ancestors* (1966), Jack Goody studied ancestor worship among the LoDagaa of West Africa. Property to be inherited by descendants is not distributed until the death of the father. Prevented from commanding the full possession of this property, a son experiences a subconscious wish for the father's death. Repression of this guilt takes the form of the belief that the dead have eternal rights to the property they formerly held. In order to enjoy those rights, the dead must receive sacrifices from the living. If sacrifices are not forthcoming, the ancestors will afflict their descendants with sickness and misfortune. Thus beliefs concerning ancestral affliction are inextricably linked to social issues of inheritance and succession.

In "Gods, Ghosts, and Ancestors," Arthur Wolf (1974) shows how Chinese concepts of a variety of supernatural beings closely correspond to social reality. In particular, the conception of ancestors replicates perceptions of parents, elders, and other kin. This is not to say that the living and dead are not distinguished, but that the same relations of authority and obedience are found among the living and in their rites for their ancestors.

ANCESTOR WORSHIP IN PRACTICE

This section describes the practice of ancestor worship in various cultural areas and in relation to several religious traditions.

Africa. Ancestor worship normally forms only one aspect of an African people's religion. A person without descendants cannot become an ancestor, and in order to achieve ancestorhood, proper burial, with rites appropriate to the person's status, is necessary. After an interval following death, a deceased person who becomes an ancestor is no longer perceived as an individual. Personal characteristics disappear from the awareness of the living, and only the value of the ancestor as a moral exemplar remains. Ancestors are believed to be capable of intervening in human affairs, but only in the defined area of their authority, that is, among their descendants.

In an important study of African ancestor worship, Max Gluckman (1937) established the distinction between ancestor worship and the cult of the dead. Ancestors represent positive moral forces who can cause or prevent misfortune and who require that their descendants observe a moral code. The cult of the dead, on the other hand, is not exclusively directed to deceased kinsmen, but to the spirits of the dead in general. Here spirits are prayed to for the achievement of amoral or antisocial ends, whereas ancestors can be petitioned only for ends that are in accord with basic social principles.

Among the Edo the deceased is believed to progress through the spirit world on a course that parallels the progress of his son and other successors. Events in this world are punctuated by rites and are believed to have a counterpart in the spirit world. Thus it may be twenty years before a spirit is finally merged into the collective dead and descendants can receive their full complement of authority. In this sense the ancestors continue to exert authority over their descendants long after death. Until that authority ceases, the son must perform rites as prescribed and behave in approved ways.

Among the Ewe of Ghana, ancestor worship is an important focal point of the whole society. It is the basis of the entire religious system and a point of reference for the conceptualization of all social relations. The Ewe believe that the human being has two souls. Before birth the being resides in the spirit world; it comes into this world when it finds a mother, and it returns to the spirit world at death. This cycle of movement through the realms is perpetual. The ancestors are invoked with libations on all ceremonial occasions. Rites range from simple, personal libations to complicated rituals involving an entire lineage. During a ritual, the soul of the ancestor returns to be fed through the ceremonial stool that serves as its shrine. In addition to individual stools, there is a lineage stool for lineage ancestors that is kept wrapped in silks or velvet.

The studies of Igor Kopytoff (1971) on the Suku of Zaire raise the question of the appropriateness of the term *ancestor worship*. The Suku have no term that can be translated as "ancestor"; they make no terminological distinction between the dead and the living. A single set of principles regulates relations between seniors and juniors. The dividing line between living and dead does not affect those principles. Thus we can say that among the Suku ancestor worship is an extension of lineage relations between elders and their juniors. Furthermore, lineages must be considered as communities of both living and dead. The powers attributed to ancestors can only be seen as a projection of the powers of living elders. In this sense the term "ancestor worship" can be misleading.

Melanesia. Ancestors are one of many types of spirits recognized by Melanesian tribal peoples. Regarding the role of ancestor worship in tribal life, Roy Rappaport's study *Pigs for the Ancestors* (1977) presents an innovative approach not seen in the study of ancestor worship in other areas. Among the highland Tsembaga, ancestral ritual is part of a complex ecological system in which a balanced cycle of abundance and scarcity is regulated. Yam gardens are threatened by the unhindered growth of the pig population, and human beings must supplement their starch-based diet with protein. Propelling this cycle is a belief that pigs must be sacrificed to the ancestors in great numbers. These sacrifices provide the Tsembaga with protein in great quantity. Pigs sacrificed when someone dies or in connection with intertribal warfare supplement the ordinary diet of yams, which is adequate for ordinary activity but not for periods of stress. Thus ancestor worship plays a vital role in the ecological balance of the tribe in its environment.

India. Ancestor worship in India takes a variety of forms, depending upon the area and the ethnic group concerned; however, providing food for the dead is a basic and widespread practice. Orthodox Hindu practice centers on an annual rite between August and September that includes offering sacred rice balls *(piṇḍa)* to the ancestors. The *Laws of Manu* includes specific instructions for ancestral offerings. Descendants provide a feast for the brahmans, and the merit of this act is transferred to the ancestors. The feast itself is called the Śrāddha. The form of this rite varies depending on whether it is observed during a funeral or in subsequent, annual observances. Texts prescribe ritual purifications and preparations in detail.

Buddhism. Based on a canonical story, the All Souls Festival, or Avalambana, is observed throughout Southeast and East Asia. The story concerns one of the Buddha's disciples, Maudgalyāyana, known for skill in meditation and supranormal powers. The mother of Maudgalyāyana appeared to her son in a dream and revealed to him that she was suffering innumerable tortures in the blackest hell because of her *karman.* Through magic Maudgalyāyana visited his mother in hell, but his power was of no avail in securing her release. Eventually the Buddha instructed him to convene an assembly of the priesthood which then would recite *sūtra*s and transfer the merit of those rites to ancestors. In other words, descendants must utilize the mediation of the priesthood in order to benefit ancestors. The result is an annual festival, traditionally observed on the day of the full moon of the eighth lunar month. At this festival special *sūtra* recitations and offering rites for the ancestors are held in Buddhist temples, and domestic rites differing in each country are performed. In addition to rites for ancestors, observances for the "hungry ghosts" and for spirits who have died leaving no descendants are performed.

Although one of the key concepts in early Indian Buddhism was the idea of no-soul *(anātman),* in fact the idea of a soul is widely accepted in East Asia. The idea of rebirth in human, heavenly, and subhuman forms is found combined with the idea that an eternal soul rests in an ancestral tablet or inhabits a world of the dead. The contradictions involved in this complex of ideas are not generally addressed as problematic by those who hold them.

In East Asia today the performance of ancestral and funeral ritual provides the Buddhist clergy with one of its greatest sources of revenue, a tendency particularly marked in Japan. The Buddhist clergy is typically employed to recite *sūtra*s for the dead and to enshrine ancestral tablets in temples.

Shamanism. Throughout East Asia ancestor worship is found in close association with shamanistic practices. Shamanism in East Asia today consists in large part of mediumistic communications in which the shaman enters a trance and divines the present condition of a client's ancestors. These practices are based on the folk notion that if a person suffers from an unusual or seemingly unwarranted affliction, the ancestors may be the cause. If the ancestors are suffering, if they are displeased with their descendants' conduct, or if they are offered inappropriate or insufficient ritual, they may cause some harm to come to their descendants. However, it is only rarely that this belief is straightforwardly expressed as the proposition that ancestors willfully, malevolently afflict their descendants.

Chinese Ancestor Worship. An important component at work in the metaphysics of Chinese ancestor cults is indigenous theories of the soul. [*See* Soul, *article on* Chinese Concepts.] First of all, since Chou times (c. 1123–221 BCE) the idea of the soul as the pale, ghostly shadow of a man has been a perduring notion found in popular stories. These apparitions are called *kuei,* meaning demons, devils, and ghosts, as opposed to *shen,* the benevolent spirits of ancestors (a word used also to refer to all deities).

Together with this idea of the ghostly soul there developed a conception of the soul in terms of *yin* and *yang.* According to this theory, the *yin* portion of the soul, called *p'o,* may turn into a *kuei* and cause misfortune if descendants do not perform proper ancestral rites. If the *p'o* is satisfactorily placated, however, it will rest peacefully. Meanwhile, the *yang* portion of the soul, called *hun,* associated with *shen,* will bless and protect descendants and their families. [*See* Afterlife, *article on* Chinese Concepts.] Thus Chinese ancestral rites have been motivated simultaneously by the fear of the vengeful dead and by the hope for ancestral blessings.

Chinese ancestor worship can be seen as two separate cults: one that expresses the unity of a lineage of lineage-segment, the so-called hall cult, and another directed to the recently deceased members of a household, the domestic cult. Lineage observances center upon an ancestral hall in which tablets representing lineage ancestors are enshrined and worshiped by descendants in a Confucian mode. Domestic rites center upon daily offerings at a home altar. [*See* Domestic Observances, *article on* Chinese Practices.] Lineage ritual tends to formality and the expression of sentiments of obedience to the authority of ancestors and elders as a group, whereas domestic ritual focuses upon the expression of individual sentiments and continued relations between descendants and particular deceased individuals.

Chinese ancestor worship is closely linked to property inheritance; every deceased individual must receive offerings from at least one descendant who will provide him with sustenance in the next life. However, a specific person is only required to worship those ancestors from whom he has received property.

Confucianism. Confucianism lays heavy emphasis upon the correct practice of ancestral ritual. Special attention is given to minute details concerning the content and arrangement of offerings, proper dress, gesture and posture, and the order of precedence in appearing before ancestral altars. According to the *Book of Family Ritual* of the Neo-Confucian scholar Chu Hsi, the *Chu-tzu chia-li,* commemoration of ancestors became primarily a responsibility of eldest sons, and women were excluded from officiating roles in the celebration of rites.

The highest virtue in Confucian doctrine is filial piety, quintessentially expressed in the worship of ancestors. When Buddhism was first introduced to China, one of Confucianism's strongest arguments against it was the assertion that Buddhism was in essence opposed to filial piety and was likely to disrupt the practice of ancestor worship. If sons took the tonsure and failed to perform ancestral rites, then not only would spirits in the other world suffer from lack of ritual attention but social relations in society would also be undermined.

In traditional Chinese society gravesites are located through a geomancer. Based upon the idea that an ideal confluence of "winds and waters" *(feng-shui)* benefits the dead and their descendants, a geomancer seeks a site in which the burial urn can be nestled in the curve of rolling hills and near running water. This combination of cosmic forces is believed to benefit the dead and to facilitate their progress in the other world. Lineages compete fiercely with one another for these scarce resources and may even forcibly remove unprotected urns so that new ones may occupy auspicious sites.

Korea. In Korea women and men hold quite different images of ancestors. A woman marries away from her natal village and enters her husband's household under the authority of his mother and father. The wife's relations with her husband's kin are expected to be characterized by strife and competition. Her membership in the husband's lineage is tenuous and is never fully acknowledged in ritual until her death. Because women's relation to the lineage is strained in these ways, they hold more negative views of the ancestors than do men. Women's negative conceptions are expressed in the idea that ancestors maliciously harm their descendants by afflicting them with disease and misfortune. Men worship ancestors in Confucian rites from which women are excluded, while women perform rites for ancestors in a shamanic mode, utilizing widespread networks of shamans, most of whom are women. This gender-based bifurcation in ancestor worship is a special characteristic of Korean tradition.

Japan. Since the Tokugawa period (1600–1868) Japanese ancestor worship has mainly been carried out in a Buddhist mode, though Shintō rites also exist. As in China, ancestral ritual reflects relations of authority and inheritance, but instead of lineage rites, rites are performed by main and branch households of the traditional family system, the *ie*. Branch families *(bunke)* accept the ritual centrality of the main household *(honke)* by participating in its rites in a subordinate status. The *honke* does not reciprocate. In addition to *honke-bunke* rites, domestic rites performed before a Buddhist altar are a prominent feature of Japanese ancestral worship.

In *Ancestor Worship in Contemporary Japan* (1973) Robert Smith demonstrates that sympathy often provokes the Japanese to enshrine the tablets of entirely unrelated persons in their own domestic altars. They may also keep duplicate tablets out of personal attachment to a deceased person and with no feeling that sanctions will be forthcoming if they fail to do so. Thus, in addition to its reflection of kinship relations, ancestor worship becomes a means of expressing affection.

The "new religions" of Japan are a group of several hundred associations that have appeared in the nineteenth and twentieth centuries. Whether their doctrine is derived from Shintō or Buddhism, most reserve a special place for ancestor worship in some form. Reiyūkai Kyōdan (Association of Friends of the Spirits) represents a rare example of a religious group in which worship of ancestors is the main focus of individual and collective rites. Reverence for ancestors in the new religions and in Japanese society in general is closely linked to social and political conservatism and to a traditionalist preference for the social mores of the past.

[*See also* Genealogy *and* Family.]

BIBLIOGRAPHY

Ahern, Emily. *The Cult of the Dead in a Chinese Village.* Stanford, Calif., 1973. A comprehensive study of ancestor worship in Taiwan that clarifies the relation between lineage and domestic observances.

Blacker, Carmen. *The Catalpa Bow.* London, 1975. An evocative study of shamanistic and ancestral practices in Japanese folk religion.

Freedman, Maurice. *Lineage Organization in Southeastern China* (1958). London, 1965. An anthropological study of lineage organization that establishes the distinction between hall and domestic ancestral cults and includes valuable material on geomancy.

Gluckman, Max. "Mortuary Customs and the Belief in Survival after Death among the South-Eastern Bantu." *Bantu Studies* 11 (June 1937): 117–136.

Groot, J. J. M. de. *The Religious System of China* (1892). 6 vols. Taipei, 1967. A comprehensive study of Chinese religions with rich data on ancestor worship, principally from Amoy.

Hardacre, Helen. *Lay Buddhism in Contemporary Japan: Reiyūkai Kyōdan.* Princeton, 1984. A study of a new religion of Japan with special reference to ancestor worship.

Hsu, Francis L. K. *Under the Ancestors' Shadow.* New York, 1948. A classic study of Chinese ancestor worship.

Janelli, Dawnhee Yim, and Roger L. Janelli. *Ancestor Worship in Korean Society.* Stanford, Calif., 1982. A study of Korean ancestor worship with special reference to gender differences in belief and practice.

Jordan, David K. *Gods, Ghosts, and Ancestors: The Folk Religion of a Taiwanese Village.* Chicago, 1969. A study of ancestor worship and related phenomena, especially spirit marriage, in Taiwan.

Kopytoff, Igor. "Ancestors as Elders in Africa." *Africa* 41 (April 1971): 129–142.

Newell, William H., ed. *Ancestors.* The Hague, 1976. A useful collection of essays on aspects of ancestor worship, especially in Africa and Japan.

Takeda Chōshū. *Sosen sūhai.* Tokyo, 1971. A study of Japanese ancestor worship with special reference to Buddhism.

Wolf, Arthur P. "Gods, Ghosts, and Ancestors." In his *Religion and Ritual in Chinese Society,* pp. 131–182. Stanford, Calif., 1974.

Yanagita Kunio. *Senzo no hanashi.* Tokyo, 1946. Translated by F. H. Mayer and Ishiwara Yasuyo as *About Our Ancestors* (Tokyo, 1970). A folkloristic view of Japanese ancestor worship and its place in Japanese culture.

8 MYTHIC ANCESTORS

Charles H. Long

Cosmogonic myths are narratives that depict the creation of the world by divine beings. In many cosmogonic myths a supreme being or high god creates the world, after which other divine beings come into being, who in the form of culture heroes or other types of gods reveal the realm of the sacred, death, sexuality, sacred geography, and the methods of food production. The narrative of the cosmogonic myth moves from the initial creation of the world to the revelation of the archetypal actions and gestures of divine beings and culture heroes, thus describing a sacred history of primordial times. [*See* Archetypes.] These divine beings and culture heroes form the ancestral lineages of the human race. The situation of the human race is based upon the activities, adventures, discoveries, and disappearance of these first creative ancestors, who appeared in sacred history. [*See* Cosmogony.]

PRIMORDIAL RUPTURES

In the Mesopotamian myth *Enuma elish,* a tension develops between the first creators and their offspring. This tension leads to a rupture in the initial creation and a struggle between its gods and their offspring. In the ensuing battle, the foundation is established for human existence. In the *Enuma elish,* the god Marduk is the leader of the offspring who fight Tiamat, the mother. In the battle Tiamat is slain, and her body becomes the earth on which human beings live. Certain archetypes for human existence are established as a result of this battle: the cooperation between the offspring gods becomes a model for cooperative enterprise among human beings, which the death of Tiamat affirms. In the biblical myth of the *Book of Genesis,* Adam and Eve live in Paradise with the creator god. When they sin they become the archetypal ancestors of the human community, for they now must experience sexuality, birth, labor, and death, the universal lot of all human beings. [*See* Fall, The.]

A Dogon myth from West Africa describes a similar situation. The god Amma began creation by first forming a cosmic egg, in which the embryos of twin deities matured; they were to become perfect beings. One of the twins became impatient and decided to leave the egg before maturation. In so doing it tore out part of the placenta and fell to what is now the earth, creating a place of habitation from the torn placenta of the egg. This was an incomplete creation, however, and Amma, to rectify the situation, sacrificed the other twin. Even with this sacrifice, the creation could not be made perfect. Instead of creating perfect beings who were both androgynous and amphibious, Amma was forced to compromise. Thus, humans are not androgynous but rather composed of two sexes; they are not amphibious but essentially terrestrial; they do not live continuously in a perfect state of illumination (composed of equal parts of dark and light), as was the original intention of Amma, but in two alternating modes of full light and darkness. In addition to this, the opposing natures of the obedient and the malevolent twin, who are the ancestors of all human beings on earth, define modes of life throughout the universe.

In myths of this kind we are able to recognize what Mircea Eliade (1969) identified as two forms of primordiality. There is, first of all, the primordiality defined by the great creator deities who brought the world into being. Their creativity is inaccessible to ordinary human beings and they appear remote and unconcerned with the human condition. [*See* Deus Otiosus.] There is another primordiality that can be recognized in the tension and rupture between the creator deities and other deities who enter upon adventures and exploits that define the archetypal modes for human existence. Through these activities, the creator deities bring the sacred into the existential modes of human existence and are seen as the ancestors of human beings.

In some cultures, the cosmogonic myths make no reference to great creator deities. The narrative begins with the second primordiality and the action is that of the culture hero, whose actions create the human condition. Among the Kwakiutl Indians of North America, the culture hero is Transformer and comes upon the scene as a human being living in a human family. Whenever he discovers human deceit or error, he transforms the human being into a bird or other animal, thus filling the landscape with the food supply necessary for human existence. In this manner Transformer sets the rules for the production and consumption of food and for reincarnation (to ensure a continuous supply of food). Prior to the actions of Transformer there is no order in the cosmos. After his participation in the production of the food supply, all other forms of order— within the family, society, and so on— come into being. The chiefs of the segmented social units *(numaym)* are each related to an animal ancestor. In fact, following upon the transformation of humans into animals, the Kwakiutl believe that animals and spirits lead lives that are exactly equivalent to those of human beings. Animals are considered to be human beings who are wearing masks and costumes created by their animal forms. [*See* Culture Heroes *and* Animals.]

The second primordiality also dominates the myth of what Adolf E. Jensen (1963) has called "cultivator cultures." In a myth cited from the Indonesian island of Ceram, he describes a type of deity referred to by the indigenous peoples as a *dema* deity. The activity of these deities goes back to the end of the first primordial period. They sometimes possess human form and at other times animal form. The decisive event in their lives is the killing of one *dema* deity by another, which establishes the human condition. Before the death of the *dema,* the human condition is not characterized by sexual differentiation or death; it is only after the death of the *dema* that these aspects come into existence. The *dema* come at the end of primordial time and are thus the first of all human ancestors. Through the death of the *dema,* human beings are accepted again within their community. In myths of this kind the ancestors are gods, heroes, or divine beings, who through their actions make possible and render meaningful the human condition as it is, with all of its possibilities and limitations, and it is through them that the human condition possesses a divine presence.

Ancestors not only set forth the general and universal human condition; they are also the founders of clans, families, moieties, and other segments of the human community. N. D. Fustel de Coulanges's classic work *The Ancient City* (1901) describes how ancient Greek and Roman families were founded by ancestors who were heroes or divine beings. The family cult was at once the basis for the order and maintenance of the family and a cult of the ancestor. Similar notions are present among Australian Aborigines, where each totemic group has its own totemic ancestor who controls the food supply and is the basis for authority and marriages among the groups. [*See* Totemism.] In almost the same manner, the Tucano Indians of Colombia understand their origins as arising from mythical ancestors, the Desána, who revealed all the forms of nature and modes of being to the human community.

An exemplary expression of the cult of ancestors is found in Chinese religions. It is the duty of Chinese sons to provide for and revere their parents in this life and the life after death; this is a relationship of reciprocity. The household is composed of the living and the dead; the ancestors provide and sustain the foundations of spiritual order upon which the family is based, while the living keep the family in motion. The living are always under the tacit judgment of their ancestors, on account of which they attempt to conduct their lives in an honorable manner.

THE FOUNDING OF CITIES

Not only do divine ancestors and culture heroes form the lineages of families and totemic groups, they are equally present at the beginnings of almost every city foundation in ancient and traditional cultures. Cain in the biblical story is the culture hero who founds the city of Enoch; Romulus is the founder of Rome; Quetzalcoatl, of Tollan. In Southeast Asia, the founding of states and kingship follow the archetypes of the Hindu god Indra.

The founding of a city may be a response to the experience of a hierophany. Hierophanies of space, or ceremonial centers, are revelations of the sacred meaning of space itself. [*See* Center of the World.] The divine beings or culture heroes who found cities derive their power from such sacred ceremonial centers. In some cases, a sacrifice is necessary to appease the gods of the location; thus, many of the myths involving the founding of cities relate a story of twins, one of whom is killed or sacrificed, as in the case of Cain's slaying of Abel, or Romulus's murder of Remus. In one of the mythological cycles of Quetzalcoatl, for example, a magical combat takes place in which Quetzalcoatl kills his uncle.

The ancestors as founders of a city establish the archetypes for all domesticated space. The normalization of activities in the space of the city, whether in terms of family structures or the public meanings of space, are guaranteed by the founding ancestor. All other establishments or reestablishments of cities will follow the model of the archetypal gestures of the founding ancestor of the city. The ruler of the city represents and symbolizes the presence of the divine ancestor, and elaborate rituals of rulership take place at certain temporal intervals to commemorate and reestablish the founding gestures. [*See* Cities.]

DEATH

In some myths death enters the world because of an action, inaction, or quarrel among the creator deities. They may have simply forgotten to tell human beings whether they were immortal or not, or the creator deity allows death to enter the world. In a myth from Madagascar two gods create human beings: the earth god forms them from wood and clay, the god of heaven gives them life. Human beings die so that they may return to the origins of their being.

In most mythic scenarios, however, death is the result of a sacred history that introduces the second meaning of primordiality. Through ignorance, interdiction, or violence, a break is made by the divine offspring from the creator deity, and in this rupture is the origin of death. The origin of the abode of the dead is equally located in this event, for, in the mythic scenarios, the rupture creates divisions in space among which a place of the dead comes into being. For example, in the Dogon myth mentioned above, the placenta of the god Amma is the earth, and at death one returns to the earth which was the original stuff of creation.

Funerary rituals are very important, for they assure that the dead will arrive in the correct manner at the abode of the ancestors. The souls of the dead must be instructed and led on the right path lest they become lost. At death the deceased is vulnerable and subject to the attack of malevolent spirits. Funerary rituals prescribe the correct behavior and route to be taken by the dead to the land of the ancestors.

[*For further discussion, see* Death *and* Funeral Rites.]

BIBLIOGRAPHY

A general discussion of cosmogonic myths can be found in my *Alpha: The Myths of Creation* (New York, 1963). For Mircea Eliade's discussion of the two types of primordiality, see "Cosmogonic Myth and Sacred History," in his *The Quest* (Chicago, 1969). For ancient Near Eastern myths, see *Ancient Near Eastern Texts relating to the Old Testament,* 3d ed., edited by J. B. Pritchard (Princeton, 1969). N. D. Fustel de Coulanges's *The Ancient City* (1901), 12th ed. (Baltimore, 1980), remains the best general introduction to Greek and Roman religion dealing with the meaning of ancestors. Joseph Rykwert's *The Idea of a Town* (Princeton, 1976) is a brilliant discussion of the myths and rituals of the founding of Rome. Paul Wheatley's *The Pivot of the Four Quarters* (Chicago, 1971) is the best work on the meaning of the ceremonial center as the basis for the founding of cities. Robert Heine-Geldern's "Conceptions of State and Kingship in Southeast Asia," *Far Eastern Quarterly* 2 (November 1942): 15–30, describes state and urban foundaton in Southeast Asia. Davíd Carrasco presents the full cycle of the myths, histories, and city foundations of Quetzalcoatl in *Quetzalcoatl and the Irony of Empire* (Chicago, 1982). For the Tucano Indians of Colombia, see Gerardo Reichel-Dolmatoff's *Amazonian Cosmos* (Chicago, 1971). Adolf E. Jensen's *Myth and Cult among Primitive Peoples* (Chicago, 1963), is the best general work on the religious meaning of culture heroes and *dema* deities. For China, see Raymond Dawson's *The Chinese Experience* (London, 1978). Dominique Zahan's *The Religion, Spirituality, and Thought of Traditional Africa* (Chicago, 1979) places the meaning of ancestors within the general structures of African religions. Hans Abrahamsson's *The Origin of Death* (Uppsala, 1951), is still the best study of the myths of death in Africa. For the ancestors of the Dinka, a cattle-raising people in Africa, see Godfrey Lienhardt's *Divinity and Experience: The Religion of the Dinka* (Oxford, 1961). Jack Goody's *Death, Property and the Ancestors* (Stanford, 1962) is a detailed study of death and funerary rituals among the LoDagaa of West Africa. Stanley Wallens's *Feasting with Cannibals* (Princeton, 1981) is a study of the meaning of ancestors among the Kwakiutl.

9 NECROMANCY

Erika Bourguignon

Necromancy, the art or practice of magically conjuring up the souls of the dead, is primarily a form of divination. The principal purpose of seeking such communication with the dead is to obtain information from them, generally regarding the revelation of unknown causes or the future course of events. The cause of the death of the deceased who is questioned may be among the facts sought.

More generally, necromancy is often considered synonymous with magic, sorcery, or witchcraft, perhaps because the calling up of the dead may occur for purposes other than information seeking, or because the separation of divination from its consequences is not always clear. There is also a linguistic basis for the expanded use of the word: the term *black art* for magic appears to be based on a corruption of *necromancy* (from Greek *necros,* "dead") to *negromancy* (from Latin *niger,* "black").

Limited to the practice of magical conjuration of the dead, necromancy does not include communication employing mediums, as in spiritualism or spiritism. Nor does it include encounters with the souls of the departed during the spirit journeys of shamans, apparitions of ghosts, or communications in dreams, with the possible exception of those in dreams resulting from incubation.

Divination is undoubtedly a universal phenomenon, to be found in all cultures. In the form of necromancy, however, it is relatively infrequent, though widespread. We possess only limited descriptions and documentation of the phenomenon and only for certain periods and regions. Necromancy presupposes belief in a form of life after death and the continued interest of the dead in the affairs of the living. As such, it may well be associated with complex funerary and postfunerary customs and with ancestor worship.

TECHNIQUES OF NECROMANCY

Necromancy is a theme often found in myths, legends, and literary works. Such texts may describe communications with the dead or state their messages, but they seldom provide information on techniques employed in a given community. Where actual descriptions exist, rather than fabulous accounts or rumors and accusations, we find inquiries connected with burial and burial preparation. Here the questioning of the corpse may concern the cause of death and the identification of a murderer. Other necromantic practices involve rites at the grave site with the use of some part of the deceased, often his or her skull, or name. The response may be in the form of an utterance produced by the diviner, either in a trance state or through ventriloquism. It may also be revealed in the form of a sign; this may involve the interpretation of an omen or the drawing of lots.

The concept of necromancy is of limited utility for at least two reasons. (1) It is linked to its history in the Western tradition and therefore difficult to employ in analyzing beliefs and practices of other cultures, with different traditions. (2) Necromancy is also only one of several types of divinatory practices, and these tend to shade into each other. For both of these reasons the term is of limited value in cross-cultural research, and it is not generally utilized in modern ethnographic studies.

NECROMANCY IN ANTIQUITY

The ancient Greeks believed that the dead had great prophetic powers and that it was possible to consult them by performing sacrifices or pouring libations at their tombs. Such offerings were also part of the funerary and postfunerary ceremonies. The visit of Odysseus to Hades to consult Tiresias, as described in book 11 of the *Odyssey,* has also been classified as an instance of necromancy. There are references in various other classical texts to formal oracles of the dead; however, these are generally to practices in remote locations or among barbarians.

Most of our information on necromancy among Nordic and Germanic peoples comes from the sagas. A number of references appear, for example, in the Eddas. Óðinn (Odin) is, among other things, god of the dead, and in one account he awakens a dead prophetess in order to consult her. In addition to conjurations, interpretation of the movement of rune-inscribed sticks appears to have been practiced. Necromancy was only one of numerous techniques of divination, and one considered to be particularly dangerous, especially when the dead were not family members. It appears to have been prohibited even prior to the conversion of these peoples to Christianity.

Necromancy appears to have been unknown, or at least unreported, among the Etruscans and in the earlier periods of Roman history. It may have been introduced with other Hellenistic and Oriental divinatory and magic practices, all of which were prohibited by Augustus. Like other forms of divination and magic, which might include the use of poisons, necromancy was perceived as a potential political tool, dangerous in a world of personal power and ambition. The emperors, however, surrounded themselves with diviners of all sorts. The concerns of medieval Christianity with necromancy and magic have their roots in this period, as well as in biblical prohibitions.

Numerous divinatory techniques are mentioned in the Bible. The account of the so-called Witch of Endor (*1 Sm.* 28) is frequently cited as an example of necromancy and of the prohibitions attached to it (cf. *Deuteronomy, Leviticus,* and *Isaiah*). Necromancy is mentioned in the Talmud among other divinatory practices. Although it is severely condemned, several examples are cited. The practice appears to have been rare, but it left its trace in rabbinic sources and medieval Jewish magical beliefs, perhaps reinforced by the beliefs of the Christians among whom the Jews lived.

Magical beliefs, many of pre-Christian origins, continued throughout the Middle Ages. It was, however, between the late Middle Ages and the beginning of the Renaissance that a great fear and persecution of witches took hold. One of the crimes of which witches were accused was necromancy, conjuring up the dead as well as (or with the help of) the Devil. Indeed, the term *necromancy* is primarily associated with this period.

NECROMANCY IN ARCHAIC CULTURES

Spanish chronicles composed shortly after the conquest of Peru record that the Inca had two special classes of diviners who consulted the dead, one group specializing in dealing with mummies of the dead and another consulting various spirit beings and their representations, which the Spaniards referred to as idols. The reports are written from the perspective of sixteenth-century Spaniards, at a time when, in their own country, the Inquisition searched out necromancers and others considered sorcerers and heretics.

In the Huon Gulf region of New Guinea, throughout the nineteenth century and prior to the arrival of missionaries, all deaths were attributed to magic. The identification of the sorcerer who had caused the death was carried out by a diviner, who conjured the spirit of the deceased into one of several types of objects. It was then questioned, and "yes" or "no" responses were obtained from the motion of the object. The most common object used was a stunned eel, whose convulsions were interpreted as "yes" responses. Other objects might be an upturned shell or a piece of bamboo held in the hand. The movements of these objects were subject to some manipulations, and the answers were often used to confirm suspicions held by popular opinion.

In Haiti, a tradition exists that is derived from both European influences of the colonial period and West African traditions. As part of postfunerary rites of Voodoo initiates, one of the two souls with which every person is endowed is removed from a temporary sojourn underwater and settled in a family shrine. During this ceremony, the soul is questioned on various matters of interest. At a later time, it may be called into a jar for purposes of consultation. Like conversations with the dead in parts of Africa, as, for instance, among the Zulu, this process appears to involve ventriloquism by the performing ritual specialist. It is also believed that sorcerers can send the spirit of one or more dead persons into the body of a victim, to cause illness and eventual death if appropriate counterrites are not performed. These involve the identification of the dead and of the sender. The diagnostic process may involve the direct questioning of the dead using the patient as a medium, or by scrying (water gazing) or other divinatory techniques. The Haitian example suggests the difficulty in drawing clear lines between divination, sorcery, diagnosis, and healing, or even among the various divinatory techniques.

[*See also* Divination.]

BIBLIOGRAPHY

Callaway, Henry. *The Religious System of the Amazulu* (1870). Africana Collectanea, vol. 35. Reprint, Cape Town, 1970.

Caquot, André, and Marcel Leibovici, eds. *La divination.* 2 vols. Paris, 1968.

Caro Baroja, Julio. *The World of Witches.* Chicago, 1964.

Godwin, William. *Lives of the Necromancers.* London, 1834.

Hogbin, Herbert Ian. *The Island of Menstruating Men: Religion in Wogeo, New Guinea.* Scranton, Pa., 1970.

Hughes, Pennethorne. *Witchcraft* (1952). Reprint, Baltimore, 1965.

Junod, Henri A. *The Life of a South African Tribe.* 2d ed., rev. & enl. 2 vols. London, 1927. The 1912 first edition has been reprinted (New Hyde Park, N.Y., 1962).

Kramer, Heinrich, and James Sprenger. *The Malleus Maleficarum* (1928). Reprint, New York, 1971.

Métraux, Alfred. *Voodoo in Haiti.* New York, 1959.

Trachtenberg, Joshua. *Jewish Magic and Superstition: A Study in Folk Religion* (1939). Reprint, New York, 1982.

Williams, Charles. *Witchcraft* (1941). Reprint, New York, 1959.

TWO

THE AFTERLIFE AND TRANSITIONS TO THE OTHERWORLD

10 THE AFTERLIFE

Jane I. Smith

Views of the afterlife, of expectations concerning some form of human survival after death, cannot be isolated from the totality of the understanding of the nature of the divine, the nature of humankind, time and history, and the structure of reality. Not all religious persons have addressed the same kinds of questions, nor have ideas always been formulated in a uniform way by those nurtured within any one of the many religious traditions of the world. Nonetheless, there is a certain commonality in the kinds of basic questions that have been addressed. This article is organized topically in terms of the ways in which peoples from a range of theological perspectives in different ages and religions have seen fit to respond to these questions.

The Nature of the Divine

The basic issue concerning the nature of the divine is whether God is to be considered a personal being with and to whom one can relate or is held to be reality itself, the source and ground of being in impersonal or nonpersonal form. Between these absolutes lie a myriad of possibilities, compounded and enriched by a variety of experiences that can be termed mystical. Monotheists have struggled through the ages with questions concerning the corporeality of God, including shape and dimension, and, correspondingly, whether humankind can actually come to gaze in the hereafter on the visage of God. Others have concluded not only that the divine being is not to be conceived in any anthropomorphic form but also that the divine being, in the most absolute sense, is removed from the realm of interaction and rests as the essence of nonmanifestation. Determinations about the nature of the divine have direct ramifications, as will be seen, for human understanding of life after death.

The tension between the two concepts (the God of form and God without form) has arisen in a multitude of ways for faithful persons of various traditions. Those who depersonalize the divine to the extent that they see it as pure reality in which the essence of all things participates must ultimately sacrifice the relationship of deity and devotee, whether this be understood on the model of master and servant, parent and child, or lover and beloved. This was the problem for the philosopher

Rāmānuja in twelfth-century India, whose qualified nondualism was the logically problematic attempt to reconcile a philosophical monism with the overwhelming need to respond to God in loving devotion. The Andalusian Muslim mystic Muḥy al-Dīn Ibn al-ʿArabī, writing about the same time, posited a series of descending levels of the godhead through which the absolute, nonmanifest divine gradually actualizes itself to the form of a Lord with whom humans can interact.

THE VISION OF GOD

Those religious traditions that have articulated an understanding of the divine in polytheistic form have tended to envision the particular gods in a concrete manner, often with the implication that the dead, or at least some of the dead, will be able to see the gods visually in the afterlife. Pictorial representations from the Middle and New Kingdoms in Egypt portray the dead person being lifted out of the sarcophagus by the jackal Anubis, taken to the Hall of Double Justice and judged, and then brought into the presence of Osiris, to be led by him to the Elysian Fields.

From the earliest times, Indian thinkers have tended to conceptualize their gods in quite specifically graphic ways. In the Vedic literature, Yama, who is at once the first mortal and the god of the dead, is portrayed as sitting under a leafy bower with his two four-eyed dogs in the presence of gods and ancestors to welcome the dead into a life that is a blissful version of earthly existence. In theistic Hinduism, the devotee expects to gaze on the face of the Beloved as Rādhā beheld Kṛṣṇa in their moments of most intense passion. The faithful Buddhist to whom access to Sukhāvatī, the Pure Land, is granted will enjoy the bliss of contemplating Amitābha Buddha himself.

Vision of the divine in the afterlife is not limited to polytheistic traditions. The sight of God in the gardens of Paradise is cherished by Muslims as the culmination of a life of piety; similar expectations have been part of the hopes of many Christians. Nor is it the case that in all polytheistic traditions there is the assumption that the dead will see those gods whom they concretely portray or conceptualize. Among the ancient Mesopotamians, the gods of the lower world were viewed as cruel and vindictive and those of the upper regions as arbitrary, with humans doomed to exist as shades in the nether regions. Thus no amount of individual effort in this life could assure one of a blissful existence in the hereafter, let alone a vision of the gods.

DIVINE JUSTICE AND JUDGMENT

Never in the Mesopotamian consideration did there seem to be any understanding that the individual who lived the good life on earth might come to an end better than that found in the cheerless underground pit of Arallu. Justice as a function of divinity never came to bear, and the hero-king Gilgamesh, in a work attributed to the second millennium BCE, could rail against the arbitrary way in which the gods meted out death to humankind while keeping life and immortality for themselves.

It is, of course, not true that justice need be a less significant factor in the consideration of the afterlife by a society that is professedly polytheistic. What often has been the case is that the concept of ethical responsibility on the part of the individual (with concomitant judgment by the deity in some form) blends with an emphasis on magic and ritual as assurance of a felicitous state in the hereafter. The ancient

Egyptian view is particularly interesting in this connection. *Maat,* the conceptual form of justice, order, and stability, became personified in the Hall of Double Justice and was understood as the means by which Osiris, the lord of the kingdom of the living dead, was finally apprised of the moral character of the one brought before him in judgment. Justice was seen as an extension of a concept of order that characterized the Egyptian worldview and that, as an essential of the eschatological reality, was in direct relationship to the establishment of stability over chaos at the time of creation. And yet it is clear from the texts that as significant as were concepts of order and justice to their view of life and death, the Egyptians never completely abandoned the feeling that the gods might not really (be able to) exercise absolute justice. Thus it was necessary to rely on ritual and magical formulas, in this way assuring that the dead would always have at their fingertips the necessary knowledge and information to answer any questions that might be posed in the final court of arbitration.

Justice, as an abstract principle of order for many ancient societies, came in monotheistic communities to be translated into a quality of the godhead itself, with the immediate ramification of justice as an ethical imperative for human beings in recognition of the nature and being of God. Thus in Islam there is a clear understanding that because God is just, he requires that a person live justly, and the quality of the individual life is actually the determining factor in the final judgment.

One of the earliest perceptions of the god who embodies this kind of justice in his very being is found in the thought of Zarathushtra (Zoroaster), the Persian prophet of the first millennium BCE. He saw in Ahura Mazdā the principles of truth, righteousness, and order upheld in much the same way as the Egyptians saw them upheld and embodied by Maat. Ahura Mazdā, however, was not for Zarathushtra the personification of truth but the great advocate of it, the divine lord into whose presence the righteous are allowed to enter at the end of time. There was never in the development of Zoroastrian orthodoxy any indication that the just could expect to see the person of Ahura Mazdā in human form, but rather there was the understanding that the soul who has lived a life of justice will be given the privilege of beholding a form of pure light.

In the development of Old Testament thought, divine justice became a particularly significant issue. In the earlier conceptions, the dark and dusty She'ol as an abode for the dead seems to have been understood much as was the Mesopotamian Arallu. There Yahveh had no jurisdiction, and gloom was assured for the righteous and wicked alike. The beginnings of hope for a more felicitous end for humankind came through reflections concerning the question of God's power and justice. If God is truly almighty, his dominion must extend to all parts of the earth and to all portions of time. And if he is truly just, then it is inconsistent that the righteous as well as the wicked should be doomed to the bitter existence of She'ol. It was with regard to God's power and justice that the seeds of an idea of resurrection to an eternal reward began to grow in the Jewish consciousness, laying the ground for the later Christian understanding of the death and resurrection of Jesus.

In Hindu and Buddhist thought, the notion of *karman* presupposes a conception of justice and judgment different from that prevailing in monotheistic traditions. Rather than the subjectivity of a judging being, there is the objective and automatic working out of cause and effect. Justice in this understanding is not so much a divine quality as an inexorable law of the universe. In its simplest form the doctrine of *karman* states that what one is now is a direct result of what one has done and been in past existences, and what one does in this lifetime will, with the accumulation of past karmic debt, be the direct determinant of the state of one's future existence. Lifetime follows lifetime in whatever form of life each successive existence takes, and liberation from the round of existences is achieved not by the intervening grace of a god but through knowledge of the truth of the realization of self. In the Vedantic understanding of the Upaniṣads, the content of this knowledge is that the self *(ātman)* is indeed identical with the Self *(brāhman),* the underlying reality of all that is.

The complex of religious responses that makes up the fabric of Hinduism and Buddhism, however, includes as a major component the understanding on the part of many that the godhead must be conceptualized in a personal way. In terms of sheer numbers, far more Hindus have placed their faith in the saving grace of Lord Kṛṣṇa than have ever held to a doctrine of absolute monism. And despite the automatic character of *karman* in determining rebirth, divine or quasi-divine figures do continue to play a judicative role in the religious imagination. In Mahāyāna Buddhism there are ten judges of the dead, one of whom is a holdover from the Vedic Yama, despite the fact that in strict philosophical or ontological terms it is a Buddhist tenet that there is no such thing as a god who can judge or even a soul that can be the object of judgment.

INTERCESSION

Issues of justice give rise to questions about the possibility of intercession for the deceased on the part of human or superhuman agency. The forms of intercession are many, from the role played by the living in providing a proper burial and maintaining the mechanical artifices of the tomb to the specific intervention in the judgment process by a figure who can plead for the well-being of the soul whose fate is in the balance. Muslims traditionally have taken great comfort in the thought that the Prophet himself will be on hand to intercede for each individual believer when he comes before the awesome throne of judgment, and through the centuries Christians have relied on the assurance that Jesus Christ sits at the right hand of God to intercede. The Buddhist concept of the *bodhisattva* is, in one sense, an extension of the idea of intercession: through the dedication or transference of merit, the saving being, who needs no more merit himself, can directly pass it on to individuals who have not reached the state of enlightenment. [*See* Merit, *article on* Buddhist Concepts.]

The role of living persons in helping to determine the fate of the dead has ranged from giving the deceased a fitting and proper interment and celebrating a communal feast in memory of the departed (often to ensure that he or she actually stays "departed" and does not return to haunt the living) to maintaining for all time, as was the Egyptian intention, the physical apparatuses of the tomb. Sometimes it is held that these responsibilities are carried out primarily for the support of the living or out of respect for the dead. Often, however, there is a conviction that the living may actually be able to influence or help determine the future condition and existence of the souls in question. Some have challenged the supposition that the fate of the soul of the deceased must rest, even in part, on the continued ministrations of those fallible individuals with whom it had a relationship while on earth. Responsibility for the dead on the part of the living has often been seen as incompatible with a belief in the justice and mercy of God. Nonetheless, some form of prayer for the deceased on the part of the living continues to be an important responsibility of pious persons in all religious traditions.

The Nature of Humankind

If it is essential to a vision of the afterlife to have some understanding of the nature of that divine being or reality to whom humankind returns at death, it is no less important to have some conception of what element in the human makeup is considered to do the returning. In every religious tradition, the way in which an individual is conceived to be constituted in this life directly determines the way in which he or she is thought to survive in an existence after death.

THE HUMAN CONSTITUTION

Conceptions of the constitution of the human being differ not only among different religious traditions but among different schools of thought within the traditions. Nevertheless, for the purpose of a comparative typology, it is possible to generalize and speak of some of the most significant of these conceptions.

The most immediately obvious distinction, and one that has been drawn in most conceptions of the afterlife, is between the physical and the nonphysical aspects of the human person. This can be understood as the body-spirit dichotomy, with a difference sometimes drawn in the latter between spirit and soul. In the Hebrew view, a person was not understood so much as having a body, something essentially different and apart from the nonphysical side of one's being, as being a body, which implies the totality of the individual and the inseparability of the life principle from the fleshly form. Spirit was said to be blown into the flesh, making it a soul, a whole person. In itself spirit was understood as a manifestation of the divine. This way of distinguishing between soul and spirit was adopted by some Islamic and Christian theologians and philosophers, although in common usage the two terms are essentially interchangeable in both traditions. When an individual is felt to be renewed in a new body in Christ, the experience is often described as spiritual; the body of the resurrection is sometimes thought of as a spiritual body different from the earthly body of flesh and soul.

The notion that an individual is, rather than has, a body is quite foreign to most Eastern thought. In Hindu Sāṃkhya, for example, the body is part of the world of nature or matter *(prakṛti)* but is absolutely distinct from the life principle or self *(puruṣa)* from which it is separated by the process of yoga. It is the very realization of the separation of these two that amounts to liberation for the individual. Advaita Vedānta, while different from the dualistic Sāṃkhya in saying that the body is only part of the world of illusion, would agree that the key to liberation from the round of rebirths is exactly the realization that the soul or self has no lasting bond with anything physical and that the soul is associated with a particular body, human or nonhuman, only temporarily, for the fleeting moments of earthly existence.

THE RELATIONSHIP OF THE HUMAN TO THE DIVINE

The question of what it is that lives on after death must be seen in relation to the basic issue of whether that which is real or lasting in the human person is identical with the divine reality or is essentially different from it. A position of monism is one end of a spectrum of possible responses. In Advaita Vedānta liberation from successive existences comes only with the realization of the identity of *ātman* (the individual soul) and *brahman* (the Absolute). In some of its Ṣūfī manifestations, esoteric Islam comes very close to identifying the eternal in humans with the eternal essence *(ḥaqq),* with the further understanding that death and resurrection come in the moment-by-moment realization of that identity.

A very different kind of conceptualization is that characteristic of some traditional societies in which not only is humanity seen to be totally separate from the gods but one exists after death only as a shade or a shadow of one's former self. That which divides the human and the divine in this context is the fact that the gods are immortal and humans are not. In between such alternatives is a range of possibilities suggesting that humans manifest some element of the divine enlivening principle. In most traditions, however, a felicitous hereafter means not the realization of identity of self and absolute, but rather some circumstance in which that which survives death comes to dwell in proximity to the divine.

A number of traditions have held that certain elements that make up an individual actually become manifested and real only at the time of death. The ancient Egyptian, for instance, was said to have come into his or her own only when after death the *ba,* or continuing personality, was fully realized through the joining with its counterpart, *ka,* which acted as a kind of guardian angel. The dead did not become *ka*s but were joined to and guided by them on the journey into the afterlife. Classical Zoroastrian texts describe the soul at death sitting on the headstone of the grave for three days, after which it is led through some good or bad circumstances (depending on one's character) and finally is met by a maiden who takes the form of the actions committed by that person while on earth. The good will thus meet a beautiful creature, while the unrighteous will confront an incredibly ugly hag.

Certain similarities can be seen here with Buddhist conceptions, such as the peaceful and wrathful deities met by the deceased in the after-death visions described in the Tibetan *Book of the Dead.* The great difference is that in the Tibetan understanding one does not meet the alternatives of good or bad but experiences a whole range of deities that represent both the most sublime of human feelings and the personification of one's powers of reason. The wrathful deities are actually only a different aspect of the peaceful ones. The point is that, in some sense, as in the Egyptian and Zoroastrian cases, one comes into contact in an apparently externalized form with aspects of one's own personality, thought, and consequent past action.

RESURRECTION OF THE BODY

The significance of the body as a continuing entity in the afterlife has been attested to in many traditions. [*See* Resurrection.] The resuscitation of the corpse expected after the elaborate processes of mummification in ancient Egypt implied the hope of permanent physical survival as well as survival of the personality. In Zoroastrian eschatology, one of the clearest statements of physical resurrection comes in the description of the Frashōkereti, or ultimate rehabilitation of the world under the dominion of Ahura Mazdā. The savior Saoshyant will raise the bones of the first ancestors and then those of all humankind, and Ahura Mazdā will invest the bones with life and clothe them with flesh for all time.

In Jewish thought, the soul was first believed to be released from the body at death, but with the development of the idea of resurrection came the belief in the continued importance of the physical body. This belief is carried over to early Christianity: Augustine in the *City of God* says that the resurrected bodies, perfect amalgamations of flesh and spirit, are free to enjoy the satisfactions of food and drink should they so desire. He finds proof for this in the example of Christ consuming a meal after his own resurrection. Proceeding from the original assurance of Jesus that not a hair on the heads of those who are granted eternal life shall perish, Augustine concludes that at the time of the resurrection of the flesh, the body will appear in that size and physical condition in which it appeared at the time of youthful maturity, or would have appeared had it had time to mature. The arguments marshaled by the philosophers of Islam have done little to shake the common faith that the reward for a life of virtue will be the experience of the pleasures of the gardens of paradise in a physical as well as a spiritual way. The kinds of proofs offered by some in the Islamic community against the resurrection of the physical form have been countered rationally, and ignored emotionally, by those for whom a purely spiritual revival seems somehow to fall short of the promises of God and the world-affirming nature of Islam itself.

CONTINUED EXISTENCE AS SPIRIT

From the earliest times, characteristic of primitive societies but certainly not exclusive to them, humankind has had a seemingly natural fear of the dead. To some extent this can be explained in terms of one's own apprehension about the meaning of death for one personally, but to a much greater extent, it seems to derive from a stated or unstated feeling that the dead have some power over the living and can actually interfere with the processes of life on earth. In more extreme cases, this has led to a kind of worship of the dead, in which those who have passed into another existence have sometimes assumed the status of gods. This has been evidenced particularly in China and Japan in the long history of ancestor worship. More generally it takes the form of concern for the proper disposal and continued remembrance of the dead, in the hope that the deceased will in no way return to "haunt" or interfere with life here on earth. [*See* Ghosts.]

Commonly held is the assumption that because a being has undergone the experience of death, it is privy to information not held by those still in the mortal condition. Echoed in much of the great religious literature of the world is the theme that if only the dead could or would return in some form, they would have much to tell the living. The vanity of this wish for information from the departed is denied by those who are convinced that the dead can and do return and have a great deal to tell us about the road that everyone, sooner or later, comes to travel. In many traditions, especially the prophetic, orthodoxy has disdained talk about the reality of ghosts and spirits functioning on earth, and it has fallen to the mythology of folklore to speculate on the best ways to propitiate the spirits of the dead and to ward off those spirits who, for a variety of reasons, are felt to be evil or malicious.

THE ROLE OF COMMUNITY

Consideration only of the destiny of the individual results in a very unbalanced picture of conceptions of the afterlife. Important to the theologies of many of the religions of the world is the relationship of each individual to other individuals, or the idea of community, whether seen from the perspective of this world (is it necessary to be a member of a community in order to reach a blessed hereafter?) or the next (is there a community of the saved, or perhaps of the damned, in a future existence?). Common to prophetic religions is the expectation that the eschaton will result in reuniting or making whole both the individual and some portion (often the totality) of the human community. It is part of Islamic eschatological tradition that on the Day of Resurrection the specific communities of all the prophets, including that of Muḥammad, will be assembled, each at its own pond, awaiting the judgment.

The notion of community, or the importance of membership in a particular group, takes on a different kind of significance when viewed from the perspective of this world. In the Hindu tradition, liberating knowledge is limited to the twice-born, although this belief is greatly modified by those to whom a devotional relationship to some aspect of the godhead implies salvation rather than liberation. The question of whether one must be a Christian to be saved has engendered among scholars and theologians of Christianity heated arguments that still have not been resolved. *Ummah,* community in the Muslim sense of a religio-political unity, is a tremendously significant element in the understanding of Islam; some contemporary Muslims still insist that one cannot be saved if one is not a Muslim, and that one cannot be Muslim outside of community.

There are some obvious instances in the history of religions in which the community of the saved is the community of the victorious in the sense of realized eschatology, that is, the establishment of a kingdom of righteousness for a specific people here on earth. This is implicit in the theme of Zionism in Jewish thought (although it is only one interpretation, or aspect, of the Zionist ideal as it has developed historically). Even Zarathushtra, if we can correctly interpret the *Gāthās,* seems at first to have envisioned the victory of *asha* ("truth, righteousness") over *druj* ("falsehood, evil") as taking place in the pastoral setting of eastern Persia within the context of this-worldly time. Realized eschatology in Christian thought refers to the understanding that Christ's life and death have, in fact, established the kingdom of God on earth for those who, in faith, are part of the body of Christ; in the mysticism of the *Gospel of John,* the Parousia, or second coming of Jesus, has already taken place. Such considerations lead directly to questions of time and history as a further category for reflection on conceptions of the afterlife.

Time and History

The way in which time, its passage and its purpose, is understood in different worldviews has a direct bearing on conceptions of the afterlife. Eastern religions and philosophies generally have conceived time as revolving in cycles, within each of which are periods of creation and destruction, with each "final" cataclysm to be followed again by the entire process of generation. In the elaborate Hindu schema of the epics and Purāṇas, there are moments of creation and destruction, eschatons when the entire universe is obliterated and reabsorbed into the body of the deity, but with the implication that this very process is endless. At the other pole are those "historical" (usually prophetic) religions that postulate a creation when time is said to have begun and a final eschaton when time as we know it will reach its conclusion. Here history is a given, a once-and-for-all process that begins with the divine initiation and is often understood as depending at each moment on the sustaining, re-creating act of the maker. Implicit is the belief that there is a plan to history, although humans may not be able to comprehend it, and that in some sense the end, when all creation will be glorified and time will give way to eternity, is already cast and determined.

IDEAL TIME

Many religious traditions envision a certain period that can be described as ideal time. This may be an epoch that existed before the beginning of time and will be actualized again when time itself ceases, or it may be conceptualized as having occurred within the framework of history and, thus, having the potential to be realized again in time. [*See* Golden Age.] In the ancient Egyptian view of the universe as static, ideal time was that continuing time established by the original creation, when order replaced chaos and *maat* was the stability of society as well as the individual ethic of justice and right. A similar understanding is expressed in the Australian Aboriginal concept of a sacred period during which the mythical ancestors lived, an epoch that is removed from any linear understanding of time. In that culture, in which language has no term for time in the abstract, the infinitely remote past is related to the present through the mythology of what has been called "the Dreaming."

For those traditions that emphasize a cyclical view of history, no time can be considered ideal. In one sense, time is not ultimately real, although, in another sense, its constant repetition means that it is perceived to be more plentiful than for people of historical traditions. Insofar as one has to deal with the illusions of reality in Indian thought, the best of times might be that represented by the beginning of each of the great cosmic cycles. From that point until the terrible *kaliyuga,* time (or rather the series of events and characteristics of the periods) degenerates and finally culminates in the awe-some destruction of flood and fire that concludes the cycle and initiates a new beginning. For the theistic Hindu, the perfect moment is actually that eternity in which he or she is able to abide in the presence of the Lord.

In the prophetic traditions, ideal time can be understood in several ways. The ideal age in one sense is that ushered in by the eschaton, the end of time that is itself the realization of eternity. Yet for most of the prophetic religions there is a time within history, theoretical or actualized, that can be described as ideal. For some Christians, this has been understood as the time of the historical Jesus and his initiation of the continued kingdom of God on earth. There have been significant differences among Christians in interpretation of the meaning of a new heaven and a new earth. The restoration of Zion for the Jew has immediate implications; some have argued that ideal time is any time in which Jerusalem is actualized as the home of the Jews. For the Muslim, ideal time in its best historical sense was the period of the Prophet and the first four right-guided caliphs of the Islamic community, a time potentially realizable again at any moment.

REBIRTH

Issues of time and history relate directly to the question of how an individual soul (or spirit or body) maintains continuity between this life and that that lies beyond death. Some traditions hold generally to the idea of one life on earth, death, some kind of resurrection or rebirth, and then continued existence on another plane. Others believe in reincarnation (metempsychosis or transmigration) with its possibilities of a series of lives on earth or elsewhere. Human imagination, or intuition, has resourcefully suggested many variations on these alternatives. [*See* Reincarnation *and* Transmigration.]

For the most part, traditions that see time as linear and progressive have rejected the idea of rebirth on this earth and relegated to the ranks of heresy those who have attempted to espouse such a theory or to combine it with the more traditional understanding of death and resurrection to propose an existence apart from the physical world. For those who hold to the idea of resurrection, final life is not automatic but is granted by the specific act of a being or beings who actually bring the dead back to life. The victory over death may be seen as occurring immediately after the demise of the individual or as coming at some final *eschaton,* as when the savior Saoshyant breathes life into the lifeless bodies of all humanity in Zoroastrian thought, or, in Islamic tradition, when the individual souls are called to the final day of judgment.

Eastern mystical thought has articulated the concept of reincarnation with some consistency, although in the Buddhist case the difficult problem arises of identifying what it is that is born in another body if there is nothing that can be called an individual soul. Buddhist thinkers have developed elaborate and complex theories for reconciling the concept of *anātman* ("no soul") with the six categories of being into which the non-soul can be reborn. Even those religions that contemplate aeons of potential rebirths, however, do project the hope of a final release from this recurring condition.

To say that one's soul is immortal is to imply that it has always existed and that it will never for a moment cease to exist. This is the basic understanding of those who postulate recurring births in a variety of incarnations, but it need not necessarily be linked to conceptions of transmigration. A great debate took place in Islam between the philosophers, whose rational directives led them to conclude that immortality was the only possibility for humans, and the theologians, whose adherence to the word of the Qur'ān dictated the necessity of belief in the specific acts of creation and resurrection from the dead. The concepts of resurrection and immortality, however, are certainly not always seen as unambiguously antithetical. Theologians have long struggled with the determination of which term is more applicable to the Christian understanding, or whether both might in some senses pertain.

ESCHATOLOGY

For those who adhere to the idea of resurrection, with the implication of some form of life eternal to follow, one of the most pressing questions concerns when that resurrection is going to occur. Millenarian expectations have taken a variety of forms in both Judaism and Christianity, with the chiliastic hope in the latter for Christ's return. This kind of eschatological anticipation is generally seen in the context of the specifics of judgment. Here again, however, there is often no clearly formulated theological statement about precisely when judgment will take place or whether it is to be an individual or a universal adjudication. Some see it as happening soon after death, while others postulate a waiting period, perhaps of great length, before the eschatological events that herald a universal judgment. [*See* Eschatology.]

In early Christianity, there was the expectation that the return of Jesus to usher in the new age would be so soon as to come within the lifetime of the community of those who had had fellowship with him. The passage of time moderated this expectation, and new theories had to be developed to account for the state of the soul in what came to be seen as a waiting period before the messianic age.

In the Persian case, Zarathushtra himself apparently had first felt that the kingdom of righteousness would be established on earth and then implied that eternal reward or punishment would instead come after death. Later, Sasanid orthodoxy, in developing its theories of three-thousand-year cycles, came to expect a kind of temporary reward or punishment lasting from death to the period of the Frashōkereti, at which momentous time a final purging through molten metal will purify all souls for their eternal habitation in the presence of Ahura Mazdā.

Other of the prophetic religions have hesitated to interpret with such exacting clarity or to understand the particulars of reward and punishment so graphically, yet in a general way have postulated a similar period between the death of the individual and the general resurrection and ushering in of the final age. The suggestions of scriptures such as the New Testament and the Qur'ān are sufficiently unsystematic that doctrines about specific aspects of life after death have often been founded on implication rather than specification.

SAVIOR FIGURES

Implicit in the eschatological expectation of Judaism and Christianity is the hope for a messiah or savior. For the Jews that person has not yet come. For the Christians he has come once and will return at the Parousia. The savior concept is somewhat different in Islam; it is embodied particularly in the figure of the Mahdi and involves a rather detailed understanding of the theological distinctions between Sunnī and Shīʿī thought as well as the relationship of the Mahdi in its eschatological framework to the restorer and final ruler of the regenerated community of Islam.

Some variation on the idea of a savior or restorer to appear at a future time is to be found in almost all of the living religious traditions, whatever their concept of the flow and structure of time. Saoshyant of the Zoroastrian or Parsi community; the Messiah of the Old and New Testaments; Kalki, the tenth incarnation of Viṣṇu, in theistic Hinduism; and Maitreya, the future Buddha—all reflect an understanding that despite the almost universal importance placed on the necessity of individual human responsibility, it is still possible to hope for the merciful assistance of some being, divine or semidivine, in the determination of one's future circumstances. [*See* Soteriology.]

The Structure of Reality

The interrelatedness of the kinds of themes one can develop in considering an issue such as life after death is obvious. The preceding discussion has touched on much of what falls also into the category of conceptions of the structure of reality. It therefore becomes a question not of considering new material as such, but of viewing some of the same concepts from a different perspective.

THE WORLD IN TIME AND SPACE

The eternality of the world, and its subsequent relationship to the eternality of heaven or the rehabilitated universe, has been postulated in a variety of ways in the history of religious thought. [*See* Eternity.] The ancient Egyptian expected that the static nature of the world and of society would mean their perpetuation eternally. In the materialistic Zoroastrian construct, the final rehabilitation of the earth implies its purification and its joining, with a purified hell, to the extension of heaven. Judaism presents an example of the constant tension between a hope for this world, renewed, and the kingdom of heaven as an otherworldly and eternal realm. In the Hindu and Buddhist conceptions, the world is not only not eternal but is in a constant process of degeneration. Even here, however, insofar as the world is constantly re-created within the realm of conditioned *saṃsāra,* it is eternal in another sense.

For many peoples, conceptions of the afterlife are directly related to the way they understand the basic divisions of the universe. The mythology of many of the ancient traditions is rich in descriptions and visual representations of the heavens, earth, and nether regions. A classic theme of religious geography has been that the heavens are located somewhere above the earth and the nether regions below, and that these have been identified to a greater or lesser extent with the location of heaven(s) and hell(s) as after-death abodes in whatever form these have been conceived. A not uncommon spatial concept is that of the land of the dead located in the west, the place of the setting sun, which is repeated in such myths as those of the jackal Anubis, lord of the Egyptian desert, and of the western kingdom of Sukhāvatī, the heaven of bliss of the Buddha Amitābha.

REWARD AND PUNISHMENT

It is often in direct relation to the existing understanding of the structure of the universe that the more specific conceptions of heaven and hell arise. These parallel places of reward and punishment were not generally present in ancient thought. The Mesopotamian *Arallu* and the Hebrew *She'ol* both designated a great pit of darkness and dust under the earth that was not a hell (in the sense of any implication of judgment), but simply an abode for the unfortunate dead. Vedic thought in India, particularly as elaborated in the descriptions of Yama and the fathers of heaven in the *Ṛgveda,* was concerned primarily with the positive fate of those who performed sacrifices and good works, the rest passing into the oblivion of nonexistence. With the introduction of the importance of knowledge over sacrifice, of *karmayoga* (liberation through works) in place of ritual performance, the kingdom of Yama was elaborated into a series of heavens, and Yama himself was gradually transformed into a judge of the dead and then a god of the underworld hells, which were correspondingly enumerated.

The greatly elaborated heavens and hells, as they came to be developed in Hindu and Buddhist thought, with their graphic descriptions of the tortures of punishment and the raptures of reward, are by nature temporary (or, at least, one's stay in them is temporary). For the Buddhist, even these abodes are part of the conditioned world of *saṃsāra* and thus by definition are ultimately unreal, as all of phenomenal existence is unreal. In any case, one is reborn from these states or conditions into another state or condition, with the understanding that not until one is reborn as a human being will final release be possible.

Quite different is the basic understanding of prophetic religions, which assumes that the eschaton and judgment result in the eternality of the final abode and resting place. The question of whether or not punishment, like reward, is eternal has long perplexed theologians. In the Judeo-Christian tradition, as well as in Islam, God's justice is always understood as tempered with mercy, and the idea of the eternality of hell has been moderated to whatever extent has seemed consistent with the prevailing theological climate.

THE INTERMEDIATE STATE

Throughout the prophetic religions it has been necessary to conceive of a kind of intermediate state or place for souls before the time of final disposition. (The very temporariness of one's stay in the Hindu and Buddhist heavens and hells suggests that they fulfill the same sort of intermediate function.) This intermediate state can be a condition of waiting, often in a specified place, for the time of final judgment. Thus, Islamic tradition developed elaborate descriptions of the *barzakh* (lit., "barrier") as a place or condition in which both good and wicked souls dwell until the day of resurrection. In later Jewish tradition, *She'ol* came to refer to a temporary place for men and women to await judgment.

In another understanding, this intermediate position is often described as being for those for whom consignment to punishment or reward is not automatic. The Qur'anic *a'rāf* ("heights"), for example, has been interpreted as the temporary abode of those whose good and evil deeds more or less balance. Christianity, in some of its forms, has elaborated the distinction between Purgatory, as a place of temporary punishment and purification, and Limbo, as a waiting state where persons such as the righteous heathen and unbaptized infants are kept.

LITERAL AND SYMBOLIC INTERPRETATIONS.

Common to many religious traditions is continuing debate as to the nature of the future abodes of punishment and reward. Are they to be understood as places of literal recompense or as representations of states of mind? If states, are they attainable now or only in the hereafter? Are the experiences that one has in these states or places real or imaginary? Or, in a rather different dimension, are the descriptions to be seen only as allegorical and not, in fact, indicative of what is actually going to happen either objectively or subjectively?

It is in this area, perhaps, that it is most difficult to generalize within traditions. The awe- and terror-inspiring vision may well be taken with absolute literalness by one believer, while another might see that such visions are only symbolic representations of internal rather than external recompense. The Tibetan *Book of the Dead,* a set of instructions for the dying and dead that is at the same time a description of the forty-nine-day period between death and rebirth, details the experience that the soul has with karmic apparitions in the form of peaceful and wrathful deities. The great insight that comes of the *bardo,* or intermediate state experience, is that not only are the apparitions the products of one's own mind but they also assume, for the purposes of instruction, a concrete and objective reality.

Despite the variations in conceptions of what the afterlife may entail, a belief that human beings will continue to exist in some form after the experience we term death is a universal phenomenon. Skeptics have never persuaded the body of believers, whatever the specifics of their faith, that with the demise of the physical body comes the extinction of the human essence. Most people through the ages have drawn a clear connection between the quality of life lived on this earth and the expectation of what will come after death. Contemporary researchers of near-death experiences claim that we now have the beginnings of a scientific proof of the afterlife in the apparent commonality of the experiences of those proclaimed clinically dead. For most persons of faith, however, such knowledge is part of a universal mystery that by definition is veiled from the eyes of the living. We have some assurances of faith, but the details of what awaits us in "the undiscover'd country from whose bourn no traveller returns" (Shakespeare, *Hamlet* 3.1) can only be anticipated, with the certainty that such knowledge will eventually, and inevitably, be ours.

[*See also* Soul *and* Immortality; *for more detailed discussions of themes of afterlife, see* Judgment of the Dead *and* Heaven and Hell.]

BIBLIOGRAPHY

Some of the older comparative studies of life after death in different religious traditions, such as Elias H. Sneath's *Religion and the Future Life: The Development of the Belief in Life after Death* (New York, 1922) and Kaufmann Kohler's *Heaven and Hell in Comparative Religion* (New York, 1923), are still useful, although somewhat elementary. More recent and valuable contributions to comparative studies of life after death are *The Judgement of the Dead* by S. G. F. Brandon (London, 1967) and *Religious Encounters with Death,* edited by Frank E. Reynolds and Earle H. Waugh (University Park, Pa., 1977). Christina Grof and Stanislav Grof's *Beyond Death* (New York, 1980) is a more journalistic overview of classical and contemporary afterlife beliefs, with fine color prints. For an understanding of the relationship of theories of time to afterlife concepts, Mircea Eliade's *Cosmos and History: The Myth of the Eternal Return* (New York, 1954) is excellent. A good addition to anthropological studies on attitudes and customs of non-Western cultures toward death and afterlife is *Celebrations of Death: The Anthropology of Mortuary Ritual* (Cambridge, Mass., 1979) by Richard Huntington and Peter Metcalf.

In addition to comparative works, a number of valuable studies deal with the afterlife as envisioned in particular religious traditions. *Death and Eastern Thought,* edited by Frederick H. Holck (Nashville, 1974), deals primarily with Indian beliefs, with brief chapters on China and Japan. Themes of death and resurrection in prophetic traditions are treated in such works as George W. E. Nickelsburg's *Resurrection, Immortality, and Eternal Life in InterTestamental Judaism* (Cambridge, Mass., 1972), John Hick's *Death and Eternal Life* (London, 1976), and *The Islamic Understanding of Death and Resurrection* (Albany, N.Y., 1981), which I wrote with Yvonne Haddad. Several excellent translations of mortuary texts are available, especially *The Tibetan Book of the Dead,* 2d ed., translated by Lama Kazi Dawasamdup and edited by W. Y. Evans-Wentz (Oxford, 1949); *The Egyptian Book of the Dead,* translated by E. A. Wallis Budge (New York, 1967) and presented as an interlinear translation with hieroglyphics; and *The Islamic Book of the Dead* of Imam ʿAbd al-Raḥmān al-Qāḍī, translated by ʿĀʾisha ʿAbd al-Raḥmān (Norfolk, England, 1977). A very good series on mythology, including myths of death and afterlife, is published by the Hamlyn Publishing Group Ltd. (1965–); it covers a broad range of literate and nonliterate societies.

A precursor in some ways to contemporary parapsychological studies is the spiritualist movement that began in the nineteenth century in Europe and the United States; it is well documented in J. Arthur Hill's *Spiritualism: Its History, Phenomena and Doctrine* (New York, 1919). Ian Stevenson's continuing research on reincarnation in cross-cultural perspective is presented in *Twenty Cases Suggestive of Reincarnation,* 2d ed. (Charlottesville, Va., 1974). Of the many recent studies of near-death experience and research, two of the best are Michael B. Sabom's *Recollections of Death: A Medical Investigation* (New York, 1981) and Kenneth Ring's *Life at Death: A Scientific Investigation of the Near-Death Experience* (New York, 1980).

11 GEOGRAPHIES OF DEATH

TH. P. VAN BAAREN

Belief in some kind of existence after death is one of the more common elements of religion, as history and anthropology show. While death is everywhere recognized as inevitable, it is seldom accepted as an absolute termination of human existence. Beliefs concerning the actual conditions of life after death, however, vary widely from culture to culture. This article will examine the variety of ways in which these afterlife conditions are represented, focusing in particular on their geography.

AFTERLIFE IN GENERAL

The different representations of life after death that we find in different religions are related to their respective conceptions of the structure of the cosmos and of life on earth, and to their different beliefs about the bodily and spiritual constitution of man. The Egyptians, for example, being agriculturalists, looked forward to a future life in the bountiful "Earu fields," whereas the Indians of the North American Plains, who were hunters, looked forward to the "eternal hunting grounds." In each case the actual economic conditions of life play an important role in determining how one will conceive of the afterlife. Similarly, the location and geography of the abode of the dead is in most cultures determined by the actual geographical conditions of their present world. Only occasionally is it determined primarily by cultural factors, as for instance by the traditions of migration among a number of Polynesian religions.

The conception of the soul is also an important factor. A soul that is conceived to be eternal and spiritual leads a different type of afterlife than one that is conceived as the double of the earthly body, or as something that gradually dwindles into nothingness after death, such as we find among certain northern Eurasian religions. A belief in multiple souls within a single individual makes possible a belief in the multiple destinations of these souls. Of the five souls of the Shipape (South America), for instance, only one goes to the hereafter.

There are also marked differences in the degree of interest that particular religions display in the afterlife. While central in one religion, it may be peripheral in another. Christianity, for example, along with a small number of other religions, has made the immortality of the individual central to its system of beliefs. But this centrality of the individual is by no means universally recognized. In many other religions the continuity of life after the death of the individual is of slight interest, because the stress falls firmly on life on earth. The continued existence of man after death may not be wholly denied, but neither is it considered to be of any importance. Thoughts about the conditions of the afterlife remain vague. Thus Godfrey Lienhardt quotes an Anuak man (Upper Nile) as saying simply that no one knows where the dead are, since no one has ever seen them. The inhabitants of Bellona Island (near the Solomons) seem equally unconcerned with what might happen to them after death. In accordance with this lack of interest we find cultures that not only allow the conditions of existence in the land of the dead to remain unclear, but even leave the question of its location unanswered. Rupert M. Downes has found this to be the case among the Tiv of Nigeria, for instance, where ideas about a future state remain nebulous. By contrast, some cultures develop extremely detailed descriptions of the realm of the dead. Here one thinks in particular of medieval Christianity.

Although today we tend to be conditioned to see life after death as an eternal state befitting an immortal soul, it is of some importance to make clear that there are also cultures in which the afterlife is considered to be a temporary prolongation of the present life, to be brought to an end by a second and final death. The Pangwe (southern Cameroon) believe that after death a man lives on for a long time in heaven, but in the end he dies and his corpse is thrown out with no hope of any further existence. The Egyptians too knew the fear of dying for a second time in the hereafter.

The manner of life after death is also closely related to the moral principles of selection for entrance into the country of the dead. In some cases such special principles of selection may be absent. In such a case, the implicit criteria are essentially social, all duly initiated adult members of a community sharing the same destiny. Children and slaves (where these exist) are often excluded. Exceptions exist of course. Among the Apapocúva-Guaraní (South America) dead children go to the "country without evil." About women the opinions vary. Islam, for example, originally excluded women from the heavenly paradise, arguing that women had no immortal soul. In fact, the idea of moral retribution after death is absent from a great number of religions.

Where the conception of reward or punishment according to ethical principles does occur, it is necessary to divide the abode of the dead into two or more sections that may be localized in different places: heaven(s) and hell(s), and in some instances a place in between where souls are purified before they are allowed to enter heaven: purgatory. This may be combined with the belief in reincarnation, as in Buddhism, such that neither heaven nor hell is eternal, the latter becoming a kind of purgatory and the former only a temporary state of conditioned bliss. In cultures where a belief in reincarnation is accepted, the question of the place of a soul's rebirth is understandably of no great importance and the ideas concerning it often remain vague or contradictory.

The distance between the world of the living and the abode of the dead may give rise to the conception of a journey from the one to the other. The Inuit (Eskimo) speak of the road the dead must follow, which seems to be identical with the Milky Way. The Tibetan *Book of the Dead* serves as a guide for the soul on the difficult and dangerous journey to the hereafter and offers detailed "geographical" instructions. The world of the departed may be separated from that of the living by a river (like the Styx in Greece), which must be traversed by boat, or may be crossed by means of a bridge, as the Parsis believe.

Generally the country of the dead is represented more or less as a copy of the world of the living, and life there follows in the main the same lines as life on earth. In these cases it is difficult to speak of a "geography" of death, which would be distinct from the geography of the living. An extreme example of this is the idea which the Admiralty Islanders on Manus (near New Guinea) have developed. In Manus, personality survives death in all respects, at least for a time. A man's property remains his own and even his profession, if he has one, remains unchanged. Reo F. Fortune reports in his book *Manus Religion* that if the deceased was a member of the native constabulary appointed by the Australian administration, he remains a policeman among the ghosts after death. There he receives the periodic visits of a ghostly white district officer of a ghostly white administration and collects the ghostly taxes paid by his fellow ghosts. It is clear that in this case the conception of the country of the dead is an exact double of the land of the living. The living and the dead coexist in space, having only different modes of being. Here it is hardly possible to speak of a distinct geography of death. Although this is perhaps an extreme example, many cases exist in which the dwelling places of the dead are considered to be in the immediate neighborhood of those of the living.

The Greek settlers in southern Italy considered some wild and eerie regions as parts of the underworld existing on the surface of the earth. "Lake without birds" was an appelation of the underworld, Avernus. The *facilis descensus Averno* of which the Roman poet Vergil speaks could be located next to one's own home. Even when the hereafter is conceived as a mirror image of the world of the living, the difference is not as great as it may seem. Things may be reversed, left and right, up and down, the cycle of the seasons may have changed places, but the general principles remain the same.

Where the dead are thought to remain present in the place where they are buried (the conception of the "living corpse"), a special country of the dead may be absent, or at least unimportant. The same is true when the dead are thought to change into animals living in their natural habitat. Nevertheless, the dead always remain separated from the living, at least by their different mode of being, whether or not they are further separated by the location of the realm of which they have become inhabitants. When we find the belief that human beings after death will be reunited again with the cosmos—often considered as divine—there is a transformation in the mode of being, but the question of a geography of the dead does not properly arise. This is the case, for instance, in the Indian concept of *ātman,* the self, which returns after death to *brahman.* Where the final destination of man is conceived negatively, as in the Buddhist *nirvāṇa,* any attempt to "locate" this final state falls under the same negative strictures.

GEOGRAPHIES OF DEATH

In those cases where there is the elaboration of a distinct geography of death, there appear to be three main possibilities, each with minor variations. The world of the dead may be on earth, under the earth, or in heaven. Numerous examples can be given of each.

In the first case, the world of the dead is situated on earth, but at a lesser or greater distance away from the dwellings of the living. The Trobriand Islanders (New Guinea) situate the village of the dead in the direct neighborhood of their own villages. The Celtic Tirnanog is an island in the far west on the other side of the immense ocean. According to the Tasmanians (Australia) the dead travel to an island nearby where they continue their existence; in parts of the Northern Territory (Australia) the island of the dead is situated far off in the direction of the Morning Star. According to the Ewe (Togo) the country of the dead lies a long way off from that of the living on the far side of a river, and the journey to arrive there is difficult and dangerous. We also frequently find peoples having traditions of migration, and here in many cases the abode of the departed is identified with the people's original home, described in myth. Starting from Southeast Asia, we find all over the Pacific variations of the name *Java,* not only as the actual island of the living, but also as the mythic island of the dead. This "principle of return," as it has been called, often appears in the orientation of the corpse at burial that is based on the idea of the return to the country of origin.

In the second case, the realm of the dead is situated beneath the earth or under the water. The idea of an underworld as the dwelling place of the departed is probably the commonest of all concepts in this sphere. The idea of an entrance to this region through a deep hole in the ground or a cave is also widespread. The Hopi (North America) locate the village of the dead, Kotluwalawa, in the depth of a lake called "Whispering Water." When located beneath the earth, the world of the dead is usually conceived as either a realm of shadowy figures or shades, as in the case of the Israelite She'ol and the Greek Hades, or as a place of punishment. On Bellona Island, for instance, the dead are believed to live in darkness under the ground, whereas the living inhabit the world of light on the earth. The Babylonian realm of the dead, the "country of no return," is pictured in the myth of Ishtar's descent to hell in similar terms:

> The house of darkness,
> The house the inhabitants of which lack light,
> The place where dust is their food
> and excrements their nourishments,
> Where they see no light and live in darkness.

The specification of the underworld as a place of punishment is closely connected with the more general phenomenon of the differentiation of destinies after death. As noted briefly above, a number of cultures believe in such a differentiation. We may distinguish two main types: one based on the principle of social or ritual status, and one according to ethical principles. Where the main criterion at first appears to be a kind of knowledge, closer inspection reveals that this type is best understood as a subdivision of the first social or ritual one. In the first type, illustrated for instance by the Delaware and Algonquin (North America), there exists a concept of a different destiny after death for different social or ritual groups. The fate of those lacking such status remains open. They are simply excluded from the regular abode of the dead without further thought being given to the problem of where and how they continue their existence.

The most common type of differentiation, however, is based upon ethical principles, which are employed to separate those who are to be rewarded after death from those who are to be punished. Along with this notion of postmortem punishment comes the notion of hell and purgatory as the locations where such punishments take place. While it is true that not all subterranean abodes of the dead are hells, it does seem to be the case that all hells are understood to be subterranean. Realms of darkness beneath the earth beyond the reach of sun and moon, they are illuminated solely by the flames that punish the damned.

In the final case, the world of the dead may be situated in heavenly spheres. This concept is also a very common one. We find it, for instance, in Egypt as one of several ideas concerning the location of the hereafter. The belief that this country is to be sought somewhere high in the mountains is only a variation, since in many religions mountaintops symbolize heaven and the dwelling place of the gods, as, for example, Olympus did in Greece. The Dusun (North Kalimantan, Borneo) situate the abode of the dead on a high mountain. Another variation is the belief that the dead continue their existence on or among the stars.

The heavenly country of the dead is often represented as a more or less idealized replica of that of the living. The Ngaju Dayak (South Kalimantan, Borneo), for example, go to Lewu Liau after death, a village of spirits situated in a lovely and fertile country, near a river full of fish and with woods filled with game nearby. Everything that is found on earth is found there too, but it is a better world where such things as criminality are unknown. We also encounter profane versions of such heavenly paradises, such as the land of Cocagne, mentioned in fairy tales and usually located in heavenly spheres.

MULTIPLE GEOGRAPHIES: THE EXAMPLE OF ANCIENT EGYPT

Ancient Egypt offers us an example of a multiple geography of death, combining in a single religion many of the different types we have mentioned above. Although there is no reason to think that the culture of Egypt was an especially somber one, it is true that its preoccupation with death and afterlife was great. Although the Egyptians believed in a judgment of the dead by Osiris, the god of the underworld, there seems to have been no concept of hell. Those souls that could not pass the divine judgment were destined to be eaten by Ammit, "she who devours." Egypt also knew the idea of a second and definitive death in the hereafter. The *Book of Going Forth by Day* in fact relates a myth according to which the entire world will in the end return to its primal state prior to creation, to a state of chaos or nothingness.

Egyptian religion is of particular interest because of the multiple ways in which it conceived of the hereafter, called in Egyptian Duat, the zone of twilight, or heaven by night. Five distinct conceptions may be mentioned.

First, the Egyptians recognized a country of the dead, named Amentet, the West. More exactly, this term applies to the western frontier of the fertile land, the edge of the desert where the necropolises were located. The idea of the dead who live on in the grave and graveyard was also known. The realm of the dead is at times situated beneath the earth, which it more or less duplicates, and at other times it is pictured as a system of caves and passages. In both of these cases, the dead living there are believed to be visited by the sun at night. Then there are the "Earu fields," conceived as a heavenly copy of the land of Egypt, complete with a heavenly Nile, yet superior to earth in every way. Finally, the country of the dead may be located in heaven among the stars, especially in the north among the circumpolar stars, which the Egyptians called the "stars that never die."

[*See also* Underworld; Otherworld; *and* Heaven and Hell.]

BIBLIOGRAPHY

Cavendish, Richard. *Visions of Heaven and Hell.* London, 1977. A useful book with many illustrations and a selected bibliography.

Champdor, Albert, trans. *Le livre des morts.* Paris, 1963. An up-to-date translation of the Egyptian *Book of Going Forth by Day.* Well illustrated. Further translated by Faubion Bowers as *The Book of the Dead* (New York, 1966).

Clemen, Carl C. *Das Leben nach dem Tode im Glauben der Menschheit.* Leipzig, 1920. Still one of the best short introductions to the theme, albeit dated as regards theory.

Cumont, Franz. *Afterlife in Roman Paganism.* New York, 1959. A standard work.

Evans-Wentz, W. Y., ed. *The Tibetan Book of the Dead.* 2d ed. Translated by Kazi Dawasamdup. London, 1949. Includes a useful introduction.

Faulkner, Raymond O., trans. *The Ancient Egyptian Book of the Dead.* Rev. ed. Edited by Carol Andrews. London, 1985. A fresh translation, lavishly illustrated.

Firth, Raymond. *The Fate of the Soul: An Interpretation of Some Primitive Concepts.* Cambridge, 1955. Short but important.

Jeremias, Alfred. *Hölle und Paradies bei den Babyloniern.* Leipzig, 1900. Short treatment of the Babylonian concepts of the hereafter. Still of value.

Kees, Hermann. *Totenglauben und Jenseitsvorstellungen der alten Ägypter: Grundlagen und Entwicklung bis zum Ende des mittleren Reiches.* 2d ed. Berlin, 1956. The standard work on Egyptian concepts of the hereafter.

Pfannmüller, Gustav, ed. *Tod, Jenseits und Unsterblichkeit in der Religion, Literatur und Philosophie der Griechen und Römer.* Munich, 1953. An anthology with a useful introduction.

12 ESCHATOLOGY

R. J. Zwi Werblowsky

The term *eschatology* means "the science or teachings concerning the last things." Derived from the Greek *eschatos* ("last") and *eschata* ("the last things"), the term does not seem to have been in use in English before the nineteenth century, but since then it has become a major concept, especially in Christian theology.

Most religions entertain ideas, teachings, or mythologies concerning the beginnings of things: the gods, the world, the human race. [*See* Cosmogony *and* Cosmology.] Parallel to these are accounts of the end of things, which do not necessarily deal with the absolute and final end or with the consummation of all things. The end may be conceived positively, as the kingdom of God, a "new heaven and a new earth," and the like, or negatively, for instance as the "twilight of the gods." Sometimes these accounts refer to events expected to take place in a more or less distant future. There is considerable overlap with messianism, which may, therefore, be considered as one form of eschatology. [*See* Messianism *and* Millenarianism.]

An important distinction has to be drawn between individual and general, or cosmic, eschatology. Individual eschatology deals with the fate of the individual person, that is, the fate of the soul after death. This may be seen in terms of the judgment of the dead, the transmigration of the soul to other existences, or an afterlife in some spiritual realm. Cosmic eschatology envisages more general transformations or the end of the present world. The eschatological consummation can be conceived as restorative in character, for example as the *Endzeit* that restores the lost perfection of a primordial *Urzeit,* or as more utopian, that is, the transformation and inauguration of a state of perfection the like of which never existed before.

ASIAN RELIGIONS

Cultures that view time as an endless succession of repetitive cycles (as in the Indian notions of *yuga* and *kalpa*) develop only "relative eschatologies," since the concept of an ultimate consummation of history is alien to them. Individual eschatology means liberation from the endless, weary wheel of death and rebirth by escaping into an eternal, or rather timeless, transmundane reality that is referred to as *mokṣa* in Hinduism and *nirvāṇa* in Buddhism. Within the cosmic cycles there are periods of rise and decline. According to Indian perceptions of time, our present age is the *kaliyuga,* the last of the four great *yugas*, or world epochs. In various traditions these periods often end in a universal catastrophe, conflagration, or cataclysmic annihilation, to be followed by a new beginning inaugurated by the appearance of a savior figure, such as the *avatāra* (incarnation) of a deity or the manifestation of a new Buddha.

Chinese Buddhism developed the idea of periods of successive, inexorable decline (Chin., *mo-fa;* Jpn., *mappō*), at the end of which the future Buddha Maitreya (Chin., Mi-lo-fo; Jpn., Miroku), who is currently biding his time in the Tuṣita Heaven, will appear and establish a kind of millennial kingdom and inaugurate a new era of bliss and salvation for all. "Messianic" and "millennial" movements in China and Southeast Asia, some of which became social revolts and peasant rebellions, have often been associated with expectations of the coming of Maitreya. Occasionally political agitation and ideologies of rebellion developed without Buddhist influences on the basis of purely Taoist or even Confucian ideas. But in these cases the ideology was "restorative" rather than eschatological in character; it announced the restoration of the lost original "great peace" (T'ai-p'ing)—as, for example, at the end of the Han dynasty or in the fourth-century Mao-shan sect—or propagated the message that the mandate of Heaven had been withdrawn from the reigning dynasty.

Taoism, like Buddhism, entertained notions concerning a postmortem judgment. According to Taoist belief, the judgment took place before a tribunal of judges of the dead who decided the subsequent fate of the soul and assigned it to one of the many hells or heavens that figured in the popular mythologies. Confucianism, however, has no eschatology in the narrow sense of the term; it has no doctrines concerning a day of judgment, a catastrophic end of this world, or a messianic millennium. Other Chinese ideas of individual eschatology were in part drawn from ancient lore and were later amalgamated with Buddhist and Taoist elements. Japanese Shintō has no cosmic eschatology and only vague ideas concerning the state of the dead. It is precisely this vacuum that was filled by Buddhism in the history of Japanese religion.

ZOROASTRIANISM

Individual and universal, or cosmic, eschatology merge when the ultimate fate of the individual is related to that of the world. In such a case the individual is believed to remain in a kind of "provisional state" (which may be heaven or hell, a state of bliss or one of suffering) pending the final denouement of the historical cosmic process. One religion of this eschatological type is Zoroastrianism, a religion in which world history is seen as a cosmic struggle between the forces of light led by Ahura Mazdā (Pahl., Ōhrmazd) and the forces of darkness led by Angra Mainyu (Pahl., Ahriman). This struggle will end with the victory of light, the resurrection of the dead, a general judgment in the form of an ordeal of molten metal (similar to the individual postmortem ordeal when the soul has to cross the Chinvat Bridge), and the final destruction of evil. Some of these Iranian beliefs, especially those concerning the resurrection of the dead, seem to have influenced Jewish and, subsequently, Christian eschatology.

BIBLICAL RELIGIONS

In the Hebrew Bible the terms *aḥarit* ("end") and *aḥarit yamim* ("end of days") originally referred to a more or less distant future and not to the cosmic and final end of days, that is, of history. Nevertheless, in due course eschatological ideas and beliefs developed, especially as a result of disappointment with the moral failings of the Jewish kings, who theoretically were "the Lord's anointed" of the House of David. In addition, a series of misfortunes led to the further development of these ideas: the incursions and devastations by enemy armies; the fall of Jerusalem and the destruction of the Temple in 587/6 BCE; the Babylonian exile; the failure of the "return to Zion" to usher in the expected golden age so rhapsodically prophesied by the "Second Isaiah"; the persecutions (e.g., under the Seleucid rulers and reflected in the *Book of Daniel*); the disappointments suffered under the Hasmonean kings; Roman rule and oppression; and finally the second destruction of Jerusalem by the Romans in 70 CE, which, after the failure of subsequent revolts, initiated a long period of exile, tribulation, and "waiting for redemption."

The predictions of the Old Testament prophets regarding the restoration of a golden age, which could be perceived as the renewal of an idealized past or the inauguration of a utopian future, subsequently merged with Persian and Hellenistic influences and ideas. Prophecy gave way to apocalypse, and eschatological and messianic ideas of diverse kinds developed. As a result, alternative and even mutually exclusive ideas and beliefs existed side by side; only at a much later stage did theologians try to harmonize these in a consistent system. Thus there were hopes and expectations concerning a worldly, glorious, national restoration under a Davidic king or victorious military leader, or through miraculous intervention from above. The ideal redeemer would be either a scion of the House of David or a supernatural celestial being referred to as the "Son of man." Significantly, Jesus, who seems to have avoided the term *messiah,* possibly because of its political overtones, and preferred the appellation *Son of man,* nevertheless was subsequently identified by the early church as the Messiah ("the Lord's anointed"; in Greek, *christos,* hence *Christ*) and was provided with a genealogy (see *Mt.* 1) that legitimated this claim through his descent from David.

Redemption could thus mean a better and more peaceful world (the wolf lying down with the lamb) or the utter end and annihilation of this age, the ushering in, amid catastrophe and judgment, of a "new heaven and a new earth," as in the later Christian beliefs concerning a last judgment, Armageddon, and so on. The doctrine of the resurrection of the dead played a major role in the eschatological beliefs held by the Pharisees and was also shared by Jesus. The chaotic welter of these ideas is visible not only in the so-called apocryphal books of the Old Testament, many of which are apocalypses (i.e., compositions recounting the revelations concerning the final events allegedly granted to certain visionaries), but also in the New Testament.

CHRISTIANITY

The message and teachings of the "historical Jesus" (as distinct from those of the Christ of the early church) are considered by most historians as beyond recovery. There has been, however, a wide scholarly consensus, especially at the turn of the century, that Jesus can be interpreted correctly only in terms of the eschatological beliefs and expectations current in the Judaism of his time. The Qumran sect (also known as the Dead Sea sect) was perhaps one of the most eschatologically radical groups at the time. In other words, he preached and expected the end of this world and age, and its replacement in the immediate future, after judgment, by the "kingdom of God." Early Christianity was thus presented as an eschatological message of judgment and salvation that, after the crucifixion and resurrection, emphasized the expectation of the imminent Second Coming. The subsequent history of the church was explained by these scholars as a result of the crisis of eschatology caused by the continued delay of the Second Coming. Some modern theologians have taken up the idea of eschatology as the essence of the Christian message, though interpreting it in a less literal-historical and more spiritual or existential manner. Karl Barth, for example, has portrayed the life of the individual Christian, as well as that of the church, as a series of decisions to be apprehended in an eschatological perspective. C. H. Dodd, in his conception of "realized eschatology," has stressed the present significance of future eschatology. Christian history has been punctuated throughout by movements of a millenarian, chiliastic, and eschatological character. Certain modern movements (e.g., Marxism) are interpreted by some thinkers as secularized versions of traditional utopian eschatologies.

ISLAM

The tradition of Islam absorbed so many Jewish and Christian influences in its formative period that it is usually counted among the biblical (or "biblical type") religions. While the eschatological aspects of these traditions were deemphasized in later Islamic doctrines, they undoubtedly played a major role in the original religious experience of the prophet Muḥammad, for whom the end of the historical process and God's final judgment were a central concern. The notion of "the hour," that is, the day of judgment and the final catastrophe, the exact time of which was known to God alone, looms large in his message and is vividly portrayed in the Qur'ān (see surahs 7:187, 18:50, 36:81, and 78:17ff.). As in the Jewish and Christian traditions on which Muḥammad drew, God will judge the living and the dead on a day of judgment that will be preceded by a general resurrection (surah 75). The agents of the final hour will be Gog and Magog (surahs 18:95ff. and 21:96), led, according to some sources, by the Antichrist.

There is also a messianic figure, the Mahdi (the "rightly guided one"), and Mahdist, or messianic, movements have not been infrequent in Muslim history. The eschatological Mahdi is more prominent in Shīʿah than in Sunnī Islam. In the latter, belief in the Mahdi is a matter of popular religion rather than official dogma. As regards individual eschatology, Muslim belief in Paradise and Hell, in spite of much variation in detail, is essentially analogous to that of Judaism and Christianity.

PRIMAL RELIGIONS

In most primal religions eschatology plays no major role, since they are generally based on the notion of cyclical renewal rather than on a movement toward a final consummation or end. While it is hazardous to generalize on the subject, in such traditions eschatological or messianic beliefs and expectations are often due to direct or indirect Christian or Western influences, whether relayed through missionaries or through more general cultural contact. These influences can precipitate crises that result in so-called crisis cults (many of which are of a markedly messianic character); they can also introduce eschatological notions concerning conceptions of time and history.

For example, according to the ancient Germanic myths recounted in the Eddas and the *Vǫluspá,* in the fullness of time all things are doomed to final destruction in a universal cataclysm called Ragnarǫk, the "doom of the gods." During this cataclysm there will be a succession of terrible winters accompanied by moral disintegration, at the end of which the Fenrisúlfr (Fenriswolf) will swallow the sun and then run wild; the heavens will split, the cosmic tree Yggdrasill will shake, the gods will go forth to their last battle, and finally a fire will consume all things. There are some vague but inconclusive indications that this total doom may be followed by a new beginning. Scholars are at variance on the question of possible Christian influences on Germanic mythology. Of greater methodological relevance to our present considerations is the question as to what extent this mythology was a response to a crisis. In other words, we may have to consider Christianity not as a hypothetical source of "influences" but as the cause of crises within the non-Christian cultures it confronted. Thus the "doom of the gods" mythology may have developed as an expression of the sense of doom that engulfed the original Nordic culture as a result of its disintegration under the impact of triumphant Christianity.

The contemporary sense of crisis and fear aroused by expectations of imminent nuclear catastrophe and cosmic destruction has reawakened an apocalyptic-eschatological mood in many circles. Some Christian groups, especially those in the United States, calling upon their particular interpretations of biblical prophecies, are "waiting for the end"—it being understood that the believing elect will somehow be saved from the universal holocaust, possibly by being "rapt up" and transferred to other spheres. This phenomenon is not, however, confined to the Christian West. Some of the so-called new religions in Japan and elsewhere similarly exhibit millenarian and even eschatological characteristics, often related to the figure of Maitreya, the Buddha of the future.

[*See also* Afterlife; Death; Heaven and Hell; Judgment of the Dead; Paradise; *and* Resurrection.]

BIBLIOGRAPHY

Since Judaism and Christianity possess the most highly developed eschatological doctrines, most of the relevant literature has been produced by theologians and students of these religions. In addition to the works of Albert Schweitzer, Johannes Weiss, and, in the first half of the twentieth century, the Protestant theologians Karl Barth and Emil Brunner, the following should be noted: R. H. Charles's *Eschatology,* 2d ed. (London, 1913); Hermann Gunkel's *Schöpfung und Chaos in Urzeit und Endzeit* (Göttingen, 1895); F. Holstrom's *Das eschatologische Denken der Gegenwart* (1936); Rudolf Bultmann's *History and Eschatology* (Edinburgh, 1957); C. H. Dodds's "Eschatology and History," in his *The Apostolic Preaching and Its Developments,* 2d ed. (New York, 1951); W. O. E. Oesterley's *The Doctrine of the Last Things: Jewish and Christian* (London, 1908); Paul Volz's *Die Eschatologie der jüdischen Gemeinde im neutestamentlichen Zeitalter* (Tübingen, 1934); Roman Guardini's *Die letzten Dinge,* 2d ed. (Würzburg, 1949); Norman Perrin's *The Kingdom of God in the Teaching of Jesus* (Philadelphia, 1963); and Reinhold Niebuhr's *The Nature and Destiny of Man,* vol. 2, *Human Destiny* (New York, 1943), pp. 287ff. For a review of the current interest in apocalyptic prophecy, see William Martin's journalistic but instructive report, "Waiting for the End," *Atlantic Monthly* (June 1982), pp. 31–37.

13 ASCENSION

Ioan Petru Culianu

In many religious traditions, the sky is the home of the gods, and a heavenly ascent is a journey into the divine realms from which the soul—living or dead—reaps many rewards. Not only is a transcendent vision (or spiritual knowledge) the result of this upward journey, but even the possibility of divinization, becoming like one of the gods.

Myths from many cultures tell of numerous ways by which the journey can be made. A mountain path, a ladder, a tree, a rope, or even a cobweb will suffice. There is the further possibility of magical flight, if the soul has wings or the person a psychopomp. [*See* Flight.] Rituals of ascent involve the living person who makes the heavenly journey in order to become sanctified as a priest who mediates between his people and their gods, to become initiated into a new, sacred status, or for purposes of healing.

ECSTATIC TECHNIQUES

In demonstrating that there are a number of parallel beliefs and rituals in all great religions of the world, Mircea Eliade cites shamanism as an example of an objective ecstatic performance. [*See* Shamanism.] Everything in the behavior and paraphernalia of the shaman is oriented toward one principal goal: the journey to heaven or the netherworld. This journey is concretely performed before the eyes of those who engage the shaman for practical purposes.

In *yoga,* an ecstatic technique of another kind, the cosmic layers are experienced in the form of a number of internal "principles," and the journey to the other world is now a journey within oneself: ecstasy becomes enstasy. This scheme of a passage from objectification to interiorization has also been applied to late antiquity. As Hans Jonas observes in his *Philosophical Essays* (1974), what was an objective ecstatic performance in gnosticism has become an inner experience in Neoplatonic and Christian mysticism.

These ecstatic techniques, both "objectified" and "interiorized," have played an outstanding role in religious experience from archaic times to the present. Yet ecstasy, whether in the form of wild Dionysiac frenzy or in the form of the shaman's "objective" journey to the netherworld, has repelled the practical Western mind.

Even in the Greek language, *ekstasis* meant nothing but a state of psychic dissociation, an illness. Pathological symptoms of ecstasy, even in its "mild," mystical forms, have been stressed too often in modern research. In addition to the psychological interpretation of ecstasy as an abnormal state of mind, sociological explanations have been adduced to show that the anomic practices of ecstatic groups were a means of compensating for their own social marginality. Another tendency in modern anthropology is to explain all forms of ecstasy as a result of an intake of hallucinogins or as a result of chemical alterations in the human organism.

The task of the historian of religions is to examine forms of ecstasy in their historical context. Archaic religions included the motifs of ascension to heaven or descent to the netherworld, magical flight, separation of the soul from the body, and so on. In attempting to explain the origins of Western beliefs about the ascent of the soul, scholars have pointed out the analogies with shamanism, but cross-cultural contacts make it difficult to sort out influences. In the least, it seems that archaic Mediterranean religions knew a pattern of prophecy and heavenly ascension that has much in common with shamanism.

WESTERN CULTURE

In the history of Western culture from Archaic Greece to the Renaissance, it appears that two religious trends have been particularly important. One of them started in Babylonia, was taken over by the Jews, and from there influenced Christian apocalypses and Muslim legends of Muḥammad's ascent. The other originated in Archaic Greece, influenced Plato, was dominant during the Hellenistic period and late antiquity, and reached the late Middle Ages through the bias of scholasticism and the Italian Renaissance through the rediscovery of Platonism.

Greek Religions. In Greece, belief and practice concerning catalepsy (state of trance) and the flight of the separable soul, either in space or into another dimension, exists apart from the belief in Dionysos, the ecstatic divinity *par excellence.* Rather, Greek medicine men, known in scholarly literature as *iatromanteis* (from *iatros,* "healer," and *mantis,* "seer"), are connected with Apollo, a divinity dwelling in Hyperborea, the mysterious land of the north. They are occasionally called *phoibolamptoi* or *phoiboleptoi* (i.e., "ravished by Phoibos-Apollo"). Besides being a medicine man, the *iatromantis* could be an *aithrobatēs* ("air-traveler"), a *kathartēs* ("purifier"), a *chresmologos* ("author of oracles"), and a *thaumatourgos* ("performer of miracles"). To the category of *iatromantis* belonged such notable personalities as Empedocles of Acragas (Agrigentum) and Pythagoras of Samos; among those *iatromanteis* perhaps less influential, but no less typical for this whole religious complex, were Abaris, Aristeas of Proconnesus, Bakis, Epimenides of Crete, and Hermotimos of Clazomenae. In general, the *iatromantis* excelled in the art of using catalepsy *(apnous)* for divination. It would be brash to say that catalepsy was induced by hallucinogenic substances. A plant called *alimos* (lit., "hungerless") or hungerbane, which might have contained a hunger-suppressing alkaloid, is mentioned in the legend of Epimenides, who is reported to have slept for some decades in the cave of Zeus in Crete. Porphyry's statement (*Life of Pythagoras* 34) that Pythagoras also used hungerbane might suggest the correct interpretation of the ancient rationalized evidence ascribing to the Pythagoreans the use of the plant *halimos (Atriplex halimus*

L.) in their poor diet. But the reverse is equally possible, since the terms *alimos* and *halimos* differ only by a rough breath.

Abaris, Aristeas, Epimenides, and Hermotimos are reported either to fly or to free their souls and leave their bodies in a state of catalepsy. Specifically, the soul of Aristeas, taking the form of a raven, was said to travel as far as Hyperborea; the soul of Epimenides, to converse with the gods; and the soul of Hermotimos, to visit faraway places and to record local events of which he could give an accurate description once it came back to its sheath (*vagina,* i.e., the body). When Hermotimos's wife delivered his inanimate body to his enemies, the Cantharidae, they burned it. Thus Hermotimos's soul lost its bodily shelter, on account of which both his wife and the Cantharidae were condemned to everlasting torture in Tartarus. Some scholars have seen Hermotimos as a marginal figure of Archaic Greece. Others have shown that, on the contrary, Hermotimos was probably a famous medium, whose art provoked the jealousy of the mighty Dionysiac confraternity *(hetairia)* of the Cantharidae.

The belief of the *iatromantis* that catalepsy was a state of separation between body and soul, in which the latter was supposed to have supernatural experiences, was resumed by Plato in the apocalypse of Er in the tenth book of the *Republic.* Er, son of Armenios of Pamphylia (Asia Minor), was wounded in a battle and appeared to be dead. His catalepsy lasted twelve days, until the very moment his body was going to be burned. Er then came back to life and reported all the secrets of afterlife that had been revealed to his soul.

Plato's pupil Heracleides Ponticus (fourth century BCE) took direct inspiration from the legends of the *iatromanteis.* In his dialogues, now lost in their entirety, he was concerned with catalepsy and its treatment (probably in the dialogue *On Catalepsy,* in which the main character was Empedokles), and with the stories of such famous ecstatics as Abaris, Aristeas, Epimenides, Hermotimos, and Pythagoras (probably in the dialogue *Abaris*). In one of these dialogues *(Abaris,* or *On Things in Hell)*, Heracleides introduced a fictitious character, Empedotimos, whose name was derived from *Empedokles* and *Hermotimos.* Some scholars have attributed to Empedotimos (i.e., to Heracleides) a very consequential innovation in Greek eschatology, namely the complete suppression of any subterrestrial place for punishment of the dead. Other scholars have claimed that the spread of celestial eschatology was due to the influence of Pythagoreanism and Stoicism, and indeed, Stoicism might have played an important role in the transformation of Hellenistic eschatology.

Hellenistic Religions. By the end of the first century CE, when Plutarch wrote his eschatological myths, the idea of an underground Hades was no longer fashionable. Plutarch's ambition was to give a "modern" version of the great myths of Plato. Accordingly, Plato's eschatology was transformed to meet the intellectual exigencies of the time.

Very interesting details about catalepsy and incubation are given by Plutarch in his dialogue *On Socrates' Daemon,* based on traditions concerning the famous oracular cave of Trophonius at Lebadea, ten miles from Chaeronea on the way to Delphis. If Lamprias, Plutarch's brother, was really a priest of the sanctuary in Lebadea, then Plutarch may have had access to the wooden tablets on which those consulting the oracle were supposed to write down the account of their experiences. The hero of this apocalypse is Timarch of Chaeronea, whose soul leaves his body through the *sutura frontalis* and visits the heavenly Hades, remaining below the sphere of the moon, which is only the first among the seven planetary spheres. In this dialogue, as well as in the dialogue *On the Face in the Moon,* the moon is the receptacle of the souls that are freed of their bodies, apart from those souls that fall again into the circle of transmigration *(metensōmatōsis).* The earth is viewed here as the lowest and meanest point of the universe; accordingly, the underground Hades and Tartarus of the Platonic myths are no longer needed.

The second important myth of Plutarch is contained in the dialogue *On the Delayed Revenge of the Gods,* in which many elements of the apocalypse of Er are resumed. Aridaeus of Soloi, whose name derives from that of the tyrant Aridiaeus in the *Republic* of Plato (615e; also known as Aridaeus in late antique sources), tries to make a fortune using dishonest means. After a fall in which he strikes his head, he enters a cataleptic state for two days. He is believed to be dead, but he wakes up just as he is about to be buried. After this experience, Aridaeus changes his name to Thespesius ("godly, wonderful") and becomes a very pious man. In fact, his soul has watched the judgment of the dead and witnessed the painful lot of the sinners.

Gnosticism. In the gnostic systems of the second and third centuries CE, a vivid polemic against astrology takes peculiar forms. The seven "planets" themselves (i.e., the five known planets, the sun, and the moon), the signs, the decans, and the degrees of the zodiac are often represented as evil archons, or heavenly rulers. These are extremely important for the embodiment and disembodiment of the individual soul.

The German scholar Wilhelm Anz, a representative of the Religionsgeschichtliche Schule, argued that the heavenly ascent of the soul through the spheres represented a central doctrine of gnosticism *(Zur Frage nach dem Ursprung des Gnostizismus,* Leipzig, 1897*).* In a way, although for reasons other than those adduced by Anz, this statement may still be maintained. [*See* Gnosticism.] In his major work, *Gnosis und spätantiker Geist* (Göttingen, 1934–1954), Hans Jonas has shown that gnosis ("saving knowledge") led to an *Entweltlichung,* or "a shedding of one's cosmic nature." Therefore, the techniques intended to assure the gnostic's soul a safe passage through the spheres of the hostile archons up to the *plērōma* ("fullness") of the godhead actually form the most important part of gnosis.

One of the first testimonies for a typically gnostic theory of the embodiment and disembodiment of the soul is the doctrine of Basilides, a Christian active in Alexandria, Egypt, around 120 CE. According to Basilides, the transcendental spirit of man is temporarily attached to a soul. During its descent, the planetary vices attack the soul and stick to it in the form of concretions of "appendages" *(prosartēmata).* The same theory is set forth by Basilides' son Isidorus in his treatise *On the Temporary Soul.*

The technical expression *antimimon pneuma,* or "counterfeit spirit" (sometimes *antikeimenon,* i.e., "evil spirit"), occurs for the first time in the *Apocryphon* (Secret Book) *of John,* one of the oldest surviving gnostic treatises, extant in four Coptic versions. The heresiologist Irenaeus, bishop of Lugdunum (Lyons), who wrote between 180 and 185 CE, based his description of the system of the so-called Barbelo gnostics on it. Some scholars claim that the *Apocryphon of John* predates even Basilides, whose theory of the *prosartēmata* is based on the *antimimon pneuma* doctrine. In fact, the *antimimon pneuma* is an appended spirit, an intermediary between the soul and the material body. The soul itself is a creation of the evil heavenly archons (i.e., the seven "planets") or, to be more precise, of the seven attributes forming conjunctions (syzygies) together with the archons.

The formation of the *antimimon pneuma* is more explicitly stated in the third book of the Coptic treatise *Pistis Sophia* (chap. 131). The "counterfeit spirit" derives directly from the archons of the *heimarmenē,* or astral destiny, which are the seven "planets." The *antimimon pneuma* follows the soul in all its reincarnations *(metabolai)* and is itself a cause of reincarnation. The goal of gnostic mysteries is to free the soul from bondage to the *antimimon pneuma.* On the basis of the order of the planets in chapter 136 of *Pistis Sophia* and in other texts of late antiquity, it appears that this doctrine derives from the Hermetic astrological treatise *Panaretos,* which includes a discussion of the degrees *(klēroi)* or positions *(loci)* of the planets, that is, the coordinates within the horoscope of nativity, where each planet is supposed to confer its principal qualities upon the subject. In their polemic against astrology, gnostics mention only the negative qualities or vices derived from the planetary influence.

The doctrine of *antimimon pneuma* became very influential in Hermetism, where it merged with the idea of the soul's descent into the world and its return to heaven. During its descent through the planetary spheres, the soul acquired from each planet the dominant vice ascribed to it in astrology. During its heavenly ascent, the soul put off those concretions and abandoned them to each planet (*Poimandres* 25–26). The ascent of the soul in gnosticism could be much more complicated. On the one hand, the archons did not represent the planets only, but also the 12 signs, the 36 decans, and the 360 degrees of the zodiacal circle, as well as the 365 days of the solar year. On the other hand, a number of the aeons, or levels that the soul had to transverse, had no connection whatsoever with astrology. They bore arbitrary names and occupied various places *(topoi)* within the system, which gnostics were supposed to learn by heart, or even to visualize in their meditation practices. Moreover, the ritual performances or "mysteries" intended to assure the soul an easy passage through the archons differed widely.

All the authentic gnostic treatises that have survived belong to an ascetic gnosis. The fourth-century heresiologist Epiphanius reported, however, that certain gnostics called Phibionites practiced *coitus reservatus* 365 times, uttering the names of the archons from the bottom to the top of the world, and again 365 times from the top to the bottom (*Panarion* 9). No doubt this would have been a strenuous practice. The ascetic gnostics, such as those who produced the two *Books of Ieū* (extant in a Coptic version), were more moderate. They had to learn by heart only some ninety names of the heavenly treasures *(thēsauroi)* and the Ieūs deriving from a primordial Ieū-Father. There were sixty treasures altogether, each one with its own configuration, occupants, gates, and watchers. The adept was supposed to learn by heart the formidable names of the aeons and of the three guardians *(phulakai)* of each treasure, together with the magic "number" *(psēphos)* and the "seal" *(sphragis)* or protective talisman corresponding to each aeon. For many adepts, this practice must have been too difficult. The Savior eventually revealed to them one complete set of names, numbers, and seals, by means of which they could open all of the heavenly gates.

Magic, Theurgy, and the Mysteries. The word *magic* is related to *Magos,* a synonym of *Chaldaean;* theurgy *stricto sensu* is the practice described by the *Chaldaean Oracles,* a second-century work composed by Julian, called "the Chaldaean," and written down by his son Julian "the Theurgist." [*See* Theurgy.] This evidence seems to indicate that the Iranian Magi, dwelling in Mesopotamia (hence "Chaldaeans") were the authors of sophisticated ecstatic techniques. In fact, the heresiologist Arnobius, who wrote at the beginning of the fourth century CE, attributes to the Magi formulas and other means for transporting their clients to heaven. It seems that Arnobius directed his polemic against a group of Neoplatonic mystics who maintained the doctrines of the *Chaldaean Oracles.* The elevation process described there, as well as the relation between the ascent of the adept's soul and the god Mithra, described in a Greek magical papyrus, actually have nothing to do with Iran. They belong instead to the intellectual products of late Hellenism, dominated by an obsession with human liberation from the world and out of the world, in or beyond the heavenly spheres.

As far as the mysteries of late antiquity are concerned, their divinities, in some cases traditionally connected with the earth and the underworld Hades, are transported entirely to heaven, where they are usually supposed to receive the souls of their adepts after death. In the mysteries of Isis, according to the second-century Latin writer Apuleius, the adept underwent an initiation consisting of either an ecstatic experience or a ritual enactment meant to give the illusion thereof. The second-century Platonic writer Celsus ascribed to the mysteries of Mithra a ritual object *(sumbolon)* consisting of a ladder with seven steps or "gates" *(klimax heptapylos),* representing the spheres of the planets. According to Celsus, this object symbolized the passage of the adept's soul through the planetary spheres. This interpretation seems unlikely, however, since the steps are arranged according to the order of the days of the planetary week, not according to any known order of the planets in the universe. Attempts to explain the meaning of the ladder and to relate it to the testimonies concerning the mysteries of Mithra themselves have yet to meet with success.

Passage of the Soul Through the Spheres. In Hellenistic culture a relationship was established between the seven "planets" and the levels that the soul had to transverse in its heavenly ascent; this link constitutes the main difference between the Hellenistic tradition and the Jewish tradition (and, later, the Islamic tradition) concerning ecstatic experiences. Gnostic polemics against astrology gave rise to the formation of the very influential theory of the passage of the soul through the spheres, which was fashionable in Neoplatonism from the third century CE down to the sixteenth. It is impossible to state whether early Neoplatonists (Porphyry, Proclus, and Macrobius) took this theory from Numenius of Apamea or from the gnostic-Hermetic tradition.

The embodiment *(ensōmatōsis)* of the soul entails a descent from the top of the cosmos to the bottom, through the planetary spheres that confer certain characteristic features upon the soul. Disembodiment is the reverse of this process. In late Neoplatonism, the ethereal body that enveloped the soul and that was formed by planetary qualities was called the "vehicle" *(ochēma).* Sometimes this "vehicle" was distinguished from others that were meant to serve as intermediaries between the soul and the material body, according to a theory of Aristotle that was very influential in Greco-Roman and Arab medicine. The theory of the passage of the soul through the spheres was taken over from Macrobius by medieval medicine and psychology. Through the works of Marsilio Ficino (1433–1499), it became one of the least controversial doctrines from the time of the Renaissance down to the end of the sixteenth century and even into the seventeenth.

Judaism. The heavenly journey belongs to the constant pattern of Jewish and Jewish-Christian apocalypses, beginning with *1 Enoch,* the oldest parts of which were completed at the end of the third century BCE. The voyage through seven or three heavens became a commonplace of Jewish apocalyptic literature with the *Testaments of the Twelve Patriarchs* (second century BCE.) Seven (heavens or palaces) is the number that prevails in the Jewish tradition of mysticism related to the *merkavah,* the chariot carrying God's throne in the vision of Ezekiel (*Ez.* 1). Under the name *ma'aseh merkavah* ("work of the chariot"), this form of speculation goes back to the Pharisees of the Second Temple. The first testimonies appear in *1 Enoch* (14:11–19) and in the Greek fragments of the second-century BCE Jewish tragedian Ezekiel of Alexandria. Important pieces of *merkavah* tradition also occur in the Jewish apocalypses *2 Enoch,* the *Apocalypse of Abraham,* and the *Vision of Isaiah,* the last of which is extant in a Christian version, slightly revised by a gnostic hand. Christian apocalypses (e.g., the *Apocalypse of Paul*), reflect the same basic ecstatic experience.

From the second or third century to the sixth century CE, *merkavah* mysticism is mainly expressed through "heikhalotic literature" (from *heikhal,* "heavenly palace"), represented by various groups of testimonies of different dates. Jewish magic, as recorded in, for example, the *Sefer ha-razim* (sixth or seventh century CE), was also concerned with the vision of seven heavens, which was fundamental to *merkavah* mysticism and heikhalotic literature. The related writings contain the revelation of seven "heavenly palaces," which the adept was supposed to attain after strenuous preparation. In Jewish mysticism, the seven heavens are never associated with the seven planets.

Iranian Religions. Ecstatic experiences induced by hallucinogens seem to be attested to in pre-Zoroastrian Iran. Among the drugs used, two have been identified as being extracted from henbane *(Hyoscyamus niger)* and hemp *(Cannabis indica),* both called in Middle Persian *bang* (Av., *banha;* cf. Skt. *bhaṅg*). Zoroastrian reform was directed against wild ecstasy, but the Younger Avestan priests reintroduced the use of *bang, mang,* and *hōm* (Av., *haoma;* cf. Skt. *soma*); these were sometimes mixed with wine.

Apart from some accounts of experiences that might be considered visionary, apocalypses seem to be completely missing from the Zoroastrian tradition until the third century CE, when the famous *mōbad* (priest) Kerdēr, defender of the true religion, committed one of his revelations to writing on a slab at Sar Mashhad. In the ninth century CE, two apocalypses were recorded in Middle Persian: the vision of Virāz the Righteous *(Ardā Wīrāz Nāmag)* and a vision attributed to Vishtāsp, the prince who protected Zarathushtra. Both works contain thoroughly Zoroastrian elements, but, among other very heterogeneous influences, they bear the decisive mark of the Christian apocalyptic tradition (e.g., the motif of the bridge to heaven that widens to let the just pass and contracts to fling the impious into hell). Traditionally Zoroastrian are the three cosmic layers, or "heavens," that the visionary crosses—

corresponding to *humata,* "fair thoughts" (the stars); *hūkhta,* "fair words" (the moon); *hvarshta,* "fair deeds" (the sun)—to arrive at *anagra raoca,* or Paradise, the layer of "infinite lights."

Islam. The Miʿrāj, or ascent of the prophet Muḥammad, is extant in three principal groups of Arabic testimonies from the eighth and ninth centuries CE, as well as in three medieval Latin versions (the first of which, the *Liber scale,* was first translated into Castilian in 1264 at the court of Alphonse X). The Islamic tradition is directly dependent on Jewish and Jewish-Christian apocalypses and shows no trace of Iranian influence. [*See* Miʿrāj.]

Accompanied by the archangel Gabriel, the Prophet is transported to the first heaven either on Burāq (a sort of winged horse) or in a tree growing with vertiginous speed up to the sky. They stop ten to fifteen times, but only the first seven or eight halts represent the "heavens." According to Jewish tradition, these heavens are never associated with the seven "planets" and therefore should not be called "astronomical heavens," as is done now and then in scholarly literature. The Hellenistic doctrine of the seven planetary spheres, which is the basis for Dante's depiction of Paradise in his *Commedia,* does not occur in Jewish-Christian, Arabic, or Iranian testimonies.

Medieval Christianity. Late Hellenistic Christian apocalypses continued to play an important role during the Middle Ages. Very influential was the Latin *Vision of Esdra,* known in a tenth-century manuscript. From the twelfth century, which was particularly productive as far as revelations are concerned, three works are among the most important: the *Vision of Alberic* (1127), written by a monk of Montecassino; the *Vision of Tundal* (1149), whose author is also known as Thugdal; and the *Purgatory of Saint Patrick* (1189). The *Vision of Alberic* was possibly influenced by the Miʿraj legends, transmitted by Constantine the African (1020–1087), a translator from Arabic who spent the last seventeen years of his life at Montecassino. The *Vision of Tundal* and the *Purgatory of Saint Patrick* belong to Irish Christianity but, despite an opinion still held by some scholars, do not seem to reflect any distinctively Celtic themes.

The *Vision of Alberic* contains an episode in which the soul of Alberic, then a boy of ten, is carried by a dove through the planetary heavens up to the throne of God. The order of the heavens is strange (Moon, Mars, Mercury, Sun, Jupiter, Venus, Saturn) and seems to reflect a failed attempt to integrate two traditions: the Jewish-Christian-Muslim on the one hand and the HellenisticHermetic-Neoplatonic on the other. Attempts at such integration did not meet with full success until Dante's *Commedia* in the early fourteenth century.

SCHOLARLY THEORIES AND NEW DIRECTIONS

The Religionsgeschichtliche Schule, represented or supported by such personalities as Wilhelm Brandt, Wilhelm Anz, Wilhelm Bousset, Richard Reitzenstein, Franz Cumont, Joseph Kroll, Rudolf Bultmann, and Geo Widengren, gave an important place to the doctrine of the ascension of the soul. Starting from ninth-century writings in Middle Persian, they inferred that these testimonies reflected an ancient Iranian lore, which they transformed into a sort of primordial religion, not only pre-Christian but also pre-Platonic. In point of fact, the reverse is true, namely that the writings in Middle Persian were directly influenced by late antique, Jewish, Christian, Neoplatonic, and even Islamic traditions.

As far as the ascent of the soul is concerned, Bousset took over Anz's theory of the Iranian origin of this doctrine and came to the conclusion that the belief in the ascent of the soul and gnostic dualism both originated in Iran and were propagated in late antiquity by means of the mysteries of Mithra. Bousset distinguished between two classes of testimonies concerning the ascent: one designating three heavenly layers, to which he ascribed an ancient Iranian background, and the other indicating seven heavens, to which he ascribed a Babylonian origin. Here Bousset based his argument on several false assumptions: that the Babylonians were not acquainted with the ascent of the soul, that they postulated an invariable number of seven heavens, and that they established a connection between these heavens and the seven "planets." In fact, the idea of ascent existed in Babylonian as well as in other religions, the heavenly layers in Babylonia varied between three and nine, and no relation between these realms and the planets could have been established before the Greek Eudoxus of Cnidus (fifth–fourth centuries BCE) came to the genial idea that the complicated trajectories of the planets could be explained as the result of the movement of several homocentric spheres around the earth. Indeed, Jewish testimonies concerning either three or seven heavens must have a Babylonian background, since they never establish any relation between heavens and "planets." The other main tradition, which extends from Eudoxos and Aristotle to Dante and Marsilio Ficino, is a purely Hellenistic one that scarcely interfered with the Babylonian-Jewish-Muslim line. With regard to Iran, it is safe to state that its influence upon the development of the two great schemes of ascent was negligible. On the contrary, it seems that during the reign of the Sasanid dynasty Iranian religion was open to various alien influences, a phenomenon that became even more intense after the Islamic conquest.

All the traditional scholarly interpretations of the ascent of the soul—of which the Religionsgeschichtliche Schule introduced only the most influential version—have one underlying feature in common: they reduce the complexity of the phenomenon to the search of a common origin, be it Iranian, Pythagorean, Greek in general, Jewish, or shamanistic (Karl Meuli). Psychological approaches have also been attempted, unfortunately too much under the influence of nineteenth-century rationalism to credit further discussion here. Much of the task of current research is necessarily oriented toward a critical reexamination and, indeed, a rejection, of ancient theories. Rather than searching for origins, it is necessary to assemble the widest possible corpus of testimonies from different traditions, with the goal of demonstrating interferences, influences, and cross-cultural contacts. At the same time, respect for the specificity of the religious fact should not obscure the researcher's ability to recognize universal categories, patterns, and typologies.

[*For further discussion of the journeys of the soul, see* Soul. *See also* Afterlife *and* Apotheosis.]

BIBLIOGRAPHY

The best single book on shamanism and related phenomena in different religious contexts remains Mircea Eliade's *Shamanism: Archaic Techniques of Ecstasy*, rev. & enl. ed. (New York,

1964). The best book on *yoga* techniques viewed in a broad historico-religious scope is still Mircea Eliade's *Yoga: Immortality and Freedom,* 2d ed. (Princeton, 1969).

An up-to-date bibliographic survey of the problem of heavenly ascension from Archaic Greece to the medieval apocalypses is included in my work *Psychanodia I: A Survey of the Evidence Concerning the Ascension of the Soul and Its Relevance* (Leiden, 1983). The texts receive an elaborated comment in my *Expériences de l'extase* (Paris, 1984).

Several materials related to ascension in gnosticism and late antiquity are to be found in *The Origins of Gnosticism,* edited by Ugo Bianchi (1967; reprint, Leiden, 1970); *Studies in Gnosticism and Hellenistic Religions,* edited by R. Van den Broek and Maarten J. Vermaseren (Leiden, 1981); and *La soteriologia dei culti orientali nell'Impero Romano,* edited by Ugo Bianchi and Maarten J. Vermaseren (Leiden, 1982). On the mysteries of Mithra and heavenly ascension, the most fascinating book remains Robert Turcan's *Mithras platonicus: Recherches sur l'hellénisation philosophique de Mithra* (Leiden, 1975). Unfortunately, Turcan's theory does not seem to stand up to the challenge of recent research. On Macrobius and the passage of the soul through the spheres, a good survey is Jacques Flamant's *Macrobe et le néo-platonisme latin, à la fin du quatrième siècle* (Leiden, 1977).

A good survey of the Jewish mysticism of the *merkavah* is Ithamar Gruenwald's *Apocalyptic and Merkavah Mysticism* (Leiden, 1980). A good bibliography concerning heavenly ascent in Iran is given in Gherardo Gnoli's *Zoroaster's Time and Homeland* (Naples, 1980).

There is no up-to-date work on the Miʿraj. Those interested in the topic must still rely on D. Miguel Asín Palacios's *La escatologia musulmana en la Divina comedia, seguida de la historia y crítica de una polémica,* 2d ed. (Madrid, 1943), translated by Harold Sunderland as *Islam and the Divine Comedy* (London, 1926), and Enrico Cerulli's *Il "Libro della Scala": La questione delle fonti arabo-spagnole della Divina Commedia* (Vatican City, 1949) and *Nuove ricerche sul "Libro della Scala" e la conoscenza dell'Islam in Occidente* (Vatican City, 1972).

A good survey of the most important medieval visions and apocalypses is given in Jacques Le Goff's *La naissance du Purgatoire* (Paris, 1981).

On the Renaissance theory of the spiritual vehicle of the soul from Ficino to Campanella, the best book remains Daniel P. Walker's *Spiritual and Demonic Magic: From Ficino to Campanella* (London, 1958). It should be supplemented by my article "Magia spirituale e magia demonica nel Rinascimento," *Biblioteca della Rivista di storia e letteratura religiosa* 17 (1981): 360–408.

14 DESCENT INTO THE UNDERWORLD

Anna-Leena Siikala
Translated from Finnish by Susan Sinisalo

Stories and accounts the world over tell of descents into the underworld. Many traditions include myths and rituals connected with journeys to the other world, journeys undertaken by both human and suprahuman beings. Experiences of such journeys are especially common in the shamanistic traditions, but they are also found in association with various ecstatic religious phenomena within the higher cultures. A visit to the underworld, particularly to the kingdom of the dead, is also one of the central themes in the myths that tell of the deeds of human or divine heroes.

The beliefs concerning descent into an underworld inhabited by the spirits are based in part on a psychological experience in which the soul is believed to leave the body during a state of altered consciousness, such as trance or sleep, or during the visions and hallucinations associated with these states. The actual content of such experiences, however, is determined to a large extent by the cultures and traditional beliefs of the persons undergoing them. They tend to be reinforced by the stories of people who were thought dead but who subsequently recovered. Such stories also conform to cultural models.

THE UNDERWORLD

Beliefs concerning the descent into the underworld are often connected with the concept of a three-layer cosmos, according to which the human world is located midway between the realm of spirits above and the realm of the dead below, the "underworld." [*See* Underworld.] The underworld itself may also be thought of as divided into layers. In certain Asian and Oceanic cultures, for example, the underworld is believed to be divided into as many as nine layers. The Scandinavians too recognized nine levels of the underworld, the lowest of which they called Niflhel. These cosmic levels are often believed to be connected to one another by a cosmic tree or mountain, which is frequently believed to be located in the north. In Inner and North Asia, India, and northern Europe, it is the "center of the world" that is to be found in the north.

The cosmic tree that connects the levels of the cosmos also acts as a path of communication between them. The Vasyugan Khanty and the Scandinavians, for example, believe that it has its roots in the underworld. In the shamanistic tales of Siberia, the opening leading to the underworld is represented as lying at the foot of the cosmic tree, or at the foot of its counterpart, the shaman's tree. The Altaic Turks, on the other hand, locate this opening at the "center of the cosmos," and describe it as a "smoke hole." Many northerly peoples locate the opening to the different cosmic levels in the North Star that shines at the center of the world.

THE REALM OF THE DEAD

In all cultural traditions the most important part of the underworld is the realm of the dead. Most of the traditions describing the descent into the underworld are in fact concerned with visiting the dead. Their realm may be described very differently in different cultures. In the high cultures of the East, and in Central Asia, for instance, it is described as the palace of the prince of death, or as a might dwelling place. In Ancient Scandinavian folklore, it is a great hall, whereas in the Finnish epic it is a large living room. Among the hunting peoples of Siberia, it is conceived of as a yurt village.

It should be noted that not all conceptions of the abode of the dead locate it in the underworld. In some cases it is located in the west, as a kingdom beyond the horizon. In other cases it is conceived of as a kingdom in the sky. According to Germanic and Inuit (Eskimo) beliefs, this heavenly kingdom was the last abode of persons of high rank or persons who had met a violent death in battle. According to the high religions of the Middle and Far East, it was the abode of the innocent and the godly. In these cases, the underworld realm of the dead represents a place where sinners are punished. Despite all this variety in representation, however, many of the concepts surrounding the realm of the dead are astonishingly similar in all parts of the world.

Beliefs in a local opening and road leading to the underworld are common in the cultures of Europe, Asia, West Africa, Melanesia and Polynesia. On the west side of Rarotonga, in the Cook Islands, for instance, one finds the Black Rock, from which the souls of the dead are thought to set off on their journey to the other world. Volcanoes, such as Etna, or caves, such as that of Lough Derg in Ireland, mark the beginning of the road to Hell or Purgatory, as in medieval Christian literature. One of the universal features of such a road to the underworld is darkness. This is why the Yakut shaman has disks representing the sun and moon sewn onto his clothing, to provide light on the route to the other world. The road is also dangerous, fraught with difficulties and preternatural obstacles that only an initiate or a spirit being can overcome. In Finnish folklore, such obstacles include a great eagle, a snake, a fiery pond or waterfall, and a river bristling with swords. Similar obstacles are also found in the mythologies of the Middle East, of classical antiquity, and of the Germanic peoples, and they were also cultivated in the Christian vision literature of the Middle Ages. Traditions familiar in both Asia and Europe tell of a stream surrounding the realm of the dead that must be crossed on a ferry, or by a narrow bridge made dangerous by swords, or speak of a wall surrounding the underworld over which the soul must leap. According to the ancient Germans and the Yakuts of Siberia, the dead had to be equipped either with shoes or a horse to protect them on their difficult journey. Another widespread concept connected with the underworld is that of the beast or dog that guards its gates. Examples include the Greek Kerberos and the Scandinavian Garmr; the Babylonian Nedu, with its lion's head, human hands, and bird's feet; and the Egyptian Ammut, who was the watchdog of the underworld god Osiris and had the body of a lion, the front limbs of a crocodile, and the rear limbs of a hippopotamus.

THE SHAMAN'S JOURNEY TO THE UNDERWORLD

A journey to the underworld under the helpful guidance of the spirits is the cornerstone of the classical shamanism of Siberia and Inner Asia, and corresponding practices connected with the activities of a seer or an ecstatic healer can be found in other parts of the world as well: in South and North America, in Oceania, in the folk religion of Indochina, and among the early ethnic religions of Europe. [*See* Shamanism.] One typical feature of this type of otherworldly journey is the use that the shaman makes of ritual techniques intended to induce ecstasy.

Where there is a belief in an underworld, it is not uncommon for people to have chance experiences of descending into it during sleep or trance. In shamanistic cultures, such spontaneous experiences were interpreted as proof that the spirits had selected a candidate for a future shaman. According to a Nentsy myth, a woodcutter once suddenly found himself on the back of a *minryy* bird, from which he next fell through a hole into the underworld. There he wandered from the dwelling of one spirit to another and had to recognze each in turn. He was then cut into pieces and put together again, after which one of the spirits guided him back to the earth's surface. This experience was taken to be the man's initiation as a shaman, particularly in view of the dissection and reassembling of his body by the spirits.

Chance visions, pains, and torments were interpreted as the shaman's sickness and were taken as signs of a person's candidacy as a shaman. While learning to use the drum and sing the shaman's songs, the candidate withdrew from the normal life of the community, fasted, and sought contact with the spirits. A journey to the underworld, experienced through visions and auditions, was a prerequisite for initiation. The central element of this journey was the experience of rebirth. The reports of such initiation visions prove that the initiate's experiences were shaped by the shamanistic tradition of the community in question. The older shamans would interpret the candidate's experiences in such a way as to channel them toward accepted, traditional patterns. During this initiation period the new shaman became familiar with that part of the spirit world to which he would later journey during his séances.

A number of the peoples of Inner Asia and southern Siberia refer to the shaman's journeying to the underworld as "black." This seems to be a reference to the fact that the underworld contained not only the abodes of the dead but also the dwelling places of various disease-causing or otherwise dangerous spirits. In order to be an accomplished shaman, one had to know the roads leading to these places and be able to recognize their inhabitants. This made it all the more important for a candidate to study the topography of the underworld during his initiation period. In the more northerly regions this study was conducted under the guidance of special spirits, usually the zoomorphic spirits of nature.

RITUAL DESCENT

The ritual descent into the underworld takes place during a shamanistic séance, in the course of which the shaman describes in song the stages of his journey. In northern Siberia and the Arctic regions in particular, the actual transfer to the other world was thought to coincide with the highest point in the shaman's altered state of consciousness and was indicated by loss of external consciousness. The shaman's soul was then thought to have left his body and to be traveling in the other world, in the form of an animal or accompanied by benevolent spirits.

The visit to the underworld was sometimes portrayed through theatrical means. The journey of the "black" shamans of the Altaic Tatars to Erlik Khan, the lord of the underworld, was expressed not only in song but also by means of mime and movement. The shaman would give a detailed description of the stages of his journey and his meeting with Erlik Khan. First he rode southward, climbed the Mountain of Iron, on whose slopes lay the fading bones of unsuccessful shamans, and then descended through a hole into the underworld. He next crossed the sea of the underworld by an extremely narrow and dangerous bridge and arrived at the dwelling of Erlik Khan. At first the lord of the underworld was angry, but as the shaman offered him drink and sacrifices, he became benevolent and promised to fulfill the shaman's wishes. The shaman then returned to earth riding on a goose.

When descending into the underworld, the shaman tried to solve problems that were thought to be caused by the spirits. The reasons for the journey to the underworld thus depended on the sorts of spirits living there and on the way they were thought to influence human life. If an illness was believed to be caused by a loss of soul, it was the shaman's task to fetch the patient's soul from the malevolent spirits who had stolen it. Other typical reasons for descending into the underworld were to acquire knowledge concerning the future, the weather, lost objects, or persons; to meet the spirits who assisted at a birth; to meet the keepers of the game during a period of famine; to escort the soul of a sacrificial animal to its destination; or to accompany the souls of the dead to the underworld. The initiatory vision of the Nganasani shaman Sereptie Djaruoskin reveals that he knew the roads leading from the foot of the shaman's tree to the spirits responsible for every kind of sickness, to the main guardians of the game, and to the spirits who provide protection at births.

If the soul of a dead person should fail to go to the underworld, but instead keep disturbing the peace of the living, the shaman was called upon to play the role of psychopomp. Indeed, among the Nanay (Goldi), the Altaic Turks, and the Nentsy, escorting the soul of the dead to its new abode was one of the shaman's most important tasks. Following a death the Nanay arranged a festival, during which the shaman caught the wandering spirit and placed it on a cushion specially made for the occasion. A big clan memorial festival was then held, and the shaman would escort the soul of the dead to Buni, the clan's own kingdom of the dead. On the way the shaman and the soul in his keeping were assisted by the spirit Buchu, who knew the way, and the bird Koori, who carried the travelers to the underworld on its back. At the séance during which all this took place, the shaman would give expression to the stages of his journey by dramatic means, giving the instructions to the spirits who assisted him and expressing in song his horror and relief over the difficulties along the way. As described at such séances, the road to Buni included eighteen stages that had special names and generally known features. The most difficult task along the journey was crossing the river separating the living from the dead. The shaman could tell when he had reached his destination from strange footmarks, the sound of dogs barking, and other traditional signs.

THE VISIONS OF ASCETICS AND MYSTICS

Visions of descending into the underworld are also part of the mystic traditions of the religions of the Middle East, of Hinduism, Buddhism, and Christianity. The visit in question is usually to the kingdom of the dead, and one of its main themes is the observation of the torment awaiting sinners in the other world and the judgment of souls. One of the earliest records of the judgment of the dead is an Egyptian papyrus of the first century CE, telling how Setne Khamuas, a high priest of Memphis, descended to the halls of Amenti under the guidance of his son Si-Osiris.

The ascetic practices known as *gyō,* practiced by Buddhist priests in Japan, sometimes led to states of trance that included visions of journeys to the underworld. Some of the visions were of an initiatory nature and had structural and thematic similarities to the shamans' visions. In the *Nihon ryōiki,* one reads how a priest called Chikō, while feigning to be dead, found himself accompanied by two messengers on the road to the underworld. The road led westward and finally to a golden palace, the door of which was guarded by two terrible beings. Three times the messengers ordered Chikō to clasp a burning hot pillar so that his flesh was burned and only his bones remained. Three times the spirits put him together again and finally sent him back to earth, ordering him to renounce the sin of envy. In addition to such reports of initiatory trials, the Japanese narratives also contain revelations of the sentences passed by the king of the underworld and the horrors awaiting sinners. One type of narrative, which has parallels in the Chinese tradition, tells of a person descending into the underworld in order to save one of his relatives from the torments of Hell.

Such descriptions of the judgment and punishment of sinners could serve as a moral warning to lead a virtuous life. These themes were also present in the Middle East and were particularly popular in the Christian literature of the Middle Ages. [*See* Judgment of the Dead.] The descriptions of journeys in Hell, Purgatory, and Paradise, one prototype of which is found in the *Apocalypse of Peter* (c. 100–150 CE), repeat beliefs in the world of the dead that are familiar from Judaism, the religions of antiquity, and from the ethnic religions. Dante gave artistic expression to such beliefs in his *Commedia.*

The journeys to the underworld made by the heroes Väinämöinen and Lemminkäinen in Finnish epic poetry are thought to have been inspired by Christian vision literature. They nevertheless lack the emphasis on the punishment awaiting sinners that lies at the heart of European vision literature. Väinämöinen descends to the underworld in the role of a sage, to seek knowledge and incantations. In this respect he is reminiscent of a shaman. A similar journey is made by the Scandinavian god Óðinn (Odin), who is described as having ecstatic powers. The episodes describing Lemminkäinen's journey have counterparts in mythical themes familiar in the Middle East.

THE HERO'S DESCENT INTO THE UNDERWORLD

The journeys to the underworld undertaken by shamans and mystics typically involve visions experienced during trance. There are, however, myths and tales in different parts of the world that tell of journeys to the underworld undertaken by humans or gods without the aid of ecstatic powers. Visiting the underworld was thought to be one of the standard deeds of mythical heroes. The heroes descending into the underworld need not necessarily be human, for we find Ishtar making the journey in the Akkadian myth and Lemminkäinen's mother in the Finnish tradition. The reasons for the descent were many. One of the most popular was the rescue of a relative or loved one who had died young. But the journey could also be undertaken in order to search for immortality, knowledge, or some special favor, to escort the dead to their final resting place, or to receive initiation in the mysteries of the underworld. Here one notices a close parallel to the reasons given for the shaman's journey.

A test of strength between love and death is at the base of the legends and myths in which one left behind in this world follows the beloved or relative "to the land of no return." The best-known representative of this type of narrative is the Orpheus theme, various forms of which are to be found not only in Eurasia but also in North America, Oceania, and Melanesia. In Vergil's version, Orpheus sets off for Hades in search of his wife Eurydice, who has died young. With his songs and his music he is able to relieve the suffering in the underworld and wins the favor of the gods. Eurydice is promised to him on condition that he not turn to look at her on the road up. The impatient Orpheus nevertheless breaks his vow and loses his wife. Greater happiness befalls the heroes of the Polynesians, including the New Zealand Maori, who rescue their loved ones by deceiving the spirits that are trying to prevent their escape. In one Maori narrative, Hutu follows Pane, who has died of love for him, to the underworld. There he entertains the spirits, having them sit on the top of a tree that has been bent over and fastened to the ground by a rope. When Hutu lets go of the rope, the spirits are hurled into the air and he is able to escape with his beloved.

In addition to a spouse or a loved one, the main characters in these tales may also be people who are attached to one another by some other tie. For example, there are stories among the Indians of North America that stress sibling attachment. And among the Tatars of the Sayan steppes, the story is told of Kubaiko, who goes to look for her brother in the kingdom of death ruled by Erlik Khan. After carrying out the superhuman tasks imposed upon her by the princes of death, she receives the body of her brother and brings him back to life with the water of life. The story gives a long description of the state after death and the punishment of sinners. A similar description of Hades is found in the story of Odysseus's journey to the land of the dead.

The related idea of the death and resurrection of a god lies behind certain invigoration rites. There is a myth connected with Akkadian Ishtar and her Sumerian counterpart, Inanna, that describes the descent of the goddess into the underworld to bring her young husband back to life. On her way, Ishtar takes off her clothes and her ornaments as she passes through the gates that lead to Arallu. On reaching her destination she dies, and the earthly vegetation wilts. When the gods sprinkle her with the water of life, she recovers and returns to earth. Tammuz, also mentioned in the poem, is a passive hero whose fate remains obscure. The annual rituals held in honor of him nevertheless contain scenes suggesting that Ishtar descended into the underworld in order to restore him to life, and with him the growth of vegetation.

In some cases a hero penetrates the kingdom of death in order to gain immortality. One of the oldest known examples is the Sumerian myth of Gilgamesh, in which Gilgamesh crosses the waters of death and reaches the land of eternal life. There he finds a plant that preserves youth, but a snake snatches it from him on his return trip and he is forced to accept his mortality. The account of Gilgamesh's journey has been compared to the account of Herakles' visit to Hades. Herakles rises victorious from the underworld, bringing with him the watchdog Kerberos.

The pursuit of immortality is also part of the tradition woven around the Polynesian trickster and culture hero Māui. Māui believed that he could make himself immortal by crawling through the body of his giant grandmother, Hine-nui-te-po. Hine-nui-te-po nevertheless wakes as Māui enters her mouth and, closing her mouth, kills the intruder. This swallowing motif, also found in the story of Jonah and the great fish, is quite common in traditions concerned with initiation, and takes both mythical and ritual forms. It is found in the Finnish folk epic, where the hero and sage Väinämöinen, in search of knowledge, enters the belly of a giant sage who had long been dead.

A further reason for traveling to the underworld may be to overcome the power of hell and rescue those condemned there, as in the medieval apocryphal tradition concerning Christ's victory over hell. Other reasons include the search for some special object, as in the descent of Psyche, or the mere satisfaction of curiosity. In each case the journey is described as being extremely dangerous and difficult, with its success depending on special conditions: the traveler should not eat any food offered him in the underworld, nor should he look back on the return journey, lest he fall under the power of the spirits giving chase from below.

BIBLIOGRAPHY

Bishop, J. G. "The Hero's Descent to the Underworld." In *The Journey to the Other World,* edited by Hilda R. Ellis Davidson, pp. 109–129. Totowa, N.J., 1975.

Blacker, Carmen. "Other World Journeys in Japan." In *The Journey to the Other World,* edited by Hilda R. Ellis Davidson, pp. 42–47. Totowa, N.J., 1975.

Davidson, Hilda R. Ellis. *The Road to Hel: A Study of the Conception of the Dead in Old Norse Literature* (1942). Reprint, Westport, Conn., 1977.

Eliade, Mircea. *Birth and Rebirth* (1958). Reprint, New York, 1975.

Eliade, Mircea. *Shamanism: Archaic Techniques of Ecstasy.* Rev. & enl. ed. New York, 1964.

Hultkrantz, Åke. *The North American Indian Orpheus Tradition: A Contribution to Comparative Religion.* Stockholm, 1957.

Kuusi, Matti, Keith Bosley, and Michael Branch, eds. and trans. *Finnish Folk Poetry: Epic; An Anthology in Finnish and English.* Helsinki, 1977.

Lopatin, Ivan A. *The Cult of the Dead among the Natives of the Amur Basin.* The Hague, 1960.

MacCulloch, J. A. "Descent to Hades (Ethnic)." In *Encyclopaedia of Religion and Ethics,* edited by James Hastings, vol. 4. Edinburgh, 1911.

MacCulloch, J. A., et al., eds. *The Mythology of All Races.* 13 vols. Boston, 1916–1932.

Popov, A. A. "How Sereptie Djaruoskin of the Nganasani (Tavgi Samoyeds) Became a Shaman." In *Popular Beliefs and Folklore Tradition in Siberia,* edited by Vilmos Diószegi, pp. 137–145. Bloomington, Ind., 1968.

Thompson, Stith. *Motif-Index of Folk Literature.* 2d ed., rev. & enl. 6 vols. Bloomington, Ind., 1955–1958.

15 THE JUDGMENT OF THE DEAD

HELMER RINGGREN

In religions where a differentiation is made between the righteous and sinners in the hereafter, the decision to which category to assign each individual can be thought to take place in different ways. Sometimes it is an automatic process, as in the Indian doctrine of *karman*; each individual's deeds in this life determine his status in his next existence. In other cases, it is believed that the deceased has to pass over a narrow bridge; if he is good there is no difficulty, but if he is evil he is thrown down. This idea is found in ancient Iranian religion, and similar beliefs exist among the Algonquin Indians, the Mari (Cheremis) in Russia, and the Bojnang of the island of Sulawesi. Here no god or personal being seems to be involved in the decision. In other cases, however, a court scene is presupposed, with divine or semidivine judges passing on each individual.

ANCIENT NEAR EAST

The evidence from ancient Mesopotamia is scanty. One Assyrian text tells the story of a crown prince descending into the netherworld and appearing before its king, Nergal, who decides that he is to return to life. It seems likely that this text presents the mythical background of an incantation rite, and thus refers only to a decision in the netherworld whether a sick person should die or recover. It does not refer to a regular judgment of the dead. Texts from the sixth century BCE, found at Susa in southwestern Iran, mention some sort of judgment that gives the good some advantage over the wicked, but they hardly represent genuine Babylonian belief; possibly they were influenced by Iranian ideas.

Ancient Egyptian religion is especially known for its concern about life in the hereafter. However, in the Pyramid Texts, the oldest funerary texts at our disposal, there is no reference to a judgment of the dead. Though we find the idea that the king still carries out his earthly function as a judge, he is not said to judge the dead in general. Several tomb inscriptions from the Old Kingdom warn that anyone who violates the tomb will be "judged by the Great God at the place of judgment." But that again is no judgment of the dead. On the other hand, autobiographical texts from the same period express the wish that the author's name "may be good before the Great God." This seems to imply some kind of judgment in the hereafter. The same is true of inscriptions in which the dead person promises to defend anyone who respects his tomb "in the judgment hall of the Great God." But in the *Instruction for Merikare* (early Middle Kingdom) there is a clear passage referring to "the judges who judge the sinner" in the hereafter as not being lenient. Therefore man should remember that he must die, and that after his death his sins will be laid beside him in a heap. Anyone who lives unmindful of the judgment in the hereafter is foolish, but anyone who has not sinned will be like a god in eternal freedom.

A different outlook is reflected in the Coffin Texts. Here magical spells are used to secure various privileges for the deceased in the hereafter. There is also reference to a court of judgment presided over by the earth god Geb, who issues decrees to the benefit of the deceased in the same way as an earthly court might. Gradually it becomes customary to add to the name of the deceased person the epithet *maa kheru*, which denotes him as cleared by the court of an accusation. This title was also given to Osiris, when he had been declared righteous in the court of Geb and had been reinstated in his royal rights (though he was now in the netherworld). As it became customary to identify every dead person with Osiris, he was also certain of being *maa kheru*.

The final result of this development appears in the well-known judgment scene in the *Book of Going Forth by Day*. Chapter 125 describes how the deceased appears before Osiris, the divine judge of the netherworld, who is assisted by forty-two assessors, one for each of the provinces of Egypt. It seems that we are here confronted with two different sets of ideas. According to the text, the deceased addresses the assessors, asserting that he has not committed forty-two specific sins; this is often referred to as the "negative confession." The scene depicted, on the other hand, shows the deceased being led before the judges by Horus; in front of Osiris there is a balance, attended by the god Anubis. On one scale is put the heart of the dead man, on the other a feather, the symbol of the goddess Maat ("truth"). The wise god Thoth takes down the result of the weighing on his scribe's palette. The illustrations always present the scales in perfect equilibrium, indicating that the dead man's life has been in accordance with *maat*, the principle of order and truth. If such is the case, the deceased is declared to be *maa kheru*, "true of voice," that is, acquitted in the court of Osiris. If not, he will be eaten by the "devourer of the dead."

All this seems to imply high moral standards. But in fact this chapter of the *Book of Going Forth by Day* is hardly more than another magic spell, intended to protect the deceased from the perils of the other world. The negative confession is rather an expression of acceptance of the validity of certain moral principles (in the last count, of *maat*) than a real declaration that one is not guilty. In addition, there are also spells to prevent the heart from "standing up against" the deceased (*Book of Going Forth by Day*, chap. 30). Thus there is a tension between moral obligations on the one hand and recourse to magical spells on the other.

INDIA AND CHINA

Ancient Indian religion seems to know King Yama as the judge of the other world. A late Vedic text (*Taittirīya Āraṇyaka* 6.5.13) states that before Yama those who have been faithful to truth and those who have spoken lies will part company. There is no explicit reference to a judgment, but it may be implied. The weighing of good and wicked deeds is referred to in the Brahmanic texts.

This same Yama appears again in the pantheon of Mahāyāna Buddhism. In China he is called Yen-lo or Yen-lo Wang. Together with nine others of Chinese origin ("the Ten Kings") he is believed to be the administrator of the punishments of Hell. It is believed that all men are to meet him after death and be judged with the strictest impartiality. It is supposed that he fixes the hour of dissolution, and that once the decision is made, nothing can alter or postpone it. In Japanese Buddhism he is called Enma-ō.

ANCIENT GREECE AND ROME

In ancient Greece, we find, in Homer and Hesiod, for example, the idea of a shadowy and dreary realm of the dead, called Hades, to which the "souls" of all dead come; but there are also at times the ideas of a miry place where the wicked are punished and of the Elysian Fields, where a few righteous are allowed to enter. But we are not told how it is decided who is going where. Homer says that Minos gives laws to the dead but does not act as judge (*Odyssey* 11.567ff.).

Gradually, however, under the influence of the mystery cults and of the Orphic and Pythagorean movements, the ideas of judgment and retribution were developed. Pythagoras taught a judgment of souls (according to the biography of Iamblichus), and the Orphic judgment is depicted on a vase that shows Aiakos, Triptolemos, and Rhadamanthos as judges.

The ideas of the Orphics and Pythagoreans are reproduced by Pindar and by Plato in some of his dialogues (*Gorgias*, *Apology*, the *Republic*). Usually, the judges are three, Minos, Rhadamanthos, and Aiakos; in the *Apology* Plato adds Triptolemos. They give judgment in a meadow, at the parting of the ways, one of which leads to the Abode of the Blessed, the other to Tartaros.

In *Gorgias* Plato says that in the beginning the dead were sent to the Island of the Blessed or to the punishment in Tartaros; the judgment was pronounced on the day of death, but apparently it was sometimes influenced by the outer appearance of the person in question. Therefore Zeus decreed that souls should be judged naked, without their earthly frame. Punishment could serve for purification and improvement; but there are some evildoers who cannot be saved. Here, in part, Plato is using traditional ideas, possibly Orphic and other; but he may have created the eschatological myth he presents here to illustrate his philosophical ideas.

Such beliefs were probably widespread among the Greeks, as is shown by numerous references to judgment and the fate of souls in Lucian's satires, and by the caricatures of Aristophanes. The classical dramatists rarely mention a judgment of the dead, but there are a few references in Aeschylus, and it figures sporadically in other authors and in grave inscriptions. In Vergil's picture of the underworld, Minos judges certain crimes, and Rhadamanthos is judge in Tartaros (*Aeneid* 6.426ff., 540ff.).

JUDAISM

The writings of intertestamental Judaism contain occasional references to a judgment of the dead. The scene in the seventh chapter of the *Book of Daniel*, where the Ancient of Days opens the books and passes judgment, is not concerned with individuals, but with the kingdoms of the earth, and it is Israel that stands acquitted. But in chapter 50 of the Ethiopic *Apocalypse of Enoch* there is an explicit mention of judgment, in which the Lord of the Spirits will show himself righteous, sinners will be punished, and the righteous will be saved. Chapter 51 then speaks of the resurrection of the dead, and says that the Chosen One will sit on God's throne, probably as judge. The same idea is found in *2 Esdras* (chapter 7): the earth will give up those who are asleep in it, and the Most High will appear on the seat of judgment. The emphasis here, however, is not on the scene of judgment but on the resurrection, and on the destiny of the righteous and the wicked.

There are occasional references in these scriptures to books in which the deeds of men are recorded, and according to which they will be judged (Ethiopic *Apocalypse of Enoch* 47:3, 90:20), but the context does not mention a final judgment in connection with the resurrection. Thus, the weighing of men's works on a balance is referred to (ibid. 41:1, 61:8) without mentioning the judgment.

CHRISTIANITY

Jesus tells the parable of the last judgment in chapter 25 of the *Gospel of Matthew.* The Son of man is to come and sit on his glorious throne, and all nations will gather before him; he will "separate them as a shepherd separates the sheep from the goats." Those who have acted in love for their neighbors will receive eternal life; those who have not will be sent away into eternal punishment.

Though this description of a final judgment is found only in the *Gospel of Matthew*, it is obvious from other occasional references in the New Testament that the idea was essential in early Christian preaching. Thus, in *Acts* 17:31, "God has fixed a day on which he will judge the world in righteousness by a man whom he has appointed [i.e., Jesus Christ]." In *Acts* 10:42, Christ "is the one ordained by God to be judge of the living and the dead"; in *2 Corinthians* 5:10, "we must all appear before the judgment seat of Christ [or, in *Romans* 14:10, of God], so that each one may receive good or evil, according to what he has done in the body." The last judgment is thus connected with the Parousia, or second coming of Christ.

In the *Gospel of John*, the idea of the judgment has been transformed in a peculiar way. Though it is stated that God the Father "has given all judgment to the Son" (5:22), we learn that one who believes "has eternal life" (here and now) "and does not come into judgment, but has passed from death to life" (5:24). In other words, the outcome of Christ's judgment is decided here and now, according to the belief or unbelief of each one; this should leave no room for a final judgment at the end of time.

The Christian church has placed considerable emphasis on the idea of the final judgment (that is, rather than on the judgment here and now). Both the Apostles' Creed and the Nicene Creed state that Christ "will come again (in glory) to judge the living and the dead."

ISLAM

In the preaching of Muḥammad the imminent day of judgment (*yawm al-dīn*) has a prominent place. Since many of the accompanying motifs correspond to Jewish and Christian ideas (not the least to the preaching of the Syriac church), it seems obvious that he has taken over the idea of judgment from these sources. The day is also referred to as the day of resurrection, the day of decision (Qur'ān, surah 77:13), the day of gathering (64:9), the day of eternity (50:34), and so forth. It is a day of great catastrophes that cause fear and terror on the earth. The judgment is individual. On that day "no soul will be able to help another, for the decision belongs to God" (82:19). Each soul must defend itself (16:112) and cannot bear the load of another (17:15, cf. 16:25); no soul will be able to give satisfaction or to make intercession for another (2:48); no ransom will be accepted (5:36). The works of each man will be documented in an irrefutable way. Books will be produced, in which "everything that they have done, great and small, is recorded" (54:52ff.). "The book will be put (before them), and you will see the sinners fearful at what is in it. . . . It leaves nothing behind, small or great, but it has numbered it. And they shall find all they did present, and your Lord shall not wrong anyone" (18:49). Every man shall find a book wide open: "Read your book! Today you are yourself a reckoner against yourself" (17:13ff.). The idea of books that are opened is found in the Hebrew Bible (*Dn.* 7:10) and in other Jewish literature (see above) in connection with a judgment scene. In addition, it may be that Muḥammad, as a merchant, was familiar with the keeping of accounts.

There is also in the Qur'ān the idea of weighing man's deeds. "We shall set up the just balances . . . so that not one soul shall be wronged anything; even if it be the weight of one grain of mustard-seed we shall produceit; and we know how to reckon" (21:49). "The weighing that day is true; he whose scales are heavy—they are the prosperous, and he whose scales are light—they have lost their souls" (7:8ff.; cf. 23:102 and 101:5ff.). There is here hardly any connection with the Egyptian ideas discussed above; the ideas of Muḥammad seem rather closer to those of the Jewish texts.

In the case of Islam, those who stand the trial will enter Paradise, and those who fail will be thrown into Hell. However, no one belief concerning the fate following judgment of the dead is common to all religious traditions. That fate is determined according to each tradition's conception of what happens after death. Just as the judgment of the dead is conceived in different ways within the different traditions, so too is the ultimate fate of the person who is judged.

[*See also* Afterlife.]

BIBLIOGRAPHY

A cross-cultural collection of sources on this topic is *Le jugement des morts: Égypte ancienne, Assour, Babylone, Israël, Iran, Islam, Inde, Chine, Japon,* "Sources orientales," no. 4 (Paris, 1961). For a treatment of the beliefs about the judgment of the dead in Egyptian religion, see *Die Idee vom Totengericht in der ägyptischen Religion* (Hamburg, 1935) by Joachim Spiegel. See also *The Dawn of Conscience* (New York, 1933), pp. 250ff., by James Henry Breasted. See my *Religions of the Ancient Near East*, translated by John Sturdy (Philadelphia, 1973), pp. 122ff., for a brief treatment of Mesopotamian ideas on the judgment of the dead. Volume 1 of H. C. C. Cavallin's *Life after Death*: *Paul's Argument for the Resurrection of the Dead* (Lund, 1974) treats the topic as it relates to Judaism. Two discussions of Christian beliefs about the judgment of the dead are John A. T. Robinson's *Jesus and His Coming* (New York, 1957) and his article "The Parable of the Sheep and Goats," *New Testament Studies* 2 (May 1956): 225–237. The only monograph on Greek ideas about judgment is in Latin: *De mortuorum iudicio* (Giessen, 1903) by Ludwig Ruhl. See also Fritz Graf's *Eleusis und die orphische Dichtung Athens in vorhellenistischer Zeit* (Berlin, 1974), pp. 79–150, and Franz Cumont's *After Life in Roman*

Paganism (1922; reprint, New York, 1959). On Plato's treatment of the topic, see *Les mythes de Platon* (Paris, 1930) by Perceval Frutiger. Two studies of the Iranian view are *The Zoroastrian Doctrine of a Future Life* (New York, 1926) by J. D. C. Pavry, and R. C. Zaehner's *The Teachings of the Magi* (New York, 1956), pp. 131ff. Arthur Berriedale Keith's *Indian Mythology* (Boston, 1917), pp. 159ff., and Bimala Churn Law's *Heaven and Hell in Buddhist Perspective* (1925; reprint, Varanasi, 1973), pp. 96ff., present Indian and Buddhist ideas of judgment.

16 TRANS-MIGRATION

R. J. Zwi Werblowsky

Transmigration denotes the process by which, after death, either a spiritual or an ethereal, subtle, and thinly material part of the personality, having left the body that it previously inhabited, "migrates" and enters (i.e., is reborn in) another body (human or animal) or another form of being (plant or even inanimate object). Other terms often used in this context are *rebirth* (especially in connection with Indian religions), *palingenesis* (from Greek *palin,* "again," and *genesis*), and *metempsychosis* (from Greek *meta,* "again," and *psuchē,* "soul"), although *metensomatosis* (from Greek *sōma,* "body"; cf. Latin *reincarnatio*) would be a more correct expression for the passage of the soul into another body. Manichaean texts in Syriac use the expression *tašpikha* or *tašpikha denafshatha,* corresponding to Greek *metaggismos* (from *metaggizesthai;* cf. Latin *transfundi*) and conveying the underlying notion of a transfusion or change of vessel whereby the soul is "poured" from one body into another. The Latin church father Augustine in his anti-Manichaean writings also uses the noun *revolutiones* and the verb *revolvi,* which happen to be identical with the later qabbalistic technical term *gilgul:* the soul "revolves" (i.e., rotates) through successive bodies. Earlier qabbalistic terms were *sod-ha-ʿibbur* ("the mystery of transition") and *haʿtaqah* ("displacing, changing place"), the latter equivalent to the Arabic *tanāsukh.*

All forms of belief in transmigration (with the exception of Buddhism, which I shall discuss below) presuppose some form of animism. Without implying commitment to all the theories of E. B. Tylor, it is obvious that the notion of a nonphysical entity (soul, or *anima*) existing separately from the physical body is assumed by all beliefs that posit an afterlife. The detailed elaboration of any one culture's views of afterlife and transmigration depends on the anthropology and psychology (i.e., the doctrines and beliefs concerning the nature of man) that culture holds, explicitly or implicitly. Thus the word *soul* may mean the whole man minus the body or a special substance or collection of substances nonphysical in nature. In the former case it is the whole albeit disincarnate man that survives (and goes on, for example, to the underworld, the land of the dead); in the latter case it is a specific soul-substance that persists and returns to its ancestral or heavenly home or haunts the living or is reborn. Many belief systems, especially among primitive societies, know of multiple souls (Tylor himself quoted many examples), but the idea is also not uncommon in more developed civilizations; examples include the *ba* and *ka* of the ancient Egyptians, the gnostic *psuchē* and *pneuma,* and the fivefold division current among Jewish qabbalists *(nefesh, ruaḥ, neshamah, ḥayyah, yeḥidah).*

ORIGIN OF CONCEPT

The doctrine of transmigration has diverse origins, explanations, and functions. The concept may have arisen in connection with the primitive view of the repetitive, cyclical nature of existence or the view that the ancestors continue to live in their descendants. It may have arisen from the assumption that disincarnate ("naked") souls seek to clothe themselves with, and unite themselves to, a physical body, a notion that relates back to the subject of animism and the attribution of souls to inanimate objects. One important function of the doctrine of transmigration is to explain the character traits (e.g., cruelty or avarice) of a particular individual by considering him as the reincarnation of a deceased person who had similar traits. There is also an inverted characterology. When transmigration is considered not merely as punishment but as another chance to accumulate more merits, atone for past sins, and fulfill one's destiny, then character traits can be interpreted as reparation for shortcomings in a previous existence. A pious man, conspicuous for his compassion, charity, and generosity, is obviously a soul that returned to this earth to make amends for his cruelty and avarice in a previous existence. Moreover, belief in transmigration provides a theodicy, an explanation of apparent injustice in the order of things. Why is one man rich and blessed, another poor and pursued by misfortune? Why is one man born a brahman or prince, another a low-caste or an outcaste? The explanation is that every man reaps the fruits of his actions in previous existences. This may be the doing and judgment of a personal god, or (as in the Hindu tradition) the automatic result of karmic causality. In fact, the doctrine of *karman* is, in Max Weber's words, the "most consistent theodicy ever produced by history."

HISTORICAL CROSS-CULTURAL OVERVIEW

The acceptance of the belief in some form of transmigration or return of the dead person to terrestrial life is a fairly general concept that is evident in many cultures. Monotheistic faith systems, however, have generally rejected this concept.

Primitive Religions. There is little evidence of belief in transmigration in most nonliterate societies to the extent that they have been reliably and systematically studied by ethnologists. In many cases the evidence is conflicting; material on the Australian Aranda (Arunta) by Baldwin Spencer and F. J. Gillen, for example, has been subsequently challenged by Carl Strehlow. George Grey, to give another example, reported *(Journals of Two Expeditions of Discovery in North-Western and Western Australia,* London, 1841) how he was welcomed in the bush by an Aborigine family as their son, adding that "this belief, that white people are the souls of departed blacks is by no means an uncommon superstition among them." Yet definitive evidence for such beliefs is lacking, and the interpretation of available evidence (e.g., regarding burial customs) is uncertain. If in some Australian tribes a woman who wants to bear children visits or worships at a site inhabited by (or otherwise associated with) the ancestors, this is not proof of primitive ignorance regarding the process of procreation (as was thought at one time by adherents of the theory of primitive or prelogical mentality). Rather, it is indicative of a certain worldview regarding the relationship of new generations to the ancestors. Although theories put forth about prehistoric religions are purely speculative and should, in any case, never confuse that category with primitive religions, it may be mentioned here that archaeological evidence of burial sites (especially those in which bodies are found in "contracted burial," the knees of the skeleton touching the chin in an embryolike position) does not warrant any conclusions regarding belief in transmigration or rebirth.

Germanic and Celtic Religions. The pre-Christian beliefs of these religions provide little solid evidence of a general acceptance of the notion of transmigration. The indications are too vague and scattered to permit definite assertions about Germanic religions. Julius Caesar's statement (*Gallic Wars* 6.14) that the druids possessed teachings concerning transmigration (see also Diodorus Siculus, 5.28) is very definite, but the subject remains doubtful in the absence of supporting evidence. The same also applies to the vague, inconclusive hints contained in Irish and Welsh epics and romances.

Egyptian Religion. The ancient Greeks considered Egypt to be the source of the belief in transmigration, but there is general agreement that the account of Herodotus (2.123) is mistaken. The Egyptian *Book of Going Forth by Day* seems to assume that certain privileged souls could transform themselves into animals (e.g., phoenix, heron, or crocodile), but this is a far cry from a general doctrine of transmigration.

Greek Religion. As the account of Herodotus suggests, the idea of transmigration was not unknown in ancient Greece. However, in ancient Greece, transmigration was but one doctrine among many, and a rather insignificant one at that. As a rule the souls of the departed were thought to descend into the underworld (Hades), though mythology and legend told of exceptional figures who were translated to the sky (e.g., as stars) or to the Elysian Fields, or otherwise transformed. The origin of the belief in transmigration in Greece is obscure. It may have evolved from certain ancient layers of primitive Greek religion. Sometimes the belief appears to be connected with the god Dionysos and thence with Orphism.

It is to the Orphic tradition that Plato and others appeal when expounding certain ideas concerning the fate and destiny of the soul, including the assertion that the physical body is the "prison of the soul" and that the latter can achieve liberation and salvation by an ascetic way of life. Here we seem to be on safer ground, provided we mean by "Orphic" not a definite body of doctrine but "a floating mass of popular belief" (William K. Guthrie), to be gleaned from, for example, Empedocles, certain passages in Pindar, and above all Plato. Once the soul is considered a distinct spiritual entity, temporarily imprisoned in a body, transmigration becomes an obvious possibility. One "Orphic" tablet reports the soul saying "I have flown out of the sorrowful weary wheel" (cited in Jane Harrison, *Prolegomena to Greek Religion,* 1976, p. 669)—a sentence that could equally well have been uttered by a Hindu soul that had escaped the wheel of *saṃsāra* and attained *mokṣa.* (On the "sorrowful cycle," see also William K. Guthrie, *The Greeks and Their Gods,* 1955, p. 323).

Greek tradition is unanimous in ascribing the doctrine of transmigration to Pythagoras (sixth century BCE), who, however, is mythologically related to Apollo rather than to Dionysos. Pythagoras (whose authority was also invoked by the medieval Jewish qabbalists, on the basis of their acquaintance with Neoplatonic texts) was even credited with remembering previous incarnations (his own and those of others)—a feat that Buddhism reserves for the possessors of the highest supernatural attainments. His contemporary Xenophanes pokes fun at him by telling a story according to which Pythagoras once cried out to someone, "Stop beating that dog—I recognize him by his voice as a friend of mine." The sources of Pythagoras may have been purely Greek; there is no convincing evidence of Indian influence, though the latter cannot be excluded.

Xenophanes' story about Pythagoras has been told here with a purpose, for it illustrates how belief in the transmigration into animals can also lead to an ascetic discipline that requires vegetarianism. Indeed, many Neoplatonic and gnostic sects (e.g., the Manichaeans and their successors) enjoined vegetarianism not only as an ascetic practice but because of the belief that animal bodies might be inhabited by human souls. The more extreme view that the same might also be true of fruits and vegetables caused some Manichaean saints not to cut up vegetables themselves but to have this service performed by lower-ranking believers. (The qabbalists had it the other way round: a soul "exiled" into an animal body could be redeemed and liberated if the animal was ritually slaughtered and eaten, piously and with the appropriate mystical intentions, by the qabbalist saints.) The Orphic tradition concerning transmigration became "canonical" after it passed into the writings of Plato (cf. *Phaedrus* 248f. and *Cratylus* 400c, where it is explicitly attributed to the Orphics; also *Meno, Timaeus, Laws,* and especially the great myth at the end of the *Republic*). From Plato this tradition passed into Neoplatonic and gnostic systems, and from there into medieval literature. The notion of transmigration does not seem to have played any role in Rome, though it is mentioned by Vergil (*Aeneid* 6.748).

Connected to the Greek notion of transmigration are the theories of preexistence, asceticism, and liberation. The Orphic-Platonic-Neoplatonic system implies several presuppositions. The one is the preexistence of the soul that enters a body (at birth or at conception) and leaves it (at death), much as a body might put on a coat and then shed it again. Another is the notion that the pure, spiritual soul is imprisoned in gross bodily matter in this lower world from which it has to be liberated: "The body is a prison" (or "a tomb"), as the popular Orphic proverb put it. The way to liberation from the weary round of rebirths is the purification of the soul of base lusts, desires, pollution, vice, sin, and so forth. Hence also the ascetic emphasis (which, of course, can also assert itself without the doctrine of transmigration, wherever the soul is supposed to aspire to immortal bliss or to a higher spiritual sphere).

When the soul is considered not to be timeless but to have a natural beginning (e.g., Aristotle) or to have been created by God (e.g., at the moment of conception, as in traditional Christian belief), then it should logically also have a natural end. The eternity and immortality of a soul that has a beginning in time is therefore a problem for philosophy as well as theology, but neither the solutions proposed for this particular problem nor the cosmological details relating to the doctrine of transmigration (is the soul reincarnated at once? where does it bide its time between one earthly life and the next?) are within the scope of this article. Suffice it to indicate here that belief in a resurrection of the body as the ultimate eschatological goal constitutes not only a rejection of the Orphic-Neoplatonic conception of man but also (theoretically, though not *de facto* in all religious systems) a denial of the doctrine of transmigration, since it views the human being as a body-soul unity and the person as an individual (in the literal sense, from "indivisible").

Western Monotheistic Religions. In the monotheistic religions originating in the western part of the ancient world, the concept of transmigration is generally absent. It is a doctrine unknown in classical (biblical and rabbinic) Judaism. The first reference to Jewish sectarians holding such views is found in the writings of the philosopher-theologian Sa'adyah Gaon (Babylonia, tenth century), but these probably percolated into Oriental Jewry from sectarian Muslim sources. The doctrine reappeared with the rise and development of Qabbalah in twelfth-century Provence, precisely at the time and place where the same belief also flourished among the so-called Christian heretics. In the latter case the belief is almost certainly derived from traditions that were ultimately Manichaean. Since the thirteenth century the notion of *gilgul* has been a central qabbalistic tenet. There were differences of opinion as to the number of possible reincarnations (a maximum of three, or more) and whether transmigration was into human bodies only or also into animals, plants, or even inanimate objects.

Orthodox Christianity in all its forms rejects the notion of transmigration as incompatible with Christian anthropology (i.e., the interpretation of the nature of man), with belief in hell (and/or purgatory) and paradise, and above all with the doctrine of redeeming grace as made available to man by Christ's sacrifice. The soul is not preexistent but created by God (as noted in the papal encyclical *Humani generis,* 1950), and man consists of two substances, soul and body ("Homo constat ex duabus substantiis, animae scilicet et corporis"), which are joined together once only before the general resurrection.

Nevertheless, at certain periods and in certain circles interest in the doctrine of transmigration was evident, especially during the Renaissance (as a result of the ascendant Neoplatonic influence). Post-Enlightenment thinkers as well as Romantics (Kant, Lessing, Lichtenberg, Lavater, Herder, Goethe, Schopenhauer) were not impervious to the attractions of this notion, though in the nineteenth century Indian influence demonstrably played a major role. Modern spiritualism, though its beginnings were in America, drew on Indian philosophy and on what was held to be the occult "wisdom of the East" in its subsequent theoretical elaboration in Europe (by, for example, Allan Kardec) as also in its Theosophical development and the latter's Anthroposophical offspring.

Like normative Judaism and Christianity, normative Sunnī Islam rejects the idea of transmigration. However, certain gnosticizing and mystical circles acceded to the notion of transmigration and rebirth. The notion of reincarnation as a valid philosophy is evident in "heretical" sects with esoteric, gnostic teachings, for instance the Nuṣayrīyah and the Druze.

Far East. Neither Japanese Shintō nor indigenous, pre-Buddhist Chinese traditions knew of metempsychosis, though spirit possessions (and their exorcism) were not unknown.

Manichaeism. In the Manichaeian belief system, the prevalent notion of transmigration is generally considered to have been influenced by the corresponding concept in the Indian religious system. Whereas the Indian connections of Pythagorean doctrines are doubtful, there seems to be better evidence of Indian influence on the

Manichaean system, since there is little reason to doubt the information given by such witnesses as the tenth-century Arab scholar and traveler al-Bīrūnī (see E. S. Sachau's *Alberuni's India,* 1910, vol. 1, p. 54). According to the Manichaeans, those who lived in a worldly state or married had to be reborn in the body. (Again, for the qabbalists everything was the other way around: to have remained childless was sufficient reason for the soul to be sent back into this world in order to make amends where it had failed in its duty toward God and the cosmos.) The best future that could befall such souls was to be incarnated as food ("in cucumbers and melons," as Augustine puts it with somewhat savage humor) and to be eaten by the Manichaean saints—a process that would translate them to their final goal of bliss.

India. The notion of transmigration and reincarnation is a pivotal aspect of the general socioreligious belief system in India. In the Hindu religious tradition, the concept of transmigration is a vital aspect of the cultural milieu and has played a dominant role in shaping the actions, ethics, and ideologies of the people. Thus, the Indian subcontinent and the cultures influenced by it are dominated by the notion of *saṃsāra,* "what turns around forever," the wheel of birth and death. Whereas in the West the idea of transmigration was always felt to be something exotic, strange, and at any rate requiring special justification, in India it came to be an accepted presupposition of life, illustrating if anything Clifford Geertz's description (in "Religion as a Cultural System," in *The Interpretation of Cultures,* London, 1975, p. 90) of "conceptions of a general order of existence . . . clothed with such an aura of factuality that the modes and motivations seem uniquely realistic."

The history and development of this notion are not yet quite clear, and scholars are at variance regarding the role of possible influences of the more popular levels of the religion of the Aryan invaders and those of the native, pre-Aryan religions. There is consensus that the weary round of *saṃsāra* is not yet part of Vedic religion. The notion seems to have evolved in the post-Vedic Āraṇyaka literature (i.e., books written by forest recluses) and developed more fully in the Upaniṣads, where it is presented as new (e.g., by Yājñavalkya in *Bṛhadāraṇyaka Upaniṣad*). There it is part of the growing interest in the question of the essential and real "self" of man, the *ātman.* The fact that the notion was taken for granted, and made the basis of their respective doctrines of salvation, by Jainism and Buddhism suggests that by the sixth century BCE it was already widespread in India. Among the presuppositions of this doctrine is the notion that space and time are endless. The identity of the self depends on (moral) karmic determinants. Life is an unending, eternal, weary round of suffering, governed by an automatic causality of reward and punishment *(karman)* that takes the soul from one existence to another through all six spheres of being, from that of the gods to that of "hungry spirits" and demons.

In Indian religious sensibility the emphasis is not so much on the duality "life and death" as on "birth and dying." The problem about rebirth is that of necessity it also implies "re-dying," that is, death recurring *ad infinitum,* unless man succeeds in escaping from the vicious circle of *saṃsāra* (also depicted iconically as the monstrous wheel of unending existences, the *bhavacakra,* and described very graphically in the Buddhist Avadāna and Nidāna literature) into ultimate liberation (Hindu *mokṣa,* Buddhist *nirvāṇa*). It should be emphasized that the ultimate goal *(artha)* is release and escape; the heavens *(svarga)* are still part of the samsaric world. Doctrinal differences of opinion relate to the method of liberation (yoga, mortifications, the "middle path") as well as to the precise definition of the liberated state.

The descriptions in the *Bṛhadāraṇyaka Upaniṣad* 6.12.15f. (cf. also *Kauṣītaki Upaniṣad* and *Muṇḍaka Upaniṣad*) still exhibit a somewhat mythological character. Those who have achieved perfection and have realized their true self go, after death, the "way of the sun," namely, the path of the gods *(devayāna):* they enter the abode of *brahman (brahmaloka)* never to return again. Those who have not achieved ultimate self-realization but have lived a life of sinless piety and devotion (through sacrifices, penance, and charity) go along the path of the ancestors *(pitṛyāna)* to the world of the moon where they become rain and subsequently food: "Gods feed on them, and when that passes away from them, they start on their return journey to be reborn as human beings. . . . Thus do they rotate." Evildoers are reborn as insects and vermin. According to the *Chāndogya Upaniṣad* 5.10.7 they are reborn as dogs and pigs. As has been noted above, heaven too is part of the samsaric cycle, and hence gods too are reborn, even as human beings can be reborn as *deva*s, to be subsequently reborn once again.

What or who exactly is it that is reborn? Unorthodox ṣramanic teachings as well as Upaniṣadic speculation provide a varied technical vocabulary *(ātman, jīva, puruṣa)* to deal with the questions of empirical ego, real self, and so forth. Some systems of thought conceive also of spiritual entities in terms of a subtle, ethereal matter; one such example in Western history would be the Stoics.

Jainism. In the Jain system, the living entity is called *jīva* ("soul" or "life"), and it is doomed to unending rebirths as long as it is covered and encumbered (as if by a thinner or thicker film) by *karman,* which is conceived as a kind of fine matter. The generation of new *karman* must be stopped, and the accumulated *karman* already present must be removed if liberation is to be achieved. That such liberation can be achieved is demonstrated by the line of *jina*s (lit., "conquerors").

Buddhism. The Buddha is sometimes called the "world conqueror," precisely because he is a "world renouncer." The very special and fascinating problem of Buddhist doctrine concerning karmic rebirth arises from the fact that Buddhism denies the existence of an *ātman*—that is, self, or ego-substance beyond the empirical ego, which is a transitory combination of "heaps" of "elements" (*skandha*s). Regardless of whether the anti-Brahmanic doctrine of *anātman* ("no-self") was already explicitly taught by the Buddha himself or was developed later, it is clearly a central concept of historical Buddhism.

If one denies the presence of an individual self, or *ātman,* yet shares the general Indian belief in rebirth, the question inevitably arises as to what it is exactly that survives to be reincarnated, that suffers rebirth, and that seeks release in *nirvāṇa* from the wheel of *saṃsāra.* The ways in which the various Buddhist schools deal with this problem need not detain us here. Suffice it to say that it is assumed that even after the dissolution of the combination of changing elements that constitute the empirical human organism and consciousness, some kind of substratum remains to become the point of crystallization for a new set of mental states (i.e., a new existence). Strictly speaking, therefore, the terms *transmigration* and *reincarnation* are not very good renderings of the Buddhist (as distinct from the Hindu or Jain) notion of *saṃsāra;* G. R. Welbon's phrase "birth-and-death-in-sequence" would be a more adequate rendering. The last thoughts before death determine the nature of rebirth: at death the "fundamental thought" is transformed into "emigrating thought," which, in turn, determines the "rebirth thought," the nucleus of a new existence.

Tibet. The application of the doctrine of rebirth in Tibet, a culture decisively shaped by one particular form of Buddhism, deserves special mention because of its relevance to the social system and its political institutions. Transfer of authority is a problem in every social system, and various techniques and mechanisms are devised to regulate it (elections, rules of hereditary succession, etc.). When the highest bearers of spiritual and/or temporal authority are bound to celibacy, hereditary succession from father to son is obviously impossible. The Tibetan system of harnessing the belief in transmigration to the mechanism of succession is unique. Competent sages identify incarnations of a high order (*tulkus*) by determining into which newborn baby a recently deceased personage has passed. The succession of Dalai Lamas and Panchen Lamas (the former representing successive incarnations of Avalokiteśvara, the latter those of Amitābha) is assured by this method.

[*See also* Reincarnation *and* Soul.]

BIBLIOGRAPHY

A good general overview of the topic is found is S. G. F. Brandon's *Man and His Destiny in the Great Religions* (Manchester, 1962) and his *History, Time, and Deity* (Manchester, 1965). Much valuable information can be found in the standard encyclopedias and history of religions texts.

For ancient Greece, one should consult, with the help of the index, Martin P. Nilsson's *A History of Greek Religion* (Oxford, 1949); Erwin Rohde's *Psyche: The Cult of Souls and Belief in Immortality among the Greeks* (1925; reprint, London, 1950); Walter Stettner's *Die Seelenwanderung bei Griechen und Römern* (Stuttgart, 1933); and H. S. Lowy's *A Study of the Doctrine of Metempsychosis in Greece from Pythagoras to Plato* (Princeton, 1948). For Manichaeism, see A. V. Williams Jackson's "The Doctrine of Metempsychosis in Manichaeism," *Journal of the American Oriental Society* 45 (1925): 246–268, and Charles R. C. Allberry's "Symbole von Tod und Wiedergeburt im Manichäismus," *Eranos-Jahrbuch* 7 (1939): 113–149. The best survey of the qabbalistic doctrines is Gershom Scholem's "Gilgul: Seelenwanderung und Sympathie der Seelen," in his *Von der mystischen Gestalt der Gottheit* (Zurich, 1962), chap. 5, and "Gilgul," in his *Kabbalah* (Jerusalem, 1974), pp. 344–350. The Christian (Protestant) position is brought out clearly in Alfred Bertholet's *The Transmigration of Souls* (London, 1909). For Islam, see "Tanāsukh" by Bernard Carra de Vaux in *The Encyclopaedia of Islam* (Leiden, 1913–1938) as well as "Die Lehre von der Reinkarnation im Islam" by Ernst Ludwig Dietrich, in *Zeitschrift für Religions- und Geistesgeschichte* 9 (1957): 129–149. Volume 9 of *Zeitschrift für Religions- und Geistesgeschichte* also contains an interesting article by Ernst Benz on "Die Reinkarnationslehre in Dichtung und Philosophie der deutschen Klassik und Romantik," pp. 150–175. On India, see Louis Renou's *Religions of Ancient India* (London, 1953) and Helmuth von Glasenapp's *Unsterblichkeit und Erlösung in den indischen Religionen* (Halle, 1938). A modern Hindu exposition is Sarvepalli Radhakrishnan's introduction to his *The Brahma Sūtra: The Philosophy of Spiritual Life* (New York, 1960), and a good scholarly discussion is Ninian Smart's *Doctrine and Argument in Indian Philosophy* (London, 1964). See also the volume edited by Joseph Head and S. L. Cranston, *Reincarnation: An East-West Anthology* (New York, 1961). On Tibet, see Franz Michael and Eugene Knez's *Rule by Incarnation* (Boulder, 1982). An example of the adoption of the doctrine of transmigration by modern Western occultist thinkers is Rudolf Steiner's *Reinkarnation und Karma* (Berlin, 1919).

17 REINCARNATION

J. Bruce Long

The doctrine of reincarnation concerns the rebirth of the soul or self in a series of physical or preternatural embodiments, which are customarily human or animal in nature but are in some instances divine, angelic, demonic, vegetative, or astrological (i.e., are associated with the sun, moon, stars, or planets). The concept of rebirth may also be expressed in such terms as *metempsuchōsis* (or more accurately, *metensōmatōsis,* "passage from one body to another") and *palingenesis* (Gr., lit., "to begin again").

The belief in rebirth in one form or another is found in tribal or nonliterate cultures all over the world. The notion is most dramatically evident in the native societies of central Australia and West Africa, where it is intimately associated with the cult of ancestor worship.

It is in ancient India and Greece, however, that the doctrine of rebirth has been most elaborately developed. In India, the precept is linked inextricably with the teachings and practices of Hinduism, Buddhism, Jainism, Sikhism (a hybrid synthesis of Hinduism and Islam founded in the fifteenth century by Gurū Nānak), and Sufism (the mystical branch of Islam); it even figures in the writings of such modern thinkers as Ramakrishna and Aurobindo. In ancient Greece, the idea is identified primarily with the philosophical lineages of Pythagoras, Empedocles, Plato, and Plotinus.

The doctrine of rebirth can also be found in certain ancient Near Eastern religions, for example, the royal cultus of the pharoahs in ancient Egypt and the mystery cult of Orpheus in second-century Greece. It is found in the teachings of Manichaeism, a third-century CE Persian religion founded by the prophet Mani. The concept of reincarnation also figures in such modern schools of thought as the Theosophy of H. P. Blavatsky and Annie Besant and the humanistic psychology of thinkers like C. G. Jung and Fritz Perls; it appears also in the "perennial philosophy" of Aldous Huxley.

ARCHAIC CULTURES

That the belief in reincarnation is of great antiquity in the history of the human species is suggested by the existence of the idea at the core of the belief systems of numerous nonliterate ethnic groups scattered throughout various parts of the world.

It is also suggested by the fact that some archaic peoples whose physical culture (domestic architecture, implements of livelihood, etc.) is of an extremely primitive nature (e.g., the Arunta, or Aranda, people who originally inhabited the wastelands of central Australia and who may be classified as a Stone Age society) espouse the ideas of preexistence and reincarnation, which may indicate that this belief arose contemporaneously with the origins of human culture per se.

It is particularly significant that a belief in reincarnation in some form or another is to be found in nonliterate cultures all over the world. Other primary cultural areas (besides central Australia) in which this precept is noticeably present are West Africa (among the Ewe, Edo, Igbo, and Yoruba), southern Africa (among the Bantu-speakers and the Zulu), Indonesia, Oceania, New Guinea, and both North and South America (among selected ethnic groups).

In sub-Saharan Africa, for example, reincarnation is not only viewed positively, but failure to be reborn and thereby gain yet another opportunity to improve the world of the living is regarded as an evil (as is the state of childlessness). Weighty emphasis is placed upon fertility rites and the efficacious powers of the shaman to promote the production of offspring (i.e., the rebirth of the ancestral spirits).

Among the Yoruba and Edo peoples, the belief in the rebirth of the departed ancestors remains a strong and vibrant cultural force to the present day. It is their custom to name each boy child "Father Has Returned" and each girl child "Mother Has Returned." The Zulu hold that the spirit of each person undergoes numerous rebirths in the bodies of various beasts, which range in size from tiny insects to huge elephants, until at long last the spirit enters a human body where it is fated to undergo yet another birth. Finally, after reaching the pinnacle of human existence, the soul is united with the supreme spirit from which it originated in the beginning. Here, as in other archaic cultures, the belief in reincarnation is linked directly with the veneration of ancestors, for it is the spirits of deceased ancestors that return in one or another life-form in association with the various totemic groups that form the organizational structure of the society.

For the Australian Aborigines, it is axiomatic that the spirits of human beings are periodically incarnated in animal or plant forms or even in such inanimate entities as water, fire, and wind, or the sun, moon, and stars. This belief is based upon the presupposition that the soul is separable from the body and from any other physical object it may inhabit. By virtue of its capacity to survive independently of a physical abode for at least a brief time, the soul possesses the capacity to travel from body to body and to inhabit a variety of forms ranging from stones and insects to animals and human beings. Because of the centrality of the totemic clan in Aboriginal religion, it was of utmost importance to establish the precise identity of the ancestor being reborn in each instance.

According to Australian Aboriginal religious beliefs, a deceased ancestor, after a sojourn of an unspecified length of time in the land of the dead, returns to the world of the living by entering the body of a mother at the moment of conception. The father is believed to play no direct role in impregnating the mother. Instead, the mother-to-be conceives new life by coming into the proximity of an *oknanikilla,* or local totem center, in which a spirit being *(alcheringa)* or soul of a deceased ancestor is lying in wait to be reborn.

Women who desire children travel to a sacred totem center with the intention of conceiving. The Aborigines also believe that if a woman happens to walk in the revered spots where the *alcheringa* ancestors are located, she will become impregnated without their intending it, even against their will. It is also commonly believed that when a woman conceives a child at a site sacred to a particular clan or totemic group (say, for example, the lizard totem), then that child will belong to the clan identified with the place of conception rather than with the clan of its parents. Thus, clan connections outweigh blood-relationships in cultural significance.

HINDUISM

The whole of the Hindu ethical code laid down in the ancient law books (e.g., *Laws of Manu*) presupposes the survival of the soul after death and assumes that the present life is fundamentally a preparation for the life to come. According to the Hindu conception of transmigration or rebirth (*saṃsāra,* "a course or succession of states of existence"), the circumstances of any given lifetime are automatically determined by the net results of good and evil actions in previous existences. This, in short, is the law of *karman* (action), a universal law of nature that works according to its own inherent necessity. [*See* Karman.] Reward and punishment are thus not decreed by a god or gods nor by any other supernatural personage. It is a person's own actions, in conformity to the moral and cosmic law *(dharma),* that is determinative. The law of *karman* finds synoptic expression in the Upaniṣadic assertion: "By good deeds one becomes good, by evil, evil."

As early as the Upaniṣads human destinies are assigned to two divergent pathways: the pathway of the ancestors (*pitṛ*s), which is traversed by those persons who follow worldly pursuits, and the pathway of the gods (*deva*s), which is taken by those who meditate with faith and austerity in the forest (*Chāndogya Upaniṣad* 4.15.5, 5.10.1–10). The former path leads to rebirth; the latter, toward brahman and liberation. After the "worldling" has resided in the postmortem realm until the effects of his previous deeds has been consumed, he returns along the same route by which he departed the world to be reborn. By contrast, those who depart by the pathway of the gods reach *brahman,* the Ultimate, and are released from the rule of *saṃsāra* forever. For them, say the scriptures, there is no returning.

The *Bhagavadgītā,* one of the most highly revered texts of Hinduism, asserts that the eternal self *(ātman)* is unaffected even to the slightest degree by the vicissitudes of finite existence. According to this text, the universal soul, or self, in its essential nature neither comes to be nor passes away, for "of the nonexistent there is no coming to be; of the existent, there is no coming not to be" (2.11–25). It is rather the body *(śarīra)* or the embodied form *(jīva)* of the self that is subject to the changing conditions of life: creation and destruction, good and evil, victory and defeat. As the eternal, unchanging, and imperishable spiritual essence of humanity, the self is invincible to alteration of any sort, whether on this side of eternity or beyond.

The succession of finite births has traditionally been regarded by Hindus pessimistically, as an existential misfortune and not as a series of "second chances" to improve one's lot, as it is often viewed in the West. Life is regarded not only as "rough, brutish, and short" but as filled with misery *(duḥkha).* Thus, the multiplication of births within this "vale of tears" merely augments and intensifies the suffering that is the lot of all creatures. Furthermore, this painful existence continues unabated until such time as a person experiences spiritual liberation *(mokṣa,* or *mukti).* [*See* Mokṣa.]

The root cause of this existential bondage to time, ignorance, and suffering is desire *(taṇhā),* or avaricious attachment to objects that at best bring only limited, and often debased, pleasure. Even the life of a deity *(deva)* is governed by the law of death and rebirth. Hence, a person's only hope of escaping the clutches of rebirth is through extinguishing all desires except the desire for perfect unification with the universal self *(brahman).* The empirical self of the liberated person "goes to the *brahman* and becomes the *brahman.*" As a result, he is free from the effects of all actions, both good and evil, and from any subsequent participation in existences determined by *karman.* This state of complete union with the universal self is known as *mokṣa* ("release" or "salvation").

Opinions differ among Indian sages as to whether final liberation is attainable while still in an embodied state or only after death. At least from the time of the *Vedānta Sūtra* (second century), the sages believed that salvation could be achieved while still alive. Thus, according to the *Mahābhārata,* the *ātman* is affected by the bonds of finite existence only under the conditions of metaphysical ignorance *(avidyā),* but once a soul is enlightened *(prakāṣita),* the self is freed from the consequences of its good and evil deeds and thereupon becomes indistinguishably identified with the *brahman* (12.267.32–38).

BUDDHISM

Śākyamuni Buddha, like his philosophical and spiritual predecessors, believed that birth and death recur in successive cycles for the person who lives in the grip of ignorance about the true nature of the world. However, he undercut the Vedāntic position by denying that the world of evanescent entities is undergirded and suffused by an eternal and unalterable Self or "soul-stuff" *(ātman).* In place of the doctrine of absolute self, he propagated the precept of "no-self" *(anātman),* namely, that the human person, along with everything else that constitutes the empirical universe, is the offspring *(phala)* of an unbroken, everfluctuating process of creation and destruction and birth and extinction according to the principle of Dependent Co-origination *(pratītya-samutpāda;* Pali, *paṭicca-samuppāda).* The technical formulation of this Law of Causation is as follows: "If this exists [e.g., an acorn], then that comes to be [an oak tree]." The entire universe perishes and is created afresh in every instant; nothing remains the same from one moment to the next, from a single microbe to an entire galaxy.

The human being or personality, therefore, is not to be understood essentially as an integral and enduring mind-body organism but rather as the manifestation of a highly complex succession of psychosomatic moments propelled along the temporal continuum by the force of *karman.* In the Buddhist view, the human person can be broken down into five constitutive elements, or strands (*skandha*s); it is continually changing but is always determined by its previous actions. As such, humans are never the same from moment to moment and therefore are in no sense the projection of a permanent self. Hence, a cardinal teaching of the Buddha is "there is nothing that transmigrates and yet there is rebirth."

If there is no absolute self that survives the death of one body and is reborn in a new one, then how is the doctrine of rebirth to be reconciled with that of "no-self"? The Buddha declares that this question, like other questions pertaining to the fundamental nature of reality, arises out of a misconstruing of the nature of *karman.*

Karman is not a unified and independently existing entity that moves from life to life, as a traveler might go from place to place. Rightly understood, *karman* is the life process itself, the blending of energy and form that coordinates an unending flow of life moments. That is, the myriad clusters of factors that constitute the universe at any given moment are nothing more than the product of all its pasts. In other words, the sprout is not the temporary projection of some universal "soul-stuff" but rather a permutation of the parent seed. As one Buddhist text declares, "One hundred thousand universes conspire in the creation of the iridescent eye that graces the feather in the peacock's tail." Birth and death, then, are to be construed as nothing more than dramatic interruptions or exceptional innovations in the ongoing life process.

Therefore, neither a single entity (however subtle and rarified) nor a conglomeration of entities passes across from the old life-form to the new, yet the continuity among the phenomena is maintained. That is, all of the constitutive elements of a person's life are present from the moment of conception, just as the sprout preexists in the seed and contains the sum total of all the effects of its antecedent causal elements, at least in a state of potentiality.

According to the doctrine of *karman,* a person may be reborn successively into any one of five classes of living beings: gods, human beings, animals, hungry ghosts, or denizens of hell. Since birth as a human being occurs at the apex of the ladder of existence and is the penultimate stage to full enlightenment, it follows that all humans have undergone a birth in each of the four other orders of existence prior to the current cycle and occupy a privileged position from which to reach the ultimate goal.

While theoretically all human beings possess the capacity to achieve enlightenment and, thence, liberation from rebirth (Zen Buddhists, for example, contend that a person can experience *satori* at any moment simply by dropping off the thinking mind), in practice only those select few who forsake the life of social responsibility in the world and follow the Buddha *dharma* exclusively as monks and nuns have a realistic hope of achieving salvation in this life. [*See* Enlightenment.]

JAINISM

According to the teachings of Mahāvīra (c. 599–527 BCE), the founder of Jainism, the unenlightened soul is bound to follow a course of transmigration that is beginningless and one that will persist for an unimaginable length of time. The soul becomes defiled by involvement in desire-laden actions and thereby attracts increasingly burdensome quantities of karmic matter upon itself. This polluting material, in turn, promotes the further corruption of the soul and causes its inevitable movement through countless incarnations.

The Jains conceive of *karman* as composed of innumerable invisible particles of material substance that pervade all occupied space. Actions of body, mind, and speech project waves of energy that, when combined with the antithetical passions of desire *(rāga)* and hatred *(dveṣa),* attract karmic "dust" to the soul and weigh it down deeper and deeper in the slough of ignorance and rebirth.

Jains also distinguish between the initial awakening to an awareness of one's bondage to ignorance, suffering, death, and rebirth (the most that the layperson can hope to achieve), on the one hand, and the ultimate state of liberation, on the other.

This ultimate state of bliss to which aspire all Jains (or at least the adherents of the monastic path) disperses and dissolves the load of karmic matter that encumbers the mind-body ego and transforms the practitioner into an omniscient and totally dispassionate soul.

ANCIENT GREECE

Whether the idea of metempsychosis was imported by the ancient Greeks from the East (more specifically, India) is subject to speculation in face of the absence of conclusive evidence to support one or another view. Be that as it may, the concept of rebirth occupied a central place in Greek thought from the time of Pherecydes of Syros (sixth century BCE), the mentor of Pythagoras (c. 582–507 BCE), and came into full flowering in the writings of Plato (427–347 BCE) and Plotinus (205–270 CE).

Herodotus, the greatest of ancient Greek historians, records that the Egyptians were the first people to embrace the doctrine of reincarnation. According to his sources, the Egyptians believed that the soul is immortal (i.e., subject to rebirth after each death) and that it passes through various species of terrestrial, marine, and aerial creatures before once again becoming embodied in human form, the entire cycle being completed at the end of a period of three thousand years.

Empedocles (490–430 BCE), under the influence of the writings of the mystic-mathematician Pythagoras, asserted that nothing in the cosmos is either created or destroyed. All living things undergo transmutation in accordance with the relationships among the four basic elements (air, fire, water, and earth). The souls of the impure are condemned to transmigrate for thirty thousand years through numerous types of incarnations. In the course of this transition, various lifetimes are affected in diverse ways by each of the four elements. Escape from this dark destiny is achieved through a lengthy purification process, the primary requirement of which is the avoidance of eating the flesh of animals whose souls once may have inhabited human bodies.

Like many other religious and philosophical traditions that hold to a belief in reincarnation, Orphism, an ancient Greek mystery cult that celebrated the life, death, and resurrection of the god Orpheus, is based upon a dualistic conception of humanity. Orphic sages declared that humans are composed of an invisible soul that was originally good and pure but that has become polluted by some kind of primordial sin or error. As a consequence of this ancient transgression, the originally pure soul has become imprisoned within a physical body that is believed to be impure or evil by nature.

The ultimate aim of this mystery was to raise the soul of each devotee to increasingly loftier and purer levels of spiritual existence. The elevation of the soul was promoted by participation in the sacramental practices of the Orphic brotherhoods *(thiasoi)*. By performing these sacraments—always in secret places and often in the dead of night—the devotee received the power of the divine life. By continually cultivating this gift through meditation, prayer, and vegetarianism, he eventually gained immortality and thereby achieved release from any future reincarnations.

Orphic eschatology emphasized postmortem rewards and punishments. Because of its essentially spiritual nature, the soul could not achieve its true state of existence until after the last of a lengthy series of lives. Complete and lasting freedom from bondage to the material order could be realized only after undergoing a series of rebirths in a variety of physical forms that were determined by the merits of the previous life or lives. Supposedly it was this mystical teaching that was the heart of the revelation that was given to each novice initiated into the Orphic religion. [*See* Orpheus.]

Plato drew together and synthesized numerous strands of thought concerning the fate of the individual soul. Under the influence of Empedocles, Pythagoras, the Orphic prophets, and others, he fashioned a theory of the nature and destiny of humanity that is as complex in its philosophical makeup as it is inspiring in its poetical contents. Like the Vedāntins, he believed that the soul *(psuchē)* is immortal. The soul is the governor and indweller of all conscious beings; it descends periodically into the physical realm of existence as a result of metaphysical nescience and bondage to the passions. Like the Vedāntins and the Buddhists, Plato declared that the soul of each human being (except for that of the "true philosopher," who is the one truly enlightened being) is entrapped by the body (and by material reality, generally) because of its attachment to the objects of transitory desire (i.e., objects of pleasure and pain). In a statement in the *Laws* (book 10) that could easily have been lifted directly from the Upaniṣads, he asserts, "Recognize that if you become baser you will go to baser souls, and if higher, to the higher, and in every course of life and death you will do and suffer what like may appropriately suffer at the hands of like."

Even the selection of a new incarnation by each soul at the beginning of a new life cycle is determined by the experiences of the former lifetime. During its journey through a series of births, the soul finds temporary abode not only in a variety of land, air, and water creatures, but, once it has achieved the status of humanity, it may pass through a number of professions of varying degrees of moral quality, ranging from that of a demagogue and tyrant at the nadir of the scale, to a lover, a follower of the Muses, and a seeker after wisdom at the apex (*Phaedrus* 248d–e).

According to Plato's famous myth of Er (*Republic* 10), those souls whose minds are governed by the baser pleasures first travel to the plain of Forgetfulness and take up residence on the banks of the river of Indifference, "where each as he drinks, forgets everything"; they then go to their respective births "like so many shooting stars."

The painful and disorienting wanderings of the soul throughout the various orders of creatures are brought to a halt, and the soul is ushered into a state of eternal and perfectly fulfilling bliss, but only after it has divorced itself completely from the pleasures of the body and the material world, placed all of its appetites and yearnings under the governance of Reason, and attained a pure and undeviating contemplation of the Absolute ("the Good"), thereby obtaining "the veritable knowledge of being that veritably is."

In the end, the liberated soul finds unending sojourn in the "place beyond the heavens" (cf. the *brahman* in Vedānta), where "true being dwells, without color or shape, that cannot be touched; reason alone, man's pilot, can behold it and all true knowledge is knowledge thereof" (*Phaedrus* 247d–e).

CONCLUSION

There is no question but that the twin doctrines of *karman* and reincarnation have done moreto shape the whole of Asian thought than any other concept or concepts.

It might be difficult to identify an idea or set of ideas that has exercised a comparable influence through the entire scope of Western thought, including the cardinal concepts in the writings of Plato and Aristotle.

Ironically, the notion of reincarnation is beginning to make inroads into contemporary Western thought (particularly in theology, the philosophy of religion, and psychology) by way of a number of circuitous routes. One of the most notable avenues along which the idea is traveling to the West is the number of Asian (primarily Indian) religious traditions that have appeared in Europe and America, along with theosophy, transpersonal psychology, and the academic study of the history of religions and comparative philosophy.

One of the most curious manifestations of the belief in reincarnation in modern times is a new approach to psychotherapy that operates in the United States under the rubric of "rebirthing analysis," which purports to help the client deal with current psychological and spiritual problems by recalling personal experiences during numerous past lifetimes with the aid of meditation, hypnosis, and in some cases, consciousness-altering drugs.

Time alone will tell whether this new imprint on the fabric of Western thought and life will endure to become an integral part of the overall design or will, in time, fade into insignificance and remain only as a vague memory of a short-lived image in Western consciousness.

[*See also* Immortality.]

BIBLIOGRAPHY

de Bary, Wm. Theodore, et al., eds. *Sources of Indian Tradition.* New York, 1958.

Ducasse, Curt John. *A Critical Examination of the Belief in the Life after Death.* Springfield, Ill., 1961.

Head, Joseph, and S. L. Cranston, eds. *Reincarnation: The Phoenix Fire Mystery.* New York, 1977.

MacGregor, Geddes. *Reincarnation as a Christian Hope.* London, 1982.

Parrinder, Geoffrey. "Varieties of Belief in Reincarnation." *Hibbert Journal* 55 (April 1957): 260–267.

Radhakrishnan, Sarvepalli, and Charles A. Moore, eds. *A Source Book in Indian Philosophy.* Princeton, 1957.

Stevenson, Ian. *Twenty Cases Suggestive of Reincarnation.* 2d ed. Charlottesville, Va., 1974.

Thomas, N. W., et al. "Transmigration." In *Encyclopaedia of Religion and Ethics,* edited by James Hastings, vol. 12. Edinburgh, 1921.

Tylor, E. B. *Primitive Culture,* vol. 2, *Religion in Primitive Culture* (1871). New York, 1970.

18 APOTHEOSIS

ROBERT TURCAN
Translated from French by Paul C. Duggan

Apotheosis is the conferring, through official, ritual, or iconographic means, of the status of an immortal god upon a mortal person. The Greek verb *apotheoun* appears first in the writings of the historian Polybius, which date from the second century BCE. The noun *apotheōsis* is found for the first time in Cicero, though it may have existed already under some form or another in the Classical Greek world. It is during the Hellenistic epoch, however, that *apotheōsis* takes on new forms that display the stamp of the Roman cult of emperors and of the dead.

ORIGINS

In principle, the immortal and blessed condition of the gods differentiates them radically from human nature. However, the Greeks regarded as "divine" *(theios)* the man whose outstanding qualities set him individually apart from the commonplace. The heroization of founders of cities or of benefactors and peacemakers assured them a kind of official cult, but only posthumously. Recipients of such honor included Brasidas, Miltiades, Gelon and Hiero I of Syracuse, Theron, and Timoleon. However, if genius, virtue, and political or military success embody divine potential in exceptional men, it is especially so while they are living. Consequently, there is no need to wait for their death before heaping upon them such homage as is accorded the gods *(isotheoi timai),* yet without identifying them with deities. Such was the case with Lysander after the victory of Aegospotami in 405 BCE: dedicated to him were statues, altars, chants, and sacred games that raised him to the status of the Olympians.

Aristotle grants that superiority in valor or virtue secures for certain people the honor of being counted among the gods (*Nicomachean Ethics* 7.1.2). The Hellenistic ideology of the savior-sovereign, beneficent and *euergetēs,* derives directly from this concept. The Stoics would apply it generally to people who excelled in services rendered, "beneficiis excellentes viros." Pliny the Elder would make this general statement: "In order to be a god, a mortal must give aid to other mortals; this is the path to eternal glory." It was the *virtus* of civilizing heroes that earned apotheosis for Herakles, for the Dioscuri, and for Dionysos. Philosophers, wise men, and miracle workers (among them Pythagoras and Empedocles, and later Plato, Epicurus, and a number of others) were regarded as god-men, benefactors of humanity. The case of the young gnostic Epiphanes, adored as a god after his death for being the founder of the Carpocratian sect, exhibits the same process.

ALEXANDER, THE DIADOCHI, AND HELLENISTIC ROYALTY

In dedicating funeral solemnities, of which some elements (particularly the eagles) prefigure certain aspects of imperial Roman apotheosis, to the memory of his friend Hephaestion, Alexander established a cult for him, ordering that sacrifice be made to him "as to a god of the highest order" (Diodorus Siculus, 17.114–115). His funeral pyre with five levels presaged the *rogus consecrationis* of the Caesars. It has been suggested that it was Alexander who proposed to the Diadochi ("successors") the plan for his own posthumous consecration. Indeed, the tomb of the conquering Macedonian became the site of a cult at Alexandria that corresponded to that of the hero *ktistēs,* or "founder." However, the Ptolemies made of it a state cult that deified the dead king by allotting to him the service of a namesake priest. Like the Olympians, Alexander was to be honored fully as a god. (His name was not preceded by the title *theos,* which fundamentally differentiated him from the Lagides kings.) When the first of the Ptolemies died, his son dedicated a temple to him as a "savior-god." The first of the Seleucids was similarly deified in 280 BCE by Antiochus I. The divinization of dead queens and kings, which was connected with the cult of Alexander by following the categories of Greek mythology, was legitimized by proclaiming that Arsinoë had been borne away by the Dioscuri, Ptolemy II by Zeus, and Berenice by Aphrodite (Wilcken, 1938, p. 318). This representation of divine abductions would long survive in the funerary imagery of the Roman era.

The posthumous deification of sovereigns that developed during the third century BCE coincides both chronologically and ideologically with the success of euhemerism. In a revolutionary book entitled *Sacred Scripture,* Euhemeros of Messene declared that religions derive from the homage rendered to beneficent kings or to civilizing conquerors. It is the epoch that witnesses the popularization of the myth of Dionysos roaming through Asia for the purpose of propagating the use of wine and also of spreading, like Alexander, Hellenic culture. Yet parallel (or correlative) to this concept—basically traditional—of the hero-*euergetēs,* there is affirmed the idea of the living god, incarnate in the active person of the sovereign. Already in 324 BCE, Alexander had laid claim to this deification: it involved a political idea, that of the unity of a universal and cosmopolitan empire in need of a religious foundation in the person of the king himself, as was later the case in the persons of the Caesars. In Egypt, the process took root in the local practice of identifying the pharaoh with Horus and of adoring him as the "son of Re." The Greeks compared the Ptolemies to Zeus, Dionysos, Apollo, Hermes, and Poseidon, and their wives to Hera, Aphrodite, Isis, and Demeter. In the same way, Antiochus I was compared to Zeus Nikator, his son to Apollo Soter. The notion was also entertained of the reincarnation of this or that deity in the person of the sovereign: Ptolemy XIII and Mithradates VI Eupator were each regarded as a "new Dionysos." Alexander too had been a "new Dionysos," a "new Herakles."

Like the Lagides, the kings of Syria and Pergamum instituted a dynastic cult alongside local cults of sovereign founders of cities. Each satrapy had its own high priest for the royal cult, just as during the Roman era each province would have its own *archiereus* for the imperial cult. This divinization was sanctioned through appeal to genealogy: the Lagides descended from Herakles or from Dionysos. There was no hesitation in proclaiming Demetrios Poliorcetes as "son of Poseidon and Aphrodite." The epodic hymn that the Athenians sang to him in 307 BCE serves as a revealing document of the new conception of deities: "You, we see you here present, not as an idol of wood or stone, but really here." The apotheosis of living beings, visible or "epiphanous," appeared as one consequence (among others) of the decline of the rule of the cities and of the cults entwined with them. The erosion of belief in the traditional gods benefited the ideology, indeed the theology, of the leader as savior and peacemaker, as effective and direct protector of the people who needed him. The same phenomenon repeated and expanded itself three centuries later to the advantage of the Roman emperors.

THE ROMAN WORLD

In Roman religions, the dead, as the *manes,* are collectively and indiscriminately dei-fied. The "sacrifices" offered to them have a negative purpose: to help them rest quietly under the ground so that they will not trouble the world of the living. Yet, under Hellenic influence, this cult tended, beginning in the second century BCE, to coincide with a kind of heroization in the case of more or less impressive individuals, such as the Scipios. The sarcophagus containing the remains of Scipio Barbatus has the shape of a monumental altar that attests to the deceased being a *deus parens* (V. Saladino, *Der Sarkophag des Lucius Cornelius Scipio Barbatus,* Würzburg, 1970, pp. 24f.). The Greek word *apotheōsis* appears in Cicero with reference to the post-humous divinization with which he attempted to honor his daughter Tullia. In the *Dream of Scipio,* the same Cicero promises astral immortality to meritorious states-men, in conformity with the Hellenistic ideology of the hero-*euergetēs.*

The altar-shaped tomb enters into widespread usage in the first century BCE (W. Altmann, *Die römische Grabaltare der Kaiserzeit,* Berlin, 1905), especially among freed slaves. The ornamentation is also significant, particularly the eagles of apotheosis, thought to bear the soul of the deceased to heaven, like the eagle of Zeus that abducted Ganymede.

In freeing the spiritual person from his carnal shell, the funeral pyre served to aid his ascension to the ethereal realm of the gods. *A fortiori,* being struck by lightning was a measure of apotheosis, as the myths of Semele, Herakles, and Asklepios show. In Egypt, drowning in the Nile assured the same result, after the example of Osiris. Yet the mode of death or the funeral rite mattered little. The mythological imagery of the sarcophagi that surpassed altars as the sepulchral fashion confirmed indirectly or by allusion the apotheosis of the deceased. Scenes of military life, hunting scenes (chases for lion or boar), and intellectual activity (Muses and philosophers) also symbolized heroization through *virtus.* Finally, untimely deaths *(funus acerbum),* as illustrated by various myths or allegories, were thought to assure the apotheosis of these dead, whom the Greeks called the *ahōroi.*

IMPERIAL APOTHEOSIS

The astral apotheosis of Caesar, cremated in the Forum and become a comet *(sidus Iulium),* shone upon Octavian, Divi Filius. However, it was not until the death of Augustus that the ritual of "consecration" of the emperors was inauguarated. [*See*

Emperor's Cult.] The Senate would gather to confer (or not confer) the honors of apotheosis upon the deceased emperor. An immense four-tiered pyre would be built upon the Field of Mars, as depicted in coins of the second and third centuries CE. This *rogus consecrationis* was constructed of planks enclosing combustible materials and was decorated on the outside with costly embroidered fabrics adorned with gold, paintings, embossments, and garlands. A funeral pallet bore the cadaver of the new *divus,* covered with spices, fragrant fruits, and perfume essences. Around the pyre the priests and horseman would move in a circle: this *decursio* is depicted in raised relief on the pedestal of the column of Antoninus Pius. The new emperor would then take a torch to kindle the pyre, and everyone participating would do the same. Finally, from the top of the pyre an eagle would take flight as if bearing the soul of the deceased Caesar to the heavenly Olympus. Coins, cameos, and the vault of the Arch of Titus in Rome illustrate this posthumous flight. However, on the pedestal of the column of Antoninus Pius, it is the spirit of eternity (Aiōn) that carries Antoninus and Faustina away on its wings (Turcan, 1975, pp. 305ff.). After the ceremony, a witness would attest to having seen the consecrated prince soar into the air. Thereafter, the deceased would be entitled to a cult served by a priestly corps comprising members of the imperial family. The ceremonial was maintained, except for certain changes necessitated by the adoption of burial, up to the end of the third century (Turcan, 1958, pp. 323ff.). This apotheosis was incompatible with Christianity. Yet upon the death of Constantine, coins of consecration were still struck on which the emperor was pictured in a chariot, extending his hand toward God's hand emerging from the sky.

The extension of the empire and of the powers of the emperor sacralized his function, and indeed his person and that of the empress, and they were compared in word and picture to the divinities of the traditional pantheon. However, even though the Hellenistic kings and the Caesars had themselves adored while alive, still there was no true apotheosis except posthumously. For, as a Hermetic writing states, "The soul cannot be divinized so long as it remains in a human body" (*Corpus Hermeticum* 10.6).

[*See also* Deification.]

BIBLIOGRAPY

Boyancé, Pierre. "L'apothéose de Tullia." *Revue des études anciennes* 46 (1944): 179–184.

Cerfaux, Lucien, and Julien Tondriau. *Le culte des souverains dans la civilisation gréco-romaine.* Tournai, 1957.

Cumont, Franz. *Études syriennes.* Paris, 1917. On the eagle of apotheosis.

Cumont, Franz. *Lux perpetua.* Paris, 1949.

Eitrem, Samson. "Zur Apotheose." *Symbolae Osloenses* 1 (1932): 31–56 and 11 (1933): 11–34.

Festugière, A.-J. *L'idéal religieux des Grecs et l'evangile.* Paris, 1932.

Koep, Leo, and Alfred Hermann. "Consecratio (Kaiserapotheose)." In *Reallexikon für Antike und Christentum,* edited by Theodor Klauser, vol. 3. Stuttgart, 1957.

L'Orange, Hans Peter. *Apotheosis in Ancient Portraiture.* Oslo, 1947.

L'Orange, Hans Peter. *Likeness and Icon.* Odense, 1973. See pages 243ff.

Pippidi, D. M. *Recherches sur le culte impérial.* Paris, n.d. (c. 1939).

Reitzenstein, Richard. *Die hellenistischen Mysterienreligionen.* 3d ed. Leipzig, 1927.

Taeger, Fritz. *Charisma.* 2 vols. Stuttgart, 1957–1960.

Turcan, Robert. "Origine et sens de l'inhumation à l'époque impériale." *Revue des études anciennes* 60 (July–December 1958): 323–347.

Turcan, Robert. "Le piédestal de la colonne antonine." *Revue archéologique* (1975): 305–318.

Turcan, Robert. "Le culte impérial au troisième siècle." In *Aufstieg und Niedergang der römischen Welt,* vol. 2.16.2, pp. 996ff. Berlin and New York, 1978.

Vogel, Lise. *The Column of Antoninus Pius.* Cambridge, Mass., 1973.

Weinreich, Otto. "Antikes Gottmenschtum." *Neues Jahrbücher für Wissenschaft und Jugendbildung* 2 (1926): 633-651.

Wilcken, Ulrich. "Zur Entstehung des hellenistischen Königskultes." In *Sitzungsberichte der Preussischen Akademie der Wissenschaften: Philosophisch historische Klasse,* pp. 298–321. Berlin, 1938.

Wlosok, Antonie. *Römischer Kaiserkult.* Darmstadt, 1978. See pages 372ff.

Wrede, Henning. *Consecratio in formam deorum: Vergöttlichte Privatpersonen in der römischen Kaiserzeit.* Mainz, 1981.

19 HEAVEN AND HELL

Linda M. Tober and F. Stanley Lusby

As symbolic expressions found in various religious traditions, heaven and hell suggest polar components of a religious vision: a state of bliss and/or an abode of deity or sacred reality on the one hand, and a state of spiritual impoverishment and/or an abode of evil or demonic spirits on the other. As a spatial referent, Heaven is generally considered to be "above," informed by the human experience of the sky as the expansive space or dome encompassing the earth and also including the sun, moon, and stars. Just as Heaven is "above" the earth, so then is deity "higher" than the human or earthly plane for those traditions in which Heaven is viewed as the abode of deity. On the contrary, Hell is generally regarded as a realm "below," a meaning reflected in the derivation of the English *hell* from the Old English, *helan,* with a root meaning of "hide," "cover," or "conceal." Thus, Heaven is often symbolized by light or brightness as a realm of bliss, whereas Hell is characterized as dark or shadowy, a realm of anguish and suffering.

JUDAISM

The worldview of the ancient Hebrews, as reflected in the Hebrew scriptures, distinguished between the world above, the "heavens" *(shamayin),* as the dwelling place of Yahveh, and the earth, the two comprising the universe of God's creation. The creation narrative of *Genesis* 1–3 portrays the heavens and the earth as the whole of God's creation. Under the earth was She'ol; the ambiguous term *she'ol* was used at times to refer to the grave or tomb itself and at other times to indicate an obscure land of shadows, the realm of the dead. Existence there was understood in largely negative terms, since in She'ol the "spirit" or "breath of life" *(ruaḥ)* through which human beings were endowed by God with life was thought to have departed. Prior to the Babylonian exile of 597 BCE, the dead were not thought of as having an existence in which individual identity was preserved beyond life on earth but rather were conceived as a faceless collective existing in a joyless realm.

With the rise of Judaism in the period following the fifth century BCE, the Jewish understanding of heaven as an ideal relationship of the righteous with God was informed both by intercultural influences and by continuing efforts to unfold the meaning and import of the covenant relationship between the community and God.

For example, life after death had been clearly and definitively envisioned by the Zoroastrians of Persia as involving a judgment of individuals at death: the righteous were destined to enjoy forever the presence of God in a realm of unending light, while the unrighteous were condemned to a torturous hell. The Greeks, both in religions such as the Orphic cults and in the thought of major philosophers such as Plato and Aristotle, stressed the immortality of the soul. By the second century BCE, both the resurrection of the dead and an event of final judgment were affirmed in some circles of Jewish thought. [*See* Resurrection *and* Judgment of the Dead.] Heaven came to be regarded as the destiny of the righteous, those in vital covenant relationship with God. Multiple heavens (seven or ten) are mentioned in Jewish apocryphal literature and in teachings preserved in the rabbinical tradition. Paradise, a state of spiritual fulfillment in which the covenantal righteous enjoy an ideal relationship with God, is variously referred to as the third of seven or the seventh of ten heavens. Messianic expectations, which developed in the centuries immediately before and following the dawning of the common era, were often associated with affirmations of the resurrection of the dead and a final judgment, with the righteous destined for a heavenly paradise. In association with these developments, a place of punishment, Gehenna, was thought to await the unrighteous after death, though the period of punishment was limited in accordance with the degree of seriousness of one's transgressions.

Traditional Judaism views the final destiny of humans in terms of the three doctrines of recompense, immortality, and resurrection. Informed by the demand of conscience that virtue be rewarded and wickedness punished, the tradition holds that even if one does not encounter equity during the earthly life, it will nonetheless be met with afterward. The interpretation of the actual form of immortality, however, is permitted wide latitude in the tradition, with deathlessness envisaged as preserving individual identity and awareness (with the attending literal images of Paradise and Gehenna) or, alternatively, as a state that is impersonal and without consciousness. Similarly, resurrection has been understood as a climactic event physically reanimating the dead and including the final judgment of bliss or damnation and also as an eternal event through which the corporeality of the resurrected is transfigured into a pure spirituality.

CHRISTIANITY

The cardinal import of heaven and hell as components of the Christian religious vision is clearly evident in the New Testament portrayal of the completion of God's redemptive activity consummated in the manifestation of a new heaven and a new earth (*Rv.* 21). Not only is heaven envisioned in early Christianity as the fulfilling state of bliss and reconciled relationship with God of which the followers of Jesus are assured, but it is also the abode of the divine, where Jesus dwelled before his earthly life and to which he proceeded following his death and resurrection. Essential to the Christian confidence in a heavenly life after death in which the total uniqueness of human personality is preserved is the concomitant affirmation that God will make possible the resurrection of the dead. This belief is to be distinguished from the Greek notion (especially of Plato and Aristotle) of the immortality of the soul understood as rationality. The reality of hell as the arena presided over by Satan and his angels and as the destiny of the "cursed" was assumed by early Christians and frequently appears in the New Testament writings (e.g., *Mt.* 25:1–46). This teaching has been taken literally by many Christian thinkers through the centuries, though alternative views have occasionally been expressed. Origen (third century BCE), for example, understood hell to involve not the eternal punishment of the cursed, but punishment of such duration as was necessary to provide for the restoration of all to the presence of God.

In Roman Catholic Christianity hell is deemed to be a state of unending punishment for the unrepentant who die without the grace of God as transmitted through the sacraments. This state is characterized both by absence from God's presence *(poena damni)* and by the suffering of fire and other tortures *(poena sensus)*. The Roman Catholic concept of purgatory, defined by the councils of Florence (1439) and Trent (1545–1563), envisions an intermediate state after death during which there is opportunity for the expiation of venial sins and compensatory punishment for mortal sins, thus providing for the ultimate restoration of fellowship with God. This teaching, likely informed by the Jewish notion of Gehenna and the Greek notion of the realm of Hades, is correlative with rituals for the dead (prayers, oblations) intended to assure their full expiation. Salvation is understood in the Roman Catholic tradition to be a process, begun in earthly life and continuing in life beyond death, through which there will ultimately be a realization of the "beatific vision," a heavenly state of full and unqualified awareness of the presence of God, a state of spiritual perfection that cannot be attained during the earthly pilgrimage. The significance and import of the Christian teaching about heaven and hell has nowhere been given more powerful aesthetic and imaginative expression than in Dante's masterful poem the *Commedia* (completed 1321). Eastern Orthodox Christianity, in sharing the teaching that hell is a destiny of eternal fire and punishment awaiting the cursed and unredeemed following the Last Judgment and that heaven is the ultimate destiny of the redeemed, has placed focal emphasis on the resurrection of Jesus as assuring the resurrection of the faithful.

Protestant Christianity, though generally lacking the teaching on purgatory or intermediate states, has retained the traditional Christian teachings respecting heaven and hell, while reinterpreting theological understandings of grace and faith as they are pertinent to salvation. With the dominance of the scientific worldview in the modern era and the theories proferred by the psychological and social sciences, literal and spatial interpretations of heaven and hell have been found untenable by some Protestant thinkers. In terms of theological argument, it is contended that it is contradictory to posit hell as eternal punishment while affirming God as one who is loving and merciful and wills all to be saved and forever seeks the lost. Karl Barth (1886–1968), for example, rejected the entire notion of eternal damnation, and instead maintained that the central message of the church is the election of all of humanity in Jesus Christ. Heaven and hell have been reinterpreted by such thinkers as indicative of qualities of life that are conducive to or detract from the realization of the full potential of persons or, alternatively, as symbols that underscore the fundamental character of the decision of faith, in which the whole of the individual is at stake, and the freedom of that decision, through which one may choose to reject God's presence or seek a full union extending beyond the confines of the earthly life.

ISLAM

In the Qur'ān and the traditions of Islam are manifold descriptions of Heaven and Hell that are expressive of the centrality of judgment as an aspect of Muslim religious anthropology. Perfect justice, one of the attributes of God, will be disclosed at the Last Judgment following resurrection. God's judgment will be pronounced on the basis of an expansive record of each person's deeds. Overriding the demerits of every believer's evil deeds will be the support provided by the Muslim confession subscribed to from the heart ("There is no god but God, and Muḥammad is his prophet.") That judgment in turn will be followed by the entrance of the believers into Heaven and the relegation of the infidels to Hell. In a manner reminiscent of the Zoroastrian Chinvat Bridge, each person will proceed across the bridge of al-Aaraf following the judgment. This will be a felicitous crossing for the true Muslim but a travesty for the infidel, whose fall from the bridge into the pits of Hell is assured. In accordance with the will of God, Muḥammad will, however, recover some who fall. The portrayals of Paradise in the Qur'ān and the traditions are graphically idyllic, in no way lacking the enjoyment of sensuous pleasures and bountiful surroundings:

> This is a Remembrance; and for the godfearing is a fair resort,
> Gardens of Eden, whereof the gates are open to them,
> wherein they recline, and wherein
> they call for fruits abundant, and sweet potions,
> and with them maidens restraining their glances of equal age.
> "This is what you were promised for the Day of Reckoning;
> this is Our provision, unto which there is no end."
> (surah 38:50–54)

Interpreters of the Muslim tradition such as al-Ghazālī (d. 1111) have called attention to the accompanying spiritual components of heavenly existence, viewing all other of the manifold pleasures of Paradise to be overshadowed by the ecstatic awareness of being with God. Equally graphic are the Qur'anic descriptions of punishment and torture in Gehenna, as indicated in the following passage:

> All this; but for the insolent awaits an ill resort,
> Gehenna, wherein they are roasted—an evil
> cradling!
> All this; so let them taste it—boiling water and pus,
> and other torments of the like kind coupled
> together. (surah 38:55–58)

Traditional Islam adheres to a conviction that the sufferings in Hell will be unending, though there are suggestions of a purgatorial realm from which, after a time, Muslims in need of purificatory restitution to the *ummah* (the Muslim community) will be recovered. Both Heaven and Hell are subdivided into seven regions in Muslim teaching, with an eighth region added to the heavenly realm of the blessed.

HINDUISM

The religious symbolisms of heaven and hell as given expression in the religious traditions of India have a distinctive role and significance when contrasted with their multiple meanings within the contexts of the religions of West Asia and Western civilizations. The ancient Vedic literature (1500–1200 BCE), especially the *Ṛgveda* (a collection of hymns associated with funereal rituals), portrays a heaven regarded as the realm of the fathers, who proceed there after death in order to be with the gods. As the practice of the funeral rite of cremation gained prominence, Agni, god of fire, was called upon to provide for the purification of the deceased. Yama, who was the first human to die and who was also the god of the dead, oversees the heavenly realm. This realm was associated with the sky and the dead were associated with the stars. Among the gods in the heavenly realm is Varuṇa, god of the high-arched sky and a source of the order in the earthly realm. The welfare of those who have passed beyond death to heaven was associated with their participation in rituals, sacrifices, and offerings to the gods while on earth.

In heaven, the distinctiveness of personal identity is preserved, and, in close communion with the gods, those who have entered heaven enjoy the pleasures and goods they have known on earth, but in full measure. Priests and warriors were portrayed among those who enter the heavenly realm, though there was no comprehensive and systematic indexing of those who do and those who do not enjoy the goods of heaven. Though there is much ambiguity regarding human destiny in the literature of the earliest Vedas, there are suggestions that the fate of those who did not achieve a heavenly state (presumably because of a neglect of proper ritual participation, since no moral tests for entrance into heaven were suggested) is either extinction or relegation to a realm of darkness under the earth (hence, hell). In later elaborate ceremonial works, specifically the Brāhmaṇas composed primarily for the ritual performances of the priests, there was presented a more definitive characterization of heaven as an abode in which were experienced the joys and goodness of earthly existence, but greatly enhanced and without the limitations known before death. The quality of heavenly life was viewed as correlative with efficacious ritual performance on earth since association with the gods of sacramental ritual communion (Agni, Varuṇa, Indra, et al.) was assured. Hell was likewise presented as a realm of retribution for ritual deficiencies.

By the era of the rise of Hinduism proper (third century BCE), a quite different worldview had come to dominate the Indian scene, shaped fundamentally by the philosophical and religious ideas of the Upaniṣads (sixth to first centuries BCE). A cyclical worldview had been given sophisticated expression. The notions of transmigration and reincarnation informed a pervasive understanding of human existence as involving, in cyclic continuity, a series of lives, deaths, and rebirths and had come to dominate a comprehensive interpretation of human existence.

Heaven and hell came to be viewed not as a vision of ultimate fulfillment or destiny, but as intermediate states intermittent with a series of earthly existences in a cycle of births and deaths *(saṃsāra).* One's *karman* (Pali, *kamma*), the reservoir of the consequences of thoughts, words, and deeds cumulative over the entire series of one's existences, determines the nature of the soul's passage from one earthly existence to another through one of the several levels of heaven or hell, which are thus intermediate states of varying degrees of suffering or relative bliss. In traditional Hindu cosmology, three realms (*loka*s)—heaven, the earth, and a netherworld (sky)—are supplemented by a vision of fourteen additional realms, seven of which rise above the earth ("heavens") and seven of which (or, in some instances, multiples of seven, such as twenty-one) are below the earth.

The goal of the continuing human pilgrimage was liberation and release *(mokṣa)* from the suffering associated with attachment to the samsaric cycle to the unqualified enjoyment and ultimate fulfillment of the bliss of *nirvāṇa. Nirvāṇa,* which is held to be resistant to definition but is accessible to experience, has been variously envisioned as the union of the soul *(ātman)* with the ultimate divine reality, *brahman* (Śaṅkara, eighth to ninth century CE, and the school of Advaita Vedānta), or as an unqualified communion of the soul with God (Rāmānuja, eleventh to twelfth century CE, and the school of Viṣiṣtadvaita). Such fulfillment was to be achieved by the spiritual discipline of one of the pathways (*mārga*s, *yoga*s), or some combination thereof, of traditional Hinduism: *jñānayoga* (liberating wisdom), *karmayoga* (actions), *rājayoga* (contemplative discipline), or *bhakti* (loving devotion, adoration of God, *pūjā*).

The twice-born castes (*brāhmaṇa*s, *kṣatriya*s, *vaiśya*s) had fullest access to these pathways of spiritual practice, especially the first three pathways mentioned. The *bhakti* movements in Hinduism stressed a mode of religious life that involved devotional and ritual practices in which adoration was centered on one of the gods of Hinduism, primarily Śiva or Viṣṇu, or one of their *avatāra*s (incarnations) or consorts. The rich corpus of Hindu religious literature provided an abundant resource for the edification and inspiration of *bhakti* devotees. The *Bhagavadgītā* (Song of the Blessed Lord; c. first century CE), a portion of the expansive epic *Māhābharata,* portrays Kṛṣṇa (an *avatāra* of Viṣṇu, the "pre server") as worthy of a devotee's total devotion, while stressing the ideal of responsible yet disinterested ac-tion in the world. Some scholars hold that the importance of the *Bhagavadgītā* lies in part in its recognition of the legitimacy of *bhakti* as a pathway to liberation alongside of *jñāna-, karma-,* and *rājāyoga.* The other great Indian epic, the *Rāmāyaṇa* (c. fourth century BCE, with the first and last of seven chapters presumed to be later additions), portrays Rāma as another *avatāra* of Viṣṇu worthy of devotional adoration, the accomplished practice of which results in intermediate stays in one of the heavens until the perfection of the practice leads to the perfect bliss of unqualified and unendingly blissful adoration of and communion with God *(nirvāṇa).*

BUDDHISM

With the Hindu tradition Buddhism shares a cyclical view of history and of individual existence. [*See* Cosmology.] The world of time and space and history, the realm of samsaric cycles, is transitory and constantly in flux. Heaven and hell are seen as parts of that transitory world, as intermediate and temporary states between one earthly existence and another. Death is thus but a transition from one earthly existence through an intermediate level of one of the heavens or hells to rebirth in yet another earthly existence. The attachment of beings to the samsaric cycle, often referred to as the "wheel of existence" and characterized by *duḥkha* (suffering, unsatisfactoriness), is caused by *tṛṣṇā* (clinging, grasping, desiring) conditioned by ignorance *(avidyā)* of the Dharma, or the truth of the Middle Path as taught by the Buddha. Though *tṛṣṇā,* in the early Buddhism of India and the later Therāvada of Southeast Asia, is the ultimate cause of rebirth, one's *karman* determines the type and level of rebirth. In this tradition, only the enlightened ones, the *arhat*s, are free from the cycle of rebirths to enjoy the equanimity and the bliss of *nirvāṇa.*

The temporary aggregation of the components of ordinary experience (the *skandhas*: form, sensation, perception, dispositions and volitions, and consciousness, including self-consciousness) that prompt the presumption of separate person or self is dissipated at death following the experience of liberation *(mokṣa).* Short of enlightenment, there is no surcease of the continuous round of rebirths. The having-been-ness of one life, with its repository of *karman*, leads to the coming-into-being of another life in another realm, though it is denied that any *ātman,* soul or self, as a separate entity transmigrates (known as the Buddhist teaching of *anātman*). Rebirth may occur in any one of the various heavens or hells, and one may be reborn as an animal, again as a human being, or in the *preta* realm, the realm of ghosts.

There is no one completely systematic account of the various hells in the Pali canon, the corpus of Theravāda texts known as the Tipiṭaka. Generally, the realm of *kāmaloka,* of the lower universe of sensuality, includes the various hells and the six lower heavens. The Pali Abhi dhamma Piṭaka reports eight "hot" hells below the earth, each involving differing forms of suffering by which the consequences of bad *kamma* are consumed.In addition, there are sixteen minor hells attached to each of these hells. The duration of a passage through any one of these hells is not definitively established, each being correlative with the measure of the evil *kamma* to be consumed. Other Hīnayāna canons preserve more systematic and detailed cosmologies.

The structure of the heavenly realms in Buddhism draws upon non-Buddhist and Hindu sources, though they are reinterpreted within the Buddhist context. The six heavens of the sensual realm of *kāmaloka* are inhabited by the kings and gods who manifest their power through various forms of sensual experience. Included in this group is the Tuṣita Heaven, from which Gautama is said to have come upon entering his last earthly existence in which he experienced enlightenment, as well as the *bodhisattvas* of exemplary compassion and saving power.

The Buddhist heavens of the other two realms, *rūpaloka* (the world of form) and *arūpaloka* (the formless world, often referred to as the world of mind or consciousness), are accessible only by those accomplished in the practice of the discipline of meditation and spiritual endeavors. The heavens of *rūpaloka* are material and are inhabited by the gods who are free from sensual yearnings. They are variously numbered in different lists, in some texts enumerated as thirteen while in other texts listed as being from sixteen to eighteen, distributed in four different groups correlative with four *dhyānas* (modes of meditation). The heavens of *arūpaloka* are likewise structured in four groups, each characterized by stages or levels of meditative attainment. For Buddhism, life in the heavenly realms is not free from involvement in the conditioned existence of samsaric cycles. The ultimate goal of enlightenment and fulfillment transcends even the highest of the heavens.

The *bodhisattva* motif of Mahāyāna Buddhism qualifies the ideas of both heavens and hells in the Buddhism of the "large vehicle." The *bodhisattvas*, moved by compassion for all beings involved in suffering *(duḥkha),* are beings who have taken a vow not to enter *nirvāṇa* until all sentient beings can do so. They are able to manifest themselves through diverse forms and beings and in any of the realms in which there are suffering beings, even into the depths of the lowest hell, to share their merit with all who are in need of liberation and enlightenment.

In no movement of the Buddhist traditions is this emphasis on the saving power of *bodhisattvas* and Buddha figures more vividly expressed than in the Pure Land schools of China, Korea, and Japan. Central to this popular Buddhist movement is the figure of Amitābha (Chin., O-mi-t'o-fo; Jpn., Amida), a Buddha who has gained inexhaustible merit through countless ages of Buddhist practice and who, as a consequence, possesses infinite saving power dedicated to the salvation of all. This Lord of the Western Paradise responds beneficiently to all who invoke his name, assuring them of both protection in earthly life and passage at death to the Land of the Western Paradise, whence their full enlightenment and entry into *nirvāṇa* is assured.

The quest for immortality had developed in Chinese religious Taoism; and with its associated belief in heavens, it made for fruitful interaction with Chinese Buddhism of the Pure Land. A notable figure who did much to extend the influence of Pure Land Buddhism in China was T'an-luan (476–542), who had turned to this form of Buddhism after an extended Taoist search for the elixir of immortality. All mortals, he held, could be assured of salvation by faith in Amitābha, given expression through the recitation of his name, thus relying on his saving power.

The dominant Pure Land schools of Japan, the Jōdoshū, founded by Hōnen (d. 1212), and the Shinshū, formed by followers of a disciple of Hōnen, Shinran (d. 1262), attest to the wide appeal of this form of Buddhism, with its inviting vision of the Western Paradise. Pure Land texts, especially *Saddharmapuṇḍarīka* (Jpn., *Hokekyō*) and the *Sukhāvatīvyūha,* contain graphic and imaginative descriptions of the Western Paradise: a bountiful land without pain or suffering; abounding in pleasure and beautiful natural surroundings, with flowing rivers and lotus-filled lakes, permeated by pleasant music, adorned by exquisite gems, and where neither a notion of nor a word for hell is to be found.

CHINESE TRADITIONS

The aspiration to achieve harmony in society that has characterized all of Chinese religion and philosophy has given to Chinese understandings of heaven a unique aspect. Rooted in the most ancient traditions of China, the worship of Heaven as well as the ruler of Heaven, Shang-ti, is evident as early as the Shang dynasty (1532–1027 BCE). During the period of the Chou dynasty (1027–256 BCE) the worship of Heaven, T'ien, was regarded as essential for the maintenance of harmony between Heaven and earth. It is in the Confucian tradition, which formatively shaped the essential character of Chinese civilization through many centuries of relative stability, that a sophisticated articulation is found of the nature and place of Heaven.

Although Confucius's teachings and the Confucian tradition advocated the quest for harmony in human affairs, especially through the five relationships (ruler-subject, father-son, husband-wife, elder brother–younger brother, and friend-friend), as the way to perfect harmony in the cosmos, there is no doubt that basic presumptions regarding Heaven provided an ontological ground for the moral teachings to be manifest in the perfection of the *chün-tzu* (sage, ideal gentleman). The focus was placed on human affairs; human beings should begin by seeking harmony in the relationships that immediately address them. Yet the underlying conviction was that if harmony is achieved in human affairs, harmony with Heaven will be assured. Thus, the full practice of *li* (tradition, propriety) informed by *jen* (human beings in relationship with each other) in the spirit of *shu* (reciprocity) along with the honoring of *hsiao* (filial piety) will manifest the kind of *te* (perfect moral virtue and power) that is the ideal of the *chün-tzu*. This is, for Confucianism, the way *(tao)* of Heaven in human affairs, and the very nature and structure of the cosmos as determined by Heaven is such that all will be well if ruler and subject both revere and follow (i.e., practice) this way. Thus, though it appears that the thought of Confucianism can most accurately be characterized as primarily a social ethic, there are nonetheless cosmic and ontological dimensions grounded in its notion of Heaven. The will of heaven *(t'ien-chih)* is the primary reality and the ultimate basis of Confucian thought. Whatever happens that is not the direct responsibility of human beings is attributed to the will of Heaven.

Unrestrained speculation about the nature of Heaven was not characteristic of Confucian thought, as evidenced in the texts of the Four Books, that is, the *Lun-yü* (Analects), the *Ta-hsüeh* (Great Learning), the *Chung-yung* (Doctrine of the Mean), and the *Meng-tzu* (Book of Mencius). In certain passages it does seem to be presumed that Heaven is an impersonal force underlying the cosmos, the ultimate source of order and morality. Yet in other passages Heaven is presumed to have the capacity to understand the plight and situation of human beings, indicating a seemingly personal dimension to heaven.

Though Confucian thought was not inclined to speculate about Heaven as a destiny awaiting human beings beyond death, its emphasis on the centrality of the family afforded a natural sympathy with ritual practices of ancestral reverence. [*See* Ancestors.] Propriety in honoring the ancestors, whose spirits survived death and whose welfare was reciprocally related to that of living persons, became an essential component of *li*. As indicated earlier, both Buddhists who presided over masses for the dead and religious Taoists in China subscribed to a cosmology that included levels of heavens above and hells below the earth.

JAPANESE TRADITIONS

There are, in indigenous traditions of Japan, concepts analogous to those of heaven and hell in other religions. The oldest traditions recorded in the *Nihongi* and the *Kojiki* contained only nascent suggestions concerning the possibility of life beyond death, though this itself was associated with the grave. Following the sixth century, Chinese and Bud dhist influences contributed to further development of religion in Japan. References are made to a realm beneath, one term for which was Yomi (literally, "dark-ness"). Though characterized as an undesirable realm from which beings threaten the welfare of the living, it is not clear that it is a repository of the dead. Gods dwell there, but they represent negative powers of death and disease. Later Yomi came to be conceived as a realm of punishment. More definite in later Japanese texts are the notions about a realm analogous to heaven, Ame. This is the dwelling place of the gods, and notable persons are thought to proceed there after death. Ame is a bounteous realm above the earth, made attractive by the presence of trees, flowers, and streams; its beauty is beyond anything known on earth. The importance Ame came to have is underscored by the tradition that Amaterasu, the sun goddess, visited there as well as Izanagi after his failure to recover his wife, Izanami. Japanese Buddhism shared as well the normative Mahāyāna visions of various levels of heaven and hell as intermediate states.

[*See also* Paradise *and* Underworld.]

BIBLIOGRAPHY

Asin Palacios, D. Miguel. *Islam and the Divine Comedy.* London, 1936. Comparative analysis of Dante's *Commedia* and Muḥammad's journey and ascension.

Baillie, J. B. *And the Life Everlasting.* London, 1936. An examination of the Christian notion of immortality by a discerning scholar of that tradition.

Blacker, Carmen, and Michael Loese, eds. *Ancient Cosmologies.* London, 1975. Cosmological structures of a variety of traditions, including Jewish, Chinese, Islamic, and Greek.

Brandon, S. G. F. *Man and His Destiny in the Great Religions.* Manchester, 1962. This publication of the Wilde Lectures in Natural and Comparative Religion presents an overview of visions of human destiny in major religious traditions through historical and comparative analysis.

Ch'en, Kenneth. *Buddhism: The Light of Asia.* New York, 1968. A valuable summary interpretation of the Buddhist tradition in interaction with the various cultures of Asia, proceeding country by country.

de Bary, Wm. Theodore, ed. *The Unfolding of Neo-Confucianism.* New York, 1975. A good collection of essays portraying the religious aspects of Neo-Confucianism in distinction from its purely moral and social functions.

Eberhard, Wolfram. *Guilt and Sin in Traditional China.* Berkeley, 1967. Morality as well as concepts of heaven and hell are examined in the context of popular religious movements in China.

Eliade, Mircea. *The Myth of the Eternal Return, or Cosmos and History.* Princeton, 1971. A comparative analysis of cyclical and linear concepts of time in history and their consequence for understanding human meaning and destiny.

Hick, John. *Death and Eternal Life.* London, 1976. An examination of responses to the question of what happens after death, based primarily Western sources.

Kitagawa, Joseph M. *Religion in Japanese History.* New York, 1966. The most complete and authoritative recent account of the religions of Japan, portraying their development and history.

MacCulloch, J. A., et al. "Blest, Abode of the." In *Encyclopaedia of Religion and Ethics,* edited by James Hastings, vol. 2. Edinburgh, 1909. A still valuable, though dated, collection of essays presenting images of human fulfillment in a comprehensive examination of a variety of traditions, primarily ancient and classical.

Parrinder, Geoffrey. *The Indestructible Soul.* London, 1973. An analysis of the structures of human existence as presented in Indian thought, including focal discussion of life after death.

Reynolds, Frank E., and Earle H. Waugh, eds. *Religious Encounters with Death.* University Park, Pa., 1977. A collection of essays, contributed by a number of specialists, that analyze the import and significance of the myths, ceremonies, and conceptions associated with death in a variety of traditions.

Seltzer, Robert M. *Jewish People, Jewish Thought.* New York, 1980. A general and comprehensive survey of Jewish experience, focusing on intellectual history from ancient to contemporary times.

Smith, Jane I., and Yvonne Haddad. *The Islamic Understanding of Death and Resurrection.* Albany, N.Y., 1981. A descriptive analysis of the basis elements of Muslim understanding of the judgment and destiny of individuals.

Zimmer, Heinrich. *Philosophies of India.* New York, 1956. A comprehensive and illuminating treatment of the classical thought-systems of India.

20 THE UNDERWORLD

J. Bruce Long

The term *underworld* refers to the subterranean region inhabited by the dead. It is often the place of punishment of the wicked, the unrighteous, the unredeemed, the unbelieving, or the lost. The concept of an underworld is an ingredient in most belief systems in the history of religions, but there is no definite evidence indicating that the idea was present in the earliest stages of human culture. In the oldest strata of Egyptian and pre-Vedic Indian cultures, however, there exists a rich store of archaeological material suggesting that the aristocratic segments of society, at least, believed in some kind of an afterlife. But even in these early records of postmortem existence, there does not seem to have been a distinction between heaven, the realm of the blessed, and hell, the realm of the damned.

Later, when the two realms came to be differentiated, each religion appealed to its own set of criteria when determining the fate of an individual after death, whether blessed or damned. [*See* Heaven and Hell.] These criteria could be defined by birth, by ritual initiation into the community, by the performance of prescribed sacramental rites, by belief in a deity or in a set of teachings, and so on. Such standards were commensurate with the way the religion defined the proper relationship to the sacred.

PRIMITIVE AND ARCHAIC RELIGIONS

Tales of heroic journeys to the underworld, often undertaken on behalf of the entire community, are extremely widespread among tribal peoples throughout the world. Particularly notable for such lore are the Maori of New Zealand; the Algonquin, the Ojibwa, and various Plains tribes of North America; the Zulu, the Ashanti, and the Dogon of Africa; and numerous other societies in North Asia (especially Siberia and Mongolia), Central America, and South America.

If one disregards for the moment the detailed differences among the various accounts of the postmortem journey to the underworld, one can observe a common theme among many such stories. A heroic figure undertakes a descent into the belly of a chthonic or marine monster, a creature often identified as Mother Earth, the Mother of Death, or the Queen of the Night. He pursues a strenuous journey through her body, during which he encounters numerous obstacles and dangers.

He finally reemerges into the world of the living, either through a natural orifice in the monster's body or through an opening that he himself creates. As numerous scholars have convincingly demonstrated, the ordeal of being ingested by a theriomorphic creature and of passing through the various channels of its body is symbolic of an initiatory ordeal whereby the hero conquers death or the fear of death and, in some cases, wins the prize of immortality.

The hero is submitted to a test or an ordeal in which he must either prove himself capable of overcoming the obstacles that lie in his path or prove himself capable of defeating the enemy that blocks his passage. The descent into the underworld is also a quest for special, esoteric knowledge or wisdom that is denied all other living beings who have not undertaken such a journey. As the possessor of this secret knowledge, the hero often serves as a mediator between the living and the dead or as a psychopomp who personally conducts the souls of the deceased to the underworld.

The typical shamanistic story of the descent into the underworld is exemplified in a tale of the Goldi peoples of Siberia. A shaman traps the soul of the deceased in a sacred pillow by beating his sacred drum. After mounting a notched tree in order to get a preview of the journey to follow, he summons two tutelary spirits to assist along the way and then, with the deceased and his ghostly companions, sets off on a specially prepared dogsled, furnished with a basket of food for nourishment. After encountering numerous obstacles along the way, the travelers arrive in the underworld. Using a fictitious name to protect his identity, the shaman deposits the deceased with his relatives in the underworld. He then returns immediately, armed with warm greetings and small gifts for the living from their subterranean kinsmen.

A prototypical example of the story in which the descent into the underworld is symbolically identified with the return to the mother's womb is found in the religious lore of the Maori of New Zealand. Māui, the heroic representative of the Maori, returned at the end of his life to the hut of his ancestress, Hine-nui-te-po, the Great Mistress (of the Night). He leapt into her body as she slept, made his way without difficulty through the various channels within her body, and had just emerged halfway from her open mouth when the birds that had accompanied him burst into laughter. Aroused by the screech of the birds' laughter, the ancestress abruptly clamped her mouth shut and cut the hero in two with her sharp teeth. Because of this misfortune, humans ever since have been mortal; had Māui successfully escaped his ancestress's body, they would have become immortal.

Many tribal peoples situate the land of the dead in the west, on the western side of the world, or simply at some distance west of the village. Many scholars (most notably E. B. Tylor and F. Max Müller) have argued that this practice is confirmation that most myths and rituals pertaining to the journey to the underworld are elaborations of a core solar myth.

While there no doubt is a kernel of truth in this view, there are other equally significant layers of meaning invested in these stories and practices. One important theme concerns the descent of a hero into the belly of a ferocious marine creature and his reemergence through the mouth or anus of the beast in an effort to conquer death and gain immortality. A second theme is of an arduous journey through wild and monster-infested areas in search of a precious object (magical ring, sacred fruit, golden vessel, elixir of immortality, etc.) that will benefit the hero or his people. In a third theme, a tribesman submits himself to a deadly ordeal in order to pass from a lower to a higher stage of existence and thereby achieves a superhuman or heroic state of being. In yet another theme, a hero shoulders the onerous task of traveling to the subterranean regions where the Mother of Death or the Queen of the Night reigns supreme, thereby gaining knowledge of the route to the shadowy realm and of the fate of those who reside there.

ANCIENT EGYPT

The afterlife of the Egyptian nobility is described in the Pyramid Texts. Royalty were believed to ascend at death to the Blessed Lands, or Fields of the Blessed, in the heavens. According to the Pyramid Texts, members of the aristocracy traveled to the celestial spheres to dwell there like gods, often traveling on the ship belonging to Re, the sun god. Highly elaborate and expensive mortuary rites, charms, and incantations were offered for the nobility to guarantee that the soul of the deceased would enjoy a blissful existence in the world beyond. The life in that world is largely similar to this one but is free of the difficulties and misfortunes that plague the lives of even the powerful and wealthy. The afterlife of the common people is outlined in the Coffin Texts. Commoners were believed either to remain near the tomb after death or to travel to the netherworld.

The dead traveled to many different realms, some to the east but most to the west. It is now believed that the dead went in different directions because the disembodied spirits were thought to move about with the sun and the stars. The west was the primary destination of the souls *(ka)* of the dead. Darkness and night were identified symbolically with death and postmortem existence. The realm of the dead was located sometimes in the sky and sometimes beneath the earth. This region was ruled by Osiris, the king of the dead. While still a mortal, Osiris was murdered by his brother Seth and then resurrected by his sister-wife Isis. He subsequently became the chief ruler of the nether realm.

ASSYRIA AMD BABYLONIA

In the views of the ancient Akkadians and Babylonians, the underworld is a dreadful place. To get there one has to pass through seven gates and remove a piece of clothing at each. The realm is organized on the order of a political state under the tyrannical rule of a king and a queen, Nergal and Ereshkigal. In the text entitled "Descent of Ishtar to the Nether World" (Pritchard, 1969, p. 107), this realm of the dead is described as

> *the Land of no Return . . . the dark house . . . which none leave who have entered it . . . the road from which there is no way back, the house wherein the entrants are bereft of light, where dust is their fare and clay their food. Where they see no light, residing in darkness, where they are clothed like birds, with wings for garments, and where over the door and bolt is spread dust.*

Once in the underworld, the fate of the deceased is improved or worsened depending on whether the body is buried according to the prescribed funeral rites and is provided by the living with food, clothing, and other accoutrements required for the journey to the other realm.

One name for the netherworld is Kigal ("the great subterranean realm"). *Kigal* is an element in the name of Ereshkigal, the "queen of the underworld" and sister of

Ishtar. This domain was also known as Kutu, the sacred city of Nergal, a chthonic deity who was lord of the netherworld. The gateway through which each soul is required to pass is situated in the west, where the Babylonians watched the descent of the sun. All graves provide entrance to this shadowy realm. Having entered the main gate, the dead are then ferried across the river Hubur by a four-handed, fierce-faced ferryman to "the Great City." This city is a gigantic metropolis, encircled by seven walls, each wall surmounted by a gate and each gate guarded by a demon. At the very center of the complex is the lapis lazuli of Ereshkigal. Befitting her position as queen of the realm, she is surrounded by numerous attendants: a plague god who executes her orders, a scribe who announces the names of the new arrivals, and seven fierce, iron-willed judges called the Anunnaki. There are a host of demons who spread pestilence and suffering throughout humanity and keep the queen plentifully supplied with new residents.

GREECE AND ROME

In ancient Greece the belief in the postmortem survival of the soul stretches back to earliest times, as is suggested by evidence of food, drink, clothing, and entertainment provided in the grave. Already in Homer a clear distinction between the corpse and the ghost was made. The *Iliad* (3.278–279, 19.259) contains the belief that the gods punished or rewarded souls at death. It was thought that the souls of the living are supplied from the stock of souls in Hades.

Despite the rich stock of ideas native to the Greek islands regarding the dead and the underworld, from the time of Homer Greek writers showed no hesitation in drawing freely from other religious traditions and in synthesizing these foreign elements with indigenous material. Most of the borrowed elements were derived from Egypt (particularly the Osiris cult and the *Book of Going Forth by Day*) and from Mycenae. From Crete they adopted the idea of *elusion* ("paradise") and the figure of Rhadamanthys (one of the three infernal judges). From Mycenae they received the idea of weighing the soul in the balance.

The earliest Greek accounts of the postmortem journey of the soul to the underworld are to be found in the *Iliad* (1.595, 3.279, 5.395–396, 15.187–188) and in the *Odyssey* (11). At the moment of death, the soul *(psuchē)* is separated from the body, transformed into a ghostly double of the person *(eidōlon),* and transported down to Hades, an enormous cavern below the surface of the earth (*Odyssey* 11.204–222). Here the souls of the dead are capable only of "flitting around as shadows while exuding shrill chirping sounds." This dismal domain is the very antithesis of the realm of the "blazing sun"; it is a place where one sees only "the cold dead" and is an altogether "joyless region." The shades of the dead are unconscious and incommunicative until they have imbibed a quantity of blood, the essence of life. So morally neutral is the life of the dead that all distinctions pertaining to social station, political position, and religious latitude are obliterated, thus rendering even a mean and destitute existence in the world highly preferable (*Odyssey* 11.487–491) to the office of rulership over Hades.

In ancient Greek cosmology, Hades lies within the ocean, perpetually shrouded in clouds and mist. Here there is no sunlight, only eternal darkness. The shades are depicted as being weak and extremely melancholy, always in search of escape from their sufferings and finding none. Especially painful are the sufferings of those who were either not properly buried on earth or not suitably nourished with sacrificial food offerings. The dire nature of the torments suffered by the inmates is graphically depicted in the story of Tantalos. Standing in water up to his chin, he found to his chagrin that the water mysteriously evaporated each time he sought to quench his thirst; surrounded by flowering fruit trees, he found that the wind blew the fruit away as he reached out to grasp it (*Odyssey* 11.582–592). Hades is separated from the realm of the living by a treacherous body of water, made up of five rivers (Lethe, Styx, Phlegethon, Acheron, and Cocytus). The entrance is guarded by Kerberos, a ferocious dog with three (earlier poets said fifty or one hundred) heads whose necks are encircled by venomous serpents. Here Minos judges the deeds of the deceased and provides the laws that govern them in the underworld. But the evidence seems to indicate that none of the laws meted out justice in the form of rewards for the righteous and punishment for the wicked.

According to Vergil, Rhadamanthys presides over a court of justice in which a variety of corporeal, mental, and spiritual retributions are distributed according to the nature of sins committed in the upper world. Nowhere in all of world literature is the drastic distinction between the two destinies after death presented in more painfully dramatic terms than in his *Aeneid:*

> *This is the place where the road divides and leads in two directions: one way is to the right and extends under the ramparts of Dis* [*i.e., Pluto*] *to Elysium* [*i.e., Paradise*], *but the left path leads to the evil realms of Tartarus, where the penalties for sin are exacted. To his left Aeneas spots a deep cave enclosed by a triple fortification around which flows Phlegethon, seething with flames and tossing rocks about in its tumultous torrents.* (6.540–579)

Aeneas encounters a gargantuan door that even the gods are powerless to penetrate, guarded by the ever-wakeful Tisiphone (one of the Furies). From inside, he hears horrifying groans and wailings from victims being lashed with whips and chains. Within this dismal kingdom of darkness and death reside a host of personifications of abstract entities: Grief and Cares, Diseases, Senility, Fear, Hunger, Toil, War, Discord, and countless other forces that afflict the life of every creature with misfortune and distress.

Not until the time of Plato do we encounter the notion that the righteous will be feted with sumptuous banquets "with garlands on their heads," or that the wicked will be plunged into a pit filled with mud, "where they will be forced to carry water in a sieve" (*Republic* 2.373c–d). Plato may have believed that the earthly experience of the fear of Hades is equivalent to being there already and that the suffering inflicted by a guilty conscience is sufficient punishment for the wicked act committed. This view coincides with the theory that Plato adopted many primitive beliefs about the fate of the soul and gave moral and psychological interpretations to allegorical tales (see *Gorgias* 493a–c). Similarly, for the poet and philosopher Empedocles the *psuchē* ("soul") is the bearer of guilt, and the world of the senses is the Hades where the individual suffers for that guilt (frags. 118, 121). Also, Plato, who perhaps more than any other ancient thinker shows a genuine concern for the immortality of the soul and the judgment it undergoes after death, presents divine rewards and punishments in terms of reincarnation into a better or worse earthly life, rather than in terms of heaven and hell. In the *Laws* (904d) he suggests that Hades is not a place but a state of mind and adds that popular beliefs regarding Hades should be invested with symbolic value only. [*See* Hades.]

JUDAISM

References to the underworld in the Hebrew scriptures are vague and derive largely from beliefs common throughout the ancient Near East (especially Egypt and Babylonia). Numerous terms are used to designate this shadowy realm, the two most popular names being *She'ol* (a word that seems peculiar to Hebrew) and *Gei' Hinnom* (Gr., *Geenna;* Eng., *Gehenna*). Some euphemistic substitutes for the latter are *erets* ("earth" or "underworld," *1 Sm.* 28:13, *Jb.* 10:21–22), *qever* ("grave," *Ps.* 88:12), *'afar* ("dust," *Is.* 26:5), *bor* ("pit," *Is.* 14:15), and *shaḥat* ("pit," *Ps.* 7:16; "the land of darkness," *Jb.* 10:21).

The historical Gehenna, or Gei' Hinnom—"Valley of ben Hinnom," or "Valley [of the son(s) of] Hinnom"— was located near the city of Jerusalem at the site of a cult in which children were sacrificed (*2 Kgs.* 23:10, *Jer.* 7:31); it was known popularly as the "Valley of Slaughter" (*Jer.* 19:5–6). Even before this time, the valley was used as a site for human sacrifices to the god Moloch(*2 Chr.* 33:8), and afterward, as a place where the city's rubbish was burned. In mythology, Gehenna was located beneath the earth or at the base of a mountain range (*Jon.* 2:7) or beneath the waters of the cosmic ocean (*Jb.* 26:5). This realm is sometimes pictured as a horrifying monster with mouth agape (*Is.* 5:14), a realm where persons of all classes are treated as equals (*Ez.* 32:18–32).

She'ol is another term used to designate the realm of the dead or the subterranean spirit world, where the destinies of the righteous and the wicked are the same. Heaven and She'ol are thought to be the two farthest extremities of the universe (*Am.* 9:2). She'ol is positioned at the nadir of a dark pit at the very base of the universe, into which the blasphemer who aspires to be equal with God will fall. But the term also refers simply to the state of death or to the grave (see *Prv.* 23:13–14, *Ps.* 89:49). The viability of this interpretation of the term is further confirmed by the fact that the Septuagint frequently translates *she'ol* as *thanatos* ("death").

The Hebrew scriptures place the domain of the dead at the center of the earth, below the floor of the sea (*Is.* 14:13–15, *Jb.* 26:5). Some passages locate the gates that mark the boundary of She'ol in the west. This realm has been depicted as a place pervaded by dust and darkness (*Jb.* 10:21–22), as it was in Mesopotamian thought. In contrast to the Babylonian netherworld, which boasted a large company of demonic creatures, both the Hebraic underworld and heaven are ruled over by one and the same God whose sovereignty extends throughout the universe (*Ps.* 139:7–8, *Prv.* 15:11, *Am.* 9:2). There is a strong suggestion in Psalm 73 that God will manifest his grace to the righteous by taking them to heaven, where they will exist eternally with him. The people of God will, therefore, be saved from She'ol to live with God forever, but the unrighteous will face a deprived existence in the chambers of the subterranean regions (*Ps.* 49).

According to the Ethiopic *Apocalypse of Enoch* (22:9–13), She'ol is not an abode of all the dead, where the souls merely exist as vague shadowy figures devoid of individual characteristics, but is a spacious realm with three subdivisions: one realm is allotted to the righteous who have been vindicated in life, one to sinners who were not submitted to divine judgment before death, and one to those whose deeds were judged during life and found wanting. In time, She'ol came to be identified with Gehenna, the pit of torment, an idea that, in turn, informed the Christian concept of Hell (*Hb.* 2:5).

In the postbiblical Jewish apocalyptic tradition, among the seven heavens that extend above the earth, sinners are confined to the second heaven to await final judgment. North of Eden lies Gehenna, where dark fires perpetually smolder and a river of flames flows through a land of biting cold and ice. Here the wicked suffer numerous tortures (*2 En.* 3–9).

Elsewhere within the same book, the Angel of Death inquires of Jehoshua whether there are any gentiles (or "descendants of Esau") in Paradise or any Children of Israel in Hell. Included in the reply is the observation that those descendants of Esau who performed righteous deeds on earth are rewarded here but sent to Hell after death; Israelites on the other hand receive punishment while living and inherit the joys of Paradise after death. According to Josephus Flavius (37–100 CE), historian of the Jewish War of 66–70, the Essenes of the Dead Sea area believed that the righteous retire to the western region, where their lives are undisturbed by rain, cold, or heat and where they enjoy cooling breezes continuously. The wicked, however, are condemned to a dark, chilly hell where they suffer eternal torments.

CHRISTIANITY

New Testament writers drew upon the postexilic Hebraic picture of Gehenna in formulating their understanding of the destination of the damned. Gehenna was imagined to be an enormous, deep pit that perpetually ejects clouds of putrid-smelling smoke from burning garbage, a pit where bodies of criminals and lepers are disposed of. Two significant alterations in the Hebraic concept of hell deserve mention: (1) there is a much sharper distinction between the realm of the blessed and the realm of the damned, and (2) the standard applied at the Last Judgment is defined by a person's attitude toward the person of Jesus and his teachings. In the Gospels the prevailing concept of the underworld is epitomized in the story of the rich man and Lazarus (*Lk.* 16:19–31). It would appear that the rich man is sent to Hell merely on account of his great wealth in this realm, whereas Lazarus is transported to "the bosom of Abraham" (Heaven, Paradise) in recompense for his sufferings and poverty. Hell is imagined as an invisible world, situated beneath the realm of the living, a blazing inferno of such intensity that even a drop of water applied to the tip of the tongue could bring welcome relief. It is also a distant land beyond a great gulf across which no movement is possible in either direction.

Whereas Hades remains at a great remove from the realm of the living, Paradise is situated in the immediate presence of God. The wicked in Hades and the righteous dead "at home with the Lord" await the final resurrection.

According to the eschatology of the *Book of Revelation,* a millennial reign is followed by the resurrection of the saints, and then by a period of universal conflict at the end of which Satan will be cast into a lake of fire and brimstone, preparatory to the resurrection of the remaining dead and the Last Judgment. Both Death and Hades are hypostatized as subterranean vaults that surrender the dead to be judged, after which Death and Hades themselves are thrown into the lake of fire, thus actualizing "the second death," that is, condemnation to the eternal fires of Hell (*Rv.* 20:11–15, 21:8). The remarkable feature of this account of "final events" is that Hell is homologized with the lake of fire to which the wicked are condemned, and it is itself punished by being cast into the same lake of torment. Supposedly the cosmic cataclysm that signals the termination of the current world order, the final defeat of Death and Satan and the Last Judgment, is a preview of the fate of the wicked in Hell. The nature of Hades can be inferred from the depiction of the realm of the blessed as a perpetually sunlit land in which the righteous are never discomfited by the blazing sun. There they are faithfully fed by the divine shepherd, refreshed by ever-flowing fountains, and relieved of their tears of grief.

Augustine (354–430 CE), the father of early medieval theology, perpetuated the concept of Hell as a bottomless pit containing a lake of fire and brimstone where both the bodies and the souls of men and the ethereal bodies of devils are tormented (*City of God* 21.10). Thomas Aquinas (1225–1274) laid much of the foundation for the philosophical concept of Hell that shaped and informed the idea of Hell in the minds of poets, painters, sculptors, and novelists for centuries to come. For him, Hell never lacks space to accommodate the damned. It is a place where unhappiness infinitely exceeds all unhappiness of this world, a place of eternal damnation and torment where the suffering of the damned is intensified by recalling the glory of the blessed while no longer able to perceive the glory firsthand.

Dante (1265–1321 CE) derived the theological framework for his notion of the underworld from the Old and New Testaments and Thomas. In the third chapter of the *Inferno* he describes the descent into Hell. Accompanied by his guide Vergil, Dante approaches the Inferno and sees the gate of Hell, the entrance to the city whose inhabitants live in suffering and eternal pain. Dante is conducted along a circular pathway leading from the gateway to the bottommost zone of Hell. He passes in succession through nine separate circular zones, each of which contains smaller cells where individuals or groups of the damned live. Charon waits on the near bank of the river Styx, ready to ferry his miserable passengers across the waters. As Dante and his guide move from circle to circle they encounter a variety of types of sinners sorted into groups according to their chief vices. On reaching the fourth ring of the ninth circle, the two travelers are confronted by Dis (Lucifer), who with his three mouths devours Judas, Brutus, and Cassius. The arduous journey of Dante and Vergil through the Inferno is completed with a horrifying descent into the interior of the body of Lucifer. Finally they arrive at a spot situated directly beneath the place of Christ's crucifixion on Mount Golgotha, from where they once more see the stars.

The history of Christianity is dotted with periodic expressions of heretical dissent concerning the existence of Hell, notably by Origen, Erigena, Voltaire, and Nietzsche. But it was not until the seventeenth and eighteenth centuries, when rationalism began to find its voice, that a widespread decline of belief in Hell developed in Western culture. The concept of Hell as an actual spatial domain has virtually disappeared or been reduced to the level of allegorical interpretation. This transformation of the idea is exemplified in *The Fall* in Camus's warning "Don't wait for the Final Judgment. It takes place every day" and in Sartre's declaration in his play *No Exit* that "hell is other people."

ISLAM

Cosmology appears to have been a matter of interest in early Islam not for its own sake but "only as a doctrinal framework for understanding the cosmic field of divine providence and human accountability" (Smith, 1981, p. 9). Muḥammad himself does not seem to have held to a clearly defined and detailed picture of a realm of the dead.

According to the Qur'ān, there are seven layers of heaven extending above the earth toward the celestial abode of God. Corresponding to the layers of heaven are seven descending depths of a vast funnel-shaped fire *(al-nār)*. The topmost level of the netherworlds is Gehenna. This realm of death and torment is connected to the world of the living by a bridge that all the souls of the dead must traverse on the day of judgment. The varieties of punishment meted out to the damned become more painful and severe with each level of descent.

At the partition between Paradise and the Fire stands Zaqqūm, a tree that exudes a stifling odor and has blossoms composed of demons' heads. Eating the fruit of Zaqqūm burns the stomach like molten metal (surah 7:46–50). The tree separates the two worlds, yet provides a point from which a person can see both realms simultaneously. Beside it is a wall or barrier that divides humanity into separate classes according to the moral quality of their deeds in the temporal world.

Each of the seven fiery realms is assigned a specific name. An inventory of these names reflects the Muslim attitude toward nonbelievers: *hāwiyah* (abyss for hypocrites), *jaḥīm* (fierce fire for idolators), *sa'īr* (blazing fire for Sabaeans), *jahannam* (purgatorial fire for Muslims), *lazā* (flaming fire for Christians), *saqar* (scorching fire for the Magi), and *ḥuṭāmah* (raging fire for Jews).

The Qur'ān depicts Gehenna in highly pictorial and terrifying terms. It is referred to as the "Fire of Hell" (89:23) and is depicted as a kind of four-legged beast. Each leg is composed of seventy thousand demons; each demon has thirty thousand mouths. Each of the seven layers of the Fire is punctuated by a gate manned by a guardian who torments the damned. The term *Gehenna* refers both to the topmost sphere and to the entire realm of seven spheres. Whenever this beast of hell is transported to the place of final judgment, it sends forth a buzzing, groaning, and rattling noise, along with sparks and smoke that shrouds the entire horizon in total darkness (15:43–44, 39:71).

The realms of the blessed and the damned are separated by a towering wall. Men who inhabit the heights of this partition can view the inhabitants of both worlds and recognize each group by their distinguishing marks. The blessed are recognizable by their smiling countenances; the damned, by their black faces and blue eyes (57:13). There is also a hint of the existence of a purgatory or limbo for beings whose deeds are neither extremely good nor extremely bad.

Both the Qur'ān and the *ḥadīth* present a wide variety of reasons why a person may be condemned to a life of torment. The fundamental cause is lack of belief in God and in the message of his prophet, Muḥammad. Other reasons include the following: lying, corruption, lack of faith, blasphemy, denial of the advent of the judgment day and of the reality of the Fire, and lack of charity. Leading a life of luxury and believing that wealth brings immortality also lead to condemnation.

The postmortem journey of the soul of the redeemed or the blessed through the various layers of Heaven in the company of the archangel Gabriel is contrasted with the difficult and painful journey of the souls of the damned downward through the many spheres of Fire. The victims of the torments of Gehenna are represented as sighing and wailing in their wretched condition (11:106). Their skins are alternately scorched to a black crisp and then renewed so that they can suffer the torments of

Fire over and over again. They are compelled to wear garments made of fire or scalding pitch, and boiling water is poured onto their heads, melting their insides and skins. Iron hooks are used to retrieve them every time they try to escape (22:19–22).

In time, Muslim theologians began to emphasize God's grace and mercy and to downplay his anger and wrath. The belief arose that after a certain period of purgation the angel Gabriel would intercede on the sinner's behalf and release him from the Fire. It was later believed that in time the Fire would be extinguished and all sinners pardoned.

HINDUISM

Vedic references to an underworld are so few in number and so vaguely conceived that many scholars have argued that Vedic religion lacked a concept of hell. More recent studies (see Brown, 1941) have demonstrated that references to a realm of postmortem suffering do signal a genuine, if relatively undeveloped, conception of hell in the Vedic literature.

According to *Ṛgveda* 7.104 and *Atharvaveda* 8.4, the Vedic Hell is situated beneath the three earths, below the created order. It is characterized as a gigantic, bottomless chasm or abyss, a place of no return. In this infinitely deep pit, there is no light, only deep darkness (cf. *Ṛgveda* 2.29.6). In the very deepest realm lies the cosmic serpent, the archdemon Vṛtra (*Ṛgveda* 1.32.10), who fell there after Indra slew him.

Some texts describe the Vedic Hell as insufferably hot or unbearably cold. It is a realm of absolute silence (*Ṛgveda* 7.104.5) and of total annihilation, a state that is depicted semi-anthropomorphically as lying in the lap of Nirṛti, the destroyer. This region of eternal torment is populated not by those who committed wrongs inadvertently but by those who consciously and intentionally pursued unrighteous ends: Vṛtra, antidivine forces (*asuras* and *dasyus*), demonic powers (*rākṣasas*), and sorceresses (*yoginīs*) dwell here. The inhabitants of Hell are those who live at cross-purposes with the universal law *(ṛta)*.

Hell stands in an antithetical relation to the ordered universe, based not on *ṛta* but *anṛta*. Here there is no order, no gods, no sun, no warmth, no fecundating waters, nor any of the elements vital to the creation and maintenance of creaturely existence. Here in the lap of destruction *(nirṛti)*, there is only death and nonexistence *(asat)*. It is the opposite of the created, ordered, and illuminated realm.

Later, in the Vedānta, hell came to be conceived in more strictly philosophical terms as the realm of pure nonbeing. Contrasted with this was the realm of being *(sat)*, the realm of living beings and of life itself that came to be referred to as *brahman*, the limitless and indefinable fulcrum of being.

In the Upaniṣads, the paths leading to the realms of the blessed and the wretched are envisioned as the way of the ancestors and the way of the gods, respectively. Little importance is accorded to the idea of hell as the destiny of the unrighteous. The emphasis is rather on rebirth as the consequence of an unrighteous past life. In the Yama-Naciketas episode in the *Kaṭha Upaniṣad*, the young man Naciketas receives instruction on the postmortem state from Yama, the lord of the dead. Rather than directly addressing a matter so subtle that not even the gods understand it, Yama informs Naciketas of two paths leading to different ends: the way of pleasure and the way of goodness. Yama recommends that Naciketas choose the latter, thereby avoiding rebirth.

But in the Purāṇas (collections of classical Hindu mythologies), hells are depicted in terrifyingly graphic terms as places of extreme suffering and deprivation. In the *Rāmāyaṇa* (7.21.10–20), Rāvaṇa, the ten-headed demon, witnesses a scene of indescribable wretchedness on entering Yama's abode. He hears the agonizing cries of the wicked being gnawed by dogs and devoured by worms. Pitiful screams shoot across the Vaitaraṇī River from parched people on hot sand who are being sawed in half. The thirsty cry out for water; the hungry, for food. Pale, emaciated specters run to and fro. The righteous, on the other hand, inhabit grand palaces and dine on sumptuous meals, surrounded by beautiful, sweet-smelling maidens dressed in exquisite garments. In the *Mahābhārata* (12.2.25) Yudhiṣthira is ushered into an enormous dark chamber that is cluttered with foul-smelling hair, heaps of raw flesh, and countless pools of blood, corpses, worms, deformed animals, hideous monsters of incomparable ugliness, and ghosts of terrifying presence. As will become standard in the later Purāṇas, a specific form of punishment is assigned to each of the subterranean chambers. In the underworld called Kumbhīpāka ("cooked victuals") the wicked are boiled alive in giant vats of boiling oil; in Śalmali, thorns from a silk-cotton tree are used to torture the wicked.

The *Agni Purāṇa* (chaps. 340 and 342), one of the eighteen major collections of classical mythology, perpetuate a theme that blossomed in the Upaniṣads. This is the idea that the course of a person's life in this world is governed by the ritual and moral quality of his deeds. One's experience in the next world is governed by the fruits of those deeds. Yama determines the infernal region to which each wicked soul repairs or the womb into which it is to be born, according to the deeds of the previous existence. The terrifying members of Yama's retinue usher the soul to a place where they prepare an account of its good and evil deeds. The soul initially reaps the benefits of its good deeds in the form of physical and spiritual delights, after which it is returned to hell for a period of suffering in order to purge the residual effects of its evil deeds. If the number of merits outweighs the demerits, the person is reborn into a pure and prosperous family; if the obverse is the case, he may be committed to a lengthy life of suffering in one of the hells or be reborn as an animal, insect, or other base form of life.

The pathways connecting this world with the various hells are dreadful to behold and extend for a total of 164,000 human miles. According to most classical cosmologies, there are a total of 28 major infernal regions situated below the lowest stratum of another 7 netherworlds. Each region lies along a vertical line of descent and is subdivided into 144 smaller chambers, to each of which is assigned an appellation describing its definitive characteristics, for example: Ghora ("horrifying"), Taralatara ("trembling"), Bhayanaka ("terrifying"), Kālarātri ("dark night of devouring time"), and Dīpta ("the blazing realm").

Each chamber is presided over by five guards with the terrifying faces of carnivorous animals and birds, who administer the form of punishment appropriate to the place. The guards cast their condemned wards into dreadful places of punishment. Some souls are cast into gigantic frying skillets or into caldrons filled with boiling oil, molten copper, or iron, while others are tossed onto the upturned tips of sharp pointed lances. Others are submitted to severe lashings with leather straps or heavy bastinados or are forced to drink beverages of boiling metals or noxious solutions of animal urine and human excreta. Still others are broken physically on the rack, dismembered, and then parceled out to vultures, hyenas, and other avaricious creatures of the infernal regions. Each of these dreadful realms is filled with the sounds of screaming, wailing, and moaning.

SECULAR VISIONS

Among a growing number of religious intelligentsia the world over, both heaven and hell are gradually being sublimated or transmuted into psychological entities or realms, with the personal and collective unconscious serving as the source of both positive and negative feelings, images, and attitudes. Even the general mass of people in industrialized countries who claim to retain a belief in an underworld of some description have, in practice, largely transposed many of the ideas and themes previously associated with the underworld (e.g., divine judgment, suffering, torment, disease, death, and mental and physical anguish) into the arena of contemporary human affairs.

[*For discussion of the underworld together with other mythic views of life after death, see* Afterlife.]

BIBLIOGRAPHY

General Works

Brandon, S. G. F. *The Judgment of the Dead.* London, 1967.

Mew, James. *Traditional Aspects of Hell (Ancient and Modern)* (1903). Ann Arbor, 1971.

Ancient Near Eastern Religions

Heidel, Alexander. *The Gilgamesh Epic and Old Testament Parallels.* 2d ed. Chicago, 1963.

Frankfort, Henri. *Kingship and the Gods.* Chicago, 1948.

Pritchard, James B., ed. *Ancient Near Eastern Texts relating to the Old Testament.* 3d ed. Princeton, 1969.

Greek and Roman Religions

Dietrich, B. C. *Death, Fate and the Gods.* London, 1965.

Farnell, Lewis R. *Greek Hero Cults and Ideas of Immortality* (1921). Oxford, 1970.

Nilsson, Martin P. *A History of Greek Religion.* 2d ed. Translated by F. J. Fielden. Oxford, 1949.

Judaism

Charles, R. H. *A Critical History of the Doctrine of a Future Life.* 2d ed., rev. & enl. London, 1913.

Ginzberg, Louis. *The Legends of the Jews* (1909–1928). 7 vols. Translated by Henrietta Szold et al. Philadelphia, 1946–1955.

Graves, Robert, and Raphael Patai. *Hebrew Myths.* New York, 1966.

Christianity

Dante Alighieri. *Inferno.* Translated by Allen Mandelbaum. Berkeley, 1980.

Jeremias, Joachim. "Hades." In *Theological Dictionary of the New Testament,* vol. 1, edited by Gerhard Kittel. Grand Rapids, Mich., 1968.

Mew, James. "Christian Hell." In his *Traditional Aspects of Hell (Ancient and Modern)* (1903). Ann Arbor, 1971.

Walker, Daniel P. *The Decline of Hell: Seventeenth Century Discussions of Eternal Torment.* Chicago, 1964.

Islam

Asín Palacios, Miguel. *Islam and the Divine Comedy.* Translated by Harold Sunderland. London, 1926.

Smith, Jane I., and Yvonne Y. Haddad. *The Islamic Understanding of Death and Resurrection.* Albany, N.Y., 1981.

Morris, James W. *The Wisdom of the Throne: An Introduction to the Philosophy of Mulla Sadra.* Princeton, 1981.

Hinduism

Brown, W. Norman. 'The Rigvedic Equivalent for Hell." *Journal of the American Oriental Society* 61 (June 1941): 76–80.

Gombrich, Richard F. "Ancient Indian Cosmology." In *Ancient Cosmologies,* edited by Carmen Blacker and Michael Loewe, pp. 110–142. London, 1975.

Jacobi, Hermann. "Cosmogony and Cosmology (Indian)." In *Encyclopaedia of Religion and Ethics,* vol. 4, edited by James Hastings. Edinburgh, 1914.

Hopkins, E. Washburn. *Epic Mythology* (1915). New York, 1969.

Macdonell, A. A. *Vedic Mythology.* Strassburg, 1897.

THREE

CONCEPTS OF THE SOUL AND ITS DESTINY

21

CONCEPTS OF THE SOUL IN THE ANCIENT NEAR EAST

STEVAN L. DAVIES

The soul can be defined most conveniently as that part (or those parts) of a person that persists after death. By this definition, the cultures of ancient Mesopotamia and Egypt may be said to have believed in a soul. But in all other details of soul concepts, these two cultures differed.

MESOPOTAMIA

Virtually no texts from the cultures of Sumeria, Akkadia, ancient Babylonia, and so forth, refer to the soul per se. All one can do in inquiring into the matter is to reason back from conceptions of the afterlife and the netherworld to the conception of the soul. If we know where and in what conditions a person persists after death we can infer (or, perhaps, invent) concepts appropriate to the soul, the persisting part.

To the ancient Mesopotamians an afterlife offered nothing good. Humans persisted for a period in conditions of unhappiness, discomfort, and despair. Various texts give similar descriptions of the place of the afterlife, thought usually to be beneath the world. It is a "house which none leave who have entered it. On the road from which there is no way back, to the house wherein the dwellers are bereft of light, where dust is their fare and clay their food. They are clothed like birds, with wings for garments, and see no light, residing in darkness" (Akkadian *Epic of Gilgamesh,* tablet 7.3.34–39, quoted in Pritchard, 1969, p. 87). The place is called here the "House of Dust" and is unusual in attributing feathers to the unlucky dead. Otherwise the account can be taken to stand for the basic concepts of the underworld. It is a place from which the dead wish to escape, yet it is a cardinal principle that none of the dead will ever leave. The central Mesopotamian myth of Gilgamesh, who seeks unsuccessfully for immortality, is indicative of the stress placed upon the impossibility of escape from the place of death. Even the great goddess Inanna/Ishtar, the queen of heaven, when she journeyed to the underworld, was sequentially stripped of her insignia of royal rank until, naked, she became a corpse and was impaled upon a stake. She, by her divine nature immortal, escaped, as no human could.

The underworld is a place modeled generally upon this world, and gods and goddesses govern there much as the earthly deities do. But the pleasures of this world are wholly lacking: the dead hunger but dwell in darkness. In accordance with this dark view of afterlife, Mesopotamians were entirely pessimistic about death, finding it bereft of moral significance. In the underworld the great would be shorn of their power and the symbols of their power. The fact of their eminence on earth might be remembered (there is some indication that princes were still known as such in the underworld), but no one on earth could work politically, morally, or religiously for a pleasant condition below. Further, because human beings, by Mesopotamian definition, were not immortal, it is likely that the dead did not persist in the underworld forever but eventually faded away into nothingness.

The above conceptions allow us to define the soul for ancient Mesopotamians as the will and consciousness and individuality of persons that persist beyond the grave. Unfortunately, in their conception, the will was thereafter frustrated, the consciousness bereft of light and hope, and individuality doomed to, at best, disappear.

There are, however, indications that the central (or offical) conceptions were not entirely and universally shared. The burial customs of ancient Mesopotamia varied from region to region and from time to time. Not infrequently, foodstuffs, drink, pottery, and other items were interred with the corpse. This might imply that the living could serve the dead and aid the dead in the underworld, but there is no reason to believe that this was thought seriously to be the case. No textual evidence exists to indicate that anything like continuing ancestor reverence on, say, the Chinese model, existed. That some in ancient Mesopotamia believed in ghosts might imply that the dead could escape from their unhappy existence in the underworld, but it is more likely that ghosts were persons who had not managed yet to enter the underworld and were, if such a thing can be imagined, more unhappy than the denizens there. There is probably no more reason to regard the grave furnishings of the common people and the belief in ghosts as significant for the Mesopotamian concept of the soul than it would be for similar beliefs and practices to be taken seriously in regard to Christian or Islamic beliefs about the soul.

There was a period of two or three generations about the middle of the third millennium BCE, when the royalty of Ur were buried in tombs containing grave goods, including human servants, in sufficient quantity to justify the speculation that at this period the souls of royalty (at least) could achieve a condition of some comfort in the netherworld. But we cannot generalize from this aberrant period anything about Sumerian or ancient Mesopotamian beliefs generally. The ancient Mesopotamian concept of the soul can be summarized as those aspects of the personality that, regrettably, persist for a time after death in an afterlife without comfort, purpose, or hope.

EGYPT

Although we may suspect that our sources of knowledge (primarily tomb inscriptions) bias our perspective, it nevertheless seems clear that the culture of ancient Egypt was persistently and substantially concerned with the fate of the soul after death. This concern led to conceptions of the soul that are of considerable complexity. If we take the definition of soul to be that part (or those parts) of a person that persists after death, the Egyptian concept of soul involved several major factors, any of which might be termed the soul. They might be thought of as the "*ka* soul," the "*ba* soul," the "*akh* soul," and the "*ab* soul," but the repetition of the English word "soul" could imply a conceptual unity that would distort Egyptian thought. Hence I shall here discuss the *ka,* the *ba,* the *akh,* and the *ab* using those terms.

The Ka. The *ka* is most often termed "vital force" in scholarly commentaries. While this is an imprecise usage, *ka* is by no means a term used with precision by the Egyptians. The hieroglyphic symbol for *ka* is two arms pointing upward that are connected at the base byslightly curved lines probably meant to suggest pectoral muscles. If the *ka* symbol derives from a representation of upraised arms it can be said to imply religious reverence, and this also is implied from the fact that the *ka* symbol is frequently depicted as placed upon a standard in the fashion of symbols of deities. A significant difference of interpretation will result, however, if the *ka* symbol is presumed to derive from an Egyptian two-dimensional representation of outstretched arms rather than of upraised arms. The *ka* symbol has been understood, with good evidence derived from three dimensional statuary, as representing an embrace (as of a son by his father) and as such a symbolic transference of vitality. Our lack of certainty in defining even the shape of the *ka* symbol is indicative of our lack of certainty in defining the *ka* itself. It is probably the most important "soul" concept of the ancient Egyptians, but this very importance leads it to appear in many seemingly conflicting contexts.

In the *Memphite Theology,* the most important statement of Egyptian philosophy known to us, it is written that at the time of creation

> *The mighty Great One is Ptah, who transmitted* [life *to all gods*], *as well as (to) their* ka's, *through this heart, by which Horus became Ptah, and through this tongue, by which Thoth became Ptah. . . . Indeed, all the divine order really came into being through what the heart thought and the tongue commanded. Thus the* ka-*spirits were made and the* hemsut-*spirits were appointed, they who make all provisons and all nourishment, by this speech. . . . So the gods entered into their bodies of every (kind of) wood, of every (kind of) stone, of every (kind of) clay, or anything which might grow upon him, in which they had taken their form. So all the gods, as well as their* ka's *gathered themselves to him, content and associated with the Lord of the Two Lands.*
>
> (quoted in Pritchard, 1969, pp. 4–5)

This text, as do many others, indicates that the individual (here, significantly, the individual gods) and his *ka* were thought of as two conjoined and associated beings; the *ka* was not simply an aspect of one single being. However, it would probably be incorrect to think of a *ka* as a double or a twin in the sense sometimes found in Manichaean writings, since the union of man (or god) and *ka* was intimate and the two could not be separated during life.

The *ka* of a person is his ability to do. It is the power of a god to do divine things, the power of a pharaoh to do divine things, and the power of a human being to do human things. If a god is thought to be resident in or symbolized by a statue (his body of wood, stone, or clay) it would be imperative to be sure that his *ka* also resided there.

The *ka*s of the gods were of a different order than the *ka*s of humans, but the gods were just as dependent upon them for their life as were humans. When Atum brought life to Shu and Tefnut, the first gods, he did so by sharing his *ka* with them by means of an embrace. It might be said that all *ka*s derive ultimately from that of the creator god, that a father's *ka* is transmitted to his son and hence that all *ka*s are in some mystical way united. But for the ancient Egyptians (the pharaoh excepted) a *ka* was a personal possession and it is doubtful that an individual thought of his *ka* as bringing him into union with other individuals.

The *ka* of the pharaoh was of a different order than the *ka* of all commoners as it was a *ka* that could exercise divine powers over the two lands or, in other words, be shared with the two lands. The central mythology of the Osiris/Horus cycle can be understood to focus on the problem of the pharaonic *ka.* Osiris (the former pharaoh) was the progenitor of Horus (the new pharaoh) and so the *ka* of the former reappears in the latter. Horus, however, must journey to the underworld to bring a share of the *ka* back to Osiris so that Osiris can return to life and engender the vital force, *ka,* that provides life and growth to nature and agriculture. On the level of the pharaoh the divine economy of *ka* provides a mediating theme relating the Osiris/Horus mythology to the late Osiris pharaoh and the living Horus pharaoh. The *ka* of the pharaoh that is the *ka* of Osiris was for the ancient Egyptians the force that provided the means of sustenance for all other *ka*s. Only the pharaoh's *ka* is commonly depicted in Egyptian art and inscriptions.

One received one's *ka* at birth and lived with it happily through life (or sadly, for one's *ka* might not be the best and might be unlucky). Its departure is the beginning of death. In the absence of one's *ka* one is a corpse. "The resting of the *ka*" is the period after death but before the rituals of final interment are completed. After interment one "goes to the *ka*" and thereafter is again alive, "master of one's *ka.*" Egyptian mortuary ritual has, therefore, its happy side, for while one might be facing an uncertain future traversing dangerous depths and coaxing grim gatekeepers, one at least will not face the future alone; the *ka* will be there too and may accompany one even into the celestial ship of the sun.

The Ba. In scholarly commentaries the *ba* is often called "soul" or "spirit," but it is unlikely that these terms are more appropriate for the *ba* than for the *ka.* The hieroglyphic representation of the *ba* is a human-headed bird that, not uncommonly, also has human arms and hands. The *ba* is the power of transformation, motion, animation of a person after death; it seems to have played little or no role in the Egyptian conception of a living person. The *ba* served to bind together the mummy and the *ka* of the deceased, provide the mobility the person needed to obtain food and drink and air, and enable the person to leave the tomb at will, travel through the underworld, and become manifest. A symbolic manifestation of a god, an especially potent amulet, or an especially significant text could be called the *ba* of that god. As such it would denote the god's presence in a particular realm. In addition to the *ka* of the god, which would be necessary to empower a sacred statue, one would need to arrange that the statue receive the *ba* of that same god so that the statue would be animated and able to receive and appreciate the offerings made to it. The *ba* of Re is the ram, the hawk is the *ba* of Horus, the crocodile is the *ba* of Sobek and so forth; these are the recognizable forms that those gods assume in communications with humans. A person wishing to assume the form of a hawk, spells tell us, must be endowed with the *ba* of Horus.

For a person recently deceased to resume human form, begin again to be able to consume food and drink, move about from tomb to heavens to the solar ship, the *ba* was absolutely necessary. But it is, perhaps, erroneous to think of "the person" and "the *ba*" as two separate but related entities along the lines of "the person" and "the *ka*." The *ba* is rarely if ever mentioned in texts dealing with living persons, although the *ka* often is. It is probably not the case that a person when dead has a *ba;* rather, the person when dead is a *ba.* A living person, then, would be ego plus body plus *ka;* a dead person (when vitalized) would be *ba* plus mummy plus *ka,* the difference being that ego cannot separate from the body during life while the *ba* is able to move about separately from the mummy. The *ba* remains in some fashion dependent upon the mummy, as the extreme care taken in embalming by ancient Egyptians makes quite clear.

The Akh. The *akh* is commonly translated by scholars as "spirit," or "transfigured spirit." The hieroglyphic character for *akh* is a crested ibis. The *akh* is the condition of a person after death when he may be described as glorious or shining. It carries the implication that he has joined the company of the happy deceased who cluster around the polestar and who therefore do not join in the daily round of the solar boat.

It is likely that the *akh* was a conception of the fate of the deceased that arose independently of that of the *ba* and *ka* and, in keeping with ancient Egypt's propensity to discuss reality by means of a multiplicity of approximations, was simply cojoined with them despite what appear to be conceptual contradictions. This should not be surprising, as we are concerned with a culture that lasted for millennia and was divided throughout that time into various competing centers of theological and necrological thinking and into various social classes. Egyptians seem to have been capable of seeing their dead both as participating in the solar cycles of nature and as transfigured and aloof from those cycles.

The Ab. The *ab* is usually translated as "heart," although "conscience" might be a more appropriate rendering. The hieroglyphic character is a glyph of the human heart, an organ thought by the Egyptians to be the center of moral and ethical judgment.

Perhaps the most well known of all vignettes in the *Book of Going Forth by Day* is that of the judgment hall where Thoth and Anubis oversee the weighing of an *ab* in a giant scale. The *ab* is balanced against a feather, symbol of *maat,* which is the Egyptian term for cosmic and social order and justice. A crocodile monster stands by to devour those hearts that are too heavy. Osiris sits enthroned above the scene, and it may be that those whose hearts are sufficiently light may continue on toward union with him.

There exist, in relation to the judgment scene, texts that are known as "negative confessions." These are ritual claims of innocence in reference to a lengthy list of potential social and ritual misdeeds. These "negative confessions" seem to imply that whether or not there ever was a time when judgment after death in a Christian or Islamic sense was taken seriously, throughout much of ancient Egyptian history judgment was not very much more than another of many trials through which the newly deceased had to pass with the aid of magical knowledge and ritual assistance.

It is probably no more correct to identify the *ab* as a soul than it would be to identify the conscience as a soul. Nevertheless the *ab* does persist after death and so falls into the general definition of soul in use here.

CONCLUSION

The ancient Egyptian conception of the soul contrasts strikingly with that of the Mesopotamians. The Egyptians were convinced that they would exist after death and that this state of existence would quite possibly be pleasurable. If the *ka* be defined as soul, Egyptians made of it a central philosophical abstraction, such that the universe could be said to be sustained by soul and religion to be focused on the mediation of soul between the gods/pharaohs, Horus and Osiris.

BIBLIOGRAPHY

As there is so little to be known about the concept of soul in ancient Mesopotamia, one may turn to virtually any book about the Sumerians, Akkadians, Babylonians, and so forth, with the expectation that the matter will be dealt with briefly and competently. Two of the best introductions to the subject are *The Sumerians* (New York, 1965) by C. Leonard Woolley, and *Ancient Iraq,* rev. ed. (New York, 1980), by Georges Roux. J. B. Pritchard's massive *Ancient Near Eastern Texts* (Princeton, 1969) provides full translations of important Mesopotamian texts (and some from Egypt) with useful commentaries.

The Gods of the Egyptians, vol. 1 (Chicago, 1904), by E. A. Wallis Budge, contains translations of a wide variety of important texts, including lengthy and detailed accounts of the journey of the soul through the afterlife. A creative and impressive recent book on ancient Egypt is R. T. Rundle Clark's *Myth and Symbol in Ancient Egypt* (London, 1959), wherein he sets forth a comprehensive and consistent theory of the meaning and development of Egyptian religion with frequent reference to various soul concepts, especially the *ka.* Henri Frankfort, a great Egyptologist, wrote both popular and technical books. The most accessible to those not knowledgeable about ancient Egypt is *Ancient Egyptian Religion* (New York, 1948); the more technical work most germane to discussion of the soul, particularly as it relates to the pharaoh, is *Kingship and the Gods* (1948; reprint, Chicago, 1978), where a full chapter is given over to consideration of the *ka.* Siegfried Morenz's *Egyptian Religion,* translated by Ann E. Keep (Ithaca, N.Y., 1973), provides a lengthy, competent account of its subject and considers various soul concepts. On practices relating to the souls of the departed, a good recent work is that of C. Jouco Bleeker, *Egyptian Festivals* (Leiden, 1967), which includes a chapter on festivals of the dead.

22 CHINESE CONCEPTS OF THE SOUL AND THE AFTERLIFE

ANNA SEIDEL

The fundamentally this-worldly orientation of ancient Chinese culture placed the world of the dead inside the universe—in the stars, in distant realms on earth, or under the earth. Death was seen not as the separation of two radically different entities like matter and spirit but as the dispersal of a multiplicity of forces (*ch'i,* "breaths"), forces that were graded but basically formed one continuous spectrum. This view accounts for the early, intense, and elaborate search for techniques to attain physical immortality, and also accounts for the vague and fluid boundary between this world and a never radically different hereafter that characterizes all Chinese religion.

SHANG ROYAL ANCESTORS

The people of the Shang period (late second millennium BCE) were in constant communication with the afterworld, that is, with the deceased members of their royal family, whom they consulted through oracles. Many of the records of these oracles, inscribed on bone or tortoiseshell, have been excavated and deciphered. They show that practically all the events of life—illness, misfortune, or defeat, as well as good harvests and victory—were ascribed to the influence of the ancestors' spirits. No description is given of the realm where the dead existed, but evidence of human sacrifices and the elaborate furnishings found in Shang royal tombs suggest that the dead were thought to exist in a style similar to the living, needing servants and possessions. Dogs interred in a pit below the coffin might have had the task of guiding the deceased to the land of the dead, a role later assumed by mythical animals such as dragons.

MAN'S TWO SOULS

Under the reign of the Chou kings (eleventh century–256 BCE) a cult arose dedicated to the deity Heaven (T'ien), an anthropomorphous celestial emperor whose court was composed of the souls of deceased nobles. [*See* T'ien.] The royal family and the families of feudal lords had ancestral temples in which the souls *(hun)* of their ancestors received a cult with offerings, to assure both their welfare in the hereafter and the prosperity of their descendants. According to the classical theory that originated in the early Chou (attested in the *Tso chuan* entry for Duke Chao, 7th year), every member of the aristocracy had two souls, which part company at the moment of death. The *hun* "soul," a spiritual and intelligent personality categorized as *yang,* goes to join the court of Heaven; a more physical vital breath, the *p'o* "soul," of *yin* character, follows the body into the grave or descends to Huang Ch'üan (Yellow Springs), a netherworld under the earth. Elaborate funerals, tomb furnishings, and sacrifices at the tomb were provided to assure the contentment of the *p'o* energy under the earth lest it trouble the family as a malevolent demonic revenant *(kuei).* The first rite after death was the Chao-hun ("summoning back of the *hun* spirit"). A rite that shows traces of early shamanistic practices, it might also have been practiced for the severely ill, whose souls were thought to stray. A poem, *Chao-hun* (c. 240 BCE), in the early anthology *Ch'u tz'u* (Songs of the South) describes to the wandering soul the pleasures it has left behind and the dangers lurking on its way into the other world. Once this rite has proved ineffective, the funeral takes place, and the *hun* spirit is fixed in a tablet that becomes the object of the ancestral cult.

This system of beliefs and mortuary practices is well known since, in an elaborated form and eventually widened to include non-nobility, it has survived throughout Chinese history in the lettered class of state officials. In Chou and Han times there certainly existed a wide variety of other beliefs, most of which have disappeared without trace.

THE NETHERWORLD

Commoners had no individualized ancestors, probably no *hun* spirit; their souls descended into the earth and were thought to assure the fertility of the family fields where they were buried. We do not know what cults were practiced for them.

Belief in the Yellow Springs, probably a feature of early folk culture, is attested mostly in poetic laments about death, but they are never described in any detail. The Yellow Springs seems to have been a sad realm of the shades, not unlike the Greek Hades. That it was imagined very close under the surface of the earth becomes clear in the tale of Prince Chuang (eighth century BCE), who had sworn never again to set eyes on his mother "until both came to the Yellow Springs." Later repenting of this oath, he dug a tunnel and, entering it, was able to meet his mother under the earth without violating his oath (*Tso chuan,* Duke Yin, first year).

IDENTITY OF LIFE AND DEATH

The philosophers also imagined destinies for man's souls. "Man's life is a coming-together of breath [*ch'i*]. If it comes together, there is life; if it scatters, there is death" (*Chuang-tzu,* chap. 22). Death was seen as a redispersing of the *ch'i* energy into the *ch'i* freely flowing between Heaven and earth, like drops of a liquid poured back into water.

Those thinkers who emphasized the universal rhythm of transformation in nature and advocated man's adaptation to this "Way" *(tao)* saw death as but one phase in the process of change. "Do not disturb the process of change!" said Li to the grieving family of a sick friend. He then asks the friend, "What is the Creator [personified Change] going to make of you next? . . . Will he make you into a rat's liver? Will he make you into a bug's arm?" (*Chuang-tzu,* chap. 6). Chuang-tzu here alludes to ancient peasant beliefs in the metamorphosis of all creatures into each other, as silkworms are transformed into moths. He applies these beliefs in physical metamorphosis to the natural transition from life to death and so brings himself to the conclusion that the afterlife can be seen in a happier light than life in this world. "How do I know that the dead do not wonder why they ever longed for life?" he asks (chap. 2). A skull confirms his view: "Among the dead, there are no such things as lords, vassals, seasons, or tasks. Peaceful as we are, we have no age but that of Heaven and Earth. A king on his throne does not enjoy greater felicity than ours" (chap. 18). Lao-tzu and Chuang-tzu both thought that death should be neither feared nor desired, advocating instead a resigned and serene acceptance of death as a part of the ever-changing mechanism of nature.

Although peasant beliefs are used as illustrations, these were the highly sophisticated views of mystics nurtured on the worldview of the *I ching* (Book of Changes). The common people's attitude was nearer that of Achilles in the underworld, who tells Odysseus that he would prefer to live on earth as the hireling of another than be king over all the dead.

PROLONGING LIFE IN THIS WORLD

Stronger than the impulse to improve one's lot after death were the efforts to prolong life in this world. Life was greatly treasured and, in the course of the first millennium BCE, the Chinese came to place more and more emphasis on longevity. This is evidenced by bronze inscriptions from the eighth century BCE onward that speak of *nan-lao* ("retardation of old age"), *pao-shen* ("preservation of the body"), and *wu-ssu* ("deathlessness"). From about 400 BCE onward the belief existed that some men had achieved perpetual life, that their souls had neither gone to the Yellow Springs nor dissipated into the vastness of the universe; instead they were preserved in a perfected spectral body, able to wander on earth and among the stars forever. These were the "immortals" *(hsien).* Their appearance in Han iconography as birdlike men, sprouting feathers over their body or fitted with wings, was influenced by the ancient bird mythology of the northeastern seaboard. [*See* Hsien.]

THE PARADISES OF THE IMMORTALS

The immortals had "transcended the world" *(tu-shih),* "ascended to distant places" *(teng-hsia),* and lived in a world of light, on holy mountains, or in paradises situated at the rim of the world. P'eng-lai, a paradise island, was imagined to be in the East China Sea. From the fourth to the second century BCE, princes and emperors sent out repeated expeditions in search of it and the drug of deathlessness rumored to be obtainable there. Chuang-tzu does not use the term *hsien,* but his description of the Perfected Ones *(chen-jen)* on Mount Ku-she gives an idea of the physical techniques they practiced and of the beneficent influence they were thought to exercise. "Their skin is like ice or snow, and they are gentle and shy like young girls. They do not eat the five grains, but suck the wind, drink the dew, climb up on the clouds and mist, ride flying dragons and wander beyond the four seas. By concentrating their spirit, they can protect creatures from sickness and plague and make the harvest plentiful" (chap. 1). [*See* Chen-jen.]

Toward the middle of the Han dynasty (206 BCE–220 CE), new geographical knowledge created a shift of interest to the northwest. Mount K'un-lun on the threshold of Central Asia had long been a mythical nine-layered mountain that led up to the

Gate of Heaven. Its deity, the Queen Mother of the West (Hsi Wang Mu), was a timeless creature with the tail of a leopard and the teeth of a tiger, reigning over the land where the sun sets. Soon she was venerated as a donor of the drug of immortality (in Ssu-ma Hsiang-ju's poems) and by the second century CE she had become the queen of a western paradise, one peopled by immortals and sought by all those who exerted themselves in the mental and bodily techniques of immortality. [*See* Hsi Wang Mu.]

TOKENS OF IMMORTALITY IN HAN TOMBS

The recent archaeological discovery of Hsi Wang Mu in fresco paintings, on stone reliefs, and on bronze mirrors in many Han tombs has added a new facet to our knowledge of this deity. Hsi Wang Mu was not only queen of those who had avoided death and achieved immortality, but she seems also to have played a major role in mortuary cults. The rich imagery of the immortality cult is expressed in tomb furnishings, which demonstrate a wish, if not a belief, that the dead too may accede to immortality. The famous silk painting of the Ma-wang-tui Tomb no. 1 in central China (168 BCE) shows the journey of the soul through what some interpret as the Isle of P'eng-lai up to Heaven; in later tombs, pictures of the deceased's journey to the mountain of Hsi Wang Mu predominate.

The contradiction between burial of the dead and deathless immortality on Mount K'un-lun was bridged by the belief that immortals die an apparent death and are buried like everyone else. Only a later inspection of their tomb reveals that the "corpse" buried was in fact only some personal item like their sandals. In 110 BCE, Emperor Wu of the Han expressed surprise at the existence of a tomb of the Yellow Emperor (Huang-ti), who was said to have ascended straight to Heaven; he was told that the tomb contained only Huang-ti's hat and robe (*Shih chi* 28). [*See* Huang-ti.]

COLLECTIVE ASCENSIONS TO HEAVEN

Popular belief in the effectiveness of elixirs created stories of immortality gained without any arduous practice. Huang-ti ascended to Heaven with his whole court and harem. The prince of Huai-nan (d. 122 BCE), a great patron of Taoist *fang-shih* masters, ascended with his household, including his dogs and livestock (*Lun heng,* c. 80 CE). [*See* Fang-shih.] Another rare glimpse into Han immortality lore is the story of T'ang Kung-fang, a petty official (c. 7 CE) who received enough elixir from a supernatural master to feed it to his family and domestic animals, and also to daub his house with it, whereupon man, beast, and house rose into the clouds (*Ch'üan Hou Han wen* 106). This story also shows the widening, during the Han period, of the social basis of these beliefs; immortality and afterlife in heaven ceased to be a prerogative of the nobles.

THE NETHERWORLD OF MOUNT T'AI

Miracle tales and a fascination with the unique Chinese concept of material immortality must not cloud our view of the ordinary fate of the dead in the centuries preceding the advent of Buddhism in China. Recent archaeological discoveries enable us to date the bureaucratization of the Chinese otherworld to rather less than a century after the establishment of the earthly centralized empires of Ch'in and

Han. In the Ma-wang-tui tombs mentioned earlier were found official lists itemizing the mortuary objects and addressed to an underworld official with the request to forward this document to the Lord of the Dead (Chu-tsang Chün). A poem of the same period links the sad underworld of the Yellow Springs with Kao-li, a peak near Mount T'ai, whence come the summons of death (*Han shu* 63). Mount T'ai, the Eastern Sacred Peak in Shantung, long since venerated as the origin of all life, in the Han dynasty becomes the seat of the otherworldly administration. It is the tribunal where the records of the living and the dead are kept on jade tablets (see especially *Feng-su t'ung-i*) and whither the *hun* and *p'o* souls are summoned. The deity of Mount T'ai is the "grandson of the Heavenly Emperor" (see *Hsiao-ching yüan-shen ch'i*); his realm is a forecourt of Heaven and the earthly branch of a developing stellar bureaucracy of destiny. The "Director of Destinies" (Ssu-ming), a stellar deity with the powers to lengthen or to shorten man's life, appeared already in the *Ch'u tz'u* in the third century BCE. *Huai-nan–tzu* (chap. 3) tells of four stellar palaces that administer rewards and punishments. The judgment of these ministries probably concerned both the living and the dead. Mount T'ai also acquires a judiciary function with the power to lengthen or shorten the allotted lifespan; a late Han *fang-shih* made a pilgrimage to Mount T'ai to petition the god for a longer life (*Hou Han shu* 112).

A rich panorama of an otherwordly bureaucracy unfolds in the popular literature of the following centuries. Those who expired after a meritorious or saintly life can reach high office in the hereafter, whereas those who had died a violent death and those deprived of proper burial or offerings at their tombs languish as prisoners or corvée laborers. The term for the underworld changes from "below the earth" *(ti-hsia)* to "earth prefecture" *(t'u-fu,* in the *T'ai-p'ing ching)* and to "prison in the earth" (*ti-yü,* which became the translation also for the Buddhist hells).

The border between this world and the other remains fluid. Messengers from Mount T'ai can be sighted on their errands and unjustly executed men can, in the otherworldly tribunals they reach, have their tormentors condemned to early death. Descriptions of these tribunals abound in stories of men who died and came back to life, having been summoned to Mount T'ai by bureaucratic error (see *Sou-shen chi; Yüan-hun chih*). The judge of the dead is the Lord of the Tribunal of Mount T'ai (T'ai-shan Fu-chün). Around the fifth century CE he is dislodged by the Buddhist King Yama, whose scribe he becomes in the Buddhist hells.

THE OTHERWORLDLY BUREAUCRACY OF TAOISM

In the emerging Taoist religion new concepts evolved that helped to shape Chinese Buddhist notions of the afterlife. One's initiation into the Celestial Master sect (T'ien-shih Tao, late second century CE) meant access to the hierarchy of the immortals and salvation from an afterlife existence as a demon in the domain of the subterranean Water Official (Shui-kuan) or in jails inside mountain caverns. The Three Officials (San Kuan, of Heaven, Earth, and Water) and the Five Emperors of the Five Sacred Mountains constituted a comprehensive otherworldly network in which the spirits of the just advanced in an administrative hierarchy that led to ever higher immortal status while the uninitiated and the wicked constituted the hordes of subservient demons (*Pao-p'u–tzu* 3; *Chen kao* 15, 16). Mediumistic revelations informed the living about the other world. They revealed the names of gods and demons that should be offered propitiatory or apotropaic rites, or summoned a deserving adept to a vacant office in the beyond (see *Ming-t'ung chi*).

Sinners were criminals, sins were crimes; atonement and advancement followed judiciary procedure. The emphasis is never on torments in hells but on continued advancement through the netherworldly hierarchy to the stellar palaces of the immortals. Attention was less on the sufferings of the wicked than on the rites performed to appease demons, the unshriven dead, who threaten to harm the living. An important concern was the supernatural inspection of man's good and bad deeds, duplicate records of which were kept in stellar offices and in the mountain tribunals. These registers determined the length of man's lifespan, his status in the world beyond the tomb, and sometimes even the destiny of his descendants (see *T'ai-p'ing ching; Pao-p'u-tzu; Ch'ih-sung-tzu chung chieh ching*).

In these basic features, which already included a judiciary concept of judgment and retribution of crimes, this Chinese underworld as yet owes nothing to Buddhism. Between the second and the seventh century it was enriched by the doctrines of *karman,* retribution in hells, and reincarnation. It in turn had a profound influence on the Chinese Buddhist concepts of the afterlife, for in Chinese Buddhism, the tribunals became the way stations of the soul on its path to reincarnation. The scenario of Buddhist judgment that emerges in the tenth century CE is a huge tribunal with the so-called Ten Buddhist Kings of Hell, who are represented as ten Chinese magistrates presiding over ten courts of justice. Among these magistrates we find King Yama and the King of Mount T'ai (see *Shih-wang ching*).

[*See also* Chinese Religion, *article on* Mythic Themes; Soul, *article on* Chinese Concepts; Alchemy, *article on* Chinese Alchemy; *and* Taoism, *overview article and article on* The Taoist Religious Community.]

BIBLIOGRAPHY

The ancestor cult of the Shang is described by Chang Tsung-tung in *Der Kult der Shang-Dynastie im Spiegel der Orakelinschriften,* edited by Otto Karow (Wiesbaden, 1970), pp. 34–166. A good general presentation of early Chinese ideas about the afterlife, especially the development of immortality beliefs and techniques, may be found in Joseph Needham's *Science and Civilisation in China,* vol. 2 (Cambridge, 1956), pp. 71–126. The quotations from the *Chuang-tzu* are from Burton Watson's *The Complete Works of Chuang Tzu* (New York, 1968). For Han myths and iconography concerning the afterlife, see Michael Loewe's *Ways to Paradise: The Chinese Quest for Immortality* (London 1979), reviewed in *Numen* 29 (1982): 79–122; and *Chinese Ideas of Life and Death* (London, 1982), pp. 25–37. Sakai Tadao's old but valuable study of the early cult of Mount T'ai, "Taizan shinkō no kenkyū," *Shichō* 7 (1937): 70–119, can today be supplemented by much new archaeological data. There is as yet no comprehensive study of the Mount T'ai tribunals or of the bureaucratic netherworld of early Taoism. The *Yüan hun chih* has been translated by Alvin P. Cohen as *Tales of Vengeful Souls,* "Variétés sinologiques," n.s. 68 (Taipei, Paris, and Hong Kong, 1982).

23 CONCEPTS OF THE SOUL IN INDIAN RELIGIONS

WILLIAM K. MAHONY

The many religious traditions of South Asia present such a variety of views regarding the psychological, metaphysical, and ethical nature of the human being and its relationship to the world that no single concept could adequately and consistently fit the English word *soul.* This may be due, in part, to the ambiguous connotations of the term itself. If by *soul* one denotes a dimension to human life that is distinguishable from corporeal existence and that to a large extent determines the nature of the human being, then one could rightly say that the various religions and philosophies of South Asia posit the existence of a soul (the most notable exception being the materialistic views of the Cārvāka and Lokāyata philosophies, which maintain that a person is nothing more than a conglomeration of physical matter). This is true even in the case of Buddhism, which, despite the fact that the doctrine of *anātman* ("no-soul") is one of the basic tenets of Buddhist teachings, still holds that the laws of *karman* apply to what is experienced as a self and that the moral aspect of one's being is subject to the cycles of rebirth. In general, South Asian religious anthropologies recognize an aspect to the human being (and, in some traditions, to all sentient beings) that either (1) survives the body's physical death and may be reborn in another form according to the actions performed in previous lives or (2) is uncreated and unchanging, does not experience the vicissitudes of mortal existence, and resides beyond the causal and normative realms.

One could not say, however, that the diverse religions and philosophies of the subcontinent that accept the notion of the self or the soul would maintain the same view regarding its ontological status or that they all hold the same values regarding its nature. Of course, this would be the case in any study in the history of complicated religious systems, but generalization is more dangerous in the case of the study of South Asian religions than it might be in others, because the teachings presented by some of those religions diametrically oppose those of other—even closely related—South Asian traditions. The monistic Advaita Vedānta argues that the soul *(ātman)* is the only reality, for example, while the equally monistic Mādhyamika school of Buddhism would hold that something is real precisely if it has *no* soul *(nairātmya, anātman).* Other religious traditions in South Asia similarly disagree on whether or not the soul is substantive or ephemeral, individual or universal, temporal or eternal, personal or impersonal.

Perhaps the best way to avoid confusion regarding the various concepts of the soul in India and Sri Lanka would be to avoid the term *soul* altogether in favor of other and various—although probably just as ambiguous—translations of the different terms used by the traditions themselves. Such an abandonment having been made impossible by the very title of this article, however, one hopes that the confusion will be less puzzling by the end of this piece.

The following discussion summarizes Vedic, Vedantic, and Buddhist concepts of the soul. This tripartite classification is given for convenience rather than as a statement of rigid categorization. Yogic, Sāṃkhya, and theistic understandings of the soul will appear here and there throughout the following sections.

VEDIC CONCEPTS OF THE SOUL

Vedic cremation hymns of the latter part of the second millennium BCE plead the fire not to burn the "unborn" *(ajobhāga)* or "undying" *(amartya)* parts of the deceased, for the ritualists held the position that a nonphysical dimension of the human being survives the death of the physical body and flies like a bird in a radiant body either to the *pitṛloka* ("world of the ancestors"), ruled by the Lord of the Dead, or to the *devaloka* ("world of the gods"), depending on the quality of the rituals the person performed while living on earth.

Thus, Vedic poets and visionaries recognized a difference between the corporeal body (*śarīra, kāya, deha,* etc.) and an immaterial spirit that might loosely be called the soul. The latter is generally understood in four ways, three of which *(jīva, manas, asu)* revolve around notions of what could be termed the individual soul while the fourth (*paramātman,* etc.) centers on the concept of a universal spirit. (1) *Jīva* ("living being") is one's biological and functional personality, that aspect of one's being that distinguishes one individual from another and that suffers or enjoys existence in earthly as well as post-mortal life according to the acts one performs while alive in this world. (2) *Manas* ("mind") is that subtle or immaterial structure of one's being by which one knows that one is related in various ways to other divine and human beings. It is that incorporeal and cognizant dimension of the human being in which awareness resides and from which the sense of being alive derives. (3) *Asu* (the "breath of life") is the vital force that brings life to inert matter, creates sentience, and which in general serves to animate the human being. In the latter part of the Vedic era, the concept of respiration (*prāṇa,* a form of *asu*) becomes one of the important images of ultimate reality.

Whether it is understood existentially and ethically (as one would infer from the connotations of *jīva*), or psychologically and epistemologically *(manas),* or ontologically *(asu/prāṇa),* the soul is said to exist independently of the physical body, which when deprived of its cognizing and animating spirit will become inert and lifeless (*śava, kuṇapa,* i.e., a "corpse"). This happens most obviously at the time of death, a moment the *Ṛgveda* sometimes describes as *asunīti* ("leading forth of *asu*"), that process by which one travels away from the physical body to the world of the ancestors or the gods and by which the soul returns to earth escorted by the celestial fire, Agni. This same disjunction may occur, in addition, during moments of unconsciousness, ecstasy, or dream sleep, states of being that in Vedic India were both feared and prized—feared because one did not want one's spirit to get lost in the otherworld (thus the warning in *Bṛhadāraṇyaka Upaniṣad* 4.3.14 and parallels not to wake a sleeping person too quickly because his life may not have time to return to his body), yet prized because these moments of disembodied existence allow one to gain knowledge of supermundane worlds and to bring that knowledge back to the waking or conscious state. The term *preta* ("one who has gone forth") is sometimes used to describe such a departed or disembodied spirit, which lives in or travels to various regions of the cosmos once it has left the physical body.

The soul as *jīva, manas,* or *asu* is regarded as a unique dimension of a human being. However, later hymns of the *Ṛgveda* reflect the idea that each distinct living being finds its origin in a common, solitary, and universal spirit. Terms that imply this transpersonal notion of the soul vary from context to context. While a generic term would be (4) *paramātman,* which would connote the universal soul as opposed to the individual soul, verses from various Vedic songs and chants refer to this generative force, the source of all being, as Puruṣa (the primordial "person" of the universe), Viśvakarman ("maker of everything"), Prajāpati ("lord of [all] living things"), Vena ("the loving one"), Paramam Guhā ("greatest secret"), Skambha ("universal prop"), Jyeṣṭha Brahman ("the highest, or ultimate, reality"), or simply Tat ("it"). Throughout the pertinent verses runs the theme that this "soul" of the cosmos is a unified reality, the sole source of all existence, out of which all diversity comes and into which all things merge. Though this ultimate reality is the efficient source of all things in the physical world, it itself is subtle and unmanifest. It is *ucchiṣṭha brahman* (see *Atharvaveda* 11.7), the ultimate reality that still remains after all phenomenal, temporal, and spatial forms have been subtracted from the universe. Notions of this unified world soul that first appear in the later parts of the Vedic Saṃhitās find their most thorough exposition and analysis in the Upaniṣads and Vedantic commentaries.

UPANIṢADIC AND VEDANTIC CONCEPTS

The seers of the early Vedic period generally understood the soul, the world, and the gods in realistic terms; all existed in an objective relationship. However, toward the end of the period in which the Vedic hymns were composed, certain poet-philosophers began to present more subjective ontologies. All the gods and all of nature were seen to be reflections of inner structures and processes. The *Atharvaveda*'s proclamation that "having made the mortal a home, the gods lived within a man" (11.8.18) and the *Jaiminīya Upaniṣad Brāhmaṇa*'s assertion that "all the gods are within me" (1.14.2) typify an emergent Vedic metaphysical anthropology that subsumes earlier objective theologies and ritual notions and establishes the important principle of the subjective identity between macrocosm and microcosm.

The contemplative search for an understanding of the subjective structures of ultimate reality was of paramount concern to the forest dwellers who composed the Upaniṣads as well as to the thinkers who expounded on those works and whose teachings form the Vedānta (the "end of the Veda"). Seeking to know the nature of the self and its relationship to the world, these thinkers came to understand that behind or beyond all of the whirling flux of one's personal existence, deep within the living and dying physical body, exists an eternal, unchanging, intelligent, incorporeal, and joyful "self," and they saw that this essential reality is identical to the very ground being of the universe itself. "A person the size of a thumb lives in the middle of the body, like a flame without smoke," reads *Kaṭha Upaniṣad* 2.1.13. "He is the lord of the past and of the future. He is the same today and [will be] the same tomorrow. This [soul], truly, is That."

The early and middle Upaniṣads (900–300 BCE) posit a distinction between material and spiritual existence, a cosmological or ontological stance that reflects the influence of early Sāṃkhya philosophies; the latter maintained that one's self is comprised of mutable physical matter *(prakṛti),* on the one hand, and immutable nonmanifest spirit *(puruṣa),* on the other. As would be consistent with Sāṃkhya metaphysics and psychology, those elements of one's self that have any content or substance are, by nature, *prakṛti,* and therefore are not spiritual. Thus, the intellect *(buddhi),* the sense of self, or ego (*ahaṃkāra;* lit., "I-maker"), and the mind *(manas)* are constitutive of the world of matter and therefore cannot be considered to be dimensions of the soul.

Middle and especially later medieval Upaniṣads similarly show the influence of yogic philosophies and practices designed to "yoke" one's individual spiritual being with the unmanifest, unchanging, and eternal spirit and thus to attain autonomy *(kaivalya)* over the fluctuations and limitations of the physical world. While the early Upaniṣads often use the word *puruṣa* ("person") and the later Upaniṣads use such terms as *kṣetrajñā* ("knower, witness") to distinguish the world soul from the individual being (*pradhāna, jīva, sattva,* and so on), the most common terms generally used in Vedānta to signify the untransmigrating, eternal, and unified self are *ātman* and *brahman. Ātman* (which in the *Ṛgveda* had meant, like *asu,* "breath") signifies the subtle, timeless, and deathless microcosmic self. *Brahman* (roughly, "expansive") refers to the equivalent intelligent and blissful essence of the macrocosm.

Said differently, *ātman* is the soul while *brahman* is the godhead. For many Vedantic thinkers the two are the same thing, a point made clear by such statements as the *Adhyātma Upaniṣad*'s assertion that "one is a liberated person who, through insight, sees no difference between his own *ātman* and *brahman,* and between *brahman* and the universe."

Upaniṣadic doctrine holds the position, therefore, that the souls of people, physical objects, otherworldly beings, and deities are all equal in that they are all *brahman:* "*Brahman* is [the gods] Brahmā, Viṣṇu, Rudra, and Indra; *brahman* is Yama [Lord of the Dead], the sun and the moon; *brahman* is the gods, spirits, and demons; men, women, and animals. . . . All of this, truly, is *brahman*" (*Nirālamba Upaniṣad* 6–20).

The composers of the Upaniṣads experienced *ātman* and *brahman* in cosmic, acosmic, monistic, and sectarian theological ways. Those who interpreted the self cosmically (*saguṇa,* "with qualities") depicted it as the subtle and stable essence of all that is, the foundation of the entire world. The sages of the *Chāndogya Upaniṣad,* for example, put it thus: "This is my self [*ātman*] within the heart, smaller than a grain of rice, or a corn of barley, or a mustard seed, or a grain of millet, or the kernel within a grain of millet. This is my self within the heart, greater than the earth, greater than the skies, greater than the heavens, greater than [all] the worlds" (3.14.3). They further proclaim that "all actions, all desires, all odors, all tastes, compassing [everything] . . . this is my soul [*ātman*] within the heart. This is *brahman*" (3.14.4). The soul, experienced cosmically, is everything that is real (see, e.g., *Kaṭh. Up.* 2.1.5–11).

Understood acosmically (*nirguṇa,* "without qualities"), *ātman* and *brahman* are the final reality that exists independently of all physical, personal, and causal terms. The acosmic soul is that imperishable and immutable reality that cannot be described or known rationally precisely because, like the notion of *ucchiṣṭa brahman,* it is nonphenomenal. *Subāla Upaniṣad* (3.1) represents such an acosmic view when it describes the soul as "nonbeing, unborn, uncreated, nonexistent, not based on anything, silent, without solidity, formless, tasteless, odorless, [and] imperishable. A wise person therefore never sorrows, for he knows the soul [*ātman*] to be vast, independent, and without origin." The *Bṛhadāraṇyaka Upaniṣad* (3.9.26 and parallels) similarly expresses this acosmic view of the soul when it repeats the lesson that the self is "not this, not this."

Interpreted theologically, the soul (here, *ātman*) is said to be the presence in the living being of a supreme deity, known generally as Īś, Īśa, or Īśvara, and more particularly as Śiva, Viṣṇu, or some other supreme deity according to the specific sectarian group. Such a position holds that the worship of a supreme god (or, as in the case with the Vaiṣṇava Upaniṣads, the adoration of God's *avatāras*) is, in fact, the worship of the *ātman.* The *Maitreya Upaniṣad* typifies a Śaiva-sectarian point of view when it states, "The body is said to be a temple. The self [*jīva*] within it is none other than Śiva. Having discarded all the residual effects of ignorance, one should worship him with [the words] 'I am He' " (2.2). The *Ātmabhoda Upaniṣad* similarly represents a Vaiṣṇava position: "I [Nārāyana, a name for Viṣṇu] am beyond all the differences in the universe, [beyond the distinction between] individual and God. I am supreme. I am not different from the personal soul [*pratyagātman*]." The *Īśa Upaniṣad* carries a similar message. Singing that "everything, whatever lives in this living world, is enveloped by the Lord" (1), the sage goes on to proclaim that "whoever that person [*puruṣa*] is, so also am I" (16).

Understood monistically, the universal soul (most often in this case *brahman* or *parabrahman,* "supreme *brahman*") is said to encompass all cosmic and acosmic, personal and impersonal, immanent and transcendent concepts. While teachings supporting this notion of the soul appear throughout the Upaniṣads, typical representatives would include the statement in the *Kaṭha Upaniṣad* that "the One Self within all beings becomes varied in shape according to whatever [it lives in] and yet it lives outside [all of them]" (2.2.10); the *Īśa Upaniṣad*'s "It moves, and it moves not. It is far, and it is near. It is within all this, and it is outside all this" (5); and the *Maitreya Upaniṣad*'s "I am the self. I am also the not-self. I am *brahman.* . . . I am all of the worlds . . . . I am not the universe. I am the seer of everything. I am without eyes" (3.1ff.).

Medieval Vedantic philosophers did not entirely agree on the particulars of the identity between *ātman* and *brahman* (and equivalent terms). For the thinkers of the Advaita ("nondual") Vedānta this identity was of monistic character. The extent of *ātman* is the extent of *brahman,* a position argued most forcefully by Śaṅkara (eighth century CE) and his students. The Śrī Vaiṣṇava theologian Rāmānuja (eleventh century CE) and his followers taught a qualified nondualist, or panentheistic, doctrine known as Viśiṣṭādvaita ("identity within distinctions") or *bhedābheda* ("difference and yet no difference"), a position that allowed for the greatness of the supreme soul beyond any cosmic or acosmic limitations. A third view, represented most articulately by Madhva (fourteenth century CE) and his school, argues in favor of *Dvaita Vedānta,* a dualistic ontology that keeps matter and spirit eternally separate.

BUDDHIST CONCEPTS

Buddhist canonical and commentarial literatures from India and Sri Lanka use many of the same terms to connote the individual person as do the Upaniṣadic and Vedantic traditions, the most common being *ātman* (Pali, *attan), jīva,* and *sattva (satta).* Buddhist Abhidharma texts frequently employ the term *pudgala (puggala)* to refer to that aspect of a living being that makes it distinct from other creatures and that in some way carries from one birth to another the moral residues of the previous life's actions. Myths, legends, and pedagogical stories such as the Pali *Petavatthu* (Tales about the Spirits) similarly use such terms as *petta* ("one who has gone forth") when telling of ancestors who now live in one of the many levels of the cosmos ranging from the hells to the heavens in accordance with their karmic residue. Such well-known works as the Theravādin *Milindapañha* employ such terms as *vedagu* to refer to a fully sentient being, and the Mahāyāna *Laṅkāvatāra Sūtra* speaks of *tathāgatagarbha* ("the womb [or abode] of suchness") and *ālaya-vijñāna* (the "store of consciousness") when discussing the process of understanding, the nature of awareness, and the place where such awareness resides in the human being.

Buddhist texts in general, then, acknowledge the existence of a self as an entity that distinguishes one individual from another, that serves as the center of intellect, will, and moral agency, and that is understood to be the source of human perfection. This attitude toward the self dates to the earliest Buddhist textual traditions. Literatures of the Pali canon, for example, often use the adverb *paccattam* (or *pati-attam*), "separately, by oneself, in one's own heart," when referring to the existential and volitional dimension of one's being. Pali collections of the Buddha's reported teachings also use such compounds as *ajjhatta* (cf. Skt. *adhyātman*) to signify the inner self that is of great importance to Buddhist ethical reflection and personal religious practice. The *Dhammapada* describes a *bhikkhu* (roughly, "monk") as one who is "in love with the inner self [*ajjhatarata*], one who is content in solitude" (2.362), and the *Suttanipāta* similarly encourages the *bhikkhu* "not to let his mind go forth to external things, [but to remain] one with his mind turned to the inner self [*ajjattacintī*]" (2.14.168).

The Buddha's reported distrust of teachings not based in experience and, accordingly, his emphasis on the importance of "self-realization" (a loose translation of such phrases as *attā va seyyo,* "the self is the best") led his followers to stress his lesson that the self is the only source of truth. This emphasis is represented by the well-known admonition *"Attadīpā viharatha attasaraṇā anaññasaraṇā"* ("Remain making yourself your island [or support], making yourself your refuge, and not anyone else as your refuge"; see, e.g., *Dīgha Nikāya* 2, *Mahāparinibbāna Sutta* 35).

We must be careful, however, not to confuse this Buddhist notion of the moral, intellectual, and volitional aspect of the human being with an Upaniṣadic or Vedantic concept of the self or of a soul. Buddhist traditions as a whole distinguish a difference between what might be termed a functional self on one hand and an ontological soul on the other. At no time should these various terms signifying the autonomous self be understood to represent the notion of an undying, unchanging, and knowable soul. Nowhere in Buddhist canonical or semicanonical writings does the term *brahman* appear in the Upaniṣadic sense of the unified ground of being, and, certainly, in no Buddhist text does one find the teaching that *ātman* (and its equivalents) and *brahman* are identical or even related. For, with only a few quite vague exceptions, Buddhism in South Asia has maintained the position that what might be termed the ontological soul is nonsubstantial and illusory. In fact, Buddhism in general has maintained that to think that anybody or anything has an unchanging and permanent self or soul is a metaphysically incorrect or even perverted view *(viparyāsa),* for everything—everything—is always changing, and to cling to anything as if it were permanent is to misunderstand the nature of reality. To hold to a self is to hold to an artificial and ignorant construction. Reality is *nairātmya* or *anātman (anattā),* meaning "devoid of self."

Buddhist anthropologies, therefore, posit very different definitions of the person than do Upaniṣadic and Vedantic traditions. Although Buddhist teachings recognize various immaterial aspects to a person, these ephemeral dimensions are never understood to have independent ontological integrity, or "own-being" *(svabhāva). Ātman* is said to be dependent on a variety of transitory conditions, to be impermanent, and therefore to lack any reality of its own.

Buddhist analysis of the nature of the person centers on the realization that what appears to be an individual is, in fact, an ever-changing combination of five constituent factors or building blocks *(skandha;* Pali, *khandha):* the physical body *(rūpa),* physical sensation *(vedanā),* sense perception *(saṃjñā, saññā),* habitual tendencies *(saṃskāra, saṃkhārā),* and consciousness *(vijñāna, viññāna).* These five aggregates fall together in various configurations to form what is experienced as a person, much in the same way that a chariot is built of various parts (see *Milindapañhā* 2.1.1). But just as the chariot as an entity disappears when its constituent elements are pulled apart, so does *ātman* disappear with the dissolution of the *skandhas*. The Theravāda philosopher Buddhaghosa (fifth century CE) uses the simile of the chariot to open his lesson in *Visuddhimagga* (The Path of Purification) regarding the soul (or lack thereof):

> *Just as the term "chariot" is nothing but an expression for an axle, wheels, a body, a pole, and other constituent parts combined in a particular manner, but when we analyze the various parts one by one we find that in the absolute sense there is no chariot. . . . In that same way, the terms "living being" and "soul" are nothing but expressions for the combination of the five* skandhas, *but when we analyze those aggregates of being one by one we find that in the absolute sense there is no "living being" or "soul" with which to form such assumptions as "I am" or "I."* (18.28)

The five *skandhas* are themselves said to be comprised of effervescent elements (*dharmas*, *dhammas*) which, like bubbles on the surface of a stream, form different shapes as they flow in and out of contact with each other. It is these different configurations that determine the nature of individuality, which would not exist without the *dharmas*.

Teachings regarding the ontological status of the *dharmas* varies from school to school, but never does the central notion of a soul appear. The Sarvāstivādins held that the *dharmas* are substantial and, being constitutive of space and time, exist eternally (*sarvāstivāda,* i.e., "the doctrine that everything exists"). Even while holding this eternalist view, however, the Sarvāstivādins remained true to the doctrine of *anātman,* for they maintained the position that the *dharmas* are independent of each other and as autonomous entities do not constitute a whole that is larger than the sum of the parts. The Sarvāstivādins teach that the *dharmas* do, however, interact with each other. This action *(karman)* follows the laws of cause and effect, thus bringing about the dynamic movements of time and space.

Some schools, notably the Pudgalavādins and other Abhidharmists, hold that a personal and moral aspect of one's being (*pudgala, puggala;* lit., "person") accumulates this *karman* and transmigrates from one birth to another according to the quality of the karmic residue. Even these schools, however, distinguish between *karman,* "action," and *kartṛ,* "actor." No school holds the ontological validity of the latter, which is a fiction of an ignorant mind.

The Mādhyamika school maintained that even the *dharmas* are devoid of any untransmutable or eternal essence and are therefore also *nairātmya.* This means that all existence conditioned by the *dharmas* and *skandhas*—in other words, what from the everyday point of view is "reality"—is by its very nature impermanent and without substance. The implication is clear. What conditions existence has no essence, and since a human being is the aggregate combination of various impermanent conditions, then that being has no permanent essence. What we experience to be a person is not a thing but a process. There is no human being, there is only becoming. There is no static and eternal soul. Human life is *anātman,* like the constantly changing patterns of insubstantial bubbles on an insubstantial stream.

The Buddha himself is reported to have understood the anxiety that may arise when one ponders the possibility that one has no soul. According to tradition, he answered such fears by analyzing the source of the anxiety itself. One is afraid of non-being only when one thinks "I have no soul." This torment ends when the realization arises that the "I" that fears such an annihilation is itself imaginary. The comprehension of the "fact of non-selfness" *(nairātmyāstika)* brings freedom from fear, doubt, insecurity, and pain. According to virtually all Buddhist traditions, this freedom from suffering is precisely what the Buddha hoped his followers would find.

BIBLIOGRAPHY

Although it will take some time and reading between the lines, readers who are interested in Vedic notions of the soul will find no better reference than the hymns of the *Ṛgveda* and *Atharvaveda.* The most accessible complete translations of the former are Karl Friedrich Geldner's *Der Rig-Veda aus dem Sanskrit in Deutsche übersetzt,* 4 vols., "Harvard Oriental Series," nos. 33–36 (Cambridge, Mass., 1951–1957), and Ralph T. H. Griffith's now outdated *The Hymns of the Rigveda,* 2d rev. ed., edited by Jagdish Lal Shastri (Delhi, 1973). Excellent partial translations appear in Louis Renou's *Études védiques et pāṇinéennes,* 17 vols. (Paris, 1955–1977), Wendy Doniger O'Flaherty's *The Rig Veda: An Anthology* (Harmondsworth, 1982), and Tatyana Takovlena Elizarenkova's Russian translation, *Rigveda: Izbrannye gimny* (Moscow, 1972). The most complete annotated translation of the *Atharvaveda* is William Dwight Whitney's *Atharva-Veda Saṁhitā,* 2 vols., edited by Charles R. Lanman (1905; Delhi, 1962).

Readers looking for translations of the Upaniṣads are referred to the bibliography s.v. *Upaniṣads,* elsewhere in this encyclopedia. Those interested in studies on Upaniṣadic and Vedantic notions of the soul might consult Paul Deussen's *The Philosophy of the Upanishads,* translated by A. S. Geden (1906), 2d ed. (New York, 1966), pp. 256–312; Arthur Berriedale Keith's *The Religion and Philosophy of the Veda and Upanishads,* 2 vols. (1925; reprint, Westport, Conn., 1971), pp. 403–416, 551–569; Baldev Raj Sharma's *The Concept of Ātman in the Principal Upaniṣads* (New Delhi, 1972); or William Beidler's *The Vision of Self in Early Vedānta* (Delhi, 1975).

Translations of Buddhist texts pertinent to concepts of the soul appear in Henry Clarke Warren's *Buddhism in Translations,* student's ed. (1896; reprint, New York, 1976), pp. 129–159. Studies of Buddhist doctrines of the soul, and the lack of the soul, can be found in Walpola Rahula's *What the Buddha Taught,* rev. ed. (Bedford, England, 1967), pp. 51–66; Edward Conze's *Buddhist Thought in India* (London, 1962), pp. 34–46, 92–106, 122–133; and Joaquín Pérez-Remón's *Self and Non-Self in Early Buddhism* (The Hague, 1980). A comparative discussion appears in Lynn A. De Silva's *The Problem of the Self in Buddhism and Christianity* (New York, 1979). The most succinct study of the *dharmas*, *skandhas*, and other constituent elements of reality according to the Sarvāstivāda is Theodore Stcherbatsky's *The Central Conception of Buddhism and the Meaning of the Word 'Dharma'* (1923), 4th ed. (Delhi, 1970). For an analysis of the Mādhyamika position, see T. R. V. Murti's *The Central Philosophy of Buddhism,* 2d ed. (London, 1970).

24 GREEK AND HELLENISTIC CONCEPTS OF THE SOUL

JAN BREMMER

The modern Western idea of the soul has both eschatological and psychological attributes, and the presence of the Greek word *psuchē,* or "soul," in concepts such as psychiatry and psychology suggests that the Greeks viewed the soul in the modern way. Yet the absence of any psychological connotations in the earliest extant usages of *psuchē* shows that at least the early Greek concept of the soul was different from later beliefs. Taking this difference as my point of departure, I shall first trace the development of the conception of the soul of the living, then look at the conception of the soul of the dead, and, finally, analyze the fate of the soul according to Hellenistic religions.

SOUL OF THE LIVING

The Greek conception of the soul in the Archaic age (800–500 BCE) might best be characterized as multiple. Following the widely accepted terminology developed by the Scandinavian Ernst Arbman (1926, 1927), we can distinguish in the oldest literary texts—Homer's *Iliad* and *Odyssey* (commonly dated to the eighth and seventh century, respectively)—two types of soul. On the one hand, there is the free soul, or *psuchē,* an unencumbered soul representing the individual personality. This soul is inactive (and unmentioned) when the body is active; it is located in an unspecified part of the body. Its presence is the precondition for the continuation of life, but it has no connections with the physical or psychological aspects of the body. *Psuchē* manifests itself only during swoons or at death, when it leaves the body never to return again. On the other hand, there are a number of body-souls, which endow the body with life and consciousness. The most frequently occurring form of body-soul in Homer's epics is *thumos.* It is this soul that both urges people on and is the seat of emotions. There is also *menos,* which is a more momentary impulse directed at specific activities. At one time, *menos* seems to have meant "mind, disposition," as appears from related verbs and the fact that the Vedic *manas* has all the functions of the Homeric *thumos.* As is indicated by the related Sanskrit *dhūmah* and the Latin *fumus, thumos* probably once meant "smoke"; it later usurped most of the connotations of *menos.* A word emphasizing the intellect more than *thumos* and *menos* is *nous,* which is the mind or an act of mind, a thought or a purpose. In addition, there are a number of organs, such as the heart and the lungs, which have both physical and psychological attributes.

In Homer, then, the soul of the living does not yet constitute a unity. The resemblance of this kind of belief in the soul to that of most "primitive" peoples strongly suggests that it belongs to a type of society in which the individual is not yet in need of a center of consciousness. Studies that relate the structural elements of Archaic Greek society to the emotional realities of that society, however, are sorely missing; in fact, studies of belief in the soul never seem to investigate this question.

In the course of the Archaic age, we hear of journeys of the soul—an important capability of the free soul that is not mentioned in Homer. Fascinating accounts tell of persons whose souls were reputed to wander away during a trance. It was told, for example, about one Hermotimos of Clazomenae, a city on the western coast of present-day Turkey, that his soul "wandering apart from the body, was absent for many years, and in different places foretold events such as great floods . . . while his stiff body was lying inert, and that the soul, after certain periods reentering the body as into a sheath, aroused it" (Apollonius, *Mirabilia* 3). Here we have a clear case of a person lying in trance whose soul is supposed to have left the body.

A similar case is reported of Aristeas of Proconnesus, an island in the Sea of Marmara. Herodotus (4.14) tells the following local legend. Aristeas entered a fuller's shop in Proconnesus and dropped dead. But, after the story of his death had spread, someone said that he had just met Aristeas outside the town. And when the relatives came to fetch the dead body from the fuller's shop, they did not find it. After six years Aristeas reappeared and composed a poem, the *Arimaspea,* in which he related a journey to the far North. A later account relates that the soul of Aristeas was seen flying from his mouth in the shape of a raven.

Aristeas's disappearance from the shop suggests that his "death" was in fact a deep trance during which his soul was believed to leave his body. The bilocation at the moment of his supposed death fits into a general pattern according to which bilocation always takes place when the free soul leaves the body—that is to say, during sleep, trance, or death. Aristeas's poem apparently used the first person to describe his journey to the Rhipaean Mountains in the North, as do the Siberian shamans when recounting their adventures during trances. Those who knew Aristeas personally would have known that he experienced his adventures only in a trance; others who knew only his poem must have concluded that he had experienced his adventures while awake. These and similar reports have been interpreted as manifestations of a shamanistic influence due to trade and colonization that had brought the Greeks in contact with the shamanistic culture of the Black Sea Scythians in the seventh century. Yet, the shamanistic parallels that have been adduced are either too general—ecstasy and the journey of the soul occur in too many places to be distinguishing traits—or cannot withstand close scrutiny. It seems more acceptable to claim these legends as valid testimonies for the existence of the free soul in Archaic Greece.

Toward the end of the Archaic age, two important developments took place. First, the gradual breakdown of the aristocratic hegemony in the later Archaic age had promoted a certain degree of individualization, and thus the idea of ending up in the unattractive and impersonal beyond that was the Homeric underworld became less and less acceptable. These changes promoted an "upgrading" of the *psuchē,* which in the middle of the fifth century even came to be called "immortal." The philosopher Pythagoras, who lived in the second half of the sixth century, introduced the speculative doctrine of metempsychosis—a doctrine probably influenced by Indo-Iranian sources. Initially, the concept of metempsychosis did not enter the mainstream of Classical Greek religion and remained restricted to marginal religious movements such as Pythagoreanism and Orphism. It was not above ridicule: a contemporary satirist relates that when Pythagoras saw a dog being beaten, he exclaimed: "Stop! Do not beat him. It is the *psuchē* of a dead friend. I recognized him when I heard his whine." However, the doctrine became very popular in post-Classical times.

The second development of the late Archaic age was the gradual incorporation by *psuchē* of *thumos,* which made the *psuchē* the center of consciousness. This transformation has not yet been satisfactorily explained, but it was most likely related to the growing differentiation of Greek society. Because of our limited sources, we can trace the course of this process only in Athens, whence, through the work of the tragedians of the second half of the fifth century, we acquire a detailed look at the changing nature of *psuchē.* Dramatic situations present persons, especially women, whose *psuchē* sighs or melts in despair, suffers pangs, or is "bitten" by misfortune—emotions never associated with *psuchē* in Homer. Characters even address their own *psuchē*, and a particular personality is referred to as, for example, a "mighty *psuchē*" or a "sweet *psuchē.*" This development evidently reflects the growth of the private sphere in Athenian society, which promoted a more delicate sensibility and a greater capacity for tender feelings, such as we find more fully in the fourth century.

The culmination of the *psuchē* as the center of man's inner life was the necessary precondition for the Socratic view that a man's most important task was to take care of his *psuchē.* This view of the soul was taken up by Plato, throughout whose work concern about the *psuchē* remains axiomatic. As Friedrich Solmsen observes, "The *psyche* which he holds to be immortal and for whose fate after life reincarnation offered some meaningful answer, is now the central organ whose vibrations respond to the individual's sufferings and emotional experiences and whose decisions initiate his activities" (Solmsen, 1982, p. 474). Plato even goes so far as to include all intellectual functions in the *psuchē* as well.

Aristotle, on the other hand, almost completely discarded *psuchē,* but "care for the soul" and "cure of the soul" remained important topics for the philosophical schools of the Epicureans, the Stoics, and the Cynics. Pursuing the concept of *psuchē* in these schools, however, belongs more to the area of the history of philosophy than to that of religion.

So far, we have been concerned only with *psuchē* as the soul of the living. However, in the second half of the sixth century, the philosopher Anaximenes seems to have used the term *pneuma,* the purely biological breath, to denote the soul of the cosmos in analogy to the soul of man (the testimony is debated, however). The Pythagoreans also believed in an "infinite breath" *(apeiron pneuma)* that was "breathed in" by the cosmos. And in the course of the fifth century, various passages appear in which *pneuma* is used where we would have expected *psuchē.* Yet *pneuma* never completely lost its biological connection and it did not replace *psuchē* in designating the eschatological soul. In Hellenistic times, *pneuma* figures notably in various philosophies, but it rises to religious prominence only among Hellenistic Jewry and in early Christianity.

SOULS OF THE DEAD AND THE AFTERLIFE

The Greeks, like many other peoples, considered the soul of the dead to be a continuation of the free soul of the living. In the Homeric epic it is always *psuchē* that leaves for the underworld; the dead in the afterlife are indeed often called *psuchai.* The body-souls *thumos, menos,* and *nous* end their activity at the moment of death—their connection with the body is the cause of their disappearance. The *psuchē,* however, was not the only mode of existence after death; the deceased was also compared to a shadow or presented as an *eidōlon* ("image"), a word that stresses the fact that for the ancient Greeks the dead looked exactly like the living.

The physical actions of the souls of the dead were described in two opposite ways. On the one hand, the Greeks believed that the dead souls moved and spoke like the living; the image of the deceased in the memory of the living play a major part in this activity. There is a corollary of this idea in the *Odyssey* (book 11) where Orion and Herakles are depicted as continuing their earthly activities. On the other hand, the souls of the dead are depicted as being unable to move or to speak properly: when the soul of Patroclus left Achilles, he disappeared squeaking (*Iliad* 23.101). The circumstance of death was also of some importance in the formation of ideas about the soul of the deceased. Homer (*Odyssey* 11.41) describes the warriors at the entrance to Hades still dressed in their bloody armor. Aeschylus (*Eumenides* 1.103) has the *eidōlon* of Clytemnestra display her death wounds, and Plato elaborately explains this idea, refining it in a way by adding that the soul also retains the scars of its former existence. On vases, the souls of the dead are even regularly shown with their wounds, sometimes still bandaged.

The idea of the soul of the dead in ancient Greece appears, then, to be influenced by the image of the deceased in the memory of the living, by the circumstances of death, and by the brute fact of the actual corpse. These ideas were never completely systematized and could occur in one and the same description. Just after his death, for example, Patroclus can be described as appearing to Achilles exactly as he was during his life. And as long as he has contact with Achilles he speaks like a normal mortal; only when the contact is over does he leave squeaking. With the passing of time the precise memories of a specific person fade away, and it is understandable that the more personal traits gradually recede behind a more general idea of the dead as the opposite of the living. In time, the individual soul becomes just a member of the countless number of "all souls." The souls move in "swarms" in the Homeric underworld and in the tragedies; the idea of the underworld found its way even into the famous description in book 6 of Vergil's *Aeneid.*

Earlier generations of scholars freely made inferences of belief in the soul from funeral rites. Nowadays we have become much more careful, but the evidence from Homer and other sources suggests that a proper funeral functioned as a rite of passage into afterlife for the dead. This seems to be reflected, for example, in the myth of Sisyphus, who instructed his wife not to perform the proper funeral rites after death so that he could persuade the queen of the underworld, Persephone, to let him return to the land of the living.

After a proper funeral the soul went to murky Hades, (the name is perhaps best translated as "house of invisibility"), which is ruled by the king of the same name and his wife Persephone, the daughter of the goddess Demeter. The comfortless picture of Hades as "the land of no return" can hardly be separated from Babylonian and Semitic ideas as they appear in the Hebrew scriptures (Old Testament). The exact location of Hades remained vague; in the *Iliad* it was situated under the earth, in the *Odyssey* at the edge of the world. In the Homeric epics, the underworld was still reached by just crossing the river Acheron, but in the course of the Archaic age the transition between life and death became less "automatic" than in Homer. The new concern for the soul reflected itself now in the introduction of the ferryman Charon and the idea of guidance by the god Hermes Chthonios.

Not everyone, though, went to Hades. In the *Odyssey,* various heroes, such as Menelaus, went to the Elysian Fields. Others, such as Achilles, went to the so-called Isles of the Blessed, where the poet Hesiod, who lived somewhat later than Homer, also situated part of the"heroic" race, which included all the Homeric heroes. From the seventh century on, initiation into the mysteries of Eleusis becomes one of the means for the common man to share in the happiness the heroes enjoyed. As the Homeric *Hymn to Demeter* (1.480ff.) says of those who have seen the secret rites: "Prosperous is that one of men upon earth who has seen them; but he who is uninitiated and has no share in the rites never has a portion of like happiness when he is dead and under the murky gloom." Any ethical requirements are still notably absent from this promise of the life eternal. At the end of the sixth century, however, clear indications of a more ethical view of the afterlife appeared, according to which the just were rewarded and the bad penalized, views especially connected with the Pythagorean and Orphic movements. These views also influenced ideas about the fate of Eleusinian initiates. However, despite the great interest in the afterlife that can be found in the literature connected with the mysteries, there is no specific mention of the soul or metempsychosis; the initiates apparently expected to arrive in the underworld in person.

On the whole, however, it must be stated that the ancient Greeks displayed only a limited interest in the life hereafter. It is in keeping with this limited interest that they did not worship their ancestors. The one festival that commemorated them had probably already ceased to be celebrated at the end of the Classical age. It is also part of this lack of interest in the afterlife that the Greeks of the Archaic and earlier Classical age rarely ever mentioned souls of the dead returning to the upperworld. Only the philosopher Plato, in the fourth century, mentions the existence of ghosts wandering around tombs and graveyards. It is true that during the Athenian festival of the Anthesteria the *kēres* were believed to appear on earth, but is is unlikely that these were the souls of the dead as earlier generations of scholars, who were strongly influenced by animistic views of Greek religion, liked to believe.

HELLENISTIC RELIGIONS

Toward the end of the fifth century the idea developed that the body remained behind on earth but the soul disappeared into the air. The celestial eschatology became highly important in the dialogues of Plato, who introduced the idea that the soul, or at least its immortal part, returned to its original abode in the heavenly area. The large-scale loss of Hellenistic writings makes it difficult to trace the idea of the soul in detail. However, a late oracle of Apollo at Claros, which contains Hellenistic views, declares:

> *When someone asked Apollo whether the soul remained after death or was dissolved, he answered, "The soul, so long as it is subject to its bonds with the des-*

> *tructible body, while being immune to feelings, resembles the pains of that* [*the body*]; *but when it finds freedom after the mortal body dies, it is borne entire to the aether, being then forever ageless, and abides entirely untroubled; and this the First-born Divine Providence enjoined."*
>
> (translated in MacMullen, 1981, p. 13)

In various of his writings, the philosopher Plutarch (c. 40–120 CE) also described the flight of the soul to the heavens, in particular to the moon, which became increasingly popular as the final abode of the soul. These views, like metempsychosis, remained popular among philosophers and the educated classes, but it is virtually impossible to establish to what extent they were shared by the lower classes.

As regards the mystery religions, which consisted of a mixture of Greek and native elements, it seems highly unlikely that the cults of Isis, the Syrian Goddess (Dea Syria), and Cybele had any specific teachings about the fate of the soul; at least there are no such indications within the considerable evidence we have regarding these cults. Rather late sources relate that the mysteries of Dionysos and Sabazios were directed to the purification of the soul, but the information is not very specific. Even the so-called Orphic Hymns do not display the otherworldly interest we might expect from hymns carrying the name of Orpheus. Mithraism is the only cult about which anything more detailed is known, that being only that the soul was supposed to pass through the seven spheres of planets after death.

When the rhetorician Menander (third century CE) composed a small handbook on oratory for such customary occasions as birth, marriage, and funerals, he also included some directions on how to speak about the afterlife: "for it is not unsuitable," he notes, "on these topics also to philosophize." He refers to Elysium,

> *where Rhadamanthus, Menelaus, Achilles, and Memnon, reside. And perhaps, better, he* [*the deceased*] *now lives among the gods, traversing the heavens and looking down on life below. Perhaps even, he is reproaching those who mourn for him; for the soul is related to the divine, descends thence, but longs again to mount to its kind—as Helen, the Dioscuri, and Heracles, they say, belong to the gods' community.* (translated in MacMullen, 1984, p. 11)

The ambivalent view of the afterlife reflected in this passage is typical of Hellenistic religions. The gods of the Hellenistic period were generally thought of as gods effective in this life, just as the more traditional gods had been. Earlier generations of scholars have often considered the mystery cults competitors with Christianity in regard to the life hereafter, but it now appears more and more clear that the interest of most people in Hellenistic times rested firmly with this life. The inscriptions that have given us innumerable epitaphs display only a negligible interest in the soul or the life eternal. It was only with Christianity that there developed a new interest in the soul and the life hereafter, but its doctrine of the resurrection of the flesh always remained repugnant to the pagan world.

BIBLIOGRAPHY

The standard study, still well worth reading, has long been Erwin Rohde's *Psyche: The Cult of Souls and Belief in Immortality among the Greeks,* translated from the original German edition (1894) by W. B. Hillis (London, 1925). Ernst Arbman's fundamental study is "Untersuchungen zur primitiven Seelenvorstellung mit besonderer Rucksicht auf Indien," pts. 1–2, *Le monde oriental* 20 (1926): 85–222 and 21 (1927): 1–185. My book *The Early Greek Concept of the Soul* (Princeton, 1983) confronts the Greek material with the latest insights from social anthropology and folklore. David B. Claus's *Toward the Soul* (New Haven, 1981) is a detailed, if conceptually limited, investigation of all the passages in Greek literature in which the term *psuchē* appears. Valuable studies of the development of the concept of *psuchē* are three by Friedrich Solmsen: "*Phren, Kardia, Psyche* in Greek Tragedy," in *Greek Poetry and Philosophy,* edited by Douglas E. Gerber (Chico, Calif., 1984), pp. 265–274; "Plato and the Concept of the Soul *(Psyche):* Some Historical Perspectives," *Journal of the History of Ideas* 44 (July–September 1983): 355–367; and *Kleine Schriften,* vol. 3 (Hildesheim, 1982), pp. 464–494. Fritz Graf discusses in detail the ideas of the hereafter connected with the Eleusinian mysteries in *Eleusis und die orphische Dichtung Athens in vorhellenistischer Zeit* (Berlin, 1974). Helmut Saake's "Pneuma," in *Paulys Realencyclopädie der classischen Altertumswissenschaft,* suppl. vol. 14 (Munich, 1974), is an up-to-date survey of notions of *pneuma.* Arthur Darby Nock's *Essays on Religion and the Ancient World,* vol. 1 (Cambridge, Mass., 1972), pp. 296–305, and Ramsey MacMullen's *Paganism in the Roman Empire* (New Haven, 1981) and *Christianizing the Roman Empire* (New Haven, 1984) demonstrate the lack of interest in the afterlife in the Hellenistic religions.

25 JUDAIC CONCEPTS OF THE SOUL

Jack Bemporad

Unlike the Egyptian and Akkadian terms that have been translated as "soul" (e.g., *ba, ka, khu, shimtu, shedu, ishtaru*), the most important Hebrew words for this concept (*nefesh, neshamah* or *nishmah,* and *ruaḥ*) do not primarily refer to appearance, destiny, power, or supernatural influences, but to respiration—the inner, animating element of life. While the Hebrew Bible distinguishes between spirit and flesh, it does not accept the type of dualism of body and soul characteristic of Greek thought. Hebrew terms for the soul usually refer to an activity or characteristic of the body or to an entire living being. To "afflict the soul" means to practice physical self-denial (*Lv.* 16:29ff.).

Hebrew *nefesh,* usually translated as "soul," refers to the breath, as does the term *neshamah* (or *nishmah*), which became the most common word for the soul in postbiblical Hebrew. The verbs formed from the roots of these words *(nafash* and *nasham*) mean "to breathe." The two words are found together in *Genesis* 2:7, which narrates how the first human *(adam)* received the breath of life *(nishmat ḥayyim)* from God and became a living soul *(nefesh ḥayyah).* Another meaning of *nefesh* is "life," particularly animal life. Here the soul is a kind of material principle of vitality, which is separable from the inert substance *(basar)* of the body. *Neshamah,* on the other hand, sometimes refers particularly to conscious life or intelligence. *Nefesh* also may refer to mental states, in particular to strong emotions or physical cravings. At times *nefesh* refers to human capabilities, such as the capacity for eloquent speech.

The word *ruaḥ,* which is often rendered as "spirit," refers to powers or actions outside the body and often has the meaning of "wind." *Ruaḥ* is the mysterious vitality in the material body, which is considered a divine gift. *Ruaḥ* sometimes denotes forces external to the body that operate in or through the body or the mental faculties. These forces are states of exaltation and depression beyond normal experience that come and go "like the wind." (The clearest example of the various meanings of *ruaḥ* in a single passage is *Ezekiel* 37:1–14, the vision of the valley of dry bones.)

According to the Hebrew Bible, a dead human being remains in possession of the soul upon entering She'ol, a shadowy place sometimes synonymous with the grave, where the vitality and energy associated with worldly life are drastically decreased.

Since both the body and the soul enter She'ol, the later doctrine of the resurrection (as expressed in *Isaiah* 24–27 and *Daniel* 12) indicates a reentry into life in both aspects. The first definite appearance in Jewish thought of a doctrine of personal survival of death in a general resurrection of the dead comes in the literature associated with the Hasmonean Revolt (166–164 BCE), from which time it increases in importance to become a central dogma, later a part of the basic doctrine of Christianity.

The work in the Hebrew canon that expresses the idea of resurrection most explicitly is the *Book of Daniel.* The final chapter of this Hebrew-Aramaic text of the second century BCE expands some details of the divine judgment of the nations with a "secret" revelation wherein it is made known that at some future time many of the dead will wake to everlasting life, while some will wake only to eternal suffering. References to the concept of resurrection are also found in *Isaiah* 26, which modern scholars regard as part of a late addition to the book. It alludes to personal resurrection, which, it suggests, will be restricted to certain categories of the dead and to the shades or *refa'im.* The original nature of the *refa'im* in Canaanite mythology is the subject of continuing debate, but in biblical contexts they are usually understood as impotent ghosts.

The "dew of light" mentioned in *Isaiah* 26, as well as in the Pseudepigrapha (e.g., *1 Bar.* 29:7, 73:2; *1 Enoch* 60:7), suggests ideas of restored fertility, and is associated in the Jewish tradition with individual resurrections as well as a general resurrection. However, thepassages in *Daniel* and *Isaiah* concerning the role of the soul in resurrection are ambiguous and have allowed for extensive and often contradictory speculation. The Sadducees, in the first century CE, followed a literal reading of the accepted scriptures and denied that the idea of a general resurrection was found there. But the Pharisees and their successors, the tannaim (first and second centuries CE) and the amoraim (third through fifth centuries CE) were convinced that the scriptures, properly understood in the light of an oral instruction passed down through Moses and the later prophets, were filled with hints and allusions concerning the world to come.

RABBINIC VIEWS

A synopsis of concepts of the soul in rabbinic literature may give an overly uniform appearance to this material, which developed over many generations. Statements scattered through this vast literature may appear when cited in isolation to be pure speculation or assertions of dogma, but they often have a primarily polemic point in context. With explicit and implicit contradictions so abundant in the Talmud, no fully articulated system (or systems) can be found, but it is possible to summarize majority views and influential positions.

The close connection between soul and body characteristic of the biblical worldview is continued in the rabbinic literature. The Palestinian Talmud (J.T., *Kil.* 8.4, 31c) attributes the origin of different portions of the physical body to human parents, while the spirit, life, and soul are attributed to God. This admits a greater duality than is acknowledged in the Hebrew Bible, but the soul is regarded as the active element, and so is responsible for sin, while the body is only its vehicle. Such an attitude is contrary to Greek views known in Hellenistic Judaea whereby the body is seen as a trap that debases or hinders the soul. According to Kaufmann Kohler and Ephraim Urbach (see, respectively, *Jewish Theology* and *The Sages,*) this view of the body as the source of sin and impurity is not found in rabbinic Judaism. Urbach also concluded that neither the concept of the soul's immortality, separate from the body, nor the idea of its transmigration into other bodies, is rabbinic. The absence of early, authoritative pronouncements on such points allowed for widely variant speculations within later orthodox and heterodox thought. Talmudic Judaism, as Urbach indicates, found moral duality existing within the soul, which contains both good and evil impulses, the latter including the ambitious, self-centered, and envious impulses in human beings that must be controlled rather than extirpated. The Talmud presents the soul as a supernatural entity created and bestowed by God and joined to a terrestrial body (B.T., *Ber.* 60a). God takes back the soul at death, but later restores it to the dead body. Similar views of the soul are elaborated elsewhere in the Talmud and early *midrashim,* although not without opposing voices. Among these is the concept of the soul's preexistence, which, Urbach argues, appears in rabbinic sayings only after the third century CE. According to some, all human souls came into existence during creation as parts of the "wind of God," understood here as "spirit" (B.T., *ʿA.Z.* 5a, *Yev.* 62a; *Gn. Rab.* 8.1, 24.4). Unborn souls abide in a *guf* ("a body"; commentators suggest "promptuary") among the treasures of the *ʿaravot,* the seventh heaven, where also are found the souls of the righteous and the "dew of light" with which God will resurrect the dead (B.T., *Hag.* 12b, *Yev.* 62a, *Shab.* 152b). The Messiah will come when the supply of souls in the *guf* is exhausted, or, according to others, when God has created those souls he has held in his intention from the beginning (B.T., *ʿA.Z.* 5a, *Yev.* 62a, *Nid.* 136; *Gn. Rab.* 24.4; cf. also *Apocalypse of Ezra* 4:35).

According to one view, God compels the selected or newly created soul to enter the womb at the time of conception. Even after the soul has entered this world, it is not entirely forgetful of its origins and is not without divine care. It is accompanied by angels (B.T., *Ber.* 60b, end; B.T., *Shab.* 119a), and nightly, while the body sleeps, the soul ascends to heaven, from which it returns with renewed life for the body *(Gn. Rab.* 14.9; probably implied in B.T., *Ber.* 60a). On the Sabbath the body enjoys an "additional soul," which is sent forth by and returns to God, as Shimʿon ben Laqish discovered by an ingenious rendering of the word *va-yinafash* in *Exodus* 31:17 (B.T., *Beits.* 16a, *Taʿan.* 27b).

Although the soul had protested at its embodiment and its birth into the world, it also protests at the death of the body. The soul hovers about the dead body for three days, hoping that life will return (*Tanḥuma',* Miqets 4, Pequdei 3; cf. B.T., *Shab.* 152a). Ultimately the soul leaves the body and awaits the resurrection, when they will reunited and judged together (B.T., *San.* 91). Concerning the fate of the soul in the meantime, one view is that the souls of the righteous will remain with God, while the souls of the wicked wander in the air or are hurled from one end of the world to the other by angels (B.T., *Shab.* 152b).

Not everyone will be resurrected. The generation destroyed in the Flood, the men of Sodom (*San.* 10.3) who were punished by complete annihilation, and, with ironic appropriateness, those who denied the doctrine of resurrection will not return to life. Attempts have been made as well to relate doctrines of the soul or of the resurrection to Jewish concepts of religious duty and piety (e.g., B.T., *Ket.* 111b), a problem that was to be taken up at length by philosophers and mystics in later centuries.

PHILOSOPHICAL VIEWS

Philosophical speculation in Judaism arose through the desire to reconcile the Jewish tradition with contemporary intellectual discourse. In medieval Jewish philosophy, the effort at reconciliation was directed at two rival forms of thought, Platonism and Aristotelianism, both of which were read under the influence of Neoplatonic commentaries and misattributed texts, such as the excerpts from Plotinus that circulated as the *Theology of Aristotle.* Isaac Husik noted (1916) that as a group, Jewish philosophers hesitated between (1) the Platonic view of the soul as a distinct entity that enters the body from a spiritual world and acts by using the body as its instrument and (2) the Aristotelian view that, as far as the lower faculties such as sense, memory, and imagination are concerned, the soul is merely a form of the physical body and perishes with it. They found biblical references to support both views, although the latter provided a clearer division between the human and the divine.

Philo Judaeus (d. 45–50 CE) sought to reconcile Greek, predominantly Platonic and Stoic, philosophy with scripture, particularly the Pentateuch. He accomplished this through a device he borrowed from the Greeks, the allegorical method of interpretation, which the Stoics had used for the Homeric epics. Philo accepted most of the Greek distinction between body and soul, including the belief that the body and its desires were the cause of the pollution of the soul, the body being a prison from which the soul must escape. Man is related to the world of the senses through the body and the lower parts (or functions) of the soul, but through reason man is related to the suprasensual, or divine, realm, to which the higher portion of the soul seeks to be reunited. For Philo, the religious task is to bring about the union of the individual soul with the divine Logos, transcending both the material world and the limits of the rational soul.

In Philo's adaptation of Plato, there is a transcendent, preexistent, incorporeal Logos, a direct projection of the ideas in the mind of God, and there is also an immanent Logos, the totality of God's powers existing in the material world. The intelligible world of the transcendent Logos is the model for our world, in which all things, including individual souls, or minds, are reflections of the ideas, or images, as these are mediated through the immanent Logos. Directly below the immanent Logos in the descent from God are the rational, unbodied souls, which have the nature of living beings. Some of these were, or will be, incarnate in human bodies; others have not and never will be so embodied. These latter beings are ranked according to their inherent level of likeness to the divine. They are found in the heavens and in the air, and are known to the Greeks as *daimones,* that is (following the etymology in Plato's *Cratylus* 398b), "knowers," but in Hebrew they are called *mal'akhim,* "messengers," because they are God's messengers in his dealings with the created world. Translators of scripture have called them "angels," that is, "heralds."

The rational, human soul, a fragment of the Logos in human form, is capable of achieving a separate existence at a new level; the angels cannot. Without the support of God, however, the rational soul would perish by dissolving into its original, undifferentiated state. This is the fate of personal obliteration awaiting the wicked. The souls of the righteous, the wise and virtuous, will be brought close to God in proportion to their merits. Not only can some reach the level of the highest angels beneath the immanent Logos, as did Elijah, but some can attain the level of the ideas of the intelligible world, as did Enoch. Moses, the most perfect man, who delivered the most perfect law by which souls are disciplined and improved, stands above all created species and genera, before God himself. Philo thus attempts to link the Platonic ascent of the soul to the Platonic ideas, using the biblical concepts of prophecy and election. No place is made for a resurrection of the body reunited with the soul. [*See* Ascension.]

Philosophical and systematic theological writings from Jewish sources appear again later in the ninth and tenth centuries in response to the philosophical schools of Islam. The work of Yitsḥaq Yisra'eli (c. 850–950) is largely Platonic in origin. Yisra'eli believed in the substantiality and immortality of the soul, of which he distinguished three kinds in every human being. The first is the rational soul, which receives wisdom, discriminates between good and evil, and is subject to punishment for wrongdoing. The second is the animal soul, which humans share with beasts. It consists of sense perception, and it controls motion, but has no connection with reality and can judge only from appearances. The third is the vegetative soul, which is responsible for nutrition, growth, and reproduction; it has no sense perception or capacity to move. These distinctions, with major and minor variations, were to become common in Jewish as well as in Muslim and Christian writings.

Yitsḥaq Yisra'eli's younger contemporary, Sa'adyah ben Yosef, or Sa'adyah Gaon (c. 882–942), summarized his ideas about the soul in the sixth treatise of his *Book of Beliefs and Opinions* (Arabic version, *Kitāb al-amānāt wa-al-I'tiqādāt,* completed about 933; Hebrew paraphrases and full translation as *Sefer ha-emunot ve-ha-de'ot*). Sa'adyah follows the less widely accepted of the Talmudic and Midrashic views that the soul is formed with the completion of the body and that there is a continuous creation of souls. He accepts, however, the predetermined limit of the total number of souls. He defends the localization of the soul in the heart with a demonstration of synonymous uses of the words in biblical texts, as well as with ancient and medieval physiological theories locating consciousness in the heart. Like the celestial spheres, the soul is perfectly transparent, so that although it permeates the body through vessels leading from the heart, it is too fine to be seen. When the soul leaves the body it is stored up until the time of general retribution, when it is restored to its own body to face God's judgment. Because of their pure, celestial nature, the souls of the wise and just rise to the heavenly spheres. The souls of the wicked, however, become turbid from the impurities of their earthly lives, and after death they drift aimlessly among the lower elements. When it first leaves the body, the soul is troubled by the thought of the disintegration of its former abode. The earthbound souls of the wicked are greatly distressed by this corruption, while pure souls are much less concerned by it and soon begin their ascent.

Sa'adyah used the resources of Arabic philosophical teachings to construct a rationalized exposition of some Talmudic views of the soul. The majority of his successors were content with more general resemblances, preferring to concentrate on the assurance of personal immortality and retribution when they discussed the soul. Shelomoh ibn Gabirol (c. 1021–1058), one of the great Jewish liturgical poets of medieval Spain, connected the soul with the nature of the universe. For Ibn Gabirol, a Neoplatonist, the individual human soul is part of the world soul and contains a higher faculty than that of the rational soul, which is that of immediate intellectual intuition. The soul contains all the forms of existence in its essence and can intuit these forms. Ibn Gabirol separates the soul from God through an intricate series of emanations, but to many his views seemed to attribute too much of the divine to the human soul.

Elaboration of the concept of soul in terms of Jewish thought was attempted by another Spanish poet-philosopher, Yehudah ha-Levi (c. 1058–1141), in his Arabic dialogue *Al-Khazarī* (The Book of Argument and Proof in Defense of the Despised Faith). Ha-Levi argues that philosophy, which has been presented as an eclectic Neoplatonism, is not absolutely wrong in teaching men to seek communion with the divine by subduing the organic and emotional, or vegetative and animal, elements of the soul to the rational. He states that there is another faculty of the soul, the religious faculty, which is capable of grasping truths and experiences beyond the reach of reason alone, so that the immaterial substance of the higher faculties of the soul becomes indestructible and immortal by assimilating universal and eternal concepts. According to ha-Levi, rabbinic Judaism is uniquely able to foster this higher, religious faculty of the soul. By leading a temperate and moral life the soul attains immortality and closeness to God.

The Neoplatonic approach of Shelomoh ibn Gabirol was resumed in later decades by another Spanish poet, Mosheh ibn ʿEzraʾ (1070–1138), who was influenced, it is thought, by the Ṣūfīs. Ibn ʿEzraʾ believed in the preexistence of the individual soul and in the transmigration of souls until they gain sufficient wisdom to be reunited with their source in the world soul. Markedly Aristotelian, in contrast, is the work of Avraham ibn Daud (1100–1180), a Spanish historian and astronomer who argued that the soul is the form of the body, that it can grasp universal ideas and discriminate between good and evil, and that it can survive the body. Ibn Daud criticized the idea of the preexistence of the soul as illogical, arguing that if a preexistent soul died with the body their union was without purpose, while if it survived the body their temporary union was also pointless.

In the twelfth century the dominant influence was not that of Ibn Daud, however, but of Moses Maimonides (Mosheh ben Maimon, 1135/8–1204). In his major philosophical work, *The Guide of the Perplexed* (c. 1190), he bases his theory of the soul on Aristotelian thought as he understood it through the great Arabic commentaries of Ibn Sīnā (Avicenna) and Al-Fārābī and on biblical texts interpreted by an elaborate theory of the meaning of scriptural language. For Maimonides, the complete soul, or *nefesh,* is coextensive with the physical body and is not separable from it. It has five functions, namely, (1) the nutritive, (2) the sensitive, which consists of the five senses, (3) the imaginative, (4) the appetitive, which manifests itself in desires and emotions, and (5) the rational. The rational function itself consists of (1) the reflective aspect, which acquires knowledge and makes ethical judgments, (2) the practical aspect, and (3) the theoretical aspect, which consists of knowledge of unchanging realities.

The rational faculty is twofold. The material intellect latent in all human beings can be developed into the acquired intellect by the proper use of the mind. The acquired intellect is a disposition of the soul and perishes with the body. The acquired intellect can realize correct general concepts about the world, and when these are realized the rational soul assimilates the corresponding thoughts of the Active Intellect, which is the emanation through which God governs the material world. In this manner elements of divinity enter into the acquired intellect. If the soul has been directed toward contemplation of the nature of God and the world, the acquired intellect is replaced by the actualized intellect, which consists of these general concepts received from the active intellect. When the body dies the lower faculties of the soul are destroyed, but the actualized intellect, being of divine origin, is reunited with God through the Active Intellect. Through rational contemplation, such souls are rewarded by immortality. The souls of those who indulged the senses and emotions will perish with their bodies. According to the *Treatise on Resurrection,* although Maimonides believed in resurrection, he considered it a temporary condition wherein the souls of the righteous remain before they depart from the physical world entirely.

The threat to traditional religious beliefs presented by Maimonidean intellectualism was not met successfully until the late fourteenth century, in the *Or Adonai* (Light of the Lord) of Ḥasdai Crescas. Crescas attacked the theory of the soul as being a form coextensive with the physical body. He also rejected the assumption that reason is the characteristic feature of the human soul. He argued that the will and the emotions are basic parts of human nature and not merely bodily distractions to be discarded with the flesh, which survive the death of the body and play a part in determining the ultimate condition and fate of the soul. He contended that religious teaching and practice are correctly directed at shaping the will and the emotions, rather than the reason.

QABBALISTIC VIEWS

According to Qabbalah, man is a spiritual being whose body is merely an external wrapping. There are three essentially different parts of the soul in qabbalistic thought, designated by the Hebrew terms *nefesh, ruaḥ,* and *neshamah.* The *nefesh* is the vital element and enters the body at birth; it dominates the physical and psychological aspects of the self. In contrast, the *ruaḥ* and *neshamah* must be developed through spiritual discipline. The *ruaḥ* comes into being when a person can overcome the body and its desires and it is thus associated with the ethical aspects of life. The *neshamah* is the highest part of the soul and is produced through study of the Torah and observation of the commandments. Torah study awakens the higher centers, through which the individual attains the capacity to apprehend God and the secrets of creation.

According to Gershom Scholem, Qabbalah took this division of the soul primarily from Jewish Neoplatonism and introduced theosophic and mythic elaborations. In Qabbalah the *neshamah* is that part of the soul that consists of the spark of the divine and is exclusively concerned with the knowledge of God. According to the fundamental text of thirteenth-century qabbalistic literature, the *Zohar,* each part of the soul originates in the world of the *sefirot* (the emanations of God). *Nefesh* originates in the *sefirah* Malkhut ("kingdom"), the lowest emanation, which corresponds to the Congregation of Israel. *Ruaḥ* originates in Tif'eret ("grandeur"), the central *sefirah,* also known as Raḥamim ("mercies"). *Neshamah* emerges from the third *sefirah,* Binah ("understanding"). The *sefirot* are assigned male and female aspects, and the soul has its origins in a union of these male and female archetypes and takes on masculine and feminine forms only in its emanations downward.

After the compilation of the *Zohar,* two additional parts of the soul were introduced, the *ḥayyah* and *yeḥidah* ("life" and "only one"; cf. *Psalms* 22:21). These were assigned higher levels than the *neshamah* and could be acquired only by spiritually evolved individuals. The soul of the Messiah, which was on the level of *yeḥidah,* had its source in the *sefirah* Keter ("crown"), the highest of the emanations.

According to Qabbalah, the *nefesh, ruaḥ,* and *neshamah* have different destinies after death. The *nefesh* hovers over the body for a time; the *ruaḥ* goes to a terrestrial realm assigned according to its virtue, and the *neshamah* returns to its home with the divine. Only the *nefesh* and *ruaḥ* are subject to punishment.

In the thought of Isaac Luria (1534–1572) and his disciples, the doctrine of metempsychosis was incorporated into concepts of the nature and destiny of creation and the mission of the Jewish people. The task of *tiqqun,* that is, the restoration or reintegration into the divine pattern of existence of the flawed material universe, is entrusted to human souls, who seek out and redeem the scattered sparks of divinity in the world. Most souls are given repeated chances to achieve this task, thus constituting a kind of reincarnation, which earlier Jewish mystics had considered primarily a form of punishment or expiation for sins. In the Lurianic system, ritual commandments are important for achieving *tiqqun,* both for the individual soul and for the whole world.

[*See also* Jewish Thought and Philosophy, *article on* Premodern Philosophy, *and the biographies of the philosophers mentioned herein.*]

BIBLIOGRAPHY

For a brief discussion of the historical and theoretical background of Jewish views of the soul, see Louis Jacobs's *A Jewish Theology* New York, 1973). Walther Eichrodt provides a useful treatment of Israelite views of the human personality and the problem of death in *Theology of the Old Testament,* 2 vols. (Philadelphia, 1961–1967); see pages 118–150 and 210–228 in volume 2. Louis Ginzberg offers an incomparable survey of the entire postbiblical period in *The Legends of the Jews,* 7 vols. (1909–1938; Philadelphia, 1937–1966). His survey includes the intertestamental literature and the writings of the church fathers on biblical events, as well as Jewish sources through the nineteenth century.

Although dated, George Foot Moore's *Judaism in the First Centuries of the Christian Era; The Age of the Tannaim,* 3 vols. (1927–1930; Cambridge, Mass., 1970), remains a classic treatment of postbiblical sectarian Jewish literature, particularly the pseudepigrapha and the earlier Talmudic and Midrashic literature. On concepts involving the soul, see especially pages 368–371, 404, and 486–489 in volume 1; pages 279–322 ("Retribution after Death"), 353, and 377–395 ("Eschatology") in volume 2; and pages 148 (note 206), 196–197, and 204–205 in volume 3. A more advanced and detailed work than Moore's, and one covering a longer period, is E. E. Urbach's *The Sages: Their Concepts and Beliefs,* 2 vols. (1969; Jerusalem, 1975). The chapter titled "Man" in volume 1 covers in great detail Talmudic and Midrashic views on ensoulment, preexistence, and embryonic consciousness, as well as related concepts, and attempts to determine the relative and absolute chronologies of statements and their attribution in the sources. Notes on pages 784–800 in volume 2 and the bibliography, pages 1061–1062, cite many earlier secondary studies. A specialized work is Shalom Spiegel's *The Last Trial: On the Legends and Lore of the Command to Abraham to Offer Isaac as a Sacrifice; The Akedah* (1950; Philadelphia, 1967), which includes a chapter on the soul's flight from the body and the dew of resurrection in Midrashic literature.

A recent, comprehensive survey from the perspective of philosophy is Julius Guttman's *Philosophies of Judaism: The History of Jewish Philosophy from Biblical Times to Franz Rosenzweig* (1933; New York, 1964). Articles on the Jewish concept of the soul from the *Encyclopaedia*

Judaica (Jerusalem, 1971) have been collected together with new material, in a single volume: *Jewish Philosophers,* edited by Steven T. Katz (New York, 1975). On the philosophy of Philo, see Harry A. Wolfson's *Philo: Foundations of Religious Philosophy in Judaism, Christianity and Islam,* 2 vols. (Cambridge, Mass., 1947); see especially chapter 7, "Souls, Angels, Immortality," in volume 1. Isaac Husik's *A History of Mediaeval Jewish Philosophy* (1916; New York, 1969) remains a standard, detailed survey of Jewish philosophies in the Middle Ages. For the concept of the soul during this period, a useful but rather narrowly focused volume is Philip David Bookstaber's *The Idea of Development of the Soul in Medieval Jewish Philosophy* (Philadelphia, 1950).

Articles by Gershom Scholem written for the *Encyclopaedia Judaica* have been collected in *Kabbalah* (New York, 1974); see especially "Man and His Soul (Psychology and Anthropology of the Kabbalah)" and "Gilgul," on the transmigration of souls.

26 CHRISTIAN CONCEPTS OF THE SOUL

GEDDES MACGREGOR

The concept of the soul in Christian literature and tradition has a complex history. Moreover, Christian thought about its destiny is by no means uniform, nor is it always even clear.

TERMINOLOGY

The New Testament word *psuchē* is rooted in the Hebrew *nefesh,* and in English both are generally translated "soul." In primitive Semitic thought *nefesh* (Arabic, *nafs*) is a fine, diminutive replica of the body. As such it can be contrasted with *ruaḥ*, an onomatopoeic word that mimics the sound of breathing and is used to designate the spirit or principle of life that in such thought is seen in the breath, which stands in contrast to the flesh. The New Testament word *psuchē,* however, has complex overtones associated with the concept of life, sometimes also signifying what today would be called the self and often assuming a special connotation as the seat of the supernatural or eternal life, the life that cannot be destroyed by the malice of men as can the body, yet can be destroyed by God (*Mt.* 10:39). So valuable is the *psuchē* that not even the whole of the material universe could compensate for its loss (*Mt.* 16:26, *Mk.* 8:36ff.).

When the *psuchē* is fully dedicated to God it acquires a special character (*1 Pt.* 1:22, 4:19), and in this dedication it can be anchored in God and be aware of possessing eternal life, assured of salvation from all that could alienate it from that inheritance (*Heb.* 6:19). Such is the "soul" or "self" that is under the care of Christ. Yet since the *psuchē* is spiritual, not material, it is not to be guarded as one guards an earthly mansion, nor to be placed like a precious heirloom in a safe deposit box, nor tended as one tends a delicate plant. On the contrary, Jesus urges his disciples to let go of it, abandoning it to God's care (*Mt.* 16:25, *Mk.* 8:35, *Lk.* 9:24, *Jn.* 12:25). Such is the paradox of self-giving, a concept that finds expression also in Hindu and Buddhist thought.

In the New Testament then, the *psuchē,* although fundamentally rooted in a Hebrew concept, encompasses so much of what we today understand as the "self" that it confronts us with many of the very complex problems to be found in modern discussions of selfhood. Yet the term carries also other connotations, as we shall see later. Furthermore, in its adjectival form, *psuchikos,* it can be used to designate the natural, biological life of man, as distinguished from the spiritual life, which is called *pneumatikos* (*1 Cor.* 2:14, 15:46; *Jude* 19). The dualistic distinction implied in this usage echoes one that is familiar to readers of gnostic literature. *Psuchē,* however, always refers to that dimension of man that is of eternal value and therefore contrasted with man's carnal embodiment.

In *Ezekiel* (13:17ff.) there is an echo of the primitivistic belief that the *nefesh* can slip out of the nostrils or another orifice during sleep (hence the old superstition against sleeping with one's mouth open) or, in the case of violent death, at the point of the assassin's sword. Ezekiel warns his hearers against women who sew frilly sleeves around their wrists, "the better to ensnare lives." This passage reflects both the old material concept of the *nefesh* and the ancient fear of witches, who made a profitable business out of nocturnal exploits in which they stole the *nefashot* of unwary sleepers, catching their souls like moths in handkerchiefs and then selling them to families with a member who, as we might say today, had "lost his mind." The Arabs entertained similar views about the vulnerability of the *nafs* to such evil agencies.

SOUL AND SPIRIT

The English words *soul* and *spirit* are attempts to represent the two sets of ideas found in the Bible: *soul* is continuous with the Hebrew *nefesh* and the Greek *psuchē,* while *spirit* is continuous with the Hebrew *ruaḥ* and the Greek *pneuma.* The one set of ideas, however, cannot be entirely dissociated from the other. For example, when we think of the ideas of wind, breath, or spirit, we would probably attach any one of them to *pneuma* rather than to *psuchē;* nevertheless, we should bear in mind that the word *psuchē* has an etymological connection with the verb *psuchein* ("to breathe"), as does the Latin *animus* with *anemos,* the Greek word meaning "wind." So some study of the concept of spirit is not only relevant to but necessary for any study of the Christian concept of the soul.

Ruaḥ, which the New Testament writers translate as *pneuma* and which is traditionally rendered "spirit" in English, does not have the quasi-physical connotation that *nefesh* has. For although *ruaḥ* is sometimes used to signify "wind" or "breath" (e.g., in *Job* 15:30), it is not accurately described as ambiguous in meaning since in Hebrew it refers simply to the principle of vital activity, however manifested. The Hebrews did not make the sharp distinction, to which our Western tradition has accustomed us, between the physical connotations of "wind" and the spiritual connotations of "spirit" or "mind." So the effects of *ruaḥ* may be heard as one hears a hurricane, or seen as one might see breath on a mirror or the dancing of branches of trees on a windy day. Or it may be perceived in more complex ways, as we perceive the results of God's action in human events. Since the ancients saw in breathing the evidence of life and in its absence the lack of life, breath would seem an obvious locus for *ruaḥ.* Nevertheless, they would so see it only as we see in the brain an obvious locus for mental activity, although not even the most positivistic of contemporary analytical philosophers would identify mental activity simply with the three pounds of pinkish-gray tissue we carry in our heads. *Ruaḥ* is also the inner strength of a man or woman, which is weakened in times of despondency and is revived in times of exhilaration. Short-tempered people are short of *ruaḥ* (*Ex.* 6:9).

The *ruah* of God (Elohim) is uniquely powerful in its effects on man, affecting him in all sorts of ways, not all of them benevolent. Since the Hebrews had no special word for nature as did the Greeks *(phusis),* one word had to do service for all seemingly superhuman activity. God sends plagues and earthquakes as well as gentle rain and sunshine. The *ruah* of the Lord, however, is that of righteousness and love, of justice and mercy, inspiring the utterances of the prophets upon whom it falls.

Behind the New Testament use of *pneuma* lie these earlier uses of *ruah.* The spirit of God is given to Jesus in baptism (*Mt.* 3:13ff.) and from Jesus to the disciples. John the Baptist distinguishes the baptism he gives from the one Jesus is to give, which is to be by the Holy Spirit *(en pneumati hagiō)* and by fire (*Mt.* 3:11). Here John is represented as anticipating the experience of the disciples on the day of Pentecost, described in *Acts* 2 as the descent of the Spirit on the assembly as if in "tongues of fire." The extent to which the New Testament writers accounted the Holy Spirit of God a separate entity, as in the trinitarian doctrine developed in later Christian thought, is, to say the least, obscure and need not concern us here. *Pneuma,* however, is very frequently used, both in a somewhat pedestrian way (e.g., the disciples are afraid, thinking they are seeing a ghost, *Lk.* 24:37) and in more reverential senses having the full range of Hebrew meanings along with special meanings arising out of the pentecostal experience. Both Paul and John make notable use of the antinomy of flesh *(sarx)* and spirit *(pneuma).* What makes one righteous is circumcision not of the flesh but of the spirit (*Rom.* 2:29). Had not the psalmist noted that the Lord was less pleased by burnt offerings than by a humble and contrite heart (*Ps.* 51)? Christians do not walk according to the flesh but according to the spirit (*Rom.* 8:13).

Although Paul follows traditional usage in such matters, he also uses *pneuma* in several less expected ways, for example, as if he were alluding to the soul (*2 Cor.* 2:13) and as if referring to the mind as the seat of human consciousness (*1 Cor.* 7:34). He also writes as if mystically identifying the soul or conscious self of the Christian with the spiritual realm or dimension to which it has been introduced through Christ; he writes as if the Christian were so absorbed into Christ that everything he or she thought or said or did issued thence. Paul has a tendency to express his dominant sense of mystical union with Christ by coalescing all such distinctions as might lie between *psuchē* and *pneuma,* focusing upon what today would more readily be called a spiritual dimension of being, one in which the human participates in the divine.

John pointedly contrasts *sarx* ("flesh") with *pneuma* ("spirit"), as in *John* 3:5–8. Because God is a spirit, all dealings with him are in the spiritual, not the carnal, dimension (*Jn.* 4:24). The words of Jesus are the revelation of God, and as such they are to be recognized as spirit *(pneuma)* and life *(zōē).* Spirit is symbolized by the physical act of breathing: in *John* 20:22 Jesus breathes on the apostles as a symbol of his bestowal of the Holy Spirit *(pneuma hagion).* Alluding to the Holy Spirit, John uses the term *paraklētos:* the one who helps or pleads one's cause. This term had been used in classical Greek in much the same way as the Latin *advocatus* ("advocate," or the English *counsel*). As used by John, it seems to recall the notion of the spirit of truth as used in the Qumran literature in the sense of "helper," where the typically gnostic contrast betweenthe spirit of light and the spirit of darkness is also notable. Jesus, as God pitching his tent awhile in the carnal world of humankind, is he who can mediate between us, in our mixed, carnal-spiritual state, and

God, who is pure spirit. In the light of such modes of conceptualizing, the distinction between soul and spirit tends to evanesce. The contrast is between the carnal realm and the spiritual realm. The characteristics of the spirit (coming "like the rushing of a mighty wind" and "blowing where it listeth") become, then, descriptions of the way in which the spiritual dimension behaves; that is, it behaves otherwise than according to the "laws" of physics or biology.

To sum up: with the translation of *nefesh* as *psuchē* in the Greek version of the Bible (Septuagint), which the New Testament writers used, the ground is laid for the tendency toward the coalescence of the ideas suggested by the terms *psuchē* and *pneuma*. For both words focus on the traditional Semitic preoccupation with the idea of life. What matters to the spiritual man is not the life we measure in days or years *(bios)* but the spiritual energy, the inner life of a man, his *zōē,* which has the capacity to become everlasting. It is to this that the soul is to be resurrected, so that resurrection then entails an ongoing, everlasting state, which Christ has made possible even for us sinful men and women. Thus our struggle in this life is not so much against flesh *(sarx)* as "against the spiritual army of evil agencies" (*pros ta pneumatika tēs ponērias; Eph.* 6:12). By extension, then, the soul, as the higher part of man, becomes indistinguishable from the spiritual dimension of man's being.

Still, one cannot easily overemphasize the fact that the New Testament Christians were heirs of a classical Hebrew view in which man does not *have* a body or *have* a soul; he *is* a soul-body unity. Flesh and spirit, however, are opposed as evil and good aspects of man. Recognition of this may have opened the way to a later accommodation to the Greek soul-body dualism. In Hebrew thought the soul was sometimes conceived as if it were a sort of liquid in the jar of the body, one that can be diminished and also replenished. In *Genesis* 2:7 God breathed his Spirit into the very dust out of which he made man, and man then "became a living soul." This imagery haunts Hebrew thought and the New Testament writers inherit the model it fostered.

ORIGIN OF THE SOUL

Within the development of Christian thought on the origin of the individual soul, three views have been maintained: (1) creationism, (2) traducianism, and (3) reincarnationism.

Creationism is the doctrine that God creates a new soul for each human being at conception. Upheld by Jerome, Hilary, and Peter Lombard, it was by far the most widely accepted view on the subject in the Middle Ages. Thomas Aquinas insisted upon it (*Summa theologiae* 1.118), and in the Reformed tradition the Calvinists generally taught it. Its consequences for certain moral questions, notably that of abortion, are clear.

Traducianism is the theory that the soul is transmitted along with the body by the parents. Forms of this view were proposed by some of the Fathers (such as Gregory of Nyssa and, notably, Tertullian), but in the Middle Ages it found little if any favor. Lutherans, however, tended to accept it, and in the early nineteenth century a modified form of it was proposed within the Roman Catholic tradition by the founder of the Rosminians, Antonio Rosmini-Serbati.

It is widely supposed that reincarnationism (a form of resurrection belief) is alien to Christian thought, but this supposition is not warranted by the evidence. The doctrine of the preexistence of the soul was certainly held by Origen and others in the tradition of Christian Platonism. Reincarnationism (not of course in its crude, primitivistic form, but in an ethical one, such as is found in Plato and in Indian philosophy) has a long and interesting, albeit partly underground, tradition in Christian thought and literature from early times down to the present day. Christian reincarnationists hold that the soul passes through many embodiments in the process of its development and spiritual growth and is judged accordingly, not on the basis of only one life of indeterminate duration. The soul, in this view, has a very long history, with origins antedating humanity itself.

DESTINY OF THE SOUL

Paul taught that since "the wages of sin is death" (*Rom.* 6:23), man has no more entitlement to immortality than has any other form of life. Thanks, however, to the power of Christ's resurrection, every man and woman of the Christian way who truly believes in the power of Christ will rise with him (*Phil.* 3:21) in a body that will be like Christ's "glorious" body *(tō sōmati tēs doxēs autou).* The resurrection of Christ makes us capable of personal resurrection, yet we can attain our own resurrection only insofar as we appropriate the power of Christ, which we can do through believing in its efficacy and accepting his divine gift of salvation from death and victory over the grave.

Indeed, although notions of immortality are inextricably woven into New Testament thought alongside the central resurrection theme, they are dependent on the latter in the thought of Paul and other New Testament writers. For all human beings, death has always been the supreme terror, the "final enemy" of man; now, Paul proclaims, it has been conquered, making possible the immortal life of the soul.

Yet we must not expect to find in the first century any clearly formulated universal doctrine of the afterlife. The expectation of the end of the age and the imminent return of Christ (the Parousia) so governed the Christian outlook during that period as to discourage speculation about the nature of the soul or whatever it is in man that survives his physical body. Paul himself pointedly discouraged idle speculation on the precise nature of the resurrected body (*1 Cor.* 15:35–58). As, however, the hope of the Parousia gradually lost much of its urgency, the need for formulation of an answer to such questions pressed itself on theological minds. Since the biblical writers had left these questions so open, and since a variety of beliefs from throughout the Mediterranean world had consciously or otherwise affected those who were thinking seriously about such matters, different and sometimes incompatible views were brought together. Even before the Christian era the Jews had been entertaining beliefs about the afterlife that had not been in the general mold of their classical thought but had been picked up from foreign sources after the Exile (587/6 BCE). In the time of Jesus, for instance, some (such as the Pharisees) believed in a resurrection from the dead which others (for example, the Sadducees) repudiated.

In classical Hebrew thought the souls of the dead went to She'ol, the counterpart of the Hades of Greek mythology, a sort of nonworld, an underground place of darkness and dust so dreary that, as Homer remarked, one would rather be a poor beggar in the land of the living than a king in the land of the dead. Yet in later Hebrew thought *sophia* ("wisdom") is seen as delivering human beings from She'ol

(*Prov.* 15:24). Unlike souls in the hell of later Christian theology, who have put themselves beyond God's benevolent power, those in She'ol could be the objects of God's care, for his power extends even there (*Dt.* 32:22, *Ps.* 139:8). In the New Testament, the concept of She'ol is sometimes replaced by that of death, for example in Paul's use of the Greek *thanatos* in *1 Corinthians* 15:55, quoting *Hosea* 13:14. However, in *Acts* 2:27, quoting *Psalms* 16:10, the term *haidēs* is retained.

In the rabbinical thought of the century before the advent of Christianity, *she'ol* came to mean a place exclusively for the wicked. The righteous go to *pardes* ("paradise," or, more strictly, "garden"), a late Hebrew term derived from the Greek *paradeisos,* the Septuagint translation for "Garden of Eden." *Pardes* was understood as a celestial restoration of the original, unfallen state of man. Sometimes, however, it represented an intermediate state between the death of the righteous and the final judgment—hence Jesus' promise to the penitent thief that they would meet that same day in "paradise" (a passage that would otherwise present grave interpretative difficulties), and other similar usages in the New Testament.

Along with such developments comes the notion of Gehenna as a pit of fire into which the wicked are to be thrown to be burned like trash. The symbolism of this transitional, intertestamental period is, however, by no means consistent; and the confusion is carried over into the New Testament, where both *haidēs* and *geenna* (*Mt.* 18:9 and *Mk.* 9:43) have been traditionally rendered "hell" in English, although they have different connotations in the Greek text. Hades, although it can function as a storehouse for the dead who await judgment (as in *Rv.* 20:13–14) and as a destructive power like death (as in *Mt.* 16:18), can also be (as in *Lk.* 16:23) a place of punishment indistinguishable from Gehenna.

The concept of Gehenna as a dumping ground for the incineration of the wicked originates with the "Valley of the son of Hinnom," the place on the boundary between Judah and Benjamin that in later Hebrew literature had an unsavory reputation as the site of a cultic shrine where human sacrifice was offered (*2 Kgs.* 23:10; *2 Chr.* 28:3, 33:6). When reference is made in *Isaiah* 66:24 to the place where the dead bodies of those who have rebelled against the Lord shall lie, this valley is the place being alluded to. In *2 Esdras* 7:6 Gehenna has become a furnace within sight of paradise. In Jewish apocalyptic literature it was often seen as a pit of unquenchable fire in which the wicked are destroyed, body and soul, a notion echoed in *Matthew* 10:28. The writer of *Revelation* calls this destination of the wicked "the second death" (21:8). In this Gehenna imagery lies the origin of the popular medieval concept of hell, in which, however, the soul, being indestructible, cannot be extinguished by the fire but is tormented everlastingly.

In early Christian thought, such a background for the concept of the soul and its destiny resulted in a confusion that no appeal to scripture could possibly clear, since the confusion was already embedded in the Bible itself. So we find that Tertullian, writing in his *De anima* (c. 210), assigns to the soul a sort of corporality. This tendency is to be found in other anti-gnostic writers of the period, including his contemporary Irenaeus. By contrast, Origen (c. 185–c. 254) and his influential Christian school at Alexandria taught that the soul preexisted in an incorporeal state and was imprisoned in a physical body as a result of its former waywardness. Origen probably also taught a form of reincarnationism. Gregory of Nyssa (c. 330–c. 395), Nemesius (who was bishop of Emesa toward the end of the fourth century), and the

Greek theologian Maximos the Confessor (c. 580–662), all interpreted the biblical concepts of the soul along Platonic lines and in the general tradition of Origen and his school.

In the thirteenth century, Thomas Aquinas follows the doctrine of the soul presented in Aristotle's *Eudemus,* teaching that, while body and soul together constitute aunity, the soul, as the "form" of the body, is an individual "spiritual substance" and as such is capable of leading a separate existence after the death of the body. This medieval doctrine of the soul, while largely determining the official teaching of the Roman Catholic church on the nature of the soul and its destiny, also indelibly imprinted itself on the theology of the Reformation. For the classical reformers, although contemporaneous with the great Renaissance movement in Europe, were thoroughly medieval in the mold of their theological thinking. The fact that Thomas described the essence of the pain of hell as the loss of the vision of God did little to mitigate the horror of hell in the popular mind.

In popular preaching during the Middle Ages and for centuries thereafter, hell was invariably depicted as a physical fire in which the souls of the damned, being somehow endowed with temporary bodies equipped to suffer physical pain, are eventually summoned on the Last Day to have their original bodies returned and enabled to suffer everlasting torture under the same conditions. The angels, however, according to Thomas, have no physical bodies; therefore Satan and the other denizens of hell must be equipped in some other way to undergo, as they certainly must, the punishment superabundantly due to them in the place of torment over which they reign. Nor could Dante's obviously symbolic treatment and allegorical vision of hell in the *Commedia* have assuaged the horror of hell in the popular mind. After all, much of Dante's genius lay in his ability to invest his great epic with an extraordinary realism that fixed itself on the minds of even those readers whose literary education had accustomed them to the allegorical methods so dear to the medieval mind.

Out of confusion in the concept of the soul, then, had sprung an increasing confusion in the Christian view of its destiny, making eschatology the least coherent aspect of the Christian theological tradition. For example, the soul has an independent existence and is sometimes envisioned, in Platonic fashion, as well rid of the burden of its physical encumbrance. Yet in the end the whole man, body and soul, must be restored in order to enjoy the fruits of Christ's redemption. In the first century, on account of the imminent expectation of the Parousia, Christians could plausibly see the separation of soul from body as a very temporary state of affairs, as represented in the catacombs by such inscriptions as "Dormit in pace" ("He sleeps in peace") and "Dormit in Christo" ("He sleeps in Christ"). As time went on, however, such a notion, although persisting to this day in pious epitaphs, could no longer serve as a theologically satisfactory account of what happens to the soul during a waiting period between death and the general resurrection of the dead. For it would suggest, if not entail, the view that heaven and hell are uninhabited until that general resurrection shall occur. Such a view is not conformable to the standard vision of Christian piety on this subject—least of all where, as in Roman Catholic tradition, the saints are already in heaven (the Church Triumphant) interceding for and otherwise helping their fellow Christians in the Church Militant on earth. Moreover, both the words of Jesus to the penitent thief (*Lk.* 23:43) and the parable of the rich man and Lazarus (*Lk.* 16:19), with their implication of a paradisial, Garden-of-Eden bliss, surely exclude the notion of a sleep till the Day of Judgment.

Furthermore, out of the doctrine of the intermediate state, which is at least foreshadowed in late Judaism and found in early Christian thought in a rudimentary form, was gradually developed the doctrine of purgatory. The concept of purgatory is of singular importance in the Christian doctrine of the life of the soul. Abused though the doctrine of purgatory was by legalistic distortions and ecclesiastical corruption in late medieval practice, purgatory has gradually come to be seen, through the influence of developments in English Tractarian thought in the nineteenth century, as a state not so much of punishment as of purification, refreshment, and growth. This theological development is adumbrated in some medieval Christian literature, notably the *Trattato (Dicchiarazione)* of Catherine of Genoa (1447–1510).

The souls in purgatory have generally been regarded as disembodied (or at least lacking our earthly embodiment), yet capable of the peculiar kind of pain that purgatory entails: a pain of waiting and longing. The duration of purgatory is indeterminate; but it is always assumed that some who enter it may be released comparatively soon and certainly that multitudes are to be released long before the Day of Judgment. What then happens to them on their release? Speculative theologians have made various proposals. According to Roman Catholic theology, each soul on its separation from the body is subjected to a "particular" judgment, as distinguished from the final or "general" judgment. In 1336, Pope Benedict XII, in his bull *Benedictus Deus,* specifically declared that souls, having been subjected to this particular judgment, are admitted at once to the beatific vision, which is heaven, or proceed at once to purgatory to be cleansed and readied for the heavenly state, or are consigned to hell. This teaching does not merely exclude explicitly the primitive Christian view represented by the *dormit in pace* type of epitaph; it makes nonsense of traditional Roman Catholic piety. For if purgatory be considered in any sense a state of punishment, hell a state of both torment and hopelessness, and heaven one of that joyful activity that comes with the full knowledge of God that is the reward of the righteous, then the traditional prayer for the dead ("Requiescant in pace"; "May they rest in peace") seems to express an inapposite wish for any of the three categories.

That ancient prayer echoes the primitive wish that the souls of the dead may not be inclined, because of their troubled state, to haunt the living but may instead pursue their business in peace and tranquillity and have no such harassing inclination. This primitive wish is, of course, transfigured in Catholic thought and sentiment, where it is illumined by the response "Et lux perpetua luceat eis" ("May perpetual light shine upon them"), expressing a loving concern for the progress of the souls of the dead and the belief that they are advancing toward the fulfillment of their destiny. Nevertheless, at the regular Roman Catholic burial service a beautiful prayer beckons the angels to come forth to meet the deceased and conduct him or her "into the heavenly city, Jerusalem."

BIBLIOGRAPHY

For the Hebrew background of the New Testament view, a reliable source is the brief article "Soul" by Norman Porteous in *The Interpreter's Dictionary of the Bible* (New York, 1962).

Rudolf Bultmann provides abundant background for an understanding of the New Testament writers' general outlook in his *Theology of the New Testament,* vol. 1 (New York, 1951). Oscar Cullmann has written an important essay on this topic, which was published in *Immortality and Resurrection,* edited by Krister Stendahl (New York, 1965). The other essays in this collection, by Harry A. Wolfson, Werner Yaeger, and Henry J. Cadbury, also merit attention. Augustine's view, articulated in his *On the Immortality of the Soul,* greatly influenced both the medieval schoolmen and the reformers. *Saint Thomas and the Problem of the Soul in the Thirteenth Century* (Toronto, 1934), by Anton C. Pegis, provides a useful introduction to the view of Thomas Aquinas as set forth in the first volume of his *Summa theologiae.* Étienne Gilson treats the subject in his study *The Spirit of Mediaeval Philosophy* (London, 1936), and John Calvin discusses the origin, immortal nature, and other aspects of the soul in his *Institutes of the Christian Religion,* 2 vols. (Philadelphia, 1960). For the Renaissance view of Pietro Pomponazzi, see Clement C. J. Webb's *Studies in the History of Natural Theology* (Oxford, 1915).

The soul plays a central role in the various forms of Christian mysticism. The notion of the "fine point" of the soul, a cell remaining sensitive to God despite the fall and consequent corruption of mankind, is a common topic of such literature: for example, see *The Living Flame of Love* by John of the Cross. For the Salesian tradition, see Henri Bremond's treatment in his *Histoire littéraire du sentiment religieux en France* (1915–1932), 2d ed. (Paris, 1967–1968), edited by René Taveneaux, especially vol. 7. Whether any form of reincarnationism is reconcilable to Christian faith is specifically considered in two books of mine: *Reincarnation in Christianity* (Wheaton, Ill., 1978) and *Reincarnation as a Christian Hope* (London, 1982).

27 ISLAMIC CONCEPTS OF THE SOUL

MICHAEL E. MARMURA

Islamic concepts of the soul vary, ranging from the traditional (and most prevalent) to the mystical. They include doctrines formulated by individual schools of Islamic dialectical theology *(kalām)* and theories developed within Islamic philosophy *(falsafah)*. It is possible to classify very broadly the different types of such concepts under four categories: traditional, theological, philosophical, and mystical (Ṣūfī). Differences (as well as overlappings) abound, not only between these categories, but also within them. Nonetheless, the various Islamic concepts of the soul all seek or claim a Qur'anic base. Hence, the proper starting point of any discussion of such concepts is the Qur'ān. Before turning to the Qur'ān, however, a few preliminary remarks on the use of the Arabic terms *rūḥ* ("spirit") and *nafs* ("soul") are in order.

As in other languages, these terms relate to the ideas of breath and wind. In pre-Islamic Arabic poetry, *rūḥ* can mean "wind," "breath," or "that which one blows" (as when kindling a fire). In post-Qur'anic Arabic, the two terms are often used interchangeably when referring to the human soul, but distinctions between them are also maintained within certain conceptual schemes. In the Qur'ān, in addition to the grammatical reflexive use of *nafs* as "self," the term is used to refer to the human soul, whereas *rūḥ* normally refers to the spirit that proceeds from God. In pre-Islamic Arabic poetry, these two terms do not have a religious or supernatural connotation. Thus *rūḥ* refers to the physical breath or wind, while *nafs* (when not used reflexively) refers to the blood, sometimes to the living body. This usage is consistent with the secular nature of this poetry, whose themes revolve around the poet's mundane loves, sorrows, heroic exploits, and concept of tribal honor. The poetry is also noted for its vivid descriptions of nature—desert scenery and animal life, wild and domestic—that convey a sense of the splendor, power (sometimes harshness), and vitality of nature, but never anything that can be construed as either teleological or mystical. There are also affirmations in this poetry that, with death, everything ends, that there is nothing beyond the grave. A seeming exception to this consists of references to the *hāmah*, a birdlike apparition resembling a small owl, which, according to pre-Islamic Arab belief, departs from the head of a slaughtered man, perches by his grave, and continues to shriek, "give me to drink," until the death is avenged. The association of this belief with the tribal law of avenging the death of a kinsman is obvious.

RŪḤ AND NAFS IN THE QUR'ĀN

As indicated earlier, *rūḥ* ("spirit") in the Qur'ān refers normally to God's spirit. The term appears in different contexts. It is the divine creative breath: God creates man (Adam) from clay, animating him by blowing into the clay of his spirit (15:29; 32:9; 38:72). Again, God blew of his spirit into Mary, causing the conception of Jesus (21:91; 66:12). Spirit is sent by God as a messenger: it is *al-rūḥ al-amīn* ("the faithful spirit") that comes to Muḥammad's heart (26:193)—hence the Qur'anic commentators' identification of "the faithful spirit" with the angelic messenger Gabriel. Mary conceives when God sends his spirit to her in the form of a perfect man (19:17). Spirit is also *rūḥ al-qudūs* ("the holy spirit") which God sends to help Jesus (2:87, 2:253). Jesus himself is referred to as a spirit from God, but it is also made clear that this does not mean that he is the son of God (4:171).

Spirit relates also to the *amr* of God (16:2; 17:85; 40:15; 42:52), a term that can mean either "command" or "affair." Muslim scholars have disagreed on the interpretation of this term as well as on the referent of *rūḥ* ("spirit") in surah 17:85: "They ask thee [Muḥammad] about the spirit. Say: 'The spirit is of my Lord's *amr;* of knowledge ye have been given but little.'" Some have understood *amr* here as "affair," not "command," and *rūḥ* as referring to the human spirit. If this interpretation is correct, then the verse provides an exception to the normal Qur'anic use of the term *rūḥ*.

The term *nafs,* when not used in the grammatical reflexive sense of "self," refers to the human soul, not God's spirit. The human soul, however, relates to the divine spirit, since, as indicated earlier, God brings life to man by breathing into him of his spirit. The equivalence of life and soul in the Qur'ān, however, is not explicitly stated. Nor is there any explicit statement as to whether the soul is immaterial or material. The Qur'ān is primarily concerned with the moral and religious orientation of the human soul, with its conduct, and with the consequences of such conduct in terms of reward and punishment in the hereafter. This concern with the moral and religious disposition of the soul is reflected in the Qur'anic characterization of the soul as either *ammārah, lawwāmah,* or *muṭma'innah.* The *ammārah* (12:53) is the soul that by nature incites or commands what is evil. Qur'anic commentators have identified this with the carnal self. The *lawwāmah* (75:2) is the soul that constantly blames itself, interpreted by some commentators as upbraiding itself in the quest of goodness. The *muṭma'innah* (89:27) is the tranquil soul of the virtuous believer that will return to its lord.

With death, the soul leaves the body, to rejoin it on the Day of Judgment. Thereafter the righteous go to Paradise, the wicked dwell in Hell. Two questions in particular that relate to the resurrection were to occupy Islamic religious thinkers. The first is whether or not it is the remains of the same body that is resurrected. To this the Qur'ān gives no detailed answer, only an affirmation that God has the power to bring back to life what has been decayed: "Who will revive these bones when they are decayed? Say: 'He who created them the first time will revive them'" (36:78–79). The second is the question of what happens to the soul between the time of death and the day of resurrection. There are Qur'anic statements (8:49; 9:101; 32:21; 47:27) that suggest that wicked souls will be punished even before the resurrection and that the souls of martyrs will be in paradise: "Do not reckon that those killed in battle are dead; they are living with their Lord, provided for" (3:169). Such statements become a basis for traditional doctrines regarding the soul's fate in the interim between death and the final day of judgment.

TRADITIONAL CONCEPTS

In Islam, the most prevalent concepts of the soul can perhaps best be termed "traditional." Their immediate inspiration is the Qur'ān, interpreted literally, and the *ḥadīth*, or "tradition." A chief source for our knowledge of the traditional concepts of the soul in Islam is *Kitāb al-rūḥ* (The Book of the Spirit), by the Damascene Ibn Qayyim al-Jawzīyah (d. 1350), a celebrated Ḥanbalī theologian and jurisconsult.

The term *rūḥ*, Ibn Qayyim maintains, is applicable in Arabic usage to both the spirit that comes from God and the human spirit. In the Qur'ān, however, it is used to refer to the spirit that comes from God. This spirit proceeds from the *amr* of God. The term *amr* in the Qur'ān, Ibn Qayyim insists, always means "command." Since the spirit proceeds from the command of God, it is a created being, although its creation antedates the creation of the human soul. The human body is created before the human soul. The latter, though created, is everlasting. Death means the separation of this soul from the body, to rejoin it permanently when the resurrection takes place. When the Qur'ān speaks of the soul that incites to evil, the soul that upbraids, and the tranquil soul, this does not mean that a human has three souls. These, Ibn Qayyim argues, are characteristics of one and the same human soul.

Ibn Qayyim gives a lengthy critique of the philosophical doctrine of an immaterial soul, incorporating in his criticism the arguments the theologian al-Ghazālī (d. 1111) had used in showing that Ibn Sīnā (Avicenna; d. 1037) had failed to demonstrate the immateriality of the human soul. Ibn Qayyim rejects the concept of an immaterial soul. An immaterial spirit or soul would be totally unrelated to what is spatial. What is unrelated to the spatial and the bodily cannot be spoken of as being in a body or outside it, or as traveling away from the body or returning to it. But this is the scriptural language expressing the activities of the soul. The human soul is hence material but "differs in quiddity [*al-māhiyyah*] from the sensible body, being a body that is luminous, elevated, light, alive, and in motion. It penetrates the substance of the body organs, flowing therein in the way water flows in roses, oil in olives, and fire in charcoal" (*Kitāb al-rūḥ*, Hyderabad, 1963, p. 310). The body, in fact, is the mold (*qālib*) of the soul. Body and soul interact, helping to shape each other's individual characteristics. Thus, when death takes place, souls leaving their bodies have their individuality and are hence differentiated one from another.

During sleep, souls leave their bodies temporarily, sometimes communicating with other souls, whether of the living or of the dead. With death, the soul leaves the body but can very swiftly return to it. The souls of the virtuous can communicate with each other, the wicked souls being too preoccupied in their torments for this. For in the interim between death and the resurrection, most souls rejoin their bodies in the grave to be questioned by the two angels of death, Munkar and Nakīr. The wicked, unbelieving souls suffer punishment and torment in the grave, while the virtuous believers enjoy a measure of bliss. Ibn Qayyim equates the period of the grave with the *barzakh*, a Qur'anic term (23:100; 25:53; 55:20) that originally meant "hindrance" or "separation." The souls of prophets are in paradise, as are those of martyrs, although there are disagreements among traditional Muslims as to whether this applies to all martyrs. These disagreements, Ibn Qayyim maintains, are reconcilable once the legal conditions governing the fate of the soul are known. To cite but one of his examples, a martyr who dies before paying a debt is excluded from entry into paradise during this interim but does not suffer torment.

The prayers of the living over the souls of the dead are heard by the latter, who are helped by them. Ibn Qayyim devotes a long section of his book to this topic. The length of this chapter indicates the importance to Muslims of the visiting of graves and the offering of prayers over the dead, for these visits are very much part of traditional Muslim piety and a source of consolation to the bereaved.

THEOLOGICAL (KALĀM) CONCEPTS

Islam's dialectical theologians, the *mutakallimūn*, no less than the more traditional Muslims, sought to uphold a Qur'anic concept of the soul. They sought to uphold it, however, within scripturally rooted perspectives of the world that they formulated and rationally defended. Their concepts of the human soul were governed largely by two questions, one metaphysical, the other eschatological. The metaphysical question pertained to the ultimate constituents of the created world: Do these consist of indivisible atoms or of what is potentially infinitely divisible? The eschatological question arose out of their doctrine of bodily resurrection: if, in the ages between the world's beginning and its end, dead human bodies decompose to become parts of other physical entities (organic or inorganic), how can there be a real resurrection, that is, a return to life of the actual individuals who once lived and died, and not the mere creation anew of replicas of them?

Regarding the metaphysical question, most of the *mutakallimūn* were atomists. Their concepts of the soul were for the most part materialist: they regarded it either as a body, or identified it with life, which they maintained is a transient quality, an accident, that occurs to a body. But there were disagreements among them, particularly among members of the "rationalist" Muʿtazilī school of *kalām*, which attained the height of its power and influence in the first part of the ninth century. Thus, one of its leading theologians, al-Naẓẓām (d. 845), rejected atomism. Moreover, he conceived of the soul (which he identified with life) as a subtle body that is diffused in all parts of the physical body. His conceptof the soul is substantially the same as that of the traditional concept defended by Ibn Qayyim. Another exception of a different type was the view of the Muʿtazilī Muʿammar (d. 835). He was an atomist and espoused a concept of the soul as an immaterial atom. Other theologians held the soul to be an atom, but not immaterial. But if it is a material atom, is life identical with it? If life is not identical with it, then could life be an accident that inheres in the single atom? The Muʿtazilah disagreed as to whether the accidents could inhere in the single atom or only in atoms that are interrelated, forming a body. They also disagreed as to whether spirit, soul, and life are identical. But the prevalent Muʿtazilī view was that the soul is material and that life, whether or not identical with soul, is a transient accident.

It is in terms of this prevalent view that the eschatological question mentioned earlier must be understood. If life is a transient accident and the dead body's atoms separate to combine differently forming other physical entities, where is the continuity that would guarantee the identity of the individual to be resurrected? Without this continuity, what appears to be the resurrected individual is only a similar being, a *mithl*. To resolve this difficulty, some of the Muʿtazilah resorted to the doctrine that nonexistence *(alʿadam)* is "a thing" *(shay')* or "an entity," "an essence" *(dhāt),* to which existence is a state that occurs. Thus a nonexistent entity *A* acquires existence for a span of time, loses it during another span, and regains it eternally at the resurrection, *A* remaining *A* throughout all these stages.

The doctrine that nonexistence is an entity, a thing, was rejected by the Ashʿarī school of *kalām*. This school was founded by al-Ashʿarī (d. 935), originally a Muʿtazilī who rebelled against his school. (Ashʿarism gradually gained ascendancy to become the dominant school of *kalām* in Islam.) But while the Ashʿarīyah opposed fundamental Muʿtazilī doctrines, they were also atomists. Their atomism formed part of their occasionalist metaphysics according to which all events are the direct creation of God. Accidents are transient and do not endure for more than one moment of time and are hence constantly recreated. Life, the Ashʿarīyah held, is a transient accident created and recreated while the individual lives. It is hence not difficult to see that the eschatological problem regarding the soul that the Muʿtazilah tried to solve persisted.

For an Ashʿarī answer to this difficulty, I will turn to al-Ghazālī. His main arguments for the possibility of bodily resurrection are found in two works. The first is his criticism of the Islamic philosophers, particularly Ibn Sīnā, the *Tahāfut al-falāsifah* (The Incoherence of the Philosophers). In this work he argues in great detail to show that Ibn Sīnā has failed to demonstrate his theory that the human soul is an immaterial, immortal substance. At the same time, he argues for the possibility of bodily resurrection in terms of a theory of an immaterial, immortal soul, maintaining that God at the resurrection creates for such a soul a new body. The second work, *Al-iqtiṣād fī al-Iʿtiqād* (Moderation in Belief), written shortly after the *Tahāfut*, gives a different explanation. Significantly, in this work al-Ghazālī repudiates the theory he advocated in the *Tahāfut*, maintaining that he had advanced it only for the sake of argument, to show that bodily resurrection is possible even if one adopts a doctrine of an immaterial soul. The true doctrine, he then continues, is the Ashʿarī, namely that life is a transient accident constantly created and recreated in the living body. Resurrection is the return to life and existence of what was originally a first creation by God. God is able to recreate what he had previously created. A copy is simply a copy, never the recreation of what was actually a new creation. Al-Ghazālī does not discuss how one can differentiate between the resurrected, recreated original being, and the copy, the *mithl,* but the implication of his argument is that this is knowable to God, who is the creator of all things.

Al-Ghazālī follows substantially the line of reasoning of his predecessor and teacher, the Ashʿarī al-Juwaynī (d. 1085). Unlike al-Juwaynī, however, al-Ghazālī does not discuss whether spirit or soul is the same as life. Al-Juwaynī is more explicit on this. Spirit is a body that pervades the physical body, animating it. Life, however, is a transient accident that inheres in spirit. With the exception of this distinction between life and spirit, al-Juwaynī's concept of the soul is in harmony with the traditional concept defended by Ibn Qayyim.

PHILOSOPHICAL CONCEPTS

The theories of the soul formulated by Islam's philosophers, the *falāsifah* (sg., *faylasūf*), derive largely from Plato, Aristotle, and Plotinus. But there are other influences—Greek medicine and Stoic thought, for example. An influential short Arabic treatise on the difference between spirit (*rūḥ;* Gr., *pneuma),* and soul *(nafs;* Gr., *psuchē)* by the Christian translator, Qusṭā Ibn Lūqā (d. 912), is of interest, not only for its ideas, but also for its listing of the sources of these ideas—Plato (his *Phaedo* and *Timaeus*), Aristotle, Theophrastus, and Galen. Spirit, according to this treatise, is a subtle body. Its less refined form spreads in the body, from the heart through the veins, causing animation, breathing, and pulsation. The more refined spirit spreads from the brain through the nervous system to cause sensation and movement. Spirit, however, is only the proximate intermediary cause of these activities; its efficacy is caused by the soul, which is an immaterial, immortal substance. With death, spirit ceases, but not soul.

It was, however, in its Neoplatonic form that the doctrine of the soul's immateriality and immortality left its greatest impact on Islamic thought. This impact was not confined to philosophy proper but is discernible in the religious thought of various Islamic sectarian groups—the Ismāʿīlīyah, for example. The other most important source for the *falāsifah*'s concepts of the soul was Aristotle. The majority accepted Aristotle's definition of the soul as the entelechy of the body, his idea of its division into vegetative, sensitive, and rational and of the latter into theoretical and practical, and his description of the states of its various parts as these change from potentiality to actuality. Within the Platonic, Aristotelian, and Neoplatonic frameworks, however, there were differences in the *falāsifah*'s conceptions of the soul. An idea of these differences can be obtained by considering the conceptions offered by some representative philosophers.

Al-Kindī (d. c. 870), the first Islamic philosopher, for example, subscribes to the doctrine of the soul as an immaterial, immortal substance and at the same time defends the Qur'anic doctrine of bodily resurrection. His surviving treatises, however, do not include anything that shows the manner in which he synthesized these two doctrines. The physician-philosopher al-Rāzī (d. 926), on the other hand, offers a theory of the human soul inspired largely by Plato's *Timaeus*. Soul is one of the five eternal principles; the others are God, atomic (disorganized) matter, absolute space, and absolute time. At a moment in time, God imposes order on matter, rendering it receptive of soul. When soul unites with matter, it becomes individuated, forming the particular living creatures. Man alone among these creatures is endowed with reason, an emanation from God. There is a lengthy but finite span of time, in which soul remains conjoined with matter and individuated. During this period there is transmigration of souls within animal and human life. The finite period ends when reason in men prevails. The individual souls then disengage from matter, returning to their original state of one soul. The initial state of the four other eternal principles resumes, continuing into the infinite future.

With al-Fārābī (d. 950) and Ibn Sīnā, we encounter two highly developed psychological theories. Both presupposed a Neoplatonic emanative scheme. The celestial world, for al-Fārābī, consists of a succession from God of dyads, intelligences, and bodily spheres; for Ibn Sīnā, it consists of a succession of triads, intelligences, souls, and bodily spheres. For both, the last successive celestial intelligence is the Active Intellect, after which our terrestrial world comes into existence. The entire process of successive emanations from God exists eternally.

According to al-Fārābī, the human rational soul is at first a potentiality in the material body. In some individuals, the objects of sensory perception, the material images, are transformed by the illuminary action of the Active Intellect into abstract concepts. These human souls that achieve abstract conceptual thought attain an immaterial status. (There are higher levels of conceptual thought, culminating with rare individuals, the philosopher-prophets, in the human soul's periodic union with the Active Intellect.) Only those souls that have attained an immaterial status are immortal. Good souls, those that have continued to live according to the dictates of reason, shunning the lower passions, live in eternal happiness, contemplating the celestial intelligences and God. Those rational souls that have betrayed their calling, surrendering to the lower passions, live in eternal misery, seeking contemplation of the celestial intelligences but unable to achieve it. The souls of the majority of mankind, however, never attain an immaterial status and, with death, cease to exist.

Ibn Sīnā, on the other hand, insists on the individual immortality of all souls. The rational soul, an emanation from the Active Intellect, joins the human body and becomes individuated by it. It is an immaterial, individual substance that exists with the body but is not imprinted in it. Souls that have lived the rational life, controlling the lower passions and remaining untarnished by vice, are rewarded in the hereafter. They live in eternal bliss, contemplating the celestial beings and God. This applies to nonphilosophical virtuous souls that have lived in accordance with the divine law, for this law is an expression of philosophical truth in the language of imagery and symbol, which the nonphilosopher can understand. Souls that have not lived the rational, virtuous life or have not adhered to the commands of the religious law are punished in the hereafter. They live eternally in torment, seeking contemplation of the celestial beings and God, but are unable to achieve this. The Qur'anic language describing the afterlife in physical terms is symbolic. Ibn Sīnā's theory of the soul culminates in mysticism. But this is intellectual mysticism. God, for Ibn Sīnā, is pure mind. The soul's journey to God includes the inundation of the souls of exceptional individuals with all of the intelligibles from the Active Intellect. This experience is intuitive, occurring all at once.

Ibn Rushd (Averroës; d. 1198) was the most Aristotelian of the *falāsifah*. In those writings addressed to the general Islamic reader, he affirms the doctrine of reward and punishment in the hereafter, insisting, however, that the scriptural language describing the hereafter should be understood on different levels, depending on one's intellectual capacity. His more technical psychological writings, notably his commentaries on Aristotle, leave no room for a doctrine of individual immortality. These writings, however, left a much greater impact on medieval and Renaissance Europe than they did on Islam. In the Islamic world, it was Ibn Sīnā's theory of the soul that had the greater influence on subsequent *falsafah* and religious thought.

ṢŪFĪ CONCEPTS

In considering this very vast subject, it is well to differentiate between three of its aspects: (1) what Ṣūfīs conceived the human soul to be, (2) the soul's purification and the path of holiness it must follow as it seeks God, (3) the relation of the soul to God, particularly in its intimate experiencing of the divine. These aspects are related, but the third represents a central issue on which Ṣūfīs were divided and which caused controversy in the general history of Islamic religious thought.

According to some, the Ṣūfī (and Ash'arī theologian) al-Qushayrī (d. 1074) observes, the term "soul" refers to those of man's characteristics that are afflicted with illness and to his blameworthy actions. It is possible, he maintains, "that the soul is a subtle entity [*laṭīfah*] placed in this [bodily] mold [*qālib*], being the receptacle of ill dispositions, just as spirit [*al-rūḥ*] is placed in this mold, being the receptacle of praiseworthy dispositions" (*Al-risālah al-Qushayrīyah*, Cairo, 1966, vol. 1, p. 249). The earlier Ṣūfī al-Tirmidhī (fl. 894) also gives expression to the view that the soul is evil. Both, moreover, reflect traditional and *kalām* concepts of the soul as material.

Al-Ghazālī, on the other hand, often uses Avicennian language in his discussions of the soul. (This fact need not necessarily commit him to Avicennian ontology, since he frequently suggests that Ibn Sīnā's philosophical language can be interpreted in occasionalist, Ashʿarī terms.) At the beginning of his *Mīzān al-ʿAmal* (The Criterion for Action), al-Ghazālī also indicates that Ṣūfīs subscribe to the doctrine of the soul's immateriality as they reject the concept of physical reward and punishment in the hereafter. Thus, within Sufism there are differences in belief as to whether the soul is material or immaterial. There is less difference (and greater emphasis), however, on the subject of its purification and the ascetic devotional course it must pursue. (Differences between Ṣūfī orders here are largely a matter of ritual, not substance.)

It is, however, the relation of the human soul—the self, the "I"—to God that is at the heart of Sufism, and it was this issue that caused conflict. The mystical experience itself is both overwhelming and ineffable. Utterances attempting to convey it are symbolic, sometimes prone to overstatement, and hence prone to being misunderstood. Central to this issue is the interpretation of the mystical experience of *fanā'*, the "passing away" or "annihilation" of the self in the divine essence, the latter representing *baqā'*, "permanence."

Ṣūfīs like al-Ghazālī interpreted *fanā'* as "closeness" *(qurb)* to God and thus helped to reconcile Sufism with the generally accepted tenets of Islam. The issue, however, remained a sensitive one, as reflected, for example, in the philosophical tale, *Ḥayy Ibn Yaqẓān*, by the Andalusian philosopher Ibn Ṭufayl (d. 1185). Ḥayy, the story's hero, who grows up on an uninhabited tropical island, undergoes a process of self-education that culminates in the mystical experience. At first he falls into the error of thinking that his soul becomes one with the divine essence; he is delivered from this mistake through God's mercy as he realizes that such concepts as unity and plurality and union and disjunction are applicable only to bodies, not to immaterial selves that have experiential knowledge of God.

The relation of the soul to God in Ṣūfī thought takes on a highly metaphysical turn in the complex theosophy of the great mystic Ibn al-ʿArabī (d. 1240) and his followers, particularly ʿAbd al-Karīm al-Jīlī (d. 1408?). Ibn al-ʿArabī is noted for his doctrine of the unity of being *(waḥdat al-wujūd)* wherein creation *(al-khalq)* is a mirroring of the Truth *(al-ḥaqq)*, the Creator. Perfect souls are reflections of the perfection of the divine essence. The prophets are the archetypes of these perfect souls: each prophet is a word *(kalimah)* of God. The perfect soul is a microcosm of reality. The idea of man as a microcosm did not originate with Ibn al-ʿArabī; it was utilized by the *falāsifah* and by al-Ghazālī. But with Ibn al-ʿArabī and those who followed him it acquires a spiritual and metaphysical dimension all its own, representing a high point in the development of the concept of soul in the history of Islamic religious thought.

BIBLIOGRAPHY

For a comprehensive study, see D. B. Macdonald's "The Development of the Idea of Spirit in Islam," *Acta Orientalia* (1931): 307–351, reprinted in *The Moslem World* 22 (January and April 1932): 25–42, 153–168. For Qur'anic, traditional, and *kalām* concepts, see Régis Blachère's "Note sur le substantif 'nafs' dans le Coran," *Semitica* 1 (1948): 69–77; F. T. Cooke's "Ibn al-Quiyim's Kitab al-Rūḥ," *The Moslem World* 25 (April 1935): 129–144; and Albert N. Nader's *Le système philosophique des muʿtazila* (Beirut, 1956); see also the work by Majid Fakhry cited below. For philosophical concepts, see Avicenna's "On the Proof of Prophecies," translated by me in *Medieval Political Philosophy: A Sourcebook,* edited by Ralph Lerner and Muhsin Mahdi (New York, 1963), pp. 112–121; Majid Fakhry's *A History of Islamic Philosophy*, 2d ed. (New York, 1983); Lenn E. Goodman's "Rasi's Myth of the Fall of the Soul," in *Essays on Islamic Philosophy and Science*, edited by George F. Hourani (Albany, N.Y., 1975), pp. 25–40; my article "Avicenna and the Problem of the Infinite Number of Souls," *Mediaeval Studies* 22 (1960); 232–239; and *Avicenna's Psychology*, edited and translated by Fazlur Rahman (London, 1952). For Sūfī concepts, see A. E. Affifi's *The Mystical Philosophy of Muḥyid Dīn Ibnul ʿArabī* (Cambridge, 1939); A. J. Arberry's *Sufism* (1950; reprint, London, 1979); Ibn al-ʿArabi's *The Bezels of Wisdom*, translated with an introduction and notes by R. W. J. Austin (London, 1980); Reynold A. Nicholson's *Studies in Islamic Mysticism* (1921; reprint, Cambridge, 1976); Annemarie Schimmel's *Mystical Dimensions of Islam* (Chapel Hill, N.C., 1975); and Fadlou Shehadi's *Ghazali's Unique Unknowable God* (Leiden, 1964).

28 CONCEPTS OF THE SOUL IN TRIBAL COMMUNITES

CLAUDE RIVIÈRE
Translated from French by G. P. Silverman-Proust

Whereas in a Christian context the human soul is thought about and overvalued in relation to the body, in the traditional thinking of so-called archaic societies an immanent power, a vital principle, an individualized dynamism, is usually recognized to exist not only in man but in certain other material and biological beings as well. Whatever moves, whatever lives, is supposed to be the abode of one or many souls.

Here I shall essentially deal with what we conceive of as the spiritual principle of the human being, the prototype of the "beings-forces" of nature, and not with the more or less anthropomorphized spirits, gods, or genies, nor with powers that are supposed to have a mineral, an animal, or a vegetable as a continuous substratum.

The essence of the soul is power, to the extent that power, soul, and life become interchangeable categories. But with regard to traditional societies we can really speak neither of the uniqueness of the soul nor of homogenous and always precise concepts. The linguistic equivalents we use remain very approximate. Since the idea of the soul is rarely the object of metaphysical discussion in these societies, it is difficult to really know if what is designated by the aborigines as "spirit of the man," or "spirit in the man," corresponds to separate realities, to distinct functions of the same reality, or to inherent potentialities of a determined substance. Nevertheless, the fact that primitive man thinks of himself as unlimited with regard to his physical potentialities shows that he examines himself in order to seize his hidden essence, which extends far beyond his body.

In the explanations relating to the subject, we observe a constant concern about concrete detail and the rejection of abstractions, which results in a correspondence between ontological pluralism and a plurality of phenomena; but nothing is represented as either purely material or purely spiritual. The quantitative character of the power of the soul is accentuated by this plurality of personal souls and by the identification of the degree of force that each individual disposes of in his relation to evil spirits, in his generative power, and in the influence he has on his fellow citizens, for example. Each of these individual powers tends to free itself and to exert itself in an independent way: for example, through the heart in courageous deeds of battle or through the mind in the wisdom of a palaver. The soul never appears as a pure essence but is identified through props and manifestations. Its power can vary from individual to individual, and even in the same individual in the course of his life.

THEORETICAL ELABORATIONS

While most of the ethnologists of religion have been interested in problems relating to the soul, E. B. Tylor (*Primitive Culture,* 1871) and Lucien Lévy-Bruhl (*L'âme primitive,* 1927) were among those who formulated the principal theories regarding this subject. In *The Golden Bough,* James Frazer remained close to Tylor's concepts. R. R. Marett, criticizing both Tylor and Frazer, coined the word *animatism* to describe the tendency of the mind to consider inanimate objects as living and endowed with feelings and a will of their own. [*See* Animism and Animatism.]

According to Tylor, who was one of the first to propose a theory of primitive religion, the evolution of religious systems had its origin in a primitive animism, defined as a belief in spiritual beings. The notion of the soul arose from the fusion of the idea of a life principle with a double, or an impalpable phantom that could separate itself from the body it resembled. Belief in a phantom double originated in the experience of the independent double of distant or deceased individuals appearing in nocturnal dreams and diurnal fantasies.

But studies in the history of religions have not validated Tylor's hypotheses. His sequential interpretation (belief in a double, attribution of a soul to animals and then to objects, ancestor and spirit cults, fetishism, idolatry, polytheism, monotheism) has been shown to be incorrect; the importance that he gave to dreaminspired revelations in the origin of myth and religion has been contested; and the historical evidence proves that monotheism appeared much earlier than Tylor thought.

According to Lévy-Bruhl, the primitive soul must be seen as participating in a unique principle. All beings function as the vehicles, and the diversely specified incarnations, of an anonymous and impersonal force that sociology has popularized under its Melanesian name, *mana.* [*See* Preanimism.] Participation in *mana,* which is at one and the same time substance, essence, force, and a unity of qualities, confers on things and beings a sacred and mysterious character that animates nature and maintains an interaction between all its parts. Belief in an essence common to certain beings and objects has been defined as totemism. But Lévy-Bruhl also viewed souls as variable and multiple powers, unequally located in the universe. Next to emanations-forces and powers of nature are placed the beings-forces, the personified souls, endowed both with intelligence and will.

It is, however, to be emphasized that both Lévy-Bruhl and Marett erred in concluding that the primitive conceives of everything in nature as being animated, even if he does believe that anything can serve as a prop for an animation under specific circumstances. The idea that all is soul is a theoretical construction. The idea that the individual soul does not exist and that it fuses either with the cosmos or with the group is also erroneous, because, on the one hand, the man's identification with the vegetable, animal, or divine world does not exclude the differentiation of powers and, on the other hand, among many African peoples (the Kikuyu of Kenya, for example), the collective soul (or family spirit) is entirely different from the soul of the individual.

The idea that primitive thought ignores any dualism separating the body and soul also lacks validation. Numerous examples show that there exists a quite noticeable distinction between the body element and the diversity of spiritual entities that we call "souls" for the sake of convenience, entities that may have the body as a prop or that, as the double of ego, constitute what Frazer called the "external soul."

VARIETIES OF THE SOUL

Owing to a lack of better and more varied terms, I use the term *soul* here, in the singular, to refer to conceptions with greater differences than those existing between Shintō and Christianity; *soul* often designates, for a single living being, plural entities, distinguished by the autochthonous peoples themselves to account for what they judge to be independent spiritual forces. As beliefs can and do contradict each other from one ethnic group to another, it is hardly possible to imagine a typology that could be valid for a single continent or even for a large cultural area; consequently, it seems more appropriate to illustrate the diversity of souls—the complexity and ambiguity of these beliefs—with some examples.

The Fang of Gabon name seven types of souls: (1) *eba,* a vital principle located in the brain, which disappears after death; (2) *nlem,* the heart, the seat of conscience, which inspires the acts of men and also disappears at the time of death; (3) *edzii,* an individual name that retains a sort of individuality after death; (4) *ki* (or *ndem*) the sign of the individual and at the same time his force which perpetuates itself after disincarnation; (5) *ngzel,* the active principle of the soul as long as it is in the body; (6) *nsissim,* both shadow and soul; and (7) *khun,* the disincarnated spirit, which can appear as a ghost.

From this example, we can see that the soul is never conceived of as an amorphous substance; rather, it is represented through functional props (brain, heart), through images (shadow, ghost), through symbols (name, character sign), or by its activities. The differentiation of souls may also occur in relation to ethical or sexual criteria or their modalities of action.

The Mbua of the Rio Branco territory in Brazil (the São Paulo littoral) believe that there exists in each individual both a beneficial soul and a dangerous soul, which manifest themselves through communication, that is to say, through speech and an impulsive process comparable to telepathy. Moreover, there is a third type of soul called *ñeē,* which is the initial core of the personality and plays the part of the protective spirit. This soul stands guard while men sleep in the forest; but unlike the guardian angel, it is not a being distinct from man. If the three souls simultaneously abandon the body, the person dies. The Mossi of Burkina Faso (Upper Volta) believe that death comes from the disunion in the soul *(siga)* of two invisible principles, one male *(hirma)* and the other female *(tule).*

Mircea Eliade has noted that the Aborigines of Australia recognize a distinction between two souls: the real ego, which preexists the individual and survives him, perhaps through reincarnation, as certain tribes believe; and the trickster-soul, which manifests itself in dreams, resists its definitive separation from the body, and may remain in the body of another person after the death of its owner. Men have to perform special rites to defend themselves against the trickster-soul.

This last example suggests what is to many theoreticians of primitive culture a fundamental distinction: that is, the distinction between soul-substance, which animates the body and which temporarily locates itself in the vital centers or in the products relating to its force (saliva, sweat, blood, sperm, tears), and the external soul, which is also plural and whose different aspects correspond to various particular functions. [*See* Blood; Tears; *and* Spittle and Spitting.]

Internal Soul. Wilhelm Wundt called the potentialities of particular parts of the body (head, heart, liver, eye) "organic souls." But if the soul is designated by the places where it shows its power, it is in the whole body that we find the substance of the soul.

Among the corporal expressions of vital dynamism, a privileged place is assigned to blood and to respiration. In one of the myths of the Iurak of Central Asia, the world perishes from a fire caused by the death of a sacred tree; as it tumbles down, the tree sheds its blood, which streams over the earth, changing itself into fire as it flows. Thus, the disanimation of the center of the world produces (as a consequence) the disanimation of all beings. Respiration is conceived of as both the sign of life and its principle. Such was the power of breath among the Celts that during the Battle of Druin Damghaire the druid Mog Ruith, using only his breath, transformed his enemies into rocks. [*See* Breath and Breathing.]

A vital spiritual force is also supposed to reside in sperm. Sexual relations are the symbol and the means of the continuity of the vital force in man. To say to an old African man that he does not have any more "force" is to tell him to his face that, on the one hand, he is impotent, and that, on the other, he is no longer capable of creation. Finally, it is to be noted that certain extraordinary potentialities of the body may be present as the result of its being possessed by a superior power.

External Soul. This term designates the powers of the soul located outside the body. Frazer spoke at length about this in *The Golden Bough.* Discovering in himself potentialities that appear to him to be superior to those shown by his ordinary physical performance, man has a tendency to conceptualize this superiority more readily outside than inside his own body.

Thus, we call external soul what can leave the body during a dream or sometimes two or three years before physical death (Dogon, Serer, Kongo of Africa); what habitually lives in an animal double (totem), in a human double, in the shadow; what expresses itself through speech and rhythm in relation to the "non-me" (the soul of communication).

Thus, the indigenous peoples of the Bank's Islands in Vanuatu fear that death will come to them if they see their reflection in the water of a cave. If the deceased does not have a shadow, he may be a shadow himself and may frighten the person who sees him as a ghost. An individual can attack another using a shadow acting as an intermediary. The Sotho of southern Africa believe that a crocodile can seize a passerby if it catches hold of his shadow at the surface of the water. But in this context the word *shadow* is used figuratively to designate some inner aspect that is *like* his shadow—clearly individual and separable from him, but at the same time immaterial despite being represented by way of material substance. This is an example of the conceptual expressing itself through objects accessible to the senses.

The "double" (which is identified with the shadow in some cultures, distinguished from it in others) is a second self, mysteriously united to an individual. It can die with the individual, or it can be seized and consumed by a witch, which action, in turn, causes a mortal sickness in the victim (a general belief in West Africa). On the island of Mota in Melanesia, the term *tamaniu* refers to a kind of double, referring to any animal that is mystically connected to man. Men are forbidden to eat the *tamaniu.* Man and animal protect and influence each other in profound solidarity, but here the double does not have the exact same traits as the original.

The fact that some of man's powers are represented by the hair and nails that continue to grow for a short time after death, and that they are symbolically transported and buried and become the objects around which family funerals are celebrated in the case of the death of a loved one in a foreign land or of an untransportable corpse (e.g., in Benin civilization), does not mean that a soul is held to live in the hair and the nails. Rather, they are viewed in very much the same way as the placenta, which, like them, is buried in most parts of Africa—which is to say, they are thought to be relics of life and power.

The souls of animals, like the souls of things (e.g., a statuette), may also enter into symbolic and participative relationship with the human soul, but an animal—for example, a bird that flies away, a fly that enters a person's ear, a snake that kills—may also temporarily become the prop of a person's external soul. Sorcerers and witches are supposed to possess, to varying degrees, this liberty to transport themselves, to live in a double, to metamorphose in order to reach the people on whom they wish to act. Sometimes, the double (e.g., the *aklama* of the Ewe of Togo) is thought of as a sort of tutelary spirit, an adviser on matters related to the luck of the individual, one that suggests a good deed or the way to avoid an accident.

ORIGIN OF THE SOUL

The soul can originate from an almighty spirit, from Mother Earth, or from special genies; it can also be obtained as a gift, by conquest, or by choice.

Among the Ewe of Togo—who use the terms *luvo* (the "substance of the soul") and *gbogbo* (the "breath of life")—the individual, before his incarnation, exists as a spirit, and together with the supreme creator Mawu-Lisa he chooses his own destiny. This choice is supposed to take place in the field called *bome,* the place of prenatal existence, a kind of reservoir of stagnant and infantile lives where the primordial mother, Bomeno, cuts clay from which to fashion the newborn, which she then sends into women's wombs. The myths relating to the origin of each individual introduce the notions of initial choice of his life *(gbetsi),* of reproduction of a character type *(kpoli),* and of reincarnation of an ancestor *(dzoto).*

The Bambara of Mali believe that man possesses twin souls called *ni* and *dya,* which are given by the deity Faro. The *tere,* which represents character, conscience, and force, is given to man by the deity Pemba. Finally, it is from the deity Mousso Koroni Koundyé that each individual obtains his *waso,* a malignant force that lives in the foreskin or in the clitoris and disappears at the moment of circumcision or clitoridectomy.

Among some peoples the generation of the soul is not the action of a divinity external to man; rather it is through traditional methods that a soul can be obtained as a power. Thus, during their lifetime the Jivaroan people of Ecuador try to obtain a soul they call *arutam wakani,* which cannot be killed by physical violence, poisoning, or sympathetic magic. The search for this soul, which takes place around the age of six, involves a pilgrimage to a sacred waterfall, fasting, and the capture of a wandering soul during a vision of large animals in combat. The individual then feels an irrepressible desire to kill. The act of killing leads to the acquisition of the victims' souls and thus confers cumulative supernatural power. Those who have an *arutam* soul and are killed by either natural or supernatural means can, at the moment of death, form a revengeful soul called *muisak,* which leaves the corpse through the mouth in order to kill the murderer. Each individual, regardless of sex, is supposed also to possess an ordinary soul *(nekas wakan)* that is relatively passive; this soul is represented by blood, and bleeding is even believed to be a hemorrhage of the soul. But the *nekas wakan* is only of secondary interest in relation to the *arutam wakani* and the *muisak.*

The Yoruba of Nigeria believe that force can be ingested and that this food possesses the quality of a soul. Thus the new king of Ifẹ had to consume the heart of his predecessor, once that organ had been reduced to powder, in order to incorporate in himself the substance of royalty. [*See* Cannibalism.]

DESTINY OF THE SOUL

The migration of the soul is the extreme consequence of the freedom of movement attributed to spiritual entities. Indeed, most primitive peoples believe that a form of soul becomes detached from the body in dreams, but there are some who also hope to reach a stage of personal weightlessness through ecstasy.

Thus the Tupi-Guaraní of Brazil believe that incessant dancing associated with strict fasting will make them become so light that they will reach the "land of no evil" beyond the seas, where they will remain eternally young and be free from work and life's trials.

The majority of the so-called primitive societies believe that after death their ancestors live in another world that either parallels the world of the living or is similar to it. The voluntary burial of weapons and food in tombs can be traced as far back as the Mousterian epoch, to Neanderthal man, and during the Upper Paleolithic period the dead were usually covered with red ochre, a sign of life and perhaps resurrection. [*See* Afterlife.]

Many African peoples believe that an ancestor identified either by divination or by some distinguishing traits, although living in the country of spirits, can be reincarnated in a newborn child, and sometimes even in several newborns, especially twins.

When detached from the body after death, certain souls can disappear, and others can reach various worlds beyond. For example, one soul makes its way to the place where its ancestors live; another is transmitted as a vital force to its descendants, usually to its grandsons. The ghost remains as a double next to the corpse or appears to the living while they sleep.

Regarding forms of life after death, an example from the Dakota is illustrative. The sky god Skan attributes to each person at birth four types of souls. (1) *Nagi,* the spirit that controls the actions of human beings until their death, when it leaves the body to await Skan's judgment. If *nagi* is deserving, it joins the world of spirits *(wanagi tamakoce);* if not, it is condemned to wander endlessly. (2) *Niya,* the vital breath, which though immaterial, is visible whenever it wills. It gives vitality to the body, making it understand what is good and bad, and it helps the body to influence other men. The *niya* can leave the body of the human being, and if the *nagi* abandons the body at the same time, it means death. After death, the *niya* gives testimony on the role of the *nagi,* which helps in the judgment of the latter. (3) *Nagiya,* the shadow, the external double, responsible for supernatural actions. A man possessed by the *nagiya* of a bear, for example, will have the nature of a bear. The *nagiya* also allows communication between animals and humans. (4) *Sicun,* the guardian spirit. It is never visible and is sent forth by the *wakan kin* ("superior spirits") to make man react differently from animals. After death, it goes back to where it came from.

Almost everywhere, the voyage of the soul after death implies a gradual purification through a series of trials (e.g., crossing a stream, climbing to the sky by means of a rope). The ultimate destination is the land of the soul, depicted as a celestial space or an underground place, a glade or a desert, or a place devoid of all tangible character. In the Solomon Islands, the beyond is said to be both a distant country and a nearby cave. The idea of the dead resting in the west where the sun sets, or underground, or in marshes does not contradict the idea of their close invisible presence.

That the individual continues to exist in a new condition does not mean that the soul is conceived of as being immortal. Life can have a circular and cyclical movement that death does not interrupt, provided that the correct rites relating to burial (cremation in the Solomon Islands), lamentation, prayer for the dead, and sacrificial offerings are carried out. [*See* Death.] Primitive peoples speak not of an eternal life but of a very long life, a kind of existence resembling the one the dead have had on earth. Behavior, good or bad, as well as the manner of death, largely determines the posthumous power. Among the Fon of Dahomey, the individual whose death was caused by lightning, drowning, or leprosy can never achieve ancestorhood, and among the Tongans of Polynesia only the nobles are totally immortal. Among other peoples, some ancestors can ascend to the heights of divinity.

Here, mutilation prevents the soul of a dead man from performing harmful acts (Bering Inuit); there, the noxious powers of a sorcerer's soul are destroyed through the burning of his body (Ganda of Uganda). While continuing his life in the other world, the dead man can be present elsewhere; as a specter or a ghost (Raketta of New Guinea) or in the form of an animal (lizard among the Samoans, python among the Kamba of East Africa). Although invisible, the souls of the dead can appear in dreams or to those specialists who know their desires and so can intercept their messages.

SUMMARY

In the religions of primitive societies, the soul is not necessarily the particularized form of a general and undifferentiated supernatural force; it is neither the genie living in a material reality nor the unique prototype of the ego or of the person considered as a moral and judicial entity. Many societies believe in the existence of several souls in the same individual, each of them having a distinct function. Generally, greater importance is given to the power of animation *(anima)* than to the faculty of representation *(animus).* And the notion that some spiritual element of the person survives after death is quasi-general.

[*See also* Immortality.]

BIBLIOGRAPHY

Centre National de la Recherche Scientifique. *La notion de personne en Afrique noire.* 2d ed. Paris, 1981.

Crawley, A. E. *The Idea of the Soul.* London, 1909.

Frazer, James G. *The Golden Bough.* 12 vols. 3d ed., rev. & enl. London, 1911–1915. Abridged and edited by Theodor H. Gaster as *The New Golden Bough* (New York, 1959).

Leeuw, Gerardus van der. *Phänomenologie der Religion.* Tübingen, 1933. Translated as *Religion in Essence and Manifestation* (1938; 2d ed., 2 vols., New York, 1963).

Lévy-Bruhl, Lucien. *L'âme primitive.* Paris, 1927. Translated as *The "Soul" of the Primitive* (New York, 1928).

Marett, R. R. *The Threshold of Religion.* 3d ed. London, 1915.

Tylor, E. B. *Primitive Culture* (1871). 2 vols. New York, 1970.

29 GHOSTS

Geoffrey Parrinder

In western Germanic languages words similar to the modern English *ghost* and the German *Geist* seem to be derived from roots indicating fury, wounding, or tearing in pieces. The spelling with *gh* in English appeared first in a work printed by William Caxton in the fifteenth century, influenced probably by a similar Flemish form. The term *ghost* has been used in various ways, to mean soul, spirit, breath, the immaterial part of man, moral nature, a good spirit, an evil spirit, and, in liturgical and dogmatic language, to designate the spirit of God as the "Holy Ghost." It has chiefly signified the soul of a deceased person appearing in a visible form, and hence has given rise to such phrases as *a ghost walking, raising a ghost,* or *laying a ghost.* It may be called "an apparition" or "a specter." In any case, the prevailing modern sense is that of a dead person manifesting its presence visibly to the living.

Other words are used to describe comparable phenomena, but with some differences. A fetch is, like the German *Doppelgänger,* the apparition of a living person. A wraith is an apparition or specter of a dead person or an immaterial appearance of someone living forewarning his own death. The Irish often speak of fetches, and the Scottish of wraiths. More generally, a phantom, from the Greek *phantasma,* is sometimes unreal or immaterial, an illusion or dream-image, a specter or ghost. A phantasm may be the same thing, but Edmund Gurney and others in *Phantasms of the Living* (1886) discussed as phantasms "all classes of cases where . . . the mind of one human being has affected the mind of another . . . by other means than through the recognized channels of sense" (vol. 1, p. 35). A poltergeist, from the German *poltern* ("to make noise") and *Geist* ("spirit") is regarded as a noisy spirit remarkable for throwing things about. Since the nineteenth century the French world *revenant* (lit., "one who comes back"), has been used in English to describe a being who returns from the dead.

The word *ghost* most commonly refers to a dead person who haunts or simply appears before the living, sometimes with a message or warning. The notion has been popular in literature. While Shakespeare wrote one play involving fairies and another involving witches, ghosts were an important feature in several of his works: Hamlet's father, Caesar, and Banquo all appear as ghosts. Hamlet's father—called a ghost, a spirit, an apparition, an illusion, and more than fantasy—expresses a belief in the activities of ghosts: "I am thy father's spirit; / Doom'd for a certain term to walk the night, / And for the day confin'd to fast in fires, / Till the foul crimes done in my days of nature / Are burnt and purg'd away" (1.5.9–13).

THE BIBLE AND THE QUR'ĀN

The Hebrew scriptures have few references to ghosts. Isaiah attacked the practice of consulting "the mediums and the wizards who chirp and mutter" (*Is.* 8:19). This refers to the spiritualistic séance, forbidden but vividly illustrated in the story of the medium of Endor, consulted by Saul. She was said to raise up the dead prophet Samuel out of the earth, saying "An old man comes up, and he is covered with a robe" (*1 Sm.* 28:14). Samuel was not a haunting ghost, although he brought a fatal warning for Saul.

In Psalm 88:12 the grave is called the land of forgetfulness, and later Judas Maccabaeus makes sacrifices to free the dead from their sins (*2 Mc.* 12:45). In the apocryphal *Wisdom of Solomon* (17:15) lawless men are said to be troubled in their sleep by specters, apparitions, and phantoms. Otherwise ghosts are not mentioned except in the older translations where death is described as surrendering the spirit, "giving up the ghost."

In the New Testament there are also few references. When the disciples saw Jesus by night, on or by the sea, they were afraid, thinking him an apparition or ghost (*phantasma; Mark* 6:49; this is the only occurrence of this word in the New Testament). In one of Luke's accounts of the resurrection the disciples were terrified, supposing that they had seen a spirit *(pneuma),* but Jesus assured them that this could not be so, for he had flesh and bones that a spirit had not (*Lk.* 24:37–39). Lazarus might be called a revenant, but he was not, strictly speaking, a ghost, since he came out of the grave alive (*Jn.* 11:44). Later Christian insistence upon the "resurrection of the flesh" *(sarx),* as in the Apostles' Creed, also precluded "ghostly" survival and postulated instead a restoration of the full personality.

In developing Christian doctrine theologians discussed the nature of angels, good spirits, bad spirits, the resurrection of the dead, heaven, hell, and purgatory. But belief in ghosts and their possible return to earth was left indeterminate, neither accepted nor rejected. All Souls' Day, the commemoration of the faithful departed, has been universally celebrated in the Western church since the tenth century, and prayers at Mass request "to the souls of all thy servants a place of cool repose, the blessedness of quiet, the brightness of light . . . forgiveness and everlasting rest."

In practice many Christians have believed in ghosts and in haunted places, and this is said to have been particularly true among Germanic peoples. The survivors owed numerous duties to the departed, and unless honor and rituals were accorded, it was thought that the dead might return to take vengeance or reclaim their former property. Those who had died untimely or unnatural deaths, such as women in childbirth, might become wandering spirits. To this day stories are related in Europe about old monasteries or rectories where restless spirits are said to appear. Rituals of exorcism have been practiced, with restrictions, both to cast out evil spirits and to lay wandering ghosts to rest.

In the Islamic world the soul or self (Arab., *nafs;* cf. Heb. *nefesh*) was at first distinguished from the breath or wind (Arab., *rūḥ;* cf. Heb. *ruaḥ*), but the words came to be used interchangeably and are applied to the human spirit, angels, and genii *(jinn).* Theologians teach that at death the soul goes to a first judgment and then remains in the grave until the final resurrection. Edward A. Westermarck stated in *Ritual and Belief in Morocco* (1926, vol. 2, p. 246) that while it was believed that dead saints might appear to the living and the dead might come to see their friends but remain invisible, "as to ordinary dead people I have been assured over and over again that the dead do not walk, and I remember how heartily my friends . . . laughed when I told them that many Christians believe in ghosts." However, the Moroccans believed that the dead would be angry if they were offended by anyone and would punish him, and if children did not visit the graves of their parents they would be cursed by them. The voices of some of the dead were thought to be audible in cemeteries, though only good people, children, and animals could hear them. If a person had been killed, the spot would be regarded as haunted, and passersby might hear him groan.

Among Berber-speaking tribes there were said to be more traces of the belief in apparitions of the dead than among Arabic-speaking Moroccans. Some of the Tuareg of the Sahara claimed that ghosts had been seen at night near cemeteries. In Egypt many stories have been told of apparitions of dead people, and Arabian bedouin believe that spirits of the wicked haunt the places of their burial and that the living should avoid passing cemeteries in the dark.

The *jinn* may be thought to haunt burial grounds and many other places, but they are fiery spirits and not dead people. Ghouls (Arab., *ghūl*) are monsters thought to haunt cemeteries and feed on dead bodies. An *ʿifrīt* is mentioned in the Qur'ān (27:39) as "one of the *jinn*," and in the *Thousand and One Nights,* in the story of the second shaykh, it is said that a benevolent Muslim woman "turned into an *ʿifrītah,* a *jinnīyah.*" She changed her shape, saved her husband from drowning by carrying him on her shoulders, and told him that she had delivered him from death by the grace of God, since she believed in him and in his Prophet. In Egypt the word *ʿifrīt* came to mean the ghost of a man who had been murdered or suffered a violent death.

AFRICA

In many parts of Africa ghosts are thought to appear to give warning or seek vengeance. Among the Ashanti of Ghana, a man who has committed suicide is called a wandering spirit, unable to find rest and refused entry into the land of spirits, roaming between this world and the next until his appointed time of death. If such a suicide is reborn, he will come back as a cruel man who might again suffer a bad end. At one time criminals who were executed had powerful charms tied on them to prevent their ghosts returning to harm the executioners. Some of the dead had their heads shaved and painted red, white, and black so that they would be recognized if they walked as ghosts.

The Ga of the Ghana coastline think that the spirit of one who dies violently or prematurely wanders about for forty days as a ghost, angry at his early death and jealous of other people's pleasures. Those who go out late at night pursuing such pleasures may be pursued in turn by ghosts until they die of heart failure. Ghosts are said to be recognizable by their fiery breath and red mouths: red is the color of witches, fairies, and ghosts, but ghosts dislike white and may be kept away if one throws white cloths on the ground.

A common belief in the Ivory Coast is that the dead may return to their homes at night to steal children from their mothers' arms. Here and elsewhere widows must keep in mourning for months or years, often in rags, lest their dead husbands return and have sexual intercourse with them, which would have fatal results. Fishermen drowned at sea, hunters lost in the forest, people struck by lightning or burnt in fires, and others who die of diseases like smallpox or leprosy may not receive burial rites and so become ghosts, living in the "bad bush." Months after the death or disappearance, the family performs mourning ceremonies and lays the ghost to rest.

When infant mortality is high, a succession of dying children may be thought to be incarnations of the same child over and over again. The Yoruba of Nigeria call such babies "born to die" *(abiku),* and if one comes a third time and dies it is said that "there is no hoe" to bury it with. Marks are made on the body of the stillborn or dying baby to prevent the ghost from returning or to make the ghost recognizable.

In central Africa the Ila of Zambia think that some spirits are captured by witches and become their ghost-slaves, causing disease and sometimes possessing people. Like poltergeists, such ghosts reputedly attack people, knock burdens off their heads, or break axes and hoes. Ghosts are often thought to speak in unnatural ways, in guttural voices or twittering like birds, and some are said to be very small, with bodies reversed so that their faces are at the back of their heads. They appear in dreams, show anger at neglect, demand sacrifice, or cause sickness. Although stories are told that seem to imply that ghosts have objective or even physical existence, they are regarded as spiritual entities who only take the essence or heart of sacrifices.

In the region of Zaire the word *zumbi* is used for spirits of the dead and ghosts, and in Haiti it becomes *zombie,* a *revenant,* or one of the "living dead," whose soul has been eaten by a witch or whose corpse has been revived by a sorcerer for evil purposes.

SOUTH AND EAST ASIA

In popular Indian belief various words may be used for ghosts. The term *bhūta,* something that has been or has become, refers to the ghost of a dead person, one who has died a violent death or has not had a proper funeral ceremony, or it may apply generally to a good or evil spirit. In the *Bhagavadgītā* (9.25) the *bhūta* is a ghost or goblin, an inferior but not necessarily an evil being. A *preta* ("departed") is the spirit of a dead person before the obsequies are performed or an evil ghost; it also may be the spirit of a deformed person or of a child that died prematurely. A *yakṣa* is generally a benevolent spirit although sometimes classed with *piśāca*s and other malignant spirits and ghosts; such terms are used loosely and often overlap.

Ghosts and demons in India are believed to haunt cemeteries or live in trees, appearing in ugly or beautiful forms and requiring food and blood. The special guardian against ghosts is the monkey god Hanuman, the "large-jawed"; his worshipers offer coconuts to him and pour oil and red lead over his images, taking some of the oil that drips off to mark their eyes as a protection. The lighting of lamps at the Dīvālī or Dīpāvali festival at the new year is also said to drive away ghosts and evil spirits.

Performance of Śrāddha funeral ceremonies is essential in India for the rest of the departed spirit, in order to provide food for it and to prevent it from becoming an evil spirit. Special Śrāddha is performed for those who died violently, as they would be likely to become haunting ghosts. Infants who die do not receive ordinary Śrāddha, but presents are given to brahmans on their behalf.

Buddhist dialogues discuss various states after death. In the *Milindapañha* (294) there are said to be four classes of ancestors *(peta),* only one of which lives on offerings from benefactors; the others feed on vomit, are tormented by hunger and thirst, or are consumed by craving. Any of these may be ghosts. In Sinhala another word *(bolman)* indicates similar dangerous beings. These appear at night as naked white figures, especially in cemeteries, and sunset, midnight, and dawn are the most dangerous times for their activities. One of them, Mahasōnā, perhaps meaning "great cemetery," puts his hand on the backs of wanderers in graveyards at midnight, marks them with his imprint, and kills them with shock. *Peta* may be offered inferior food, as well as drugs or excrement, and if they act as troublesome poltergeists they are exorcized. Another term for ghostly creatures, *bhūtayā* ("has been") may be substituted for *peta* and other words for demons and harmful spirits.

Burmese Buddhists believe that although all beings pass on to rebirth, most go first to one of four "states of woe" as an animal, demon, ghost, or inhabitant of hell. Rebirth as a human being is an exception, one of "five rarities." Monks may be reborn as ghosts. One account of five heads of a monastery who died in quick succession attributed the premature deaths to the ghost of the original incumbent, who had owned the monastery personally and died before appointing a successor. Those who followed were usurpers, and as a ghost he caused their deaths. As a consequence the villagers decided to abandon that monastery and build a new one for the next abbot.

In Thailand the Indian word *preta* is used for the ghosts of the recently dead, who may have been condemned to hell or to wander the earth. Although not harmful to humans they may be disgusting and gigantic in appearance. Because of their tiny mouths they suffer from constant hunger and thirst. Relatives may transfer merit to the *preta*s by extra gifts to monks; some writers consider *preta*s to be the inversion of the Buddhist monk. Mural paintings in Buddhist temples of South Asia often depict both the joys of paradise and the sufferings of unhappy spirits.

In China a ghost *(kuei;* f., *yao)* was the spirit of someone who had died an unusual death, often as the result of crime. Ghosts of bandits were thought to linger near the place of their execution, and if a woman had a difficult labor it was attributed to her having passed near such a place during pregnancy and having offended one of the bandit ghosts. The ghost might try to oust the rightful soul during labor and be born as the woman's son.

Under Buddhist influence souls were thought to live in zones of formlessness until the time of rebirth. They were fed by surviving relatives, and if nobody cared for them they would haunt people. In the seventh month after death there was a great festival for "hungry souls," when the priests would recite texts not only for relatives but for the souls of strangers and those without anyone to care for them. Meals, models of houses, and paper money were dedicated to the dead and burned as offerings. Especially in southern China, paper boats, often with a host of deities aboard or with lanterns in the shape of lotus flowers, were set drifting down rivers to light the way for spirits and ghosts to cross the river of transmigration. If sickness or calamity afflicted the community, however, it was attributed to inadequate propitiation of ghosts.

In Japanese belief one category of the ancestral dead is that of wandering angry ghosts. Neglected ancestors may quickly change from benevolent beings to vicious, cursing tyrants, attacking their families in painful ways until proper food and potent texts are offered to them. There are also spirits with no particular affinity *(muenbotoke),* those who die childless or without kin to worship them, and they may attack any stranger whose weakness lays him open to spiritual possession.

The most dangerous ghosts are those of people who die violently, are murdered, or die in disgrace. They become angry spirits *(onryō)* requiring rituals for appeasement. In the literature of the eighth to the tenth century there are striking examples of these furious ghosts, such as the story of Prince Sawara. After horrifying starvation, exile, and death by poison, he was said to have brought a whole series of calamities on the country. And a minister who died in 903 in disgrace and exile was credited with a succession of natural disasters thanks to his furious ghost. In early times discontented ghosts were depicted in animal or natural form, but in later *nō* plays they appear as ordinary men and women who are finally revealed as ghosts in horned masks and long red wigs.

Notions of ghosts and spirits as restless, perhaps unburied or unavenged, beings with a message to convey or a task to fulfill abound in popular belief in many countries, although there may be little formal doctrine or orthodox teaching in the scriptures to support these ideas.

[*See* Soul *and* Afterlife.]

BIBLIOGRAPHY

The larger dictionaries provide examples of the ways in which *ghost* and similar words have been used, especially the complete or the "compact" edition of the *Oxford English Dictionary,* 2 vols. (Oxford, 1971). Biblical and ecclesiastical dictionaries rarely discuss ghosts, but the *Shorter Encyclopaedia of Islam* (1953; reprint, Leiden, 1974) has a useful article on the soul *(nafs).* Edward A. Westermarck's *Ritual and Belief in Morocco,* 2 vols. (1926; reprint, New Hyde Park, N.Y., 1968), is a treasury of popular beliefs. African beliefs have been collected in my *West African Psychology* (London, 1951). For Indian rituals Margaret S. Stevenson's *The Rites of the Twice-Born* (1920; reprint, New Delhi, 1971) is still valuable. There have been more recent studies of Buddhist countries: Richard F. Gombrich's *Precept and Practice* (Oxford, 1971) on Sri Lanka; Melford E. Spiro's *Buddhism and Society,* 2d ed. (Berkeley, 1982) on Burma; Stanley J. Tambiah's *Buddhism and the Spirit Cults in North-East Thailand* (Cambridge, 1970) on Thailand; and Carmen Blacker's *The Catalpa Bow* (London, 1975) on Japan.

30 IMMORTALITY

JULIEN RIES
Translated from French by David M. Weeks

The concept of immortality can be understood and expanded upon on three levels. In its first sense, immortality is the quality attributed to divine beings, mythical or angelic, who by their very nature are not subject to death. The second sense concerns those heroes who have attained a divine status that they share with the gods. In its third sense, the concept of immortality has to do with the human being who enters upon a new form of eternal and incorruptible existence after death. The present article will deal only with immortality in this third sense, treating the permanence of the human being beyond the phenomenon of death.

Human life is recognizable in the animation produced by life-giving breath, and it is likewise attested to by a whole series of expressions and activities. It may also be defined, following Aristotle's use of the word *organon,* as that which is organized and self-organizing. Whether understood as organization, animation from without, or expression and activity, human life is subject to the final wearing away that is death. Hence, immortality, in the third sense given above, is the infinite prolongation of human existence and of the human personality beyond death. Life is then followed by another form of organization, the afterlife. Other concepts, such as eternity, paradise, hell, and transmigration, are then associated with the afterlife. These, however, will not be discussed in this article.

APPROACHES TO POPULAR BELIEF

Two fundamental approaches to an examination of conceptions of immortality as found in popular belief must consider (1) the celebration of death as a transition to the afterlife and (2) the traditions and texts of the various cultures and religions. The first has to do with the attitude of the living in the presence of death and the dead, including appropriate actions, behavior, rituals, prayers, treatment of the corpse—in short, a vast symbolic network. Thus, archaeology and history reveal various methods of handling the body of the deceased: burial, embalming, mummification, exposure, and cremation. In addition to these activities there is the environment created for the deceased: the type, materials, and decoration of the grave, the covering of the corpse, funeral furnishings and offerings, and the presence of signs and symbols. Mention must also be made of funerary ritual: rites of opening of the mouth, eyes, ears, and nose, purification rituals, rites to celebrate the funeral ceremonies, and postmortem rites—all are indicative of beliefs.

The study of written documents and oral traditions allows us to comprehend the meaning of these beliefs directly, and thus to begin to interpret the symbolism of the rites. In this approach via documents and oral traditions we make use of three types of information. First there are the written texts of the world's various religions, then come myths and folk tales, with the material added by cultural tradition, and finally we have the texts of funerary rituals.

PREHISTORIC PEOPLES

The people who lived during the two million years before 9000 BCE have left us broken messages and mute testimony: bones, skulls, stone tools, grave furnishings, wall carvings, and cave and rock paintings. Analysis of these records reveals that early *Homo sapiens* was also a *homo religiosus.* Aside from the symbolic interpretation of cannibalism as a reembodiment of the dead person by the living (Louis-Vincent Thomas, *Le cadavre: De la biologie à l'anthropologie,* Brussels, 1980, p. 169), we possess early Neanderthal graves (80,000 BCE), with funerary deposits, orientation of the body, supine and fetal burial positions, and red ocher. Grave VI at Shanidar in Iran (50,000 BCE) shows that the body was laid on a litter of flowers. Upper Paleolithic sculptures (35,000 to 9000 BCE) show numerous ornamental objects and the importance of red ocher as funeral makeup, a substitute for blood. Paleolithic strata continually yield deposits of bones and skulls that have been manipulated or arranged according to a deliberate plan. In Upper Paleolithic wall art, symbols like the rainbow and the earthly bridge suggest connection with the world beyond.

Mesolithic and Neolithic Periods. Funerary records become more plentiful in Mesolithic and Neolithic times. In the ancient Near East, the funeral practices at the Natufian (7800 BCE) seem to reveal a "cult of the dead." At Jericho, skulls have been found arranged in a circle, looking inward, as have three groups of three skulls each, all facing in the same direction. The Neolithic city of Çatal Hüyük in central Anatolia (6500-5600 BCE) has yielded numerous shrines whose plaster walls are decorated with paintings referring to death and skulls adorned and surrounded with everyday objects. The civilization of Lepenski Vir, on the southern bank of the Danube in eastern Serbia, has enriched our knowledge of Neolithic burial practices, including inhumation under or near houses and, in the center of the house, a rectangular hearth with a decorated altar or an egg-shaped stone behind it; skulls and long bones were buried between the hearth and the altar. For two millennia following 5800 BCE, megalithic tombs covered northern and western Europe, extending to the Mediterranean. In these collective tombs are found bodies with grave goods, decorative objects, offerings of food, cultic objects, and reliefs on the walls. In the course of the third millennium the image of a protector-goddess of the dead appeared.

The Dawn of Historical Time. The Bronze Age sees the birth of spirit worship at Carnac, France, at Stonehenge, England, and in Egypt and Mesopotamia. In the late Bronze Age the collective ossuary and the individual tumulus give way to "urnfields." Cremation destroys the corpse in order to free the spirit through fire, which becomes the vehicle of the soul. Cremation takes its accustomed place in the Uranian religions and in astral cults. Urnfields from western Europe and stelae from Valcamonica, Tyrol, and the upper Adige take on new significance in light of the great discoveries of Georges Dumézil concerning ancient Indo-European ideology. From the Neolithic period on, belief in an afterlife is clearly demonstrated in the context of cosmic religions and the worship of the mother goddesses.

NONLITERATE PEOPLES

Having considered the beliefs in immortality of early prehistoric man, we go on to the study of such beliefs in traditional societies, that is, in nonliterate cultures. Our primary reason for this is that such research permits us to discover the symbolic value of the beliefs and rites practiced by primitive peoples, most specifically in the area of the encounters of the living with the dead. The study of this symbolism affords insight into a number of the living values of these peoples, their relations with their ancestors, their initiation rites, their sense of time, and their eschatological myths, and in this way we arrive at a better comprehension of the basic patterns of the activity of *homo religiosus*. A second point of interest for our investigations, one especially conspicuous in the works of Mircea Eliade, is that through the study of the beliefs and rituals of traditions that have survived into the contemporary era, we gain a comparative perspective that enables us to understand more deeply the records left behind by prehistoric man.

Sub-Saharan Africa. A discussion of traditional beliefs in Africa presents a number of difficulties, given the variety and nature of the ethnological evidence, much of which is drawn from an oral tradition of myths and proverbs, as well as from personal inquiries and testimony. Moreover, sub-Saharan Africa contains more than two thousand ethnic groups separated by pronounced specific differences, so that any discussion of traditional beliefs necessarily presupposes a great many choices and omissions.

One element of African beliefs in immortality arises from eschatological concerns. For the African there are two kinds of time: mythical time, the time of the eternally valid group and its continuity, and real time, in which the life of the individual and the discontinuity of death take place. Between these two times lies the symbolic mediation of funeral rites, through which the deceased leaves contingent time and passes into mythical time, the time of the pyramid of beings. The funeral rites are the collective response to the death of an individual; they allow the group to endure. This conception of the immortality of the ethnic group, coupled with the dual reality of time, is found in most African cosmogonies.

Alongside this vision of the undying ethnos exists the belief in the deathlessness of the personal being, indispensable for the continuity of the group. Among the Bobo of Burkina Faso, real time lies under the sign of Dwo, an unchanging divinity who rules over spirits and genies, the life force *(nyama),* and the ancestors. Also in Burkina Faso, in the eschatology of the Dagaī, a cyclic conception of time is accompanied by the notion of the reincarnation of the deceased—all new births arise from the transformation of the ancestors. After death, the deceased passes first to the land of the spirits, either to become an ancestor or to be reincarnated in the body of a totemic animal. Among the Luba and other Bantu-speaking peoples of Zaire, the *muntu,* the essence of each person's being, goes after death either to the world of the ancestors or to that of the shades. Whenever a birth occurs, the ancestor invests the infant with his own life force. The Samo teach that the *mere,* the immortal double of the dead person, passes initially to a first village of the dead and then, after another death, to a second village. At the end of this double life-death operation, the *mere* takes up residence in a tree, and when the tree is destroyed it enters another tree of the same species. In Yoruba belief, *emi* ("breath"), the life force, leaves the body and passes into the abode of the blessed ancestors, where it becomes one with *ori* ("head"), its tutelary spirit. But in all African cultures, the evil dead, whose life energy has been banished from society, wander about in the air and become imprisoned by the forces of evil. In Africa, immortality is marked by a reference to the past, through which the dead play an important role in the society of the living. Reincarnation symbolically returns the dead to the circle of the living, so that the invisible living exist side by side with the visible living (Thomas, 1982, pp. 122–136).

A second basic aspect of immortality is the belief in the ancestors. There are two classes of ancestors, those who are mythical and primordial and those who have entered this state after their life on earth. Ancestor worship holds a most important place in African belief and ritual. The conception of the ancestor is made up of two components: on the one hand, the purity of the social and religious ideal, and on the other, a concern with the continuity and identity of the community. Together the two components form the concept of individual and collective immortality. The ancestor represents the symbolic transposition of the human condition to a numinous plane while continuing to be a part of the world of the living. It is in the role of ancestor that the most important stage of one's destiny after death is realized. A true solidarity binds together the dead who have attained ancestral status and the living who remain in communion with them so as to live according to the exemplary past, the highest ideal of life. The organization of the ancestral world is ruled by a complex hierarchy, one both social and familial, based on descent and function. There are close or immediate ancestors, those who have died recently, and distant ancestors, who make up a faceless crowd. The more eminent among the dead are watchful ancestors, while others are ordinary dead people who never leave the mass of collective anonymity. To the African mind, the ancestors are ranked according to the strength of their life force, for example Bantu-speaking peoples distinguish the *vidye,* spiritual beings who take an active part in the life of the community, from the *fu,* the ordinary dead. Among the latter are the ghosts, who must be appeased by the living with offerings and sacrifices.

The ancestors provide more than a personal and ethnic immortality, however. The hierarchical ancestral community is the repository of the accumulated knowledge of successive generations, and in this sense it is the memory of the ethnic group, the product of its origins and its past. It represents the law of the fathers, and it exercises a permanent regulatory function over the life of the group. This explains the importance of cult and ritual in African society.

Before they can attain a final, lasting rest, the dead undergo profound changes. This rest depends partly on the remembrance of the living and their ability to keep alive the memory of those who have gone before. As long as their descendants honor and pray to them, they remain among the "living dead," but as soon as they fall into oblivion they enter a collective afterlife. According to the Bambara of Mali, the most perfect of the ancestors are allowed to gaze upon God. In any case, the world of the ancestors provides the community with a model, a tradition of norms, and the assurance of its continuity. Ancestrality and immortality are bound together.

Another aspect of ancestral immortality is found in African beliefs in reincarnation. Ethnologists have emphasized the complexity of the idea that the person is composed of multiple elements (see Zahan, 1963). One can say that it is the person's life force that is reincarnated, but the actual conditions of reincarnation depend upon many variables or choices, including those of sex, time, the will or condition of the deceased, and that of the group. Reincarnation brings about a reactualization of the deceased that partially interrupts his postmortem fate. Reincarnation implies that the returning ancestor is recognized and present in the memory of the living, and it can only occur in a child of the same lineage and sex. The ancestor transmits a portion of the genetic inheritance, which is why the various ethnic groups attach so much importance to respect for the body and its preservation at death and in the funeral ceremony. The ancestor also transmits the spiritual elements: the *kili,* in the belief of the Serer of Senegal, the *ri,* or "thought," among the Samo of Burkina Faso. But the reincarnated ancestor continues to live in the beyond. "The belief in reincarnation serves to bring back the dead, to return him, symbolically at least, to the circle of the living" (Thomas, 1982, p. 135).

In all cultures, funeral rituals serve as primary expressions of belief in immortality while at the same time serving as instruments that help to make it real by symbolically absorbing the shock caused by a death. Like the rites of birth and initiation, they effect a passage that is at once a separation and a coming together. In all African communities, funeral rites mark out the successive stages traversed by the deceased. The actors are many: the deceased, the master of the ceremony, gravediggers, bierbuilders, family, clan, the deceased's stand-ins, priests, and chiefs. In the performance of the ritual due emphasis must be laid on the sonorous background of chants and cries, which are thought of as a collective release but also as a symbol of fertility; also to be considered are the purification of the corpse, a plentiful supply of speech-making and food, rituals making light of death, burial of the corpse, and in some cases a second funeral, in which the bones are retrieved from the grave, washed, adorned, and placed on the altar of the ancestors. The Fali of Cameroon ritually prepare the skull, place it in an urn, and replace it in the grave.

In the rites of revitalization performed on the deceased we perceive the beliefs concerning their transformation with a view to their new life. The preparations are conducted with care so as not to bruise the body and to protect its appearance, like the bathing of a newborn. The ritual continues with makeup and adornments involving ashes, kaolin (fine white clay), red ocher, and gold dust. Kaolin is the symbol of life, and it is used in fertility rituals for sprinkling on seeded fields. The priest and the initiate are covered with it in initiation ceremonies. Applied to the corpse, white kaolin signifies rebirth and life. Red ocher is commonly used as facial makeup. The sacrifices and funeral meals make up the provisions needed for the journey, and the dead person's escort is represented by metal and carnelian jewelry and figurines of birds, snakes, and crocodiles, symbolizing eternity. The rites of separation and completion set the deceased on the road to the beyond through graduated stages extending through time. The rites that follow the death ensure passage from one stage to the next. The family altar, masks, and icons will evoke the presence of the ancestors; the *ases*, or metal family trees, found in Benin are another symbolic support for this presence. In Gabon, the Mpongwe keep relic chests in which the red-painted skulls lie on a bed. Identical customs are found among the neighboring Mitsogo and Fang tribes. The arrangement of African funeral rituals helps to maintain the balance between the two elements which make up society, the living and the dead.

The perception of time, ancestorism, and funeral rites are three essential features of culture and religion in sub-Saharan Africa. They offer an impressive convergence of facts and symbols that shed light on the dual conception of immortality, that of the ethnic group and that of the individual. Time is the pillar of generations. Past, present, and future, the three instants of duration, can only be thought of in human terms, but they must be viewed in their relation to the world of the ancestors, the ideal world of the living. Thus immortality is linked to the past and to ancestral tradition. This tradition is the attainment of successive generations; it is the sum total of the wisdom and the fundamental value of life. Through the experience of the deceased and the ever-growing ancestral community, the living unceasingly enrich their spiritual wealth. Linear time and cyclic time intersect each other to form the axis of immortality. The other world is associated with the notions of rest, tranquillity, and peace, a paradise toward which the society of the living progresses so long as it lives in conformity with tradition. It is by way of the ancestral community and worship of the ancestors that the African reaches immortality.

Australia. In 1770, the explorer James Cook arrived in Australia, claiming it for England. By 1788 around five hundred Aboriginal groups had been counted, each one comprising a group of individuals linked by a common descent. Numerous ethnological studies have been devoted to these peoples, who are known especially for their totemic practices and their systems of kinship classification. Australian myths, the subject of particular study in recent decades, refer to supernatural creator beings who fashioned the world out of a preexisting cosmic substance. The appearance of man in his present form is placed in the Dreaming, a primordial era called *alchera* or *alcheringa* by the Aranda, a central Australian people who are especially interesting for their social and religious life, and who are very well known thanks to the studies of Carl Strehlow, Baldwin Spencer, and F. J. Gillen. The creation myths revolve around the great gods and the civilizing heroes, so that primordiality is fundamental. The cosmogonic and primordial myths play a pivotal role because all the rites of initiation, reproduction, and fertility are reenactments of these myths. In sum, "all of the Australian's religious acts can be thought of as so many means, different yet related, of reestablishing contact with the Supernatural Beings and reentering the sacred Dream Time" (Eliade, 1973).

As a single cell of the sacred universe created by the supernatural beings, a cell that has become profane by being born, each individual must rediscover his spiritual origin through rites of initiation: circumcision, which is a symbolic killing amid the howls of the bull-roarers and anointing with blood; rites of purifying and spiritualizing fire; the rite of water-purification; and the ritual return of the *alcheringa.* The Aranda word *alcheringa (churinga, tjurunga)* means "mythical time, dream time"; it refers to both the ancient times and the heroancestors. In the form of a material object, a stone or a piece of wood, the *tjurunga* is given back to the initiate as an effective symbol of his recovered spiritual being. Through the *tjurunga* the initiate is put back in touch with the primordial Dreaming—he becomes *altjira,* "sacred." The sacred symbols are of prime importance for the life of the individual and the tribe, for they enable one to achieve contact with primordial time and to relive the ancient events through myths, rites, visitation of sacred places, and contact with the

God of heaven and the Dreaming. An extraordinary abundance of objects created by native art allows us to realize the coherent functioning of this symbolism.

Death is a shock to the tribe and is felt as a disruption of the collective life, hence the cries and wailing, the mourning rituals, the rhythmic chanting, and the search to discover the evil spirit who caused this death. But the Australians believe that death is the final rite of passage that leads one from the profane world to the sacred universe. Man has two souls. The true self, the primordial and preexistent spirit, comes from heaven, the totemic center. At death, the true soul leaves the body and goes back to live forever in the eternal Dreaming, where it was before the individual's birth, while the other soul remains on earth, taking up residence in another person and moving about among the living. Eliade believes that death is thought of in Australia as an ecstatic experience, patterned after the first journey of the supernatural beings and the mythic ancestors (Eliade, 1973). The soul does what was done at the very beginning. All Australian tribes profess a belief in the indestructibility of the human soul, a spiritual entity that has its origin in the Dreaming.

The funeral rites take various forms. The body is treated in different ways by different tribes—buried, mummified, cremated, exposed on a platform with delayed burial, or deposited in the crotch of a tree. Double funerals, with an intervening period of mourning, are very common. Mummification is intended to help separate the body from the spirit, for the mummy is burned at the end of the mourning period, and the cremation frees the soul completely. The combination of funeral rituals must bring about this separation so that the spirit can return to its primordial home among the civilizing heroes. Through the funeral rites, the preexisting spirit regains its spiritual domain, sometimes thought of as the primordial totemic center. A whole ritual symbolism punctuates this journey, for example the occasional placing of bones within a totemic coffin. Beliefs in reincarnation, however, are rare and confused. For human beings the life cycle is simple: from the preexisting spirit, birth into a body and entry into the profane world, to the first stage of reintegration into the Dreaming via initiation, and finally the return to the original state through funeral rites.

The Americas. We come now to American Indian beliefs in immortality, as they are found outside the more advanced American civilizations. These are forms of religion that have survived through the post-Columbian era and still exist in some areas of North and South America. The belief in a life beyond the grave seems to have been firmly established in Indian thought in early times, to judge from their conception of the world and of life, from ancestral traditions, and from the testimonies of seers. These seers are sometimes persons who undergo dreamlike experiences, and sometimes medicine men who travel, in their imagination or in trance, to the borders of the realm of the dead. Funeral rituals also constitute a valuable source of knowledge about beliefs in an afterlife.

Among the American Indian peoples we find a conception of the soul that forms the basis of their beliefs in immortality. In North America the idea of a double soul is extremely widespread. The corporeal soul gives life, consciousness, and the faculty of movement to the body, whereas the dream soul is separate from the body and can move about in space and go to distant places. Death occurs when the separate soul becomes trapped in the realm of the dead. Then the corporeal soul is also detached from the body. Among the Inuit, the corporeal soul, called *tarneg,* survives after death, keeping the form of the deceased in the realm of the dead. The Yuchi and Sioux tribes speak of four souls, splitting the notion of a double soul to bring it into accord with the sacred number four. In South America, the same dichotomy is found in the case of the Mundurucú, but the Waica of the upper Orinoco and the Jivaroan people of Ecuador appear to have no concept of a separate soul.

In *The Religions of the American Indians* (Berkeley, 1979), Åke Hultkrantz makes two important observations. First, in both North and South America, the great civilizations share a monistic conception of the soul, a fact which may be attributed to the decline of shamanism in these cultures. Second, the belief in two souls, one of which can be separated from the body even during life, could have been motivated by shamanistic experiences of the journey of the soul. Indeed, the wanderings of the shaman and other people in dreamlike trances provided abundant information about journeys to the realm of the dead. In North and South America these tales report obstacles set up in the soul's way: curtains of fire, expanses of water, and monsters who threaten the traveler and try to make him lose his mind. The Ojibwa and Choctaw of North America speak of the slippery pine-trunk joining the banks of a rushing stream which the soul must get across. In South America, the Manacica believe that the deceased begins the journey to the realm of the dead as soon as the funeral is over. The medicine man guides him through virgin forests, seas, swamps, and mountains to the river that separates the land of the living from that of the dead. He has only to cross the bridge joining the two, which is guarded by a divinity.

In the American Indian conception of immortality, the Milky Way occupies a special place. It is also likened to the rainbow; the Kwakiutl of Vancouver Island think of it as the *axis mundi.* In British Columbia, the path of souls is the world tree. The *axis mundi,* the world tree, the road linking earth and sky, and shamanism are features of the mythic context of ecstasy and immortality. The Indians believe that the soul goes to the region of the dead, which is known through myths and tales to be patterned after the world of the living. Thus in North America it is sometimes called the "happy hunting ground." The Plains tribes imagine the dwelling place of the dead as a wide rolling prairie with feasting and dancing, whereas east of the Mississippi River and in South America, the cultivation of maize and agrarian festivals color the images of this realm. The afterlife of immortality is a reflection of earthly life.

The location of the land of the dead varies widely. For the Cubeo of the Amazon Basin, the country of the ancestors lies close by the villages of the living; the Blackfeet of Montana and Alberta speak of the "sandy hills" a few days' walk from the camps of the living, most of the Amazonian tribes think of a place beyond the setting sun, and the Pueblo Indians imagine it underground, an uncommon idea among American Indians since most of them locate the soul in a brightly lit place. Indian thought is marked by an ancient dualism: the "evil ones" and those who have died "badly" are doomed to a wandering life as ghosts, for the realm of the dead is open only to those who, after normal death, have received funeral rites.

These rites provide us with some valuable data. There are various methods of entombment: inhumation in South America, and in Canada placement of the body on a platform, in a tree, or on the ground. There is also incineration. Among the Iroquois, the Algonquians to the south of the Great Lakes, there are second funerals, involving the burial of the disinterred bones in a common grave or funeral urn. The provision of grave goods—food, drink, weapons, clothing, and jewelry—is widespread in the Andean region. The occasional addition of mummification in this practice allows us to speak of the "life of the corpse." In Colombia, archaeologists have discovered funeral wells, symbols of the afterlife, as well as traces of human sacrifices and anthropophagy. The Waica of the Amazon Basin practice cremation of the corpse, believing that the soul of the dead person, called *nobolebe* ("cloud"), rises to the sky where it is joined by *nonish,* the shadow soul. The funeral rites are intended to facilitate the deceased's journey to the region of the dead and to prevent his return. Belief in reincarnation is present both in the South and in the North, especially among the Inuit. The extent of ancestor worship is not so great; we find it in particular among the Zuni of New Mexico, in the Andes, and in the West Indies among the Taino. H. B. Alexander has emphasized the "wanderings of the soul" that appear in various initiation ceremonies, such as those of the Great House of the Delaware tribe and the Midewiwin of the Algonquian tribes (*The World's Rim: Great Mysteries of the North American Indians,* Lincoln, Nebr., 1953). Such initiations are meant to enable the initiate to grasp the meaning of life, which begins in this world and continues in the other world after death.

Inner Asia and the Finno-Ugric Peoples. A great similarity in beliefs concerning the soul can be noted on both sides of the Urals. The Khanty (Ostiaks) and Mansi (Voguls), Ugrians from the Ob River region, believe in the existence of a double soul comprising the breath or bodily soul and the shadow or dream soul, which is free and quite incorporeal but is tied to the dead person after death. Thus, after the person's death, the soul that was free and immaterial in life takes on a bodily form because of its ties to the corpse. Corpse and soul together stand for the complete, personal identity of the deceased person. Thus while the body is in the grave, it is also somewhere else thanks to its soul. The Khanty and Mansi believe that the free soul enters a subterranean realm where it represents the deceased and his personality. The same idea is found among the Samoyed of Europe and Siberia: the free soul survives, allowing the dead to lead lives in the underground world comparable to those which they lived on earth. In the dualistic eschatology of the Tunguz of the Yenisei River region, the free soul goes after death to the celestial land of the souls, along "the upper course of the tribal river," to heaven, where it becomes an *omi,* an "infant soul," so that it can be reincarnated. The body and soul that sojourned in the body go to the subterranean world, and the free soul, becoming an infant soul, remains in heaven until it is reborn. The Yukagir, who occupied Siberia before the Tunguz and the Yakuts, also have a twofold conception of the soul: man possesses a free soul, which has its seat in the head and which goes to the realm of the dead after death, plus bodily souls located elsewhere in the body.

Finnic pneumatology is identical to that of the northern Eurasian world. The free soul (image soul, shadow soul) is the extracorporeal manifestation of the person, which can become separated from the body even during life, in dreams, ecstasy, or trance. The corporeal soul, bound to the body, animates physical and psychic life. This dualism has faded under the influence of Christianity, but has left numerous traces in religious practices. The Mari (Cheremis), a Finnic people studied by Harva, say that after death, *ört,* the free soul, remains near the corpse and follows it to the grave. During the memorial ceremonies a feast is given in its honor, after which it is led back to the grave. The corporeal souls have ceased to exist, while the free soul continues to represent the human being. Thus throughout northern Eurasia death is conceived of as twofold: there is the corpse, abandoned by the corporeal souls, and then there is the soul of the deceased that continues to prolong the person's life. This dual status of the dead explains the funeral rites and the concept of the afterlife. The family handles the corpse with care, washing and dressing it and providing it with funeral furnishings and gifts for the other deceased members of the family. The Finns believe that the living and the dead form a family that is cemented together at the funeral and the memorial services. To discourage the soul from coming back into the house, the corpse is taken out through a hole cut in the wall. The grave is sacred, and it is located in a pleasant and picturesque spot, since it is the deceased's home; the cemetery is the "village of the dead." However, the Finnish language also carries traces of ideas about an underground abode of the dead and the dead person's continuing his work. Finnic eschatology, like that of all northern Eurasian cultures, is focused on the present, and conceives immortality not as an eternity, but as a present. The Finns continue to recognize this "presence" of the dead through feasts and memorial ceremonies. Many such rituals have been retained even after the conversion of these populations to Christianity.

Summary. To complete this brief overview of the beliefs in immortality among the preliterate populations of Africa, Australia, America, and Asia, a few further details must be mentioned. I have touched only in passing on the important area of reincarnation as a realization of the afterlife. Further, I have stressed the fact that immortality is linked to ancestor worship on the one hand and to the worship of the dead on the other. It should of course be noted that there is a difference between these two types, for not every dead person becomes an ancestor. If ancestor worship represents an important datum for the understanding of immortality in African thought, it must nevertheless always be distinguished from the veneration of the dead. The latter forms part of postmortem rituals, whereas ancestor worship is among the basic elements that make up certain archaic religions. Such a distinction takes on great importance in primitive religions such as the tribal cults of Indonesia: the ancestors worshiped there are a select group who have played a pivotal role in the life of the people. The creation of an ancestor is the work of the whole society, performed in a solemn initiation festival. In such a case we turn from the study of the worship of the dead to that of the worship of kings.

The study of immortality among American Indian and Eurasiatic peoples has revealed the existence of the "road of the dead." Study of these routes of the deceased is of value for our knowledge of these peoples' beliefs in immortality. They are of two principal kinds. The first is the heavenly road, reserved for chiefs, initiates, and those among the moral elite. The second is underground, or horizontal; it is the normal road leading to the world of the dead, or quite simply to the deceased's familiar haunts. In the "discovery" of the roads of the dead, a major role has been played by shamanism, for it is through the shamans' journeys to the transcendental world that the living have been informed about the paths to the beyond. By his ability to make such journeys the shaman has helped to etch in the memories of many peoples the landmarks of the funerary landscape and the road of the dead. Moreover, because this "revelation" is instructive for the life of archaic peoples, we should emphasize one idea that dominates these myths and rituals: "Communication between Heaven and Earth can be accomplished—or could be *in illo tempore*—by some physical means (rainbow, bridge, stairway, liana, rope, 'chain of arrows,' mountain, etc.). All the symbolic images dealing with the connection between Sky and Earth are merely variations on the World Tree or the *Axis Mundi*" (Eliade, 1964). The road of the dead, shamanism, and immortality bring us back to the basic realities for *homo religiosus:* the symbolism of the center, the cosmic tree, and the primordial time when contacts between heaven and earth were normal. The belief in immortality has led various archaic peoples to the discovery of the mythic, paradisiacal moment before the fall and the loss of contact between heaven and earth.

MESOAMERICAN RELIGIONS

The Mesoamerican cultural and religious complex includes various civilizations dating from 3500 BCE to the Spanish conquest in the sixteenth century CE. There are three major periods: the Preclassic concludes in the third century CE, and the Classic era extends from that time to the year 1000, followed by the Postclassic era. I shall consider here only the last period, for which we have relatively abundant archaeological and historical records.

The Aztec. The religion of the Aztec—the dominant people in Mexico at the time of the conquest—is a syncretic one in which three principal gods are found: the sun god Huitzilopochtli, the rain god Tlaloc, originally from Teotihuacán, and Quetzalcoatl, the feathered serpent of the Toltec, the culture hero and cosmic embodiment of wisdom. For the Aztec, the present world—which has already been preceded by four others—has the shape of a cross whose northern end is the land of darkness, the abode of the dead. It was created by Quetzalcoatl, who wrested the bones of the dead from the underworld and restored them to life by sprinkling them with his blood. This world is threatened with a calamity that can only be averted by means of human blood, and this is why there are wars, which are necessary for finding prisoners for sacrifice.

After death, people are subject to different fates, according to the choice of the gods. Stillborn children go to the thirteenth heaven, where the "tree of milk" is found that provides them with nourishment for an eternal infancy. Warriors slain on the battlefield and all those who have been sacrificed on an altar, as well as traders who have died on their journeys, become companions of the Sun, who has chosen them to take part in the cosmic salvation. Cremation prepares them for this solarization: the corpse is adorned with precious materials, the face covered with a mask, the head decorated with plumes, and the legs and arms are bound. Before consigning this mummy to the flames, it is provided with a precious stone, *chalchihuitl,* meant to take the place of its heart in the afterlife. Warriors, sacrificial victims, and tradesmen become the "companions of the eagle," *quauhteca,* accompanying the Sun from his rising until he reaches the zenith. Women who have died in childbirth are ranked with the warriors. They accompany the Sun from noon until sunset, carrying him on a litter of quetzal plumes. Thus there is immortality for this select group, and the warriors are reincarnated after four years.

The second category of the deceased is made up of men and women chosen by Tlaloc, those killed by drowning, lightning, and marsh fevers. These are buried, and go to the eastern abode, to the gardens of the god. The agrarian creed of Tlaloc envisages for them a happy life ever after amid luxurious vegetation—immortality in the paradise of Tlaloc. A fresco from Teotihuacán depicts this tropical garden and the elect who sing of their happiness there.

All other dying people go to the northern realm, the land of night. Their bodies are burned together with those of dogs, their companions on the road of the dead, a route beset with dangers—eight steppes and nine rivers. At the end of a four-year journey, during which their families carry out funeral ceremonies, they reach the underworld of the god Mictlan, who will annihilate them.

The Maya. Maya religion is known through the discovery of great cities such as Tikal, Copan, Palenque, and Uxmal. The period of its highest attainment extends from the third to the tenth centuries. In its funeral practices we find again three categories of the dead. The privileged groups are warriors who fall in battle, women dying in childbirth, priests, and suicides by hanging. These are immortal and enjoy eternal gladness in the Maya paradise beneath the sacred ceiba, the tree that crosses all the celestial spheres. This is the "tree of the beginning," Yache, which creates the junction between heaven and earth. The recent discovery of the tomb of Pacal, the king of Palenque from 615 to 633, offers irrefutable evidence of the Maya belief in immortality: the deceased falls into the mouth of the setting sun and, transformed into the bird Mohan, the symbol of immortality, rises into the sky again with the rising sun. The cross-shaped cosmic tree sends its roots into the world below and spreads its branches into the heavens. The *Book of the Dead* of the Maya religion also expands on the doctrine of reincarnation.

INCA RELIGION

At a time when various civilizations shared the Andean region (Peru, Bolivia, and Ecuador), new populations came on the scene. Chief among these were the Inca, named after their founding tribe, who settled the town of Tiahuanaco and the area around Lake Titicaca around 1445. Their empire would last only a century, crumbling under the impact of the Spanish invasion.

The highest god in the Inca pantheon was the Sun, the creator god, called by the name Viracocha in the mountains and Pachacámac in the coastal areas. The chiefs of the country were the "sons of the Sun." Alongside the worship of the sun (solar temples which were built in all the great cities), there was also the worship of Pachamama, the earth goddess, the embodiment of fertility.

Various witnesses of the Spanish conquest left accounts of Inca religion, all of which agree that the Inca believed in immortality and imagined the afterlife as a continuation of the present life. The evidence found in Peru attests to funeral customs such as the preservation of the corpse, the giving of a deceased ancestor's name to a newborn child, and the placing of the body in a fetal position in the grave or funeral jar. The belief in an afterlife accounts for the care devoted to the arrangement of graves, the embalming of the bodies of princes, and the strict punishment for any violation of graves. For the funeral of the ruler, the ritual prescribed embalming, special treatment of the face and eyes, the sacrifice and embalming of his wives and servants, and the placing of his furniture and possessions in the tomb.

RELIGIONS OF CHINA

The discovery of the Yang-shao culture in 1921 provided the first data on the early Chinese Neolithic period (4115 or 4365 BCE) and revealed something of early Chinese conceptions of sacred space, fertility, and death. Belief in the afterlife of the soul is attested by the placing of tools and foodstuffs in graves. The funeral urns of children were furnished with an opening at the top that allowed the soul to go out and to return. The funeral urn, the deceased's home, attests to the worship of ancestors. Red decoration in three motifs—triangle, checkerboard, and cowrie—forms a complex symbol of life, afterlife, and rebirth. These houses for the soul, which are numerous in Chinese prehistory, are the precursors of the ancestral tablets. Under the Shang dynasty (1751-1028 BCE), there are an increasing number of Bronze Age oracular inscriptions incised on bones and oyster shells that reveal the dialectic of the opposites (the *coincidentia oppositorum,* which foreshadows the doctrines of Taoism) and conceptions of the renewal of time and spiritual regeneration. Sacrifices to the supreme god Ti and to the ancestors make their appearance, and the royal graves have revealed animal and human sacrifices meant to accompany the ruler in his afterlife.

The year 1028 BCE marks the beginning of the Chou dynasty, which ruled China until 256 BCE. From its earliest days, the fundamental feature of the country's organization is lordship founded upon the family group and the possession of manorial land, thus the religion rests on the twin bases of the ancestors, who make up the divinized family, and the god of the earth, the apotheosis of lordship. Every family has its ancestors, who act as its protectors, and the king's forefathers are the guardians of the entire country. The funeral rites demonstrate a belief in the afterlife of souls, but this belief is somewhat inconsistent with regard to the fate of the dead. To begin with it must be recognized that every person was supposed to have multiple souls. The abode of the dead can be either the grave, the Yellow Springs, ruled by the earth god, the celestial world of Shang-ti ("lord on high"), or the ancestral sanctuary. The correct observance of the funeral rites is an essential condition for the afterlife.

Under the Chou dynasty, from the eighth to the third centuries BCE, Chinese civilization was transformed and expanded, and philosophical thought reached a high point. The celestial god T'ien ("heaven"), or Shang-ti, was all-knowing and all-seeing but impersonal; this "omniscient heaven" tradition was inherited by the philosophers. In the worship of the ancestors, the urn-house was replaced by the depositing of a tablet in the temple. The pattern of macrocosm-microcosm in the oppositional cycle of *yang* and *yin* was also integrated into Chinese thought, as the ancient symbolism of polarity and alternation underwent a remarkable development to become a system of cyclic totality, involving cosmic alternations and ritual separation of the sexes, the ordering principle upon which the philosophy of the Tao was based. According to Eliade, this is an archaic cosmogonic vision of the original unity-totality: "For Lao-tse, 'One,' the primitive unity/totality, already represents a step toward 'creation,' for it was begotten by the mysterious and incomprehensible principle of the Tao" (Eliade, 1982). The Tao exists before heaven and earth; it is a primordial wholeness, living and creative, and also a paradisiacal state.

The attempts of Taoist adepts to reintegrate this paradisiacal state constitutes their search for immortality, an exaltation of the primordial human condition. The attempt of Confucius (K'ung-tzu) was similar to that of Lao-tzu, in that both were based on ancient fundamental ideas—the Tao as the principle of wholeness, the *yin-yang* alternation, and the application of the analogy between macrocosm and microcosm to all levels of existence. Lao-tzu and his followers sought out the original unity within their own lives; Confucius looked for it in a balanced and just society. Lao-tzu was in search of the Tao, the ultimate, mysterious, unfathomable reality underlying all existence, seeking out the living wholeness through a reconciliation of the opposites and a return to the beginnings. Confucius (551–479) rejected neither the Tao, nor the god of Heaven, nor the veneration of ancestors. For him, the Tao was a decree from Heaven. He recommended a system of education that could transform the ordinary individual into a superior person, so that society might become an embodiment of the original cosmic harmony.

China did not produce a hierarchical classification of its beliefs about the fate of the dead. Most of them were destined for the kingdom of the Yellow Springs, while the kings and princes ascended to be near the Lord on High. The lords lived out their afterlives in the temples of the family ancestors, near their graves. This ancient agrarian religion dissolved along with the early social structure once the Han dynasty came to power, beginning in 206 BCE. Taoism then developed spectacularly, reaching its peak under the Six Dynasties, from the fourth to the sixth centuries of our era. As a religion of salvation, it had to offer an afterlife, and as the human being was thought to have many souls, but only one body for them to live in, it was along these lines that thinkers sought immortality. Some envisioned a melting pot of souls, out of which the deceased would receive an undying body, provided that the living were assiduous in practicing the funeral rites. But most tended to the view that the living body was preserved and became an immortal one. To this end they felt one should develop certain organs to be substituted for the corporeal ones. This gave rise to various practices to which the adepts, *tao-shih,* applied themselves in the desire to ensure the immortality of the living (body)—dietary practices to kill demons and maintain bodily vigor, embryonic circular breathing to induce ecstatic experiences, and sexual practices involving a mixing of the semen with the breath in order to stimulate the brain (Henri Maspero, *Taoism and Chinese Religion,* Amherst, 1981). Spiritual techniques such as insight, meditation, and mystical union came to be added to these physical ones. Between the second and sixth centuries, these techniques were supplemented by ceremonies for the dead, rites intended to melt the souls in a fire that would transform them into immortals *(hsien).*

ANCIENT EGYPT

At the center of the Egyptian belief in immortality lies the theme of life. The whole history of Egypt—its architecture, its art, its writings, its religion—proclaims the joy of life. From the deepest antiquity the *ankh* appears, a symbol of life, a symbol that even the Christians adopted as a precious legacy of three millennia of Egyptian religious tradition.

From the time of the Old Kingdom, the Egyptians envisaged a complex spiritual pattern, modeled on the divine life and made up of three elements necessary for life to exist. *Akh* is divine energy. *Ba* is the faculty of movement, human consciousness, and the ability to take various shapes. The divine breath and support of all created beings, *ka,* is the collection of qualities of divine origin that give eternal life; it is the life force connected with Ptah and Re, and it is the divine, living part of man. When the *ka* becomes separated from the body, it disintegrates, and the person must then be re-created through mummification and funeral rites if an afterlife is to be possible.

The Pyramid Texts, from the Old Kingdom, deal solely with the fate of the pharaoh. They assert that the dead king flies or climbs heavenward, to become a star or a companion of Re, the sun god, on his daily journey. In fact, we see that the deceased pharaoh has a dual destiny. Becoming one with Osiris, he returns to life through mummification, which gives him an everlasting body that must be fed and clothed by means of offerings, after which he goes to the realm of Re to live in the celestial world. The synthesis of this double doctrine of the pharaoh's assimilation to both Osiris and Re, which took place during the fifth dynasty, forms the foundation of the ancient Egyptian belief in immortality.

The mastabas, erected by their eventual occupants during their lifetimes, give an idea of the nature of Old Kingdom beliefs. Everything in these structures speaks of life as if in a house, for the afterlife is an extension of life beyond death. To go on living is to go on eating, so the walls of the mastabas are covered with bearers of offerings, funerary meals, and scenes of everyday life. A false door allows the deceased to come and go symbolically between the worlds of the dead and the living. The funeral scenes pictured in the mastabas show the two goddesses Isis and Nephthys, the sisters of Osiris, accompanying the deceased. The notion of rebirth in Osiris is current among the people already in the Old Kingdom. The earliest depiction of the afterlife is an image of the deceased sitting at his table, but the luxuriance of decoration down to the smallest detail shows that every aspect of immortality was already being imagined.

In the second millennium BCE, the Middle and New Kingdoms left behind a codification of their beliefs in the Coffin Texts and the *Book of Going Forth by Day.* Alongside older ideas recast in a somewhat democratic mold, new beliefs appear. The *ba,* the life force connected with Ptah and Re, is the dead person's soul. It remains near the mummy, but can also enter the *tuat,* the increasingly important realm of the dead, where Osiris reigns beneath the earth. The *ba* can also rise up to heaven, but its greatest joy lies in leaving the tomb during the day to move among human beings. Thanks to the *ka,* the soul can assume different shapes. Placing incantations from the *Book of Going Forth by Day* on the mummy's heart allowed the *ba* to go out in the daytime and do what the living do, returning to the tomb at night.

The *Book of Going Forth by Day* represents a confluence of various doctrines concerning immortality—mummification, psychostasia, or weighing of the *ba,* the judgment of the dead, the kingdom of the dead, the freedom of the *ba,* and the happy fate of those who have led their lives in accord with Maat. These seemingly contradictory features can be reconciled in terms of the trial of the soul before Osiris and his court. Mummification was intended to bind the *ba* to the body of the deceased and to this world. After vindicating himself before Osiris, the blessed one, *maa kheru,* was free to move about among the gods and spirits of the *tuat.* Meanwhile he also maintained ties with the world of the living, a world of joy in Egyptian eyes. Although Egyptians observed the Osirian funeral, the dependence of immortality on the preservation of the mummy need not be overemphasized. Even if the disintegration of the mummy broke the connection between the *ba* and the world, the deceased who had been consigned to the *tuat* continued to live happily in the Field of Reeds. The happy lot of the just person living in the boat of the Sun was reserved for those who were too poor to secure an Osirian funeral. The vast world of the immortals in the Middle and New Kingdoms was composed of Osirian immortals tied to their preserved mummies, and thus free to move about in the beyond and in this world of the living, Osirian immortals whose mummies had been destroyed but who were still happy in the *tuat* kingdom, where they were constrained to stay, and solarized, blessed immortals in the boat of the Sun. Their happy everlasting life had been prepared for by an ethical life in conformity with Maat ("justice") by the arrangement of the tomb and mummification, and all that went into the construction of the eternal home. The necropolises are testaments to life. Such a conception of immortality is further clarified by the illustration of the weighing of the *ba* and the trial of Osiris. The presence of the monster who devours the dead person seems to refer to a second death for the evildoer, and perhaps his total destruction.

In Hellenistic and Roman times the religion of Isis was to undergo a great expansion. Although immortality remains centered around the theme of life, water also assumes great symbolic importance. Life-giving, purifying, a symbol of rejuvenation, water is "the identification of the Nile and Osiris," which the goddesses Isis, Nephthys, or Nut procure for the deceased. In imperial times the "fresh water of the dead" is mentioned. According to Françoise Dunand, the dead person who receives the life-giving water of Osiris wins immortality, for by drinking the water he absorbs the strength of the god (*Le culte d'Isis,* vol. 3, Leiden, 1973, p. 212). In addition, the god Anubis opens up the roads to the otherworld and becomes himself a solar god. Plutarch makes Osiris the god of the celestial world, a pure and invisible world that the deceased enters after being transformed into Osiris, and in this context the rite of initiation takes its place as a doctrine of salvation and a path to immortality.

INDIA

In all three of the great directions in Indian religious thought—Vedic, Brahmanic, and *bhakti*—the belief in immortality is clear and constant.

Vedic India. The Sanskrit word *amṛta* (Pali, *amata*) is formed from privative *a* plus *mṛta* ("death") and means "nondeath." Related are the Greek *am(b)rotos* ("immortal") and *ambrosia* ("elixer of immortality"); the Avestan *Ameretāt,* the name of an abstract divine entity meaning "deathlessness, immortality"; and the Latin *immortālitās.* Thus our word *immortality* is of Indo-European origin and means literally "nondeath." As Georges Dumézil showed in the early days of his studies on comparative Indo-European mythology (*Le festin d'immortalité,* Paris, 1924), *amṛta* is an essential concept in Indo-European thought. In the Vedic texts, particularly in sacrificial contexts, *amṛta* appears together with *soma. Amṛta* is the heavenly elixir of immortality, as *soma* is a sacrificial libation offered to the gods by the priests. *Amṛta* is the drink of immortality of gods and men; *soma* is the elixir of life that has come from heaven to bestow immortality *(amṛtam).* Both words contain the idea of the winning of immortality, conceived as a perpetual renewal of youth and life.

In the *Ṛgveda* a distinction is made between the body and the invisible principle of the human being, designated by the words *asu,* the life force or breath, and *manas,* the spirit, the seat of intellect and internal feelings, located in the heart. The nature of the soul can be seen in the Vedic attitude toward death, for the dead are simply the shadows of the living. What survives is the individuality, the essence of the human person, which becomes immortal by being indefinitely prolonged in time, as part of a perfectly ordered cosmos. Immortality is a perpetual remaking in accord with universal law, and consists in being born everlastingly. The Ṛgvedic hymn 10.129.1–3 speaks of "the One that was before being and nonbeing, before death and non-death." Nondeath is understood in relation to both the birth of organized time and the womb that is synonymous with death and renewal.

The Vedic sacrificial symbolism through which the belief in immortality is affirmed revolves around the sun, *soma,* and *agni* ("fire"). The motion of the sun and the cosmic drama in which it is destroyed only to be restored again are deeply ingrained in Vedic India. The sun appears as the substance of rejuvenation and the prototype of the sacrificial fire. The fire is the god Agni, ever renewed and hence forever young (*Ṛgveda* 3.23.1), the navel of immortality, whose eternal youth lies in his ability to be reborn. The immortality symbolized by *agni,* the divine fire, and *soma,* the drink of life, is perpetual rebirth. Agni, the golden embryo, the sun, *soma,* and the celestial tree (the *Ficus religiosa*) are all symbols of immortality. The immortal world is *sukṛta,* "well-made," and *saṃskṛta,* "perfected," and within its dynamically interwoven patterns lies the basis of immortality. For the *Ṛgveda,* "to be born limitlessly is deathlessness, and those who are born, the sun and fire, are also immortals, the very guardians of the immortality that they obtain for man (Lilian Silburn, *Instant et cause: Le discontinu dans la pensée philosophique de l'Inde,* Paris, 1955, p. 45).

Brahmanic India. By laying stress on perpetual renewal, the Brāhmaṇas deepen and systematize this idea of the infinite extension of the cosmic order. Their foundation is threefold: fire, the sacrificial altar, and Prajāpati. Already present in the *Ṛgveda* as the patron of reproduction, Prajāpati becomes the central figure of the Brāhmaṇas. The thirty-fourth god, beside the thirty-three Vedic divinities, he is the creative force, the concentrated spiritual act preceding creation, the energy that is scattered about in creating the world in all its multiplicity and that must reassemble and lead to the unity of the beginnings. Prajāpati is the sacrifice, an earthly copy of the great cosmic drama. The cyclic rhythm of the cosmos is repeated in that of the sacrificial ritual, a replica of the cycle of the sun and its alternation without beginning or end. The ritual must restore the lost unity, it must reassemble it and provide structure and continuity. Thus the ritual becomes a transcendence of death.

The symbolism of immortality in the Brāhmaṇas goes beyond the Vedic symbolism. The sacrifice confers long life and immortality, symbolized by the cosmic year; the days and nights are symbols of human lives, of mortal, transient time. The seasons make up the year in its real sense, a limitless rebirth; the year is the symbol of divine life and immortality, and Prajāpati is the year. The sacrificial altar is constructed in the course of a year using 10,800 bricks, each one representing an hour. The *gārhapatya* fire represents a womb, into which a special *mantra* inspires the breath of life. Through the *āhavanīya* fire the sacrificer rises to heaven, to be born a second time and attain immortality. Thus the sacrifice constitutes the transcendence of death by means of ritual.

With the Upaniṣads India enters a period of deep reflection on consciousness and liberation. The concept of the *ātman,* or self, comes to the fore: it is thought of as the undying basis of man, whose task is to free itself from the human body to attain perfect oneness with *brahman.* The *ātman* is unchanging, immortal *(amṛta),* indestructible, eternal, imperishable. *Brahman* is the creative principle, the phenomenal reality and totality of the universe, the sacred principle.

Upaniṣadic thought takes India out of its Brahmanic ritualism and confers a new importance on human action, attributing to it an energy that will continue to bear fruit until it is spent. Under the influence of *karman* with its doctrine of retribution of acts through reincarnation, the *ātman* will experience a continual unfolding of existence beyond death. Here we become involved more deeply in the idea of deliverance, which can proceed via two possible routes. The first is a return to a body, a reincarnation, and the second is the route of the gods, the royal road, the development of the metaphysical and mystical consciousness needed to discover the *ātman,* the *brahman,* and the identity of *brahman-ātman.* This quest for the Absolute is the search for immortality, the *tat tvam asi,* "thou art that." Immortality is the absorption of the individual in *brahman;* it is attained by seeing the underlying oneness of things. To the ritualism of the Vedas and the Brāhmaṇas, the Upaniṣads oppose a release from rebirths through the knowledge that unites man once and for all with *brahman.*

Bhakti. In the last centuries before the common era, a religious current known as *bhakti* spread across India. It was a form of Hinduism that implies a relationship between God and his creatures based on grace, and conversely one of total devotion to God on the part of his creation. *Bhakti* is a loving devotion that gives the believer a greater knowledge of the Lord (Kṛṣṇa or Īśvara) than any meditation or reflection, and it is a divine gift given only to those who have prepared themselves by a loving attitude. Within the wider context of the transmigration of souls, the *bhakti* movement affirms a monotheistic tendency and an emphasis on salvation. Devotion should be accompanied by knowledge, but it is superior to knowledge, as two stanzas from the *Bhagavadgītā* will illustrate: "I will reveal that which is to be known and by knowing which, eternal life is gained. / It is the Supreme *brahman,* who is without beginning and who is said to be neither being nor nonbeing" (13.12). Along with this knowledge, utmost devotion to the Lord is necessary: "And whoever, at the time of death, gives up this body and departs, thinking of Me alone, he comes to My status (of being)" (8.5; trans. Radhakrishnan, New York, 1948). *Bhakti* takes the place of the elixir of life, conferring eternal life with Kṛṣṇa. A number of texts emphasize the destiny of the *bhakta,* who is *siddha* ("perfect"), *amṛta* ("immortal"), and *tṛpta* ("happy").

Summary. As we have seen, although the forms taken by the Indian belief in immortality are diverse, they are linked together by a rich and overlapping symbolism with many points in common. In this symbolism we touch on a subject that has been strongly emphasized by Eliade (1969): the techniques for the winning of immortality. I have already referred to symbolism such as that of Agni and the sacrificial fire, the mystic flame produced by *tapas,* the bridge leading to the supreme *brahman,* the great journey reminding us of the importance of reincarnation, the master charioteer, the sun and the cosmic wheel, the celestial tree, and *soma.* Eliade has also stressed two further aspects of this long development of Indian philosophy, namely yogic practices, already apparent in the Upaniṣads, and the tendency, incipient in the Vedas and firmly established in the Brāhmaṇas and the Upaniṣads, to assert the existence of several layers of reality. In the quest for complete reintegration, the ultimate aim of existence, transmigration too is described in very lively terms.

In the symbolism of *amṛta,* funerary worship holds pride of place. In the Vedic ritual the dying person is laid in a purified place, the head turned toward the south, the direction of the land of the dead. After death, the corpse is scrupulously prepared for the cremation. Gold pieces, symbols of deathlessness, are placed on the facial openings. The fire is carried at the head of the funeral procession, always in new vessels. The cremation place is selected carefully, near the water, with a pleasant view to the west. On the spot where the pyre will be built a gold piece is laid. The pyre is lit from three sacrificial fires, symbolized by three layers of grass, for the cremation is considered a sacrifice. After the body is consumed by the fire, the bones are cleansed, reassembled, and placed in an urn or a grave. In household rites, an offering of rice is made, representing an offering to the fathers and a meal for the dead. Several kinds of Vedic and Brahmanic rituals have been observed for millennia, and all are symbolic enactments of the fundamental tenet of India, expressed in the words of the *Bṛhadāraṇyaka Upaniṣad:* "Lead me from death to nondeath" (1.3.28).

BUDDHISM

The Upaniṣads taught that there exists within every person an *I,* the *ātman,* an enduring and eternal entity, an immutable substance underlying the ephemeral world of phenomena. Hence the way to immortality was easily found. The *ātman,* they said, becomes immortal not through sacrifice or ritual or ascetic discipline, but by taking possession of the immortal, the *brahman.* For the Upaniṣads, it is the identification of *ātman* and *brahman* that bestows immortality. The Buddha denied the existence of the *ātman,* teaching instead the doctrine of *anātman,* or "no-self," in which every person is a collection of aggregates, a functioning whole for which ceaseless change is the true reality. The Buddha replaced the vital principle of *ātman* with these "aggregates," or *skandhas*, and by the "chain of being," *santāna,* whose links are related by cause and effect. He recognized the act and its fruit but not the actor, believing that there is no *sattva,* or independent self that can be reincarnated. But the whole functions, the "contingent self" exists from moment to moment, laden with its previous actions and carrying with it the potential for unceasing rebirth. Death marks the instant when retribution for another set of actions must begin; it is a rebirth, but not a transmigration. The individual is an unceasingly renewing flow, for he has within him, in his actions and desires, the seeds of his continued existence.

The belief in an afterlife and immortality is not ignored by the Buddha. Like the brahman, the yogin, and the mendicant, he seeks "that which endures," "deliverance," and "what is undying." "The first words of Śākyamuni on becoming Buddha are to proclaim that he has attained the Immortal, and has opened the gates of the Immortal" (Louis de La Vallée Poussin, *Nirvâna,* Paris, 1925, p. 50). "The inexpressible Immortal is the goal of the holy man, because it means release from birth and death" (ibid.). This goal is called *nirvāṇa.* The Buddha did not define *nirvāṇa;* we know it by its attributes: unshakeable happiness and blessedness, unborn, unproduced, undone, unconditioned, perfect, unconstructed gladness. *Nirvāṇa* is release, an unseen dwelling, immortal, never returning to the world below. Speaking of the saint who has attained perfect enlightenment in this world, one text says: "The *arhat,* already in this life, restrained, having attained *nirvāṇa (nibbāna),* feeling happiness within him, passes his time with *brahman*" (*Aṅguttara Nikāya* 2.206). To arrive at *nirvāṇa,* and thus immortality, one must follow the method and the way of the Buddha. La Vallée Poussin and Eliade have stressed the yogic nature of this path to deliverance.

A discussion of the debates concerning *nirvāṇa* among the various schools of the great movements of historical Buddhism—Hīnayāna, Mahāyāna, Tantric, and Pure Land—is outside the scope of this article. Let us cast a brief glance, however, at Tibet, for the tradition of Tibetan Buddhism constitutes a unique synthesis of the ancient Bon religion and highly fragmented Buddhist doctrines. The Tibetan *Book of the Dead* is an invaluable source for our knowledge of the journey of the soul. By reciting the texts at the dead person's bedside, the lama is supposed to restore the life force, *bla,* to the deceased's body for its journey of forty-nine days through the intermediate stage between death and rebirth. If this rebirth does not occur, the deceased appears before the god of the dead to be judged. (Several details indicate an Iranian influence.) Giuseppe Tucci (*The Religions of Tibet,* Berkeley, 1980) emphasizes among other ceremonies the various rites performed around the *maṇḍala* especially constructed for the funeral. After a purification ritual, a piece of the dead person's bone *(rus)* or a piece of paper or wood with his name written on it is placed on the *maṇḍala;* the bones are the supports of the deceased and the seat of his soul. The ceremony is meant to induce rebirth, but it is reminiscent too of the journeys of the soul in the world of the shaman. The Tibetans have retained their belief in a direct link between earth and the paradisiacal spheres of heaven. They also believe that in eternity, the deceased keeps the appearance he had when living on earth. Carried in a fabric sling, the symbol of his meritorious deeds, he can rise to the celestial regions, in an ascension ritual revealing the shamanistic influence of Inner Asia.

CELTS, GERMANS, SCANDINAVIANS, THRACIANS, AND GETAE

The work of Georges Dumézil has pioneered the discovery of the tripartite organization, based on sovereignty, force, and fertility, of ancient Indo-European religious ideology. Thanks to this insight, the study of the religion of the Indo-European peoples has been made considerably easier by revealing both the consistency of Indo-European thought and the importance of the Indo-European inheritance. These factors prove to be invaluable in the study of peoples who have left behind only scattered remains, in archaeological records and epigraphy, eyewitness accounts handed down by neighboring peoples, and mythological remants.

A firm belief in an afterlife is attested by the funerary practices of the Celts, Germans, and Scandinavians. Archaeological evidence is abundant, including megalithic tombs, dolmens, and individual burials in coffins marked with solar symbols, and cremation is known from the urnfields as early as 1500 BCE. Everything in these graves speaks in the symbolic language of the afterlife: the preservation of skulls, the location of graves near the living, bodies turned to face the house, and the inclusion of the dead person's possessions. The widespread nature of cremation around the middle of the second millennium BCE (a practice finally prohibited by Charlemagne) points to an Indo-European presence.

The belief in the soul's immortality among the Celts and the Gauls is attested by numerous early witnesses. Caesar (*Gallic Wars* 6.14) says that the druids asserted that souls are immortal, that after death they pass into another body, and that this belief explains the reckless fearlessness of their warriors. For the Germans, the soul is reborn within the *Sippe* (the clan). Diodorus Siculus speaks of the Gaulish custom of throwing letters addressed to the deceased onto the funeral pyre. Various Celtic traditions give accounts of an *aes sídh,* or "paradise of the dead," an open world connected by a bridge to the land of the living, sometimes also appearing as an island in the ocean. Eggshells found in graves are an especially important symbol; the broken egg is a sign of newly born life.

In Germanic religion, Valhǫl (Valhalla) is a lodging reserved for warriors who have fallen on the field of battle, and for all those who have died a heroic death. It is the home of the *einherjar,* the heroes who pass a pleasant life there; part of their time is taken up with the feast of immortality, in which the flesh of the wild boar Sæhrímnir is recovered intact every night so that the banquet can go on the next day, and the sacred mead is served by the *valkyrjar* (valkyries). Another symbol of the Germanic world is the tree Yggdrasill, which stands at the center of the world, sending one root into the land of the dead, another into that of the giants, and a third into the world of men. It symbolizes fate, the link between the living and the dead, as well as the continual rebirth of life.

The cult of Zalmoxis among the Thracians and the Getae (Herodotus, 4.94–95) also entails the belief in the deathlessness of the soul, obtained through an initiation ritual that belongs among the mystery cults of the Mediterranean world, particularly those having to do with the preparation for a happy existence in the other world.

RELIGIONS OF ANCIENT IRAN

Turning to Iran, we do not leave the Indo-European world. In fact, we enter an area heavily indebted to the inheritance of Indo-European trifunctional religious thought, as Dumézil has shown. However, the theme of immortality here has to be examined from a new angle, since the religious reform of Zarathushtra (Zoroaster) had a profound effect on Iranian thought.

In the *Gāthās,* the opposition between body and spirit is everywhere, for the human soul is complex. *Vyana* is the breath-soul, the spiritual self. *Manah* is mind, the activity of consciousness, thought, and memory. *Urvan* is the part of the personality that deals with the spiritual and religious domain; it corresponds to the Indian *ātman. Daēnā* is the religious intelligence that allows for knowledge of the revelation. The *Gāthās* lay great stress on the spiritual part of the human being.

The word *fravashi,* absent from the *Gāthās,* is of preZoroastrian origin, being derived from *fravarti* ("protector, guardian"), according to Söderblom (1901). It is used elsewhere in the Avesta; *Yasna* 23.1 says, "I call to the sacrifice all the holy *fravashi*s, whoever they are, who are on the earth after their death," recalling the Indo-European notion of the "fathers," the "ancestors," or spirits of the dead. Söderblom thinks that the *fravashi*s go back to pre-Avestan popular beliefs and worship of the dead. There are traces of a vague notion of the continuation of the dead person's life near the house, and hence the idea of a preexisting soul that survives death. At the end of the year, the *fravashi*s of the dead come to earth to ask for food and clothing from the living, in exchange for their protection.

Priest and prophet, Zarathushtra brought about a profound religious reform. Departing from Indo-Iranian polytheism, he conferred the status of supreme god on Ahura Mazdā, the creator of light, living creatures, and mental faculties. An all-knowing god and lord of wisdom, Ahura Mazdā lives in a realm of light, surrounded by his celestial court, who are six trifunctional Indo-Iranian gods transposed into archangels (Dumézil). Three are on his right side: Vohu Manah ("good thought"), Asha ("justice"), and Khshathra Vairya ("strength"). Three are on the left: Ārmaiti ("piety"), Haurvatāt ("wholeness, health"), and Ameretāt ("immortality"). These divine entities arose from Ahura Mazdā. In creation, energy and activity are the privilege of two spirits: Spenta Mainyu ("good spirit"), who is very close to Ahura Mazdā, acts as his deputy in the creation, and is charged with bestowing health and immortality; and Angra Mainyu ("evil spirit"), the creator of nonlife and sower of disorder. Man must choose between the two. The choice between good and evil is paramount, since eternal happiness depends on it.

The ancient Indo-European belief in immortality takes on a new aspect, as the theistic and mystical conception is succeeded by one of a religion of salvation. Beside the universal eschatology, the *Gāthās* propound an individual soteriology. Thus immortality results from the salvation of the soul, which is realized after death on the basis of merit gained through the choices made in life. Salvation depends upon judgment, and it is Ahura Mazdā who bestows immortality. In this area we find a very rich symbolic background, as in descriptions of the passage between earth and heaven via the Chinvat Bridge (*Yasna* 46.10–11; 32.13). Whoever does not cross this bridge successfully ends up in the house of *druj,* the hell of damned souls. The journey of the soul and the crossing of the bridge reveal a shamanistic influence, recalling the soul's ecstatic journey to the sky and its journey to heaven after death. Zarathushtra thus spiritualized Iranian eschatology and the Indo-European concept of the afterlife. The reward is an immortal life, a life of eternal happiness, a transfiguration and rejuvenation. There is no question of the Indian *saṃsāra* or of cyclic time; immortality is final after death, new youth being bestowed by Ahura Mazdā himself. Haurvatāt and Ameretāt, material and spiritual happiness, are part of this reward. The soul finds itself in the house of Ahura Mazdā, amid fields of justice and mercy (*Yasna* 33.3).

Zarathushtra's revelation had a definitive influence on the Zoroastrian belief in immortality. The most indicative of the later Avestan texts is undoubtedly the *Hadhōkht Nask;* dating in its present form from the Sasanid period, it describes the vicissitudes of the soul's journey after death. For the first three nights the soul remains near the body. The just person's soul sings the praises of Ahura Mazdā; that of the evildoer cowers in anguish. At the end of the third night, the soul of the righteous person feels the coming of a bracing, sweet-smelling breeze from the south, bringing to it its own *daēnā,* in the form of a radiant young girl. Who is this *daēnā?* For H. S. Nyberg (*Die Religionen des alten Iran,* Osnabrück, 1966) it is a luminous virgin who represents the celestial realm of the Zoroastrian community. Geo Widengren (*Die Religionen Irans,* Stuttgart, 1965) sees in it the heavenly counterpart of the soul. *Urvan* and *daēnā* are the two parts of the soul, and the *daēnā,* the celestial part, is conditioned by the person's earthly life. In *Zarathustras Jenseitsvorstellungen und das Alte Testament* (Vienna, 1964), after analyzing the *urvan*'s conversation with its *daēnā,* Franz König discusses the eschatological doctrine of these twins: by its thoughts, words, and deeds in this life, the *urvan* creates its heavenly *daēnā,* a mirror image of its earthly life. Immortality begins with the reconciliation of the *urvan* and the *daēnā.* Thereupon the righteous soul crosses three heavenly spheres before appearing at the entrance to the kingdom of light, where it receives the "butter of spring," followed by its judgment and entry into heaven, Asan or Asman, "the radiant world above, which rises over the earth" (*Yashts* 13.2). There it meets the two divine entities Haurvatāt and Ameretāt. The evil soul is thrown into a cavern.

Thus it may be seen that although the popular religion of the Zoroastrian community introduced some substantial new elements, the broad outlines of Zarathushtra's doctrine of immortality were preserved.

MESOPOTAMIA

Through scraps of texts, archaeological records, funerary rituals, and other hints we are able to recover a few features of the Mesopotamian concept of the afterlife. A pair of myths provide some details about the search for immortality, and show that this was a question that preoccupied the thinkers of the time. The myth of the sage Adapa recounts how he was summoned before the court of Anu for having broken the wings of the south wind. Adapa admits what he has done, but he refuses to eat the "bread of life" or drink the "water of life" that the god has offered to him, and thus he loses his chance to become immortal. Another myth concerning the quest for immortality is the epic about Gilgamesh, the ruler of Uruk. This epic, written in Akkadian, tells of the defeat of a hero who tries to overstep the human condition. Although Gilgamesh fails to pass the initiation test, which requires him to go without sleep for six days and seven nights, Utanapishtim reveals to him the secret of the gods, the whereabouts of a youth-restoring plant. Gleefully Gilgamesh descends to the bottom of the sea and harvests the sweet-smelling plant. On the return route he stops to bathe, and a snake takes advantage of this to rob him of the plant that would confer immortality.

In Mesopotamia, death is seen as the universal and inescapable fate. The body becomes a corpse and disintegrates, leaving behind two elements. The first of these is the skeleton of the human being—hence the great respect accorded the tombs in which the dead lie—and the second is the "ghost," or shade, attested around 2500 BCE in the Sumerian word *gedim.* The afterlife of the deceased is spent down below, in the lower hemisphere beneath the land of the living, which explains the funeral rites in which bodies were placed in the ground, in pits, graves, or caves. As a rule there is neither exposure of the corpse nor cremation. The world below was also inhabited by the *anunnaki*s, divinities of the lower world.

Entry to the world of the dead was gained through the grave or through the west, where the sun sets in the evening. There is thus a road of the dead, an entry into the domain of the dead, an enormous dark cave. The question of whether there was a postmortem trial among the Assyro-Babylonians is still open, but in any case the journey is one of no return. Inequalities in the fates of the dead, attested in various records, are to be understood primarily in terms of the attitudes taken toward them by the living. The dead were interred, preferably under the house, their grave goods comprising a dish, ornaments, tools, weapons, and toys. Because the dead had to receive food and drink, water was poured into the grave through a tube. At the end of the lunar month, the memory of the dead and the ancestors was celebrated in order to help them and to turn their wrath away from the living. In short, what is known for certain about the Assyro-Babylonian world is that there was an afterlife and the dead descended to the realm below and lived an unhappy life there.

THE HEBREW SCRIPTURES

From remotest times the Hebrews practiced inhumation, placing various objects, weapons, and provisions in the grave for the use of the dead, gestures which seem to constitute at least one facet of a *votum immortalitatis*. The Hebrew Bible sees the human being as a composite of flesh *(basar),* the breath of life, or soul *(nefesh),* and spirit *(ruaḥ). Basar* is functionally equivalent to *caro,* and *nefesh* to *anima,* as *ruaḥ* is to *pneuma* (Lat., *spiritus*). The hierarchic structures of this triad reveal a dualistic trend of *soma* versus *psuchē;* the Septuagint, a Greek version of the Bible, uses the word *psuchē* about a thousand times to refer to *nefesh,* and it is quite clear that Palestinian Judaism, just as much as the Greek version, assimilated a view of man on the pattern of body and soul (see Albert Descamps, "La mort selon l'écriture," in Ries, 1983, pp. 52–55).

After death, people go to She'ol—an immense, underground place, deep, dark, and bolted shut, the abode of shadows—to lead lives that are shadows of their lives on earth, and according to *Job* 7:9–10, this life is one of no return. This idea contrasts with the archaic concept of the "afterlife" of a corpse that makes use of objects and food, and is undoubtedly later. She'ol is not to be confused with the grave, the habitat of the corpse. The shade in She'ol is not the remnant of the mortal being in the grave, it is a "double"; She'ol is an extension of the grave.

The doctrine of She'ol was of popular origin and remained quite vague, but it demonstrates a spiritualistic tendency in the belief in an afterlife found in the Hebrew scriptures. References to an afterlife are found in the Bible. The human being is not destroyed after death, but is reunited with his ancestors. The miracles performed by Elijah and Elisha (*1 Kgs.* 17:17–24, *2 Kgs.* 4:31–37) show that life can be restored to the body. Moreover, the evocation of the dead, characteristic of popular beliefs in an afterlife, shows that the living attempted to get in touch with the deceased. According to *Genesis* 2 and 3, man was immortal (by nature or through grace) in God's original plan, but showed himself to be unworthy of this fate. The story reflects man's refusal to accept death, the deep desire to live unendingly in a long and happy life. This is the theme of the earthly paradise, the *votum immortalitatis* in which man partakes of the divine *ruaḥ* (*Gn.* 1:26–27, 5:1, 9:6). This participation vouchsafes to man, after the Fall, the afterlife of She'ol. The faith of Israel admits of no failure of Yahveh in regard to She'ol.

The *refa'im* of She'ol are the biblical forerunners of immortal souls. Several passages in *Job* and *Psalms* allude to a union with God that death will not destroy. During the persecutions of Antiochus Epiphanes, the fate of the dead is foremost among Israel's preoccupations; the vision of dry bones in *Ezekiel* 37:1–14 serves as the basis of a meditation on resurrection and God's power to bring his believers out of She'ol. In the *Book of Daniel* 7:9, the motif of the "book of life" marks a gradual shift toward individual judgment, and the faith in individual eschatological resurrection is clearly attested in both *Daniel,* which dates from 165 BCE (*Dn.* 11:40–12:13), and in *2 Maccabees* (chaps. 7, 9, 11), written in Greek sometime after 124 BCE.

In the *Wisdom of Solomon,* written in Greek around 50 BCE, the concept of the afterlife is rendered for the first time by *aphtharsia,* "immortality" (1:11–15, 2:23–25), and the immortality of the souls of the righteous is clearly affirmed. They are in the hand of God (3:1–4), and their souls enjoy a never-ending life with God in peace, rest, love, grace, and mercy (3:9, 4:7, 5:15). After the destruction of the Temple in the year 70 CE, a doctrine of resurrection for everyone—not only the righteous but also for nonbelievers—appears within the circle of the tannaim.

THE QUMRAN TEXTS

The Essenes, as described by Josephus Flavius, believed in the immortality of the soul and its future life freed from bodily ties, hence their renunciation of even the most legitimate of the pleasures of this world. As for the Qumran texts, the *Manual of Discipline* says that those who let themselves be guided and inspired by the spirits of truth and light will be blessed in this world and will enjoy eternal gladness in a world without end. The wicked will be punished in the darkness of an everlasting fire (2.8, 4.7–8). The community forms an eternal alliance with God in this world and beyond, so that the immortality of the souls of individual members is closely bound up with that of the community, envisaging a home in the world of light above, the world of God and his angels (J. P. M. van der Ploeg, "L'immortalité de l'homme d'après les textes de la Mer Morte," *Vetus Testamentum* 2, 1952, p. 173). Psalm 3 seems to refer to a resting place for the blessed, an unending height or a vast plain, in a symbolism matched by expressions in *Psalms* 16:9–10 and 73:23–28. Belief in a happy future life appears to be common in the thinking of the composers of these psalms.

THE GRECO-ROMAN WORLD

The imagination of the ancients endowed the land of Greece with many mouths of the underworld, called the "gates of Hades." For some, these were the paths through which people vanished after death, for others they were the wombs of perpetual rebirth; the Greeks were divided over these two views of the afterlife (André Motte, *Prairies et jardins de la Grèce antique,* Brussels, 1973, p. 239). This phenomenon accounts for one of the earliest notions of the afterlife in the Greek world, the idea of a cycle of successive deaths and rebirths. In Homer the belief in the beyond is marked by a deep-seated pessimism. Hesiod is more optimistic, speaking of the islands of the blessed where the dead carouse. The theme of immortality, barely outlined in Homer and Hesiod, begins to gain ground from the sixth century on. Thus the works of Pindar are permeated by a deep longing for immortality. One particular religious movement, Orphism, came to play a decisive role in the diffusion of doctrines of immortality.

Orphism. Monuments to Orpheus are found as early as the sixth century BCE, and allusions to his descent into the underworld appear in the fifth century. Priests who preach salvation in the name of Orpheus and promulgate an initiation that sets people free for their lives in the next world are reported in Classical times. In the Hellenistic period references to Orpheus become more frequent, and Orphism finds fertile ground in Ptolemaic Egypt, where it encounters the cult of Osiris.

From the confused obscurity of a mixture of traditions, Eliade has unraveled the important fact that Orpheus is a founder of initiations and mysteries, a religious figure of a type formally parallel to Zalmoxis, the culture hero of the Getae, the Thracians who believed themselves to be immortal. Certain elements also recall shamanistic practices. Introducing a religious message predating Homer, Orpheus makes inroads into the Olympian religion. He extols vegetarianism, asceticism, purification, and initiation; herein lies the conjunction with Apollo and Dionysos.

The Orphic anthropogony is a dualistic one, and the early records are corroborated by the recently discovered Derveni Papyrus. It refers to the myth of the Titans, who were burned to ashes by Zeus's thunderbolt in punishment for the murder of

Dionysos. From these ashes arose the human race, composed of Titanic matter and the pure soul that stemmed from the blessed race of the undying gods, which was sent forth as a falling star to earth, where it was united with a body and became subject to fate. Hence the present race of men carries a dual inheritance, from both the gods and the Titans. The evidence of gold lamellae found in graves in Italy and Crete is invaluable, providing references about the journey of the soul of the dead extending from the second to the fourth century CE.

In contrast with Homeric thought, which was oriented toward earthly pleasures and very little concerned with the next world, Orphism professes the belief in a happy afterlife. The seed of salvation is within man, since his immortal soul is a piece of the divine stuff, and the purpose of life on earth is to come to a permanent choice. The Orphic doctrine of purification allows for the reincarnation of souls. We know from Plato that the Orphians offered rather gloomy descriptions of the torments of the guilty soul and the evils awaiting the damned, plunged into a pool of mud (*Republic* 2.363d). The disciple's initiation and asceticism and the permanent change in his behavior were meant to prepare him for a happy eternity, the future life about which the golden plates furnish some details. A plate from Petilia in northern Italy pictures the soul coming to two springs, one near a cypress tree and the other near the Lake of Memory. It drinks from the second spring and rediscovers its divine origin. A lamella from Thurium in Italy shows the soul, freed from its bodily prison, hearing these words: "O happy and fortunate one, you will be a god and not a mortal" (Guthrie, 1952). Another has the soul say, "I have lost myself in the bosom of the Queen." In such an apotheosis, Persephone carries out the mystical act of divine filiation, and the initiate becomes once more divine and immortal.

Early Pythagoreanism. Pythagoreanism stands out against a background of dualistic doctrines. Settling in Magna Graecia in the second half of the sixth century, Pythagoras founded at Croton a brotherhood shrouded in secrecy, which introduced its followers to a new kind of life meant to point the way that led to salvation. In religious matters Pythagoras espoused Orphic views and brought about, as Eliade (1982) has indicated, a large-scale synthesis of archaic elements (some of them "shamanistic") and bold reevaluations of ascetic and contemplative techniques. The Orphic and Pythagorean doctrines regarding the soul display many features in common: immortality, transmigration, punishment in Hades, and the soul's eventual return to heaven. Pythagoreanism, however, developed its teaching independently, in a closed society. For Pythagoras the human soul is immortal; it is held within the body as if in a prison and can live independently of the body. After death, the soul passes into Hades to be purified, and to the extent that it is not completely cleansed it must return to earth and seek a new body. The soul's journey back to the celestial world is made possible by many incarnations and after a life of ascetic discipline marked by purifying ceremonies. The goal of human life is to withdraw the soul from earthly existence so as to restore its freedom as a divine being.

Plato. To understand Plato's conception of the immortality of the soul one must begin with his theory of Ideas, or Forms, which are thought of as a reality separate from the objects of the senses. The highest principle of the universe is the Idea of the Good. Starting from the Ideas, or Forms, the Demiurge creates the visible world and thus disrupts their original oneness. The world is built on the model of the Ideas, and is alive thanks to the soul that confers order and harmony on it. Plato uses myths to outline his approach to the concept of the world soul and the souls that are divine sparks or pieces of it, thus prolonging the old doctrine of archetypal patterns.

At the beginning of the myth of the winged chariot in the *Phaedrus,* immortality is declared to be the original condition of the soul, as it was in the beginning, leading an ideal life absorbed in contemplation of the Forms and enjoying immortality as a dynamic principle. Thus the soul is seen as a purely spiritual and incorporeal celestial body (*Phaedrus* 245d, 247b) and the source, ground, cause, and origin of life, unbegotten, incorruptible, and undying.

The human soul is a combination of three constituents. The first of these is the *nous,* the rational soul, a remnant of the material of the world soul created by the Demiurge. It contemplates the world of Forms and is immortal. Incarnated in a body, it falls into its prison, with modifications introduced by the other two (mortal) elements, the *thumos* ("heart, spirit, passion") and *epithumētikos* ("desire"). The symbolic illustration of the chariot is expressive: the charioteer is the *nous,* the head and driver of the chariot, the immortal part of the soul, which aims toward its original state of connaturality with the Forms. The two horses are the *thumos* and the *epithumia.* The wings of the chariot are the urge toward spiritual reality.

Once incarnated in a body, this immortal soul will have to free itself through multiple reincarnations, and the first of these has very important consequences for those that follow. If it becomes a philosopher, the *nous* keeps the soul very close to the contemplation of the Forms, its celestial immortality is not far off, and its liberation will come soon. Plato proposed a scheme involving nine incarnations. Thus reincarnation is only a conditional immortality, and true immortality is the prerogative of the incorporeal soul, the celestial body. The doctrine of the tripartite nature of the soul condemns the two lower constituents to the dissolution common to all matter. Only the immortal part will finally escape the cycle of reincarnation, for it is a divine spark. Souls are immortal and are as old as the universe, endlessly migrating through a succession of living mortals; a divine lineage underlies the Platonic view of the immortality of the soul.

The Platonic doctrine had a profound influence in the Mediterranean world during the Hellenistic age. The church fathers readopted it, but in a radically altered form. Both Platonists and Christians agreed on the word *immortality,* but they were deeply divided over its nature and that of the soul. For the Platonists, the soul was supraindividual, and as such it was immortal because it remained within the universal Soul after its final liberation. For the Christians each soul was created immortal and individual by God, committing it irrevocably to the afterlife. A different disagreement separates Platonism from the views of the Stoics, who also saw man as a composite of soul and body, but for whom the soul too is material. For the Stoics the soul survives the body in a temporary and limited afterlife, and thus Stoicism takes an intermediate position between the Platonic conception of immortality and the Epicurian denial of it.

Summary. The Orphic, Pythagorean, and Platonic doctrines thrived and soon found a new area of expansion in the opening of the Orient after the conquests of Alexander. The Mediterranean world in Hellenistic times was a place of great ferment of religious ideas, as Mediterranean man was in quest of salvation. Mystery cults, Osirism, Hermetism, and the teachings of the magi came to the aid of those who saw themselves as strangers in this world, and it is into this milieu that Christianity would come in full bloom to play the role of catalyst. The Oriental gods found in Greece and Rome are savior gods. All eyes are turned toward heaven, the dreamt-of place of salvation, as solar theologies and astral religions add their own prescriptions. Gnosticism and Mithra worship put themselves forward as rivals of the salvation offered by Christianity.

Franz Cumont, in *Lux perpetua* (Paris, 1949), coined the apt phrase *celestial immortality* to identify the common denominator of the various currents of thought regarding immortality in the Hellenistic world. In pharaonic Egypt, Minoan Crete, Vedic India, and Avestan Iran alike, man's gaze was raised toward an eternal life in the glow of the heavens. The teachings of Zarathushtra added important details to this idea of immortality in the divine light, and were taken up by the magi, who added many Babylonian features to it and circulated it throughout the Near East. We know for certain that Pythagoreans and magi had contacts with one another, and astronomy too came to the support of theology. The popular notion of the *fravashi*s and the Platonic theory of the preexistent soul also had an impact on the thinking of Hellenistic man.

Rome fell in early with this syncretistic trend. Pythagoreanism won full citizenship there and was soon established as both a church and a school. Some of the elements that account for its success in Rome are its rules of strict observance, meditation, music, its effectiveness as a celebrational ritual, and its funeral rites in which the white shroud symbolizes the immortal soul. With Posidonius, astrological doctrines took on a religious and mystical tinge. Cicero, following his example, adopted the mystic quality of astral eschatology in the *Dream of Scipio;* in *De Senectute* he sums up the traditional proofs of immortality and shows the aspiration toward a divine congregation of light.

The astral concept of immortality retrieved old mythological material concerning the relationships of souls with heavenly bodies, thereby forming a learned doctrine that would serve as a foundation for the pagan mysticism of the first centuries of our era. The Pythagoreans thought that the space between the earth and moon was filled with souls on their way toward their destiny. The eclectic Stoics also cast a sidelong glance at the stars. The crescent moon appeared often on Roman funeral monuments, but solar cults also developed, and in imperial times the sun became more and more usual as the god of the dead.

Although the creed of solar immortality claimed many followers, the astrology of the planets was also not abandoned. The sequence of seven gates in the mysteries of Mithra indicates the extent of the syncretism possible within the context of celestial immortality. Thus the Mediterranean world in late antiquity was dominated by the concept of man's immortality in the radiance of the world beyond, a world of repose in eternal light. The Christians expanded on this while rejecting pagan astrology and introducing the doctrine of the eternal contemplation of God.

GNOSTIC RELIGION

The central element in gnostic philosophy is a dualistic teaching that the human being possesses a divine spark that originated in the world above but has fallen into the lower material world and is held captive there. This divine spark—the soul—has to regain the knowledge of its heavenly origins, escape the material world, and return to its native home. Each sect of this gnostic religion, with its own creed and method of salvation, teaches and practices the release of souls in its own way. Gnosis implies the identity of three factors—the knower, the celestial substance, and the means of salvation. This threefold assimilation makes it a transforming faith reserved for a select group of initiates. To the transitory material world of birth and death, gnosticism opposes the higher world, the world of life, permanence, incorruptibility, and immutability. The gnostic thinks of himself as a complete stranger to the world—he is "allogenous," of another race. He rejects the world, feeling that empirical existence is evil and opposed to the only true, transcendent reality.

Thus the gnostics viewed man as a combination of matter and spirit and saw the body as the prison which holds the soul after its fall. Within this mixture, the soul, an aeon of the same substance as the celestial world, remains intact, for it is incorruptible. The technical term *aphtharsia* ("incorruptibility") is part of the theological vocabulary of all gnostic systems. Incorruptibility is part of the soul's makeup because of its divine origin and is the essence of its immortality, even though by being imprisoned in the body the soul has become steeped in matter.

Salvation consists in the liberation of the soul. A heavenly savior intervenes to stir the captive soul's memory, to remind it of its origin and make it recognize its true "self." This revelation is made through a series of initiatory trials, by the end of which the soul has discovered a luminous vision of its own essence; the vision awakens in it a burning desire to return to its home. Then begins the second stage, that of the return to the "realm of life." The description of this ascension (or *Himmelsreise*) is found in the texts of all the sects; it includes deprivation and release from material bonds, a path passing through many dangers, the presence of a heavenly guide, and a triumphant entry into celestial Paradise for an immortal destiny amid the blessed light. The gathering of all the souls that have been held in bodies reconstitutes the Pleroma.

MANICHAEISM

Within the wide range of gnostic sects, Manichaeism holds a special place. Mani wished to establish a universal, definitive religion that would bring together all the previous revelations. It is based on a radical dualism of two eternal realms that stand opposed to one another from *Urzeit* to *Endzeit,* representing light and darkness, matter and spirit, body and soul, a dualism that pervades cosmology, anthropogony, soteriology, and eschatology. Claiming to possess the most perfect gnosis, Manichaeism divides mankind into the two categories of pneumatics and hylics and further divides its own church into elect and catechumens.

In the Manichaean scheme, man is a mixture of light and darkness. His body is the work of the archons, but his soul is a divine spark, a portion of the eternal realm of light that has fallen into the material world and been imprisoned in the body by birth. The saving element in the earthbound soul is the *nous,* while the *psuchē* is the part that must be saved; this is the task of Gnosis, a hypostatic divine entity from the realm of light. The gnostic message awakens the *psuchē,* makes it aware of its divine origin, and stirs in it the desire to return on high. This awakening of the soul is the beginning of salvation. The gnostic strives to realize the separation of light and darkness within himself. By an unceasing choice he carries out a *katharsis* within himself, a preliminary salvation that will take full effect after death, in a final liberation of the radiant and eternal soul.

The body is mere matter, destined for destruction as in Zoroastrianism, and is abandoned to the darkness from which it arose. The soul can regain the paradise of light, but if it is not reinstated at the hour of death, it remains enslaved to the archons and will have to continue its existence by being reincarnated into another body. In contrast, the souls of the elect are completely free to begin their triumphant ascension to the realm of light. The Coptic hymns of Medinēt Mādi give numerous examples of this ascension. It is the hour of final victory, completed by the bestowing of a crown (254.64.10–11). Stamped with the seal of purity, the elect join the angels in the shining city (254.64.14–15). Jesus himself, as the spouse of the perfected soul, awaits it and ushers it into the nuptial chamber where it becomes a holy bride of light (265.81.13–14). Three angels come toward it to present it with the crown, the trophy, and the robe (267.84.17–20), as trumpets sound in joyful welcome of the one who will forevermore taste of plenty and rest in the city of light (261.75.11–16).

In the *Fihrist* of the Arabic chronicler al-Nadīm (d. 995), it is the Primordial Man who sends a guide of light to the soul, accompanied by three angels bearing a crown of water, a robe, a diadem, and a crown and band of light. A virgin, the replica of the elect's soul, comes out to meet it, echoing the symbol of the *daēnā* that comes to meet the *urvan,* the earthly part of the soul, in the Avestan *Hadhōkht Nask.* The fate of the souls of the Manichaean *auditores* is not the same as for those of the elect. For them purification in the cycle of reincarnations is required, to enable them one day to follow in the footsteps of eternal salvation of the elect. There is also a third category of people, the sinners who have rejected the gnostic message. For them there is no escape; they are doomed eternally to make up the *massa damnata* of the realm of darkness.

ISLAM

The proclamation of the Day of Judgment comes at the beginning of the Qur'ān, and it is seen from the standpoint of the resurrection, *qiyāma.* On that day all the race of Adam will be gathered together, each one to receive judgment and everlasting retribution according to his deeds. Fear of the Last Day and of the punishment of Hell is a fundamental feature of the Prophet's teaching. The chosen ones on the right, the believers, will be called to enjoy Paradise, while the unbelieving will be condemned to torture. This preaching of Muḥammad's left its traces in every surah of the Qur'ān and gave rise to various systematizations within the currents of Islamic thought. Tradition has never ceased to enliven and enrich this central theme, and it is from this starting point that the elements that make up the common belief in immortality can be brought together.

Islamic Anthropogony. The Islamic view of the nature of man is not particularly clear. The word *rūḥ* means *pneūma,* "breath"—the subtle breath that comes from the brain, that is, the mind. In some traditions it dies with the body only to be brought back to life with it. This is the spiritual part of the human being. There is also the *nafs* (Heb., *nefesh*), commonly translated as "soul," the carnal breath that comes "from the viscera." The philosophical debates of Islamic scholars show the influence of Iran and Greece in the argument that *rūḥ* or *pneuma*, is the truly spiritual part of the human being, the immortal element destined for the afterlife.

Various Ṣūfī traditions distinguish between *nafs* as the seat of lust and *rūḥ* as the spiritual breath that can communicate with God.

The spiritualist doctrine of Shiism views the *rūḥ* as the pure breath of all matter, a spiritual substance that is immortal by nature. In this perspective man is not a body with a soul, but a spirit which temporarily inhabits a body as its instrument. Only on leaving the body does it find its true nature, for it is made to live independently; the soul's pleasure lies in the spiritual world. This tradition sees the spirit as a celestial, radiant substance, imperishable and immortal.

As against the spiritualistic tendency of Shiism, the traditional Sunnī theologians held that man is rather a compound of substances, body and soul, and entirely material. The central question is this: what happens at the moment of death? For those who take man to be a material composite of body plus soul, the soul "disappears" at death and is brought back to life on the last day, while those who see in the body only a temporary instrument of the soul believe the human soul to be made for the spiritual life, even after its separation from the body. In the first case the resurrection of the body is indispensable, whereas in the second the afterlife can do without it. As may be seen, the possible viewpoints can differ sharply.

After Death. The early tradition of the Sunnī faith, based on surahs 40:45–46 and 40:11, holds that the body and spirit both die but that God resuscitates them in the grave for a brief afterlife and a judgment followed by a second death, the latter being abrogated for those who have been killed in the cause of God (3:169–170). The short afterlife in the grave, which has been extensively embellished by popular imagery, is devoted to a personal judgment and settling of individual accounts, with a cross-examination by two angel assessors and the divine judge. Islamic scholars wondered about a death of the body and soul at the time of this second death, but no clear answer to this question was ever arrived at, although some insisted that the soul must have an afterlife because it is inherently immortal.

Spiritualist trends discarded the afterlife of the grave, claiming that the human spirit is immortal and can begin to live its own life from the moment of death. From then on the souls of believers who love God join him in a spiritual, radiant world, where they live until the day of the resurrection. After their bodies arise and are given back to them for the judgment, they enter Paradise once and for all. The wicked and the unbelieving remain in unhappiness and suffering until the last day, when they will be reunited with their bodies for an everlasting punishment.

Resurrection. The resurrection of the body is an essential article of Islamic faith. The usual term used to refer to it is *ba'th* ("awakening"). Where the Qur'ān speaks of *qiyāmah,* theologians often use *ma'ād* ("return"), referring to the return of the being who has ceased to exist. The word *yawm* ("day") appears 385 times in the Qur'ān to designate the end of the present world, the resurrection of the dead, and the universal judgment followed by the beginning of the torments of Hell for unbelievers and a new life in Paradise for the faithful. On this promised day, awful and inescapable, the dead will rise to their feet as God grants them life. (A second creation is also alluded to in surah 22:5.) Details about the ceremony are not lacking: two books are brought forth, one for the unbelievers and one for the pure, and witnesses are present. Every person is introduced to a new life, in Hell or in Paradise, that must go on forever. For the believers Paradise awaits, where they will live in divine reward *(ridwān),* while Hell is reserved for unbelievers, polytheists, and detractors of the Prophet.

The descriptions of this afterlife are plentiful and make use of a rather remarkable symbolism. As Louis Massignon has shown, surah 18 of the Qur'ān speaks of a future life parallel to the present one, to be led in accordance with the will of God, and also lays stress on the submission of man to God and his ardent desire for justice that will blaze forth at the final resurrection. It is recited at the mosque on Friday, and expresses the central theme of immortality in the Qur'ān, the belief that the end of humankind on the final day of resurrection will allow true life to burst forth.

CHRISTIANITY

In order to understand the Christian doctrine of immortality, the message of the New Testament must be located within its twofold setting in the biblical tradition of Israel on one hand and the context of religious beliefs and philosophical ideas of the Greco-Roman world on the other. At the time of the birth of Christianity, the Platonic doctrines of the human composite of *soma* and *psuchē,* the dissolution of this composite by death, and the immortality and afterlife of the *psuchē,* were widely held in Mediterranean thought. With this in mind, the central question concerns not the immortality of the soul as such but the originality of Christian revelation concerning the immortality of man, as he is created in the image of God and redeemed by Christ. Such a problem calls for an examination of the two aspects of Christian immortality, the resurrection of the body and the afterlife of the spirit.

The Hope of Resurrection. As we have seen, the faith in an individual and eschatological resurrection is clearly attested in the *Book of Daniel* and in the *Second Book of the Maccabees*, in the second century BCE. But where did the idea of bodily resurrection fit into the eschatological thought of Jesus? In an early presentation, Jesus affirms that those who enter the kingdom will receive a share in a life of unending peace and happiness, a point of view both communal and personal. The divine gift of eternal life is one of a spiritual nature; whosoever will enter the kingdom easily will be transformed (*1 Cor.* 15:51). This presentation ends by proclaiming the Messiah's passage through death and the reopening of his kingdom after it. This is the idea behind the earthly pilgrimage of the church, through which Jesus shared his own victory over death with his disciples (*1 Cor.* 15:20).

How did apostolic Christianity interpret the resurrection of Christ? After living first in the hope of the Lord's coming (*1 Cor.* 16:22), the apostles focused on the message of resurrection. Jesus is resurrected as the first fruit of the believers who die before his second coming. Later the church gradually accorded more importance to resurrection for all. As Albert Descamps notes in "La mort selon l'Écriture" (in Ries, 1983, p. 46), "Always sustained by the Jewish hope of the resurrection of the body, and even more by the memory of a Paschal event that is taken as a model, the faith in resurrection will become the Christians' main response to the problem of the other world, a resurrection expected by virtue of Christ's own and somehow understood as being in its image (*1 Thes.* 4:14; *Rom.* 6:5; *1 Cor.* 15:20, 15:23; *Col.* 1:18; *John* 11:24)." This doctrine, for nineteen centuries the central belief of Christianity, fulfills the biblical Jewish hope in an eschatological resurrection and replaces it with the inclusion of all Christians within the resurrection of Christ. For this reason the resurrection of non-Christians and sinners is devoid of Paschal glory (*1 Thes.* 4:14).

Afterlife of the Soul. The immortality of the souls of the righteous is clearly affirmed fifty years before the common era in the *Wisdom of Solomon* (1:15, 3:9, 5:15). The setting of the biblical text is a world under the influence of Platonism, with the addition of traditional ideas from Israel. The place of the immortal soul in the teaching of Jesus is evident in his proclamation of the kingdom. It offers eternal life, which implies the expectation of a spiritual afterlife as suggested by the *Gospel of Matthew* 10:28. But the disciples' questions would be answered by apostolic Christianity, beginning with Paul (*2 Cor.* 4:7–5:10), who felt that existence after death is independent of the body. In the *Letter to the Philippians* 1:19–26, where Paul affirms even more clearly his certainty that he will never be separated from Christ (cf. *Rom.* 8:37–39, 14:7–12). Here we see the revival and christianization of Hellenistic Judaism and Greek wisdom, the Christian evaluation of the doctrine of Plato's *Phaedo:* the presence within man of a basic and incorruptible spiritual principle. The reflection of this Greek view of man appears also in the confirmation of an afterlife of the soul in *Matthew* 10:28, and in the parable of the evil rich man and Lazarus the beggar in *Luke* 16:19–31 the same idea is developed in popular terms. Jesus' answer to the second criminal on the cross (*Lk.* 23:43) openly declares the certainty of an immediate afterlife in the spirit.

In the light of the texts of the New Testament, the belief in immortality is an affirmation of the eschatological resurrection as a consequence of that of Christ and his presence on earth during the intermediate period after his death. This belief is the culmination of a millennium of earlier biblical reflection and piety, and has for nineteen centuries been the basis of the theology and faith of Christian believers.

CONCLUSION

The course of our research into beliefs in immortality, spanning the wide cultural and religious range of humanity from prehistory up to the great monotheistic systems, has uncovered several essential traits in the character of *homo religiosus.* Thrown into a universe to which he attempts to give some order, in search of a direction that will enable him to know where he is going, man discovers a dimension that transcends his earthly life. Through his day-to-day experiences, he ponders the mysterious phenomenon in which all his actions and all his behavior are rooted—the phenomenon of life. Such reflection marks the beginning of an unceasing quest into the nature and the density of life, which is revealed as a hierophany. The recognition of a sacred dimension in his own existence impels man to seek out the origin of life and to return to it. His ceaseless encounter with death all around him intensifies his questioning, and it is in this "nostalgia for the beginnings" that the search for immortality and the never-ending effort to transcend the human condition take root.

Our survey has revealed a *homo symbolicus,* for indeed it is through a symbolic language that man attempts to express his perception of the mystery of life, a life which he tries to comprehend as something absolute. The combination of this symbolic language with the efforts that have been made to solve the mystery of life is the source of an impressive fund of cultural and religious wealth in the form of art, literature, and ritual. The spirit attempts to approach the mystery of life and the afterlife through a series of universal symbols: the tree as a symbol of life and as *axis mundi,* the water that heals, rejuvenates, fertilizes, and becomes *soma;* the fire, the youth-restoring *ignis divinus* that can transform the body and become a divine messenger; the symbolism of ascension in the flight of birds; the sun and moon, signs of resurrection and guidance; and the rainbow, the link between heaven and earth.

Ritual symbolism too represents an important aspect of the efforts of *homo religiosus* to comprehend and realize his afterlife, as seen in such details as the fetal position of the corpse; the preparation and decoration of the tomb; the special attention given to the skull; funeral furnishings and offerings; stelae recalling the memory of the deceased; red ocher as a substitute for blood; inhumation, cremation, and mummification; gold foil on the funeral pyre; postmortem rituals for accompanying the soul on its journey; rites of opening the mouth, nose, ears, and eyes; and the placing of a book of the dead in the grave. What is most striking is the similarity between the rites for birth, initiation, and funerals. *Homo religiosus* believes that his life does not end, for death is a birth into a new life and an initiation into the afterlife.

Sacred, symbolic, and ritual converge in peoples' beliefs in immortality, and myths that underlie these beliefs are also numerous. The phoenix, for example, appears often in the mythic structure of immortality; Herodotus and Plutarch present this legendary bird in unequaled splendor. As the hour of its death nears it builds itself a nest of aromatic branches, and is consumed by a fire kindled by its own heat, after which it is reborn from the ashes. In ancient Egypt, it was associated with the daily cycle of the sun and the annual flooding of the Nile, and in pharaonic funerary symbolism, after the weighing of the soul, the deceased became a phoenix. In India it stands for Śiva, and in Greece it was a substitute for Orpheus. From Origen on, Christians took the phoenix as a sign of the triumph of life over death, and it is a symbol of Christ's resurrection throughout the Middle Ages.

[*See also* Soul; Afterlife; *and* Resurrection.]

BIBLIOGRAPHY

Alger, W. R. *A Critical History of the Doctrine of the Future Life.* New York, 1981.

Anati, Emmanuel, ed. *Prehistoric Art and Religion: Valcamonica Symposium 1979.* Milan, 1983.

Beier, Ulli. *The Origin of Life and Death.* London, 1966.

Bianu, Zeno. *Les religions et la mort.* Paris, 1981.

Camps, Gabriel. *La préhistoire: À la recherche du paradis perdu.* Paris, 1982. See pages 371–445 for a remarkable synthesis on prehistoric religious man.

Choisy, Maryse. *La survie après la mort.* Paris, 1967.

Cullman, Oscar. *Immortality of the Soul or Resurrection of the Dead? The Witness of the New Testament.* London, 1958.

Cumont, Franz. *Lux perpetua.* Paris, 1949.

Dumézil, Georges. *Le festin d'immortalité.* Paris, 1924.

Edsman, Carl-Martin. *Ignis divinus: Le feu comme moyen de rajeunissement et d'immortalité; Contes, légendes, mythes et rites.* Lund, 1949.

Eliade, Mircea. *Shamanism: Archaic Techniques of Ecstasy.* Rev. & enl. ed. New York, 1964.

Eliade, Mircea. *Yoga: Immortality and Freedom.* 2d ed. Princeton, 1969.

Eliade, Mircea. *Australian Religions: An Introduction.* Ithaca, N.Y., 1973.

Eliade, Mircea. "The Religions of Ancient China." In his *A History of Religious Ideas,* vol. 2, *From Gautama Buddha to the Triumph of Christianity.* Chicago, 1982.

Fröbe-Kapteyn, Olga. "Gestaltung der Erlösungsidee in Ost und West." In *Eranos Jahrbuch 1937*. Zurich, 1938.

Goossens, W. "L'immortalité corporelle." In *Dictionnaire de la Bible: Supplement,* vol. 4. Paris, 1949.

Guiart, Jean, ed. *Les hommes et la mort: Rituels funéraires.* Paris, 1979.

Guthrie, W. K. C. *Orpheus and Greek Religion.* 2d ed., rev. London, 1952.

Heiler, Friedrich. *Unsterblichkeitsglaube und Jenseitshoffnung in der Geschichte der Religionen.* Basel, 1950.

Heissig, Walther. *The Religions of Mongolia.* Translated by Geoffrey Samuel. Berkeley, 1980.

James, William. *Human Immortality* (1898). 2d ed. New York, 1917.

Klimkeit, Hans J., ed. *Tod und Jenseits im Glauben der Völker.* Wiesbaden, 1978.

La Vallée Poussin, Louis de. *Nirvâna.* Paris, 1925.

Lemaitre, Solange. *Le mystère de la mort dans les religion de l'Asie* (1943). 2d ed. Paris, 1963.

Parrot, André. *Le refrigerium dans l'au-delà.* Paris, 1937.

Pfannmüller, Gustav. *Tod, Jenseits, und Unsterblichkeit.* Munich, 1953.

Preuss, K. T. *Tod und Unsterblichkeit im Glauben der Naturvölker.* Tübingen, 1930.

Ries, Julien, ed. *La mort selon la Bible, dans l'antiquité classique et selon le manichéisme.* Louvain-la-Neuve, 1983.

Silburn, Lilian. *Instant et cause: Le discontinue dans la pensée philosophique de l'Inde.* Paris, 1955.

Söderblom, Nathan. *La vie future d'après le mazdéisme à la lumière des croyances parallèles dans les autres religions.* Paris, 1901.

Stendahl, Krister, ed. *Immortality and Resurrection.* New York, 1965.

Stephenson, Günther. *Leben und Tod in den Religionen.* Darmstadt, 1980.

Théodoridès, A., P. Naster, and Julien Ries, eds. *Vie et survie dans les civilisations orientales.* Louvain-la-Neuve, 1983.

Thomas, Louis-Vincent. *La mort africaine: Idéologie funéraire en Afrique noire.* Paris, 1982.

Tucci, Giuseppe. *The Religions of Tibet.* Translated by Geoffrey Samuel. Berkeley, 1980.

Wenzl, A. *L'immortalité: Sa signification métaphysique et anthropologique.* Paris, 1957.

Zahan, Dominique, ed. *Réincarnation et vie mystique en Afrique noire.* Strasbourg, 1963.

CONTRIBUTORS

Th. P. van Baaren, Rijksuniversiteit te Groningen
Jack Bemporad, Temple Sinai of Bergen County, Tenafly, N.J.
Erika Bourguignon, Ohio State University
Jan Bremmer, Rijksuniversiteit te Utrecht
Ioan Petru Culianu, Rijksuniversiteit te Groningen
Stevan L. Davies, College Misericordia, Dallas, PA.
Tamara M. Green, Hunter College, City University of New York
Helen Hardacre, Princeton University
Marilyn J. Harran, Chapman College
Charles H. Long, University of North Carolina at Chapel Hill
J. Bruce Long, Claremont Graduate School
F. Stanley Lusby, University of Tennessee at Knoxville
Geddes MacGregor, University of Southern California
William K. Mahony, Davidson College
Michael E. Marmura, University of Toronto
Geoffrey Parrinder, University of London
Kay A. Read, University of Chicago
Julien Ries, Université Catholique de Louvain-la-Neuve
Helmer Ringgren, Uppsala Universitet
Claude Rivière, University of Oxford
Anna Seidel, École Française d'Extrême-Orient, Kyoto
Anna-Leena Siikala, Helsingin Yliopisto
Jane I. Smith, Harvard University
John S. Strong, Bates College
Louis-Vincent Thomas, Université de Paris V
Linda M. Tober, University of Tennessee at Knoxville
Robert Turcan, Université Lyon III
R. J. Zwi Werblowsky, Hebrew University of Jerusalem

Lawrence E. Sullivan is professor of the History of Religions and acting director of the Institute for the Advanced Study of Religion at the University of Chicago

FINDING LIST OF ARTICLE TITLES

The following table lists the article titles (in parentheses) as they originally appeared in *The Encyclopedia of Religion.* Titles not listed below are unchanged

Human Sacrifice (Human Sacrifice: An Overview)
Ancestor Worship (Ancestors: Ancestor Worship)
Mythic Ancestors (Ancestors: Mythic Ancestors)
The Afterlife (Afterlife: An Overview)
Geographies of Death (Afterlife: Geographies of Death)
Eschatology (Eschatology: An Overview)
Concepts of the Soul in the Ancient Near East (Soul: Ancient Near Eastern Concepts)
Chinese Concepts of the Soul and the Afterlife (Afterlife: Chinese Concepts)
Concepts of the Soul in Indian Religions (Soul: Indian Concepts)
Greek and Hellenistic Concepts of the Soul (Soul: Greek and Hellenistic Concepts)
Judaic Concepts of the Soul (Soul: Jewish Concept)
Christian Concepts of the Soul (Soul: Christian Concept)
Islamic Concepts of the Soul (Soul: Islamic Concepts)
Concepts of the Soul in Tribal Communities (Soul: Concepts in Primitive Religions)